FROM WAR TO PEACE
Fateful Decisions in International Politics

FROM WAR TO PEACE

Fateful Decisions in International Politics

CHARLES W. KEGLEY, JR.
University of South Carolina

GREGORY A. RAYMOND
Boise State University

Bedford / St. Martin's

Boston ♦ New York

For Bedford/St. Martin's

Political Science Editor: Marilea Polk Fried
Developmental Editor: Heidi L. Hood
Senior Editor, Publishing Services: Douglas Bell
Production Supervisor: Dennis J. Conroy
Marketing Manager: Jenna Bookin Barry
Text Design: Stratford Publishing Services, Inc.
Cartography: Mapping Specialists Limited
Cover Design: Donna Lee Dennison
Cover Photo: AP Photo/Stanton R. Winter
Composition: Stratford Publishing Services, Inc.
Printing and Binding: Haddon Craftsmen, Inc., an R.R. Donnelley & Sons Company

President: Charles H. Christensen
Editorial Director: Joan E. Feinberg
Publisher for History, Political Science, and Communication: Patricia Rossi
Director of Marketing: Karen R. Melton
Director of Editing, Design, and Production: Marcia Cohen
Manager, Publishing Services: Emily Berleth

Library of Congress Control Number: 2001089956

Manufactured in the United States of America.

7 6 5 4 3 2
f e d c b a

For information, write: Bedford/St. Martin's, 75 Arlington Street, Boston, MA 02116
(617-399-4000)

ISBN: 0-312-39468-3

PREFACE

The causes of war and the building and maintenance of peace are complex and understudied subjects. *From War to Peace: Fateful Decisions in International Politics* has been inspired by our belief that without devoting sufficient attention to their dynamics, progress toward a more just and less violent world will be frustrated. Without international security other serious threats to humanity, such as poverty, environmental despoliation, and human rights abuses, cannot be adequately addressed. Through this textbook we aim to help students understand the fundamentals of war and peace and to begin to formulate their own prescriptions for building a lasting peace. In so doing we also aim to help them better appreciate the ethical dilemmas intrinsic to making choices about war and peace and to recognize how normative issues affect world politics. To be most useful in the classroom, we have built a multipurpose book that provides basic introductions to the study of war and peace, foreign policy decision making, and international relations in general while stimulating critical thinking.

From War to Peace teaches students to think critically about foreign policy by asking two profound questions: Why do states go to war? And how can they create a lasting peace? By examining the decisions made in key wars and peace settlements throughout history, this book encourages students to think about the consequences of alternative foreign policy choices and about the conditions under which particular strategies are likely to succeed. We concentrate especially on how the winners of wars should treat their defeated foes as a determining factor in creating a lasting peace. One school of thought counsels leniency: Victors should be magnanimous to extinguish any desire for revenge by the vanquished. Another school calls for sterner measures: Victors should be harsh to ensure that the enemy's defeat is irreversible. The first approach seeks stability by building trust between adversaries; the second, by eliminating an adversary's capacity to mount a future military challenge. *From War to Peace* prompts students to consider which of these contending approaches to peace is more likely to yield a lasting peace and provides them with a range of cases from which they can formulate their conclusions.

However, this is not simply a text about war and its termination; it is also about broader issues in international relations. It introduces international relations ideas and concepts that students need to better understand the cases — concepts such as levels of analysis, liberalism and realism, rational choice, enduring rivalries, irredentism, grand strategy, just war theory, and more. In this way *From War to Peace* supplements and makes concrete many of the key concepts and theories surveyed in introductory texts on world politics and world order.

Through the information laid out in the introductory chapter and the examples in the cases themselves, this book also gives students the opportunity to move beyond war and peace decision making to draw conclusions that apply to international decision making as a whole. How individual preferences form around specific options, how these preferences are converted through collective processes of policy making into national strategies, and how the strategies chosen by different countries combine to yield outcomes of international significance are widely applicable topics. What students can learn about influences on war and peacemaking decisions has ramifications for understanding many other areas of foreign policy decision making.

From War to Peace also emphasizes the rival realist and liberal theoretical philosophies that have guided states' foreign policies throughout history. By looking at the policy implications of liberalism and realism on the choices made in the historical cases presented in this book, students can consider the advantages and limitations of these two contested theoretical traditions.

Another important feature of this focus on decision making is that it prompts students to consider the place of morality in foreign policy. Whenever actors have choices, questions of right and wrong arise. There exists a regrettable tendency to ignore or dismiss discussions of ethical behavior in world affairs, even though questions of injury, retribution, and reconciliation are central to the human condition and, we argue, to most issues on the global agenda. By examining theories of just war and just peace, this book helps rectify this oversight and gives students additional tools for critical thinking when comparing the cases.

THE DEVELOPMENT OF THIS BOOK

Readers familiar with our previous text, *How Nations Make Peace,* will note that *From War to Peace* builds on and improves on that prior book. We have striven to create an even more useful and thought-provoking text, while maintaining the strengths of the prior version. One of the first things we did was to place an increased emphasis on revealing the importance of the nature of each war to the resulting peace settlement. Because no peace can be considered without first considering the war that preceded it, we worked to better illuminate this connection, and changed the title of this book to better reflect its content. Thus, the book *How Nations Make Peace* became *From War to Peace.*

Among the things we retained from the last edition is the comparative case-study approach to the study of international politics and war and peace. Inspired by our experiences as Pew Faculty Fellows in International Affairs at the John F. Kennedy School of Government, we chose this approach because of its value in promoting critical thinking. Historical cases encourage readers to draw inferences that they can use to generate theoretical propositions and policy prescriptions. We carefully chose cases for this book that will encourage students to think theoretically and normatively about the consequences of alternative foreign policy choices and to draw conclusions about which strategies are likely to succeed.

Aided by the advice of instructors who commented on our earlier book, we introduced a number of changes that will make this text more useful in the classroom. First, to provide students with the basic tools for examining case studies and to allow comparisons between the ancient and modern eras, we incorporated the cases of the Peloponnesian War and the Punic Wars from antiquity into one introductory chapter. Next, to further enrich the comparative approach of this book, we added two cases to this edition. The chapter covering the Thirty Years' War rounds out the historical foundations of modern statecraft and provides a basis for understanding the origins of the contemporary international system. Paired with the Persian Gulf War, a new chapter on the war in Kosovo provides a basis for exploring the changing character of war and peace at the dawn of the twenty-first century.

In addition to these changes in structure and coverage, we have incorporated other enhancements throughout. We expanded the book's coverage of the ethical dimensions of the study of war and peace through additional consideration of moral analysis, introducing, for example, a new discussion of just war theory. We also draw on the most recent scholarship on the material we present. Finally, to make the book easier for students to follow, we have reworded several subheadings to better signal the content of each section.

Part Organization

The chapters in *From War to Peace* are organized into five parts. Part I introduces the key concepts for analyzing war and peace decision making, including the options available to victors for dealing with defeated adversaries, the underlying assumptions of the realist and liberal theoretical approaches, and the core arguments in the moral philosophy about just war and the ethics of peacemaking. It also provides questions to guide student analysis of the cases in the book and outlines a levels-of-analysis framework from which students can examine decision making in international relations.

The cases presented in Parts II through IV have all registered a lasting impact on today's global landscape. The fateful choices taken by the belligerents in these pivotal wars alert readers to what can go wrong with lenient as well as with harsh postwar policies. They show how the seeds of future wars are often sown by the manner in which the vanquished were treated, and how a failure of vision can leave victors and vanquished alike without a viable design for international order capable of meeting postwar security challenges.

Part II underscores the timeless nature of the problems inherent in constructing a viable peace settlement by focusing on three of the most well-known wars of the early modern period of the interstate system: the Thirty Years' War, the Napoleonic Wars, and the Wars of German Unification. Taking place during an age of empire building and balance-of-power diplomacy, these conflicts reveal how national interests and ethical values framed foreign policy options, including when to create an organization for international consultation and how to treat the vanquished. These cases also provide ample opportunity to examine the hypothesis that the choice between lenient and punitive policies can be a key factor in determining whether the postwar era is one of peace or war.

Part III surveys the First and Second World Wars, two total wars that marked the end of the classical, multipolar state system that existed from the seventeenth through the nineteenth centuries. These cases provide potent examples of how the seeds of new conflicts are often sown in the past. They also highlight the different policy prescriptions emanating from realism and liberalism and how these two traditions produce divergent visions of ethics and justice for the waging of war and peace.

Part IV looks at the face of war and peace after the Cold War, on the eve of the twenty-first century, by juxtaposing two contemporary cases. The Persian Gulf War and the war in Kosovo exemplify many of the things that promise to become more common in the future: wars within states, collective security actions, humanitarian intervention, and the difficulty reaching a conclusive end to such conflicts. Part IV asks students to consider the criteria needed to justify military intervention for humanitarian purposes. It also asks them to assess the practicality of collective security and the effectiveness of collective action.

Finally, Part V provides students with a thought-provoking summary that prompts critical thinking about rival approaches to peacemaking in contemporary international politics. Turning to the cases for examples, it focuses on four main categories of inquiry about war and peace: the value and limitations of the realist and liberal schools of thought, the factors that constrain the ability of victors to make rational and moral choices, twelve key peacemaking policy prescriptions, and arguments about waging just wars and building just peace. By examining these issues along with the current trends and conditions in international politics, this chapter provides the basis for evaluating the prospects for peace in the twenty-first century.

Chapter Organization

Each case chapter is organized to help students master factual material and prompt critical thinking. To guide students toward a purposeful reading of each case, each chapter begins with a brief **preview** section that signals the important concepts, theories, and questions the case at hand addresses. Bold **key terms,** which are also defined in the **glossary** at the end of the book, alert students to concepts important to the study of war and peace and international politics. A **chronology** summarizes the important events in each case, and **controversies to contemplate** at the end of each chapter provide thought-provoking questions to stimulate critical thinking and prompt classroom discussion. A **suggested reading** list at the end of each chapter facilitates student research.

ACKNOWLEDGMENTS

We are indebted to the Pew Faculty Fellows in International Affairs at the John F. Kennedy School of Government at Harvard University, and especially to the director of teaching development in that fellowship program, John Boehrer, for inspiring us to prepare a textbook grounded in the case method of instruction. We are convinced that this method is a powerful pedagogical tool for giving students concrete referents for the abstract analytic concepts found in general theories about war and peace. We expect instructors to find this format useful in encouraging student participation in class discussion. Our experience suggests that students not only probe the causal processes operating within a given case, but they also grapple with the larger question of how the insights they have gleaned might shed light on other situations.

We also wish to acknowledge the contributions of others from whom we have benefited while writing this book. On a personal level, we wish to thank the two people most important to us, Debbie Jump and Christine Raymond, for their unwavering support and constant encouragement. On a professional level, many scholars contributed to our efforts to make this text both informative and interesting. At the project's inception, constructive comments were provided about our prospectus by several anonymous reviewers. Thanks also go to our colleagues who reviewed manuscript drafts of *How Nations Make Peace,* including H. Carl Camp, the University of Nebraska; Christopher Joyner, Georgetown University; Lawrence Katzenstein, the University of Minnesota; and Robert Kerstein, the University of Tampa. Other colleagues made useful suggestions on how to improve that earlier book which resulted in this sequel. We are particularly grateful to the following reviewers for their help: Richard Foster, Idaho State University; Joe Hagan, West Virginia University; Edward Mihalkanin, Southwest Texas State University; John Molloy, Michigan State University; Steven Lamy, the University of Southern California; Jeffrey Morton, Florida Atlantic University; Joel H. Rosenthal, the Carnegie Council on Ethics and International Affairs; Alpo Rusi, Helsinki University; Paul Senese, SUNY–Buffalo; John Vasquez, Vanderbilt University; and Thomas Walker, the University at Albany.

We are grateful for the research advice provided by Róger Coaté, Don Puchala, Wendy Foster Halbert, and Min Ye, and for the dedicated manuscript preparation assistance provided by Ruth Cooper, Holly Gastineau-Grimes, and Linda Logan. In addition, we are thankful for the support that allowed us to conduct research in various European archives and libraries, especially, the Bibliotheek van het Vredespaleis in The Hague that provided valuable assistance in obtaining copies of rare historical documents and legal manuscripts.

At Bedford/St. Martin's, we are grateful to President Charles H. Christensen and Editorial Director Joan E. Feinberg for their support of this project. We also wish to thank Sponsoring Editor Marilea Polk Fried and Developmental Editor Heidi Hood who offered professional guidance and assistance throughout the manuscript development process, and Senior Editor Doug Bell who ably shepherded the book through production. In addition, Leslie Connor and the staff at Publisher's Studio also contributed significantly to the preparation and polish of the book.

From War to Peace builds on three decades of our friendship and research collaboration. We hope that readers will find our latest joint effort helpful in thinking through the moral dilemmas and policy problems that states face when confronted with the threat of war and the task of building an enduring peace.

Charles W. Kegley, Jr.
Gregory A. Raymond

CONTENTS

ABOUT THE AUTHORS

Charles W. Kegley, Jr. (Ph.D., Syracuse University) is Pearce Professor of International Relations at the University of South Carolina. A past president of the International Studies Association (1993–1994), he has held appointments at Georgetown University, the University of Texas, and Rutgers University. With Eugene R. Wittkopf, his books include *American Foreign Policy: Pattern and Process,* Sixth Edition (2002); *World Politics: Trend and Transformation,* Eighth Edition (2001); *The Global Agenda: Issues and Perspectives,* Sixth Edition (2001); and *The Nuclear Reader: Strategy, Weapons, War,* Second Edition (1989). Kegley has also published *Controversies in International Relations Theory: Realism and the Neoliberal Challenge* (1995), *The Long Postwar Peace: Contending Explanations and Projections* (1991) and *International Terrorism: Characteristics, Causes, and Controls* (1990), along with many articles in a wide range of scholarly journals.

Gregory A. Raymond (Ph.D., University of South Carolina) is director of the Honors College at Boise State University. Selected as the Idaho Professor of the Year (1994) by the Carnegie Foundation for the Advancement of Teaching, his books include *The Other Western Europe: A Comparative Analysis of the Smaller Democracies,* Second Edition (1983); *Third World Policies of Industrialized Nations* (1982); and *Conflict Resolution and the Structure of the State System* (1980). He has also published many articles on foreign policy and world politics in various scholarly journals. Raymond has spoken on international issues at numerous professional conferences throughout Europe, the United States, and Latin America.

Together Kegley and Raymond have previously coauthored *Exorcising the Ghost of Westphalia: Building World Order in the New Millennium* (2002), *How Nations Make Peace* (1999), *A Multipolar Peace? Great-Power Politics in the Twenty-First Century* (1994), *When Trust Breaks Down: Alliance Norms and World Politics* (1990); and *International Events and the Comparative Analysis of Foreign Policy* (1975). They have also coauthored over two dozen journal articles in such periodicals as the *International Studies Quarterly,* the *Journal of Conflict Resolution,* the *Journal of Peace Research,* the *Journal of Politics, International Interactions,* and the *Harvard International Review.* Both Kegley and Raymond were Pew Faculty Fellows at the John F. Kennedy School of Government at Harvard University.

PART I

How States Make Decisions
for War and Peace

The chapter in this introductory section provides a road map for examining the case histories of war and peace that follow. It introduces the concepts and theories that will be used to investigate the difficult policy problems faced by political leaders whose states are locked in mortal combat. In addition, it supplies a framework for identifying the most potent factors that influence decisions about waging war and making peace. Chapter 1 thus sets out the principles for analyzing historical events so we can draw meaningful conclusions about why states go to war and how the conduct of hostilities affects the eventual peace settlement.

To set the stage for the decision-making perspective emphasized in this text, Chapter 1 begins with a brief overview of some timeless issues surrounding the practice of statecraft. Although weapons, tactics, and logistics have changed over the centuries, certain perennial questions about justice and expediency in foreign policy have been raised by every generation. Because political leaders frequently seek answers to these questions in either liberal or realist theories, we next summarize what each theory identifies as the causes of war and the conditions that sustain a durable peace. Drawing on the policy prescriptions of liberalism and realism, we then inventory the range of options that the victors in a war have when trying to craft a lasting peace.

To highlight the difficulties in choosing the most effective option for dealing with a defeated adversary, we briefly compare two famous cases from antiquity: Sparta's relatively lenient treatment of Athens at the end of the Peloponnesian War, and Rome's brutal, pitiless treatment of Carthage after the Punic Wars. Historical cases with parallels to present problems are especially useful when they juxtapose contending ethical traditions and encourage a consideration of the costs, benefits, and risks associated with the policy recommendations advanced by each side. As will be shown, both Spartan leniency and Roman brutality had drawbacks. Without a political grand strategy for the postwar world, neither victor foresaw the side effects and long-term consequences of its actions. They each tried to solve certain

1

immediate problems but did not consider what new problems their solutions would create. Their experiences offer an enduring lesson: Unless victory on the battlefield is complemented with a clear, coherent, and nuanced strategy for dealing with allies and adversaries, political leaders intoxicated by military success will suffer nasty political hangovers.

Having sketched some of the difficulties in building robust peace settlements, the chapter concludes with a presentation of those factors that most influence decisionmakers as wars wind down. Organized according to three levels of analysis (international environment, internal domestic setting, and individual leadership characteristics), they provide a guide for exploring the tangle of competing interests, objectives, and values woven throughout the processes governing war and peace, laying the foundation for comparing wars and peacemaking efforts from throughout the past to the most recent times.

Comparisons with cases in later chapters reveal that prudence in victory requires an understanding of the larger political context of the war. It recognizes the roles of distributive, retributive, corrective, and restorative justice in crafting a peace agreement, and seeks to balance competing goods and lesser evils in a firm but fair settlement. Because many of the questions surrounding decisions about waging war and making peace are anchored in deeper ethical quandaries, Chapter 1 and the chapters that follow stress the moral dimensions of foreign policy choices. Statecraft, it is often argued, responds to strategic necessities defined by national interests. Yet what one deems necessary will appear compelling only to the extent that certain values are accepted as important enough to warrant sacrificing other values. Choosing one set of values over another entails a moral judgment. The historical case studies in this introduction and the chapters beyond were explicitly selected to provoke interest in and awareness of the moral aspects of policy choices in international politics.

· 1 ·

WAR AND THE MAKING OF PEACE:
AN INTRODUCTION

You have to take chances for peace, just as you must take chances in war.
— JOHN FOSTER DULLES

"All history shows," the political scientist Hans J. Morgenthau once remarked, "that nations active in international politics are continuously preparing for, actively involved in, or recovering from organized violence in the form of war."[1] For observers of international politics like Morgenthau, peace is but a temporary interlude between rounds of armed combat. Because these clashes are endemic in a state system lacking global institutions to police aggressors, national leaders are advised to be vigilant and ready to engage any potential adversary on the field of battle.

We do not question the importance of thinking about how preparations for war might affect its likelihood, but believe the traditional emphasis on restraining predators overlooks the equally important dynamics governing how states forge strategies to preserve international peace. This book is about the linkage between the end of war and the maintenance of peace. Its purpose is to help us to understand two types of national choice critical to international security. The first is the age-old question: What conditions justify waging war? The second is the related question: When a war ends, how should victors treat the defeated in order to promote an enduring peace?

The latter question is as important as the former. Battlefield success, no matter how impressive, does not automatically yield a durable peace settlement. The choices national leaders face when wars conclude are among the most consequential they ever make, because winning is not an end in itself. The geopolitical landscape is littered not only with decisions to wage wars that led to defeat, but also with military victories that never translated into stable political orders.

Perhaps the most famous example of a battlefield success resulting in failure occurred over two millennia ago, when King Pyrrhus of Epirus overwhelmed a Roman army at Asculum in 279 B.C.E. The Greek king had

3

recently defeated the Romans at Heraclea, but only after his troops had suffered enormous casualties. Another victory over the Romans, he reasoned, would cement his position on the Italian peninsula and allow him to conquer the wealthier cities of Sicily. Pyrrhus achieved victory. After two days of bitter fighting in the woods and marshes around the Aufidus River, some six thousand Roman soldiers lay dead. Yet the victory came at a terrible cost, with Pyrrhus's forces again suffering staggering losses. "One more such victory," he grumbled, "and I am undone."

Exhaustion and resource depletion often prevent victors like Pyrrhus from capitalizing on their military accomplishments. However, these constraints are not the only reasons why military mastery alone is unlikely to provide an enduring triumph; victors need a coherent peace plan for the postwar world. Peace is not something that happens spontaneously when the infernal engine of war is shut off; it must be cultivated and nourished by people of vision. As President Woodrow Wilson noted in a 1917 speech to the U.S. Senate, without a judicious, well-designed strategy for the treatment of vanquished opponents, the terms of peace "would leave a sting, a resentment, a bitter memory . . . [and would rest] upon quicksand."[2]

The underlying theme of this book is that a victor's policies toward the vanquished are fateful, heavily influencing whether the defeated will accept or reject the postwar settlement and whether their role in the postwar world will ultimately be constructive or destructive. How the vanquished are treated can determine whether political defeat will be snatched from the jaws of military victory — or whether a peace treaty is simply an interlude before a bitter foe resumes hostilities. Most scholarship focuses on the decisions undertaken at the start of a war, during its course, and on the so-called endgame tactics in the waning days of the war seeking to persuade an adversary to surrender.[3] Our focus in this book is different: We examine the influence different types of peace settlements have had on relations between the former belligerents.

JUSTICE AND EXPEDIENCY IN INTERNATIONAL POLITICS

Wars are initiated for various reasons. Whether inspired by offensive or defensive aims, they breed mutual enmity, which can lead each side to demonize the other as a means of rationalizing violence. Whereas states take up arms amid conflicting and often quixotic expectations about what the fighting will be like, campaigning against a determined opponent can harden attitudes about the adversary, especially as a war grows in destructiveness and duration. How wars begin and how they are fought thus shape the passions and philosophies of the belligerents toward one another when wars end.

Few human activities evoke stronger emotions than combat. Fear, rage, and grief all attend the battlefield. To think about warfare without acknowledging these powerful emotions is to overlook some of the most important forces motivating human behavior, forces that can destroy the prospects of a negotiated cease-fire and tear apart the very fabric of a peace agreement. Consider the **enduring rivalry** between Spain and France. Between 1494 and 1683, these neighbors went to war, on average, every 12.6 years. Clearly, this series of lethal engagements suggests that truces struck between Spain and France were not prompted by a sincere desire to resolve the issues that divided them; the peace treaties did not dispel the hostilities — they were pauses in an ongoing feud, animated by deep-seated passions. Similar patterns of protracted warfare punctuated by lulls can be found among other rivals. For example, over the course of two hundred years from 1678 to 1878 Russia and Turkey maintained a rivalry that erupted in fighting ten times. Peace, in these types of long-standing rivalries, rarely endures; it is an interlude during which one side or the other longs for revenge and methodically works to settle old scores.

People who harbor an acute sense of injustice do not easily forget the suffering caused by others. Every emotion, argued the philosopher Ludwig Wittgenstein, is its own world. An angry person lives in an angry world. A person deeply resentful over some past injury lives in a bitter world. Emotions are not just psychological predispositions coloring our view of life, they are specific feelings about particular objects that structure experience.[4] They endow life with meaning and therein alert us to what is important. While at times painful, passions such as those aroused during warfare affect people's actions toward others. Yet, as political scientist David Welch points out, perusing much of what is written in the field of international relations, "one would never suspect that human beings have right brains as well as left"[5] — an intuitive side and a cognitive, logical side, independent but mutually influencing perceptions and decisions. Indeed, the social sciences have long ignored the role of emotions in decision making. But people do not always behave like the self-concerned egoists found in interpretations based on **rational choice;** they can be driven by emotions ranging from love to hate, often disregarding calculations of self-interest.

> "Against war it may be said that it makes the victor stupid and the vanquished revengeful."
>
> — FRIEDRICH NIETZSCHE

The inescapable part that human emotions play in molding decisions on war and peace highlights the ageless philosophical controversy over the proper roles of justice and expediency in statecraft. Grievances frequently arouse intense emotions. Although sometimes feelings of anger and resentment are justifiable and it is appropriate to act in accordance with them, they can also sour the relations between former belligerents long after the fighting is over. Victors face complex trade-offs when attempting to assuage the rancor of a bitter past. Forced to balance competing ideals and interests in an emotionally charged environment, they can be drawn one way by moral principles while being yanked another way by the quest for advantage. The following list of questions illustrates some of the ways in which policymakers are pulled in opposite directions when ethics and opportunism offer different counsel.

- *Distributive Justice versus Expediency*   Despite the fact that conquest can pay off through acquisition of land and resources,[6] does the victor have any moral duty to disavow the spoils of war that can be seized from the defeated?
- *Retributive Justice versus Expediency*   Should the victor temper the punishment for immoral or illegal acts committed by the defeated, because punitive retribution may create significant **opportunity costs** for the victor in the form of forgone gains from trade?[7]
- *Corrective Justice versus Expediency*   Because defeated industrial powers can rapidly regain their antebellum power position unless they are occupied and exploited,[8] should a victor be ruthless and exact a heavy toll from the defeated to retard the vanquished nation's military recovery?
- *Restorative Justice versus Expediency*   Inasmuch as security threats abound and today's adversary may be tomorrow's ally, should the victor forgo justifiable penalties against the defeated to heal the relationship with its former enemy?

These questions exemplify the dilemmas created by the tension between justice and expediency in international politics. To what higher ideals beyond the pursuit of national self-interests are victors obligated? What duties do they have toward the vanquished? Who has responsibility for postwar policies when they are cobbled together by many people, each of whom, driven by diverse emotions, may labor on only one element of the overall design? To better understand these topics of ethical judgment and prudent choice it is helpful to define the domain of investigation to which these questions will be applied.

THE SCOPE OF THE INQUIRY

International politics can be defined as the pattern of interactions unfolding between and among actors in the global community. The most powerful of these actors are **states,** those sovereign actors that possess a permanent population, a well-defined territory, and a government capable of managing public affairs. Because of their prominence on the world stage, states and their relations are at the center of this book's attention, with the acknowledgment that other types of nonstate actors play important roles.

The relations of states are sometimes cooperative, frequently competitive, and often conflictual. The emphasis in *From War to Peace* is on interstate wars that ended with decisive victories. Although most readers will disagree little with the wars that were selected, some may wonder about the ones left out or mentioned only in passing. This book focuses on well-known wars with decisive outcomes because they accentuate the unique political and ethical dilemmas facing decisionmakers struggling to construct a lasting peace with a bitter enemy. These fateful choices warrant separate investigation, given the frequency with which victors have failed to convert battlefield successes into durable peace settlements. This is not to argue that peace building after a mili-

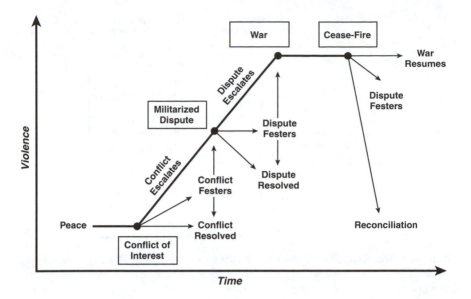

FIGURE 1.1 Phases and Trajectories in the Evolution of Armed Conflicts. Conflicts can move through various stages between peace and war. At each stage there are several divergent paths that the conflict might follow, each leading to different outcomes.

tary stalemate is unimportant. It is simply another subject, one that introduces a different set of research questions and requires separate treatment.

From War to Peace inspects fateful decisions regarding both war making and **peacemaking,** because there is a direct linkage between the two. How wars start and how they are fought affects choices about peace; conversely, how peace is made affects the probability of future wars. To envision the properties that the cases illuminate, it is helpful to think of the transition from peace to war and back to peace, with a possibility of a resumption of warfare, as a multistage, branching process. Figure 1.1 depicts the major decision points in this process and the various trajectories conflict may follow over time. This process begins when a nonviolent conflict of interest occurs between two parties that had previously been at peace. Although conflicts of interest are common in international affairs, most are resolved before either side resorts to heavy-handed tactics. The issue causing the conflict may dissipate on its own, the parties may resolve their differences through bilateral negotiation, or they may use a third-party intermediary to help them reach a settlement through such amicable conflict-resolution procedures as **mediation, arbitration,** or **adjudication.**

If the issue is not resolved, the conflict may fester, becoming a chronic source of discord before ultimately being settled or turning more violent. Alternatively, the conflict of interest may rapidly escalate to a serious dispute involving the threat, display, or use of military force. **Militarized disputes** can evolve in different ways: some are resolved, others fester for generations without resolution, and still others escalate to war. Just as there are numerous causal sequences that can lead a conflict of interest to escalate to a

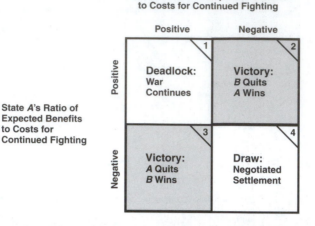

FIGURE 1.2 War Outcomes Based on Belligerent Cost-Benefit Ratios. Peacemaking decisions are made when a war ends, but the circumstances for choice depend on the way wars conclude. This text investigates situations in which there was a clear winner and loser (shaded cells)and evaluates the winner's decisions for dealing with the defeated. Source: Adapted from Stam, 1996.

dangerous militarized dispute, there are many ways that a militarized dispute can escalate to full-scale war. This potentiality highlights the possibility that an armistice and peace settlement are no guarantee that peace will prevail. Indeed, the postures of both victors and the defeated even in the aftermath of a reconciliation will affect their long-term relationship (see Chapter 9); a reconciliated settlement that is not reciprocal and mutually acceptable to both parties can fail to resolve the underlying hostilities, fueling anger and resentments that can lead to the resumption of war.

Figure 1.2 displays the possible outcomes of a war between two parties. When both sides believe the ratio of expected benefits to costs for continuing the fighting is positive (cell 1), the war will most likely continue. If both are convinced that the ratio is negative (cell 4), a negotiated settlement is probable. But when one side expects the benefits of continued fighting to exceed the costs while the other does not (cells 2 and 3), a cease-fire eventually will be declared with the side making the negative assessment surrendering. As shown in Figure 1.1, once the war is over and a cease-fire is in place, there are three possible outcomes: (1) the parties may reconcile and resume peaceful intercourse; (2) the conflict may fester as a bitter, unrepentant loser resorts to terrorism or other unconventional uses of military force short of war to keep pressure on the victor; or (3) the conflict may reignite into another round of warfare once the defeated party regroups.

The thesis of this book is that *the trajectory of a conflict after one of the belligerents wins a decisive military victory will be heavily influenced by the character of the peace settlement.* Whether a lasting peace emerges will depend largely on how the victor treats the vanquished following a cease-fire.

Each of the historical cases presented in the chapters that follow explores how the postwar policies implemented by the victor in a given war influenced the durability of the peace settlement. As such, they focus on wars terminating with a clear winner and loser (cells 2 and 3 in Figure 1.2), not those ending inconclusively in a draw (cell 4). Because decisions made by winners on how to deal with the defeated are shaped by the process of escalation and the conduct of the fighting, a brief history of the entire trajectory, from conflict of interest through cease-fire, is provided for each war to help readers better interpret each case's peacekeeping choices.

THE CALCULUS OF CHOICE: LIBERAL AND REALIST PERSPECTIVES

Most of what has been written over the centuries about the tension between justice and expediency in the termination of warfare has been informed by ideas derived from the intellectual traditions of "liberal" and "realist" thought in international relations. Both **liberalism** and **realism** purport to explain entrenched behavior patterns and predict future trends; and, most important, both offer advice to policymakers on what they ought to do to realize their foreign policy goals.[9] Liberalism and realism have many adherents, and it would be unfair to mask the diversity within these traditions by claiming that the members of each respective group all agree with one another. There are many streams of thought within these contending traditions. While it is beyond the scope of this book to trace all of the streams of thought within these contending traditions, Box 1.1 describes their core assumptions.

The chapters that follow present a number of policymakers strongly associated with each of these two traditions. Woodrow Wilson, for example, is often viewed as a pillar of liberal theory, which is embodied most prominently in his "Fourteen Points" speech given in the closing days of World War I. Franklin Delano Roosevelt echoed this vein of liberalism in his "Four Freedoms" speech during World War II. On the other hand, the actions of Klemens von Metternich and Otto von Bismarck exemplified realist theory during the Napoleonic and German unification wars, respectively. To prepare the way for examining the wartime and postwar policies advocated by these and other statesmen in the historical cases assembled, it is first helpful to take up the question of how liberals and realists respond to the demands of justice and the lure of expediency as wars wind down.

Liberalism

At the heart of liberal theorizing about issues of war and peace is the contention that an unbridled pursuit of national self-interest is destructive. Rather than emphasizing **self-help**, in which states use their own resources for self-promotion and protection, liberalism seeks ways in which states can organize themselves to promote economic growth and avoid war, without sacrificing either economic or political freedoms.[10] According to liberals, power resides in

BOX 1.1
THE ESSENTIALS OF LIBERALISM AND REALISM

The Liberal World View

Liberals hold divergent views of world politics. What joins them is their shared assumptions about reality. Collectively, liberals embrace the following beliefs:

1. Human nature is essentially "good" or altruistic and because people are capable of mutual aid and collaboration, the attainment of moral virtue and justice in international affairs is a meaningful aspiration.
2. The fundamental human concern for the welfare of others makes progress possible.
3. Bad human behavior is the product of evil institutions, global anarchy, and the absence of a global moral consensus that motivates people to harm others.
4. War is not inevitable and its frequency can be reduced by eradicating the anarchical and ethically normless conditions that encourage it.
5. War and injustice are international problems that require collective or multilateral, rather than national, efforts to eliminate them.
6. International society must reorganize itself institutionally to eliminate the lawless anarchy that makes problems such as war and competitive vengeance likely.
7. Global change and cooperation are possible because history records humanity's continuing efforts to successfully engineer reforms that build collaborative problem-solving institutions.

The Realist World View

Realists also hold diverse views on world politics. Nevertheless, all realists believe that conflicts of interests among nations are inevitable and that the purpose of statecraft is to ensure national survival by acquiring power. The following beliefs comprise the central tenets of realism:

1. History teaches that people are by nature sinful and wicked.
2. Of all people's evil ways, no sins are more prevalent or dangerous than the lust for power and the desire to dominate others.
3. The possibility of eradicating the instinct for power is a utopian aspiration.
4. Under such conditions, international politics is a struggle for power, "a war of all against all," as the sixteenth-century English philosopher Thomas Hobbes put it.
5. The primary obligation of every state in this environment — the goal to which all other national objectives and moral considerations

should be subordinated — is to promote the "national interest," defined in terms of survival and national security through power.

6. The anarchical nature of the international system necessitates the acquisition of military capabilities sufficient to deter or subdue any potential rival.

7. Economics is less relevant to national security than military might and is important primarily as a means to acquire national power and prestige.

8. Allies might increase the ability of a state to defend itself, but their loyalty and reliability should not be assumed.

9. International law and international organizations cannot be trusted to preserve peace.

10. International stability results from maintaining a balance of power.

adhering to ethical principles. Following a war, liberal theory counsels against approaching peacemaking from a **zero-sum** outlook that permits the winner to extract the greatest possible gains at the loser's expense, stressing the principle of **reciprocity** that is predicated on the expectation that behavior sent will be returned in kind. To maximize the prospects for enduring peace, liberal theorists reason that harsh punishments and staggering penalties will backfire, while clemency and compassion will produce cooperation and compliance.

Realism

In contrast to liberal theorists, realists see international politics as a ceaseless struggle for power. They believe that efforts to construct a postwar peace through clemency and compassion ignore the nasty, brutish facts of international life: Without a central authority to settle disputes, the strong will dominate the weak, the powerful will take advantage of the powerless, and relations between former enemies will be determined more by a myopic quest for self-advantage than by a principled concern for cooperative security. From the realist point of view, security is a function of power, and power is a function of military strength. Peace settlements, they argue, should not be grounded in expectations that an adversary will reciprocate conciliatory acts, because defeated states are likely to interpret magnanimity as weakness and use lenient treaties as an opportunity to resume the pursuit of power. Apprehensive over the possibility that an indignant loser will try to avenge its battlefield humiliation, many realists recommend firm settlements as the most reliable method of maintaining postwar peace.

In Search of a Path to Peace

Within victorious governments, we usually find considerable debate over the advisability of a lenient conciliatory versus a harsh, punitive peace settlement. Liberalism and realism, the two most common theoretical lenses policymakers use when inspecting the calculus of fateful choices regarding war and peacemaking, usually advance diametrically opposed recommendations (although, at times, they find common ground). Policymakers need a theory backed by evidence that answers the questions of how states should make peace. Which theory — liberalism or realism — offers the strongest basis for developing policy prescriptions to guide peace making in the wake of war? It is this very theoretical question that dominates the efforts of contemporary **peace research** scholars who seek to test empirically the conditions under which various approaches to the preservation of peace will succeed.

The cases in *From War to Peace* provide the opportunity to look at the dilemmas of peacemaking through both theoretical lenses, and to balance your evaluation of liberalism and realism by considering the findings produced by rigorous social science and informed by the normative analyses of moral philosophers. History is the social scientist's only laboratory and the moral philosopher's only available object of observation. It is from historical inquiry that better decisions can be made about how states ought to act if they want to cement a lasting peace. To help with the task of weighing the usefulness of rival liberal and realists approaches, it is important to first look at the possible options for peacemaking.

APPROACHES TO WAR TERMINATION

Every peace settlement is influenced by the manner in which an agreement to cease fighting is reached. One way wars may end is through the mere cessation of combat. With costs mounting and no victory in sight, the belligerents may simply stop fighting. Sometimes a temporary cease-fire is declared in a given locale for purposes such as tending to the wounded or burying the dead. On other occasions a more general armistice may be arranged in order to conduct peace negotiations.[11] And on still other occasions military activities may be halted without any collateral effort to reach a peace agreement.

Although various wars have ended through this kind of reciprocal cessation (e.g., in 1720 between Spain and France and in 1801 between Russia and Persia), belligerents usually prefer to bring hostilities to formal closure. By abstaining from an explicit settlement, the issues that initially caused the dispute to become militarized continue festering. Thus, settlements are preferred to cessations, even if all of the outstanding issues cannot be immediately resolved. For instance, the Treaty of Ghent, which brought the War of 1812 to a close, provided for the restoration of property and an exchange of prisoners between England and the United States but left various issues open for resolution at a later time.

Figure 1.3 shows the ways in which hostilities between hypothetical states A and B may be brought to a definitive conclusion. If either A or B achieves a complete victory, it can demand the unconditional surrender of its adversary. *From War to Peace* looks at those disputes in which one warring state forced

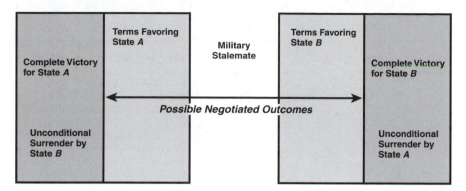

FIGURE 1.3 The Range of Peace Settlements.

the utter capitulation of its opponent (the darkest shaded area in Figure 1.3) or won decisively enough to obtain peace terms just short of unconditional surrender (the lightly shaded area). In contrast to instances of military stalemate, where neither party is in a position to dictate the peace settlement, these two forms of categorical victory allow the winner to impose its will upon the vanquished.

While each side may hope for resounding battlefield success, military and financial constraints normally stop the fray before total submission occurs. Table 1.1 lists the arguments typically taken into account when deciding whether or not to terminate hostilities.[12]

When neither combatant can conquer the other and both seek a formal end to hostilities, they usually will negotiate a peace treaty. Most treaties are couched in terms of perpetuity, though occasionally they have a fixed time limit. For instance, the 1713 Treaty of Adrianople between Russia and Turkey was limited to twenty-five years. Regardless of the time limit of a peace treaty, each side has an interest in ensuring the other does not violate its terms. A welter of techniques is used to ensure that peace treaties are upheld. They may be sanctified through religious rites (as was the 1559 Treaty of Cateau-Cambrésis between Spain and France), secured by an exchange of valuable objects (as were the treaties of 1756, 1764, and 1768 between Genoa and France), or guaranteed by third parties (as was the 1815 Act of Paris reestablishing the Swiss policy of neutrality). In addition, the legal norm that treaties are binding —*pacta sunt servanda*— also supports the promissory obligations incurred in a formal peace agreement.[13]

Peace treaties reflect a complex interplay of many influencing factors, including calculations of the opportunity costs or trade-off of gains and losses among competing options, the amount of domestic and international pressure on the combatants to lay down their arms, as well as the balance of national capabilities, risk-taking propensity, and resolve. Barring a military stalemate, either A or B will enjoy a position of relative superiority and emerge victorious, though the margin of victory can range from modest to decisive. War, as political scientist Thomas Schelling reminds us, is "a bargaining process — dirty,

TABLE 1.1
The Calculus of War Termination

Arguments Weighing in Favor of Termination	Arguments Weighing against Termination
The situation is deteriorating politically, militarily, or economically.	Circumstances are in our favor or show signs of improving politically, militarily, or economically.
Time is on the enemy's side; cut losses while still possible.	Time is on our side; maintain the pressure on the enemy.
No external support is expected.	External support is forthcoming.
Battlefield casualties are excessive.	The sunk costs are high; the number of lives already sacrificed requires pushing on regardless of the costs.
The domestic situation is unstable; social and political unrest hampers the war effort.	The domestic situation is stable; morale is high and the public continues to support the war effort.
The enemy has offered reasonable terms for concluding the war.	The enemy offers demanding terms for concluding the war.
Participating in peace negotiations will work to our advantage.	Participating in peace negotiations will weaken our position.

Source: Adapted from Handel, 1978, p. 37.

extortionate, and often quite reluctant bargaining on one side or both — nevertheless a bargaining process."[14] Almost every bargain that is struck furnishes advantages for victors and disadvantages for the vanquished. The greater the magnitude of the victory, the greater the opportunity for the winner to translate its military gains into favorable treaty terms.

PEACEMAKING OPTIONS

Victors have many options they can pursue when dealing with the defeated. As shown in Table 1.2, their choices range from actions that can be taken for the purpose of retribution to those that can promote reconciliation. As we shall see in the chapters that follow, victors typically combine several of these actions. Moreover, they may at times resort to different combinations when they have engaged the same adversary in successive wars.

Forging a Punitive Peace

There are several ways for victors to deal with the vanquished. The most severe forms of retribution fall under what the Romans called *deballatio,* a term that had three usages in antiquity: (1) subjugation of the defeated state,

TABLE 1.2
Selected Policy Options for Victors

Actions That May Be Used for Retribution	Example
Subjugation	Under the Peace of Vereeniging, which brought the 1899–1902 Anglo-Boer War to a conclusion, the Afrikaner republics of the Orange Free State and Transvaal became extinct as states and thus lost international legal personality.
Partial Annexation	Following the Russo-Ottoman War of 1828–1829, by the Treaty of Adrianople Russia appropriated the mouth of the Danube River and the Black Sea littoral of the Caucasus.
Occupation/ Colonization	In 1849, following the Second Sikh War, the kingdom of the Punjab was placed under British imperial rule in India.
Partition	At the end of World War II, Germany was divided into British, American, Soviet, and French zones and subjected to four-power control. In 1949, the Soviet zone was converted into a separate state, the German Democratic Republic. The remaining western zones became the Federal Republic of Germany.
Neutralization	Under the Austrian State Treaty of 1955, the occupation of Austria, which had been in effect since the end of World War II, was ended contingent upon Austria not acceding to future military alliances.
Demilitarization	Under the 1919 Treaty of Versailles, restrictions were placed on deployment of German military forces in the Rhineland.
Reconstitution	After World War II, the United States imposed a democratic political system on Japan.
Reparation	Under the terms of the 1842 Treaty of Nanking, China was required to recompense England for costs emanating from the Opium War.

. . . to Promote Reconciliation	Example
Rapprochement	After the defeat of Napoleon in 1815, France was permitted to join the Concert of Europe.
Restoration	Following the Ottoman Empire's victory in the 1861–1862 Montenegrin War, to placate the vanquished, in the Convention of Scutari, the Ottomans restored the frontiers of 1859.
Compensation	After France and Piedmont defeated Austria in 1859, by the Treaty of Zurich Austria was forced to cede most of Lombardy, but, to diminish Austria's humiliation and strengthen peace, Napoleon III in turn ceded Lombardy to Piedmont.
Resuscitation	In 1947, the United States instituted the Marshall Plan to rebuild the war-torn economies of Germany and Italy.

(2) occupation of the defeated state until a successor government is established, and (3) controlling portions of the defeated state's territory until it
fulfills certain conditions. Of the three, subjugation was the most common.
Traditionally, it has been defined as the "extermination in war of one belligerent by another through annexation of the former's territory after conquest, the enemy's forces having been annihilated."[15] From the time of
Sargon I (2350 B.C.E.), depicted in Akkadian lore as the "King of Battle" and
known today as the founder of the world's first recorded empire, armies have
obliterated beaten enemies and subjugated their lands. Conquest tended to
be beneficial, because ruthless overseers could extract resources from
defeated countries for less than the costs of administration and repression.[16]
Moreover, according to custom, conquest gave the victor title to the territory
of the defeated.[17] Francisco de Vitoria, a sixteenth-century Spanish professor
of theology, was among the first people to wrestle with questions about the
legality and morality of such imperial claims rationalized by the stern realist
belief that "might makes right."[18] His analysis of the respective rights of
Spaniards and the indigenous population of the Americas drew on **just war
theory** in Christian doctrine[19] and encouraged a humanitarian reassessment
of the long-standing belief that conquerors acquired legal title over the conquered. "Arms, of themselves," the Abbé de Mably would later insist in the
spirit of liberal thinking, "give no title,"[20] a view that did not gain prominence until after World War I with the promulgation of the 1928 Kellogg-
Briand Pact, the Stimson Doctrine of 1932, and the 1938 Lima Declaration
of the Nonrecognition of the Acquisition of Territory by Force.

Under Article 10 of the League of Nations Covenant and Article 2(4) of the
United Nations Charter, involuntary cession by military conquest is now illegal.
Still, many people agree with legal scholar H. B. Jacobini, who contends that
"however meritorious such positions may be from the standpoint of abstract
justice, prevailing international practice seems to support the contrary view."[21]
Consequently, although the 1970 Declaration of Principles of International
Law adopted by the UN General Assembly declares "the territory of a state
shall not be the object of acquisition by another state resulting from the threat
or use of force," three qualifications to this assertion have been proposed:

1. a state acting in lawful exercise of its right of self-defense may seize and
   occupy foreign territory as long as such seizure and occupation are necessary to its self-defense;
2. as a condition of its withdrawal from such territory, that state may require
   the institution of security measures reasonably designed to ensure that the
   territory shall not again be used to mount a threat or use of force against it
   of such a nature as to justify exercise of self-defense; and
3. where the prior holder of the territory had seized that territory unlawfully,
   the state which subsequently takes that territory in the lawful exercise of
   self-defense has, against that prior holder, better title.[22]

Whereas the desires for wealth and glory are among the various impulses
that stimulate conquerors, other motives and ethical values also frequently

influence how they treat the defeated. "The vanquished can never be the friends of the victors," asserted the Mongol conqueror Genghis Khan; "the death of the former is necessary therefore for the safety of the latter."[23] To be sure, numerous conquerors have not annihilated their victims in a genocidal bloodbath. Defeated states have been occupied, partitioned, neutralized, demilitarized, or forced to make reparations in retribution for past transgressions and in the name of future defense needs. Yet these acts can create new security problems. A punitive peace often inspires another round of warfare aimed at undoing the harsh settlement. The *Dhammapada,* an early collection of Buddhist verses, tells us that "victory breeds hatred, for the conquered sleep in sorrow."[24] The *Mahabharata,* an ancient Hindu epic, takes a similar position: "A king should never do such an injury to his foes as could rankle in the latter's heart."[25] "The conqueror can have vengeance or he can have justice," observes historian Geoffrey Blainey, "but he cannot have both in the same treaty. If he chooses the path of vengeance, he may keep his hobnailed boot on the neck of the vanquished for a generation or so, but this may be the limit."[26]

Constructing a Lenient Peace

Recognizing the limitations of a boot on the neck, some conquerors have defined national interests in accordance with liberal moral values and not pressed their victories to the point of humiliating the defeated. Rather than establishing a vindictive peace that might fuel an international vendetta, they have sought a restorative peace designed to reconcile former adversaries and would-be belligerents.

One long-standing approach to constructing a restorative peace has been for the victorious party to make symbolic concessions, however minor they might be. Roman emperor Julius Caesar, for example, showed clemency after victory and restored the status of many defeated foes. Similarly, Kautilya, an exponent of ancient Hindu **realpolitik,** recommended that the conqueror "should never covet the land, things, and sons and wives of the king slain by him." Rather, "he should reinstate in their own estates relatives of the kings slain."[27]

Another approach to establishing a restorative peace involves granting aid to the defeated. Various forms of assistance, ranging from territorial compensation to financial support, have been employed to revive the opponent and allay feelings of bitterness. Compassion is here thought to be more beneficial than resorting to retaliation for past injuries. As summarized by the maxim in the ancient Indian "Advice to Kings" *(Rajovada),* the most effective policy is to overcome "wrath with kindness, evil with good, greed with charity and falsehood with truth."[28]

In sum, when making decisions about national security, victorious leaders are pulled in opposite directions. Advocates of stern punishment counsel that a punitive peace treaty will disempower the defeated enemy and force it to refrain from future fighting. Proponents of rehabilitative policies proclaim that generous terms will assuage the vanquished, build trust, and secure their cooperation in building a lasting framework of mutual security. As we shall see in the cases presented in the chapters that follow, rationally choosing between these consequential alternatives is so difficult that it can be labeled the ultimate test of wise statecraft.

CHOOSING BETWEEN RECONCILIATION AND RETRIBUTION

"Victory in the true sense," the strategist Basil Liddell Hart wrote, "implies that the state of peace . . . is better after the war than before."[29] In an effort to achieve a better peace, victors draw inspiration from a vast reservoir of values when choosing which policy options to pursue as they deal with the defeated. As the views quoted in Box 1.2 demonstrate, some of these values accentuate magnanimity. Defeated troops receive mercy, and noncombatants are treated with compassion. Alternatively, victors may espouse values that downplay clemency in favor of harsh punishment. Preoccupied with preserving the gains won in battle, they try to incapacitate former foes. Joseph Stalin's suggestion on how to prevent German military revival after World War II illustrates the kind of policies derived from this sort of brutal value system. According to Winston Churchill, Stalin proposed liquidating the remaining fifty thousand men in the German officer corps.[30]

At issue is which value position helps political leaders craft viable postwar policies. The best approach is not always obvious. To illustrate the difficulties in choosing between lenient versus punitive policies, consider the following example from Sparta's victory over Athens at the end of the fifth century B.C.E.

Sparta and the Peloponnesian War

On a beautiful spring day in the year 404 B.C.E., as the sound of flutes drifted through the crowd, Spartan dignitaries adorned in flowers watched with satisfaction as the once mighty Athenian fleet burned in its home port at Piraeus. Twenty-seven years earlier, Sparta had gone to war with Athens. It was, as the Athenian historian Thucydides recorded, the greatest upheaval that had ever shaken the ancient world.[31] Nature itself seemed to agree: the tiny island of Delos, long a center of Greek religious life, was jolted by an earthquake just before the fighting began. No one could remember anything like this happening there before. Was it an omen? Would some terrible tragedy befall Greece once its two most powerful city-states clashed?

Nothing was farther from the minds of the Spartans on that spring day. After dismantling the defensive walls surrounding Athens, they proclaimed all Greeks were free from Athenian imperial control. To commemorate their military triumph, they unveiled a group of bronze statues in Delphi that depicted gods laying wreaths upon Spartan heads. The victors in what we now call the Peloponnesian War could scarcely contain their pride. Not only

---

BOX 1.2
CONTENDING VIEWS ON HOW TO DEAL WITH ENEMIES

On Magnanimity

"In war, resolution; in defeat, defiance; in victory, magnanimity."
—Winston Churchill

"Let us never negotiate out of fear; but let us never fear to negotiate."
—John F. Kennedy

"Treat the enemy that has been conquered with courtesy and generosity."
—Kwan-Tsz

On Malevolence

"For great evils, drastic remedies are necessary, and whoever has to treat them should not be afraid to use the instrument that cuts the best."
—Prince Klemens von Metternich

"Nothing should be left to an invaded people except their eyes for weeping."
—Otto von Bismarck

"Bear thou thy foe upon thy shoulders till the time cometh when thou canst throw him down, breaking him into pieces like an earthen pot thrown with violence upon a stony surface. The foe must never be let off even though he addresseth thee most piteously. No pity shouldst thou shew him but slay him at once."

—Kanika

---

was peace at hand, but it appeared to be a peace cemented by Spartan **hegemony.** The years of brutal combat and staggering losses were finally over. With an unrivaled army and numerous allies, Sparta was positioned to reshape the Hellenic state system.

Greece at the time of the Peloponnesian War (see Map 1.1) was not unified; it contained a welter of small, autonomous poleis, or city-states, scattered throughout the Balkan Peninsula, the Aegean Archipelago, and what is today western Turkey. Though fiercely independent and often harboring territorial jealousies, the city-states of fifth-century B.C.E. Greece shared a common culture, language, and religious practices. Most poleis were small, not exceeding a few hundred square miles and a population of approximately twenty thousand. Sparta and Athens were much larger than the average

MAP 1.1 The Hellenic World during the Peloponnesian War 431–404, B.C.E. At the onset of the Peloponnesian War, the Athenian Empire consisted of city-states scattered throughout Ionia and the Aegean Sea. Sparta's allies were concentrated in the Peloponnesus.

polis, however. Laconia, the region around Sparta, contained roughly 270,000 inhabitants within an area of over three thousand square miles. Athens boasted a population of approximately 300,000 and an area of some one thousand square miles.[32] Herodotus, touted by many as the "father" of history, indicates that relations between these two powerful city-states had long alternated between hostility and cooperation and says that oracles warned the Spartans that "many deeds of enmity would be done against them by the Athenians."[33]

Sparta was admired throughout Greece for the courage and skill of its soldiers. Despite this reputation, oligarchic Sparta was a cautious, conservative land power. Its rival, democratic Athens, was a bold, innovative sea power that possessed a vast maritime empire. As Athens grew in power and prosperity, Sparta became apprehensive about how that military and economic strength might be used. The Corinthians, a Spartan ally, warned of an insatiable Athenian appetite for expansion; all Greece would eventually fall under an Athenian yoke unless Sparta took action. In response, the Spartans made a series of demands on the Athenians. Pericles, the leading Athenian of the day, urged no concessions: "If you give way," he cautioned, "you will instantly have to meet some greater demand."[34] Convinced by the wisdom of his advice, the Athenians refused to accede to the Spartan ultimatum. Each side now prepared for war.

Hostilities began in 431 B.C.E. when the Spartan king, Archidamus, invaded the Attic Plain which adjoined Athens. Rather than confront Sparta and its Peloponnesian allies in a series of set-piece battles, Pericles encouraged people living throughout Attica to abandon their homes for the safety of the walled city. Archidamus might be able to pillage the countryside, but he could not breach Athens's walls or sever the city's maritime links with commercial centers around the Mediterranean and Black Seas. On the other hand, Athens could employ its formidable naval forces to strike anywhere along the coastline of Laconia. If Athens had patience, Pericles reasoned, the Spartans would exhaust themselves in costly, inconclusive campaigns. Furthermore, if it showed restraint by fighting a limited, defensive war, it would be possible to negotiate a peace settlement with those Spartans who feared a protracted conflict.[35]

The Athenians' plans for success were dealt a severe blow in the second year of the war when a terrible epidemic struck Athens, killing roughly one-fourth of the population. With disease ravaging the city and Spartan soldiers laying waste to surrounding farmland, Pericles came under heavy criticism. In his last public speech before succumbing to the plague, he told the Athenians to stop grieving for their private losses and work for the public good. Persuaded by Pericles' appeals to honor and past glories, the Athenians recommitted themselves to the war effort. Showing phenomenal resilience, they continued to fight even under the most bleak conditions.

As the war dragged on, internal disputes within Greek city-states between democrats favoring Athens and oligarchs sympathetic to Sparta became commonplace. Both Athens and Sparta tried to break the military stalemate by undertaking daring offensives, but neither enjoyed long-term success. Eventually, a new leader rose to prominence in Athens. Handsome, charismatic, and daring, Alcibiades was an imaginative military strategist. Yet he also possessed serious character flaws: ostentatious, brash, and self-centered, his behavior offended almost everyone. As one contemporary described him, Alcibiades had a lengthy career "as an adulterer, as a stealer of the wives of others, [and] as a perpetrator of acts of lawless violence in general." Though claiming to be a friend of the people, he was an extortionist who used state revenues for personal gain.[36]

Whereas at the beginning of the war Pericles could boast of government guided by free and open political discussion, during this later stage passion eclipsed prudence. The moderation of Periclean leadership had given way under the pressure of a long, grinding war to the megalomania of Alcibiades. As Thucydides reported, reckless ambition led Athenians into "projects both unjust to themselves and to their allies — projects whose success would only conduce to the honor and advantage of private persons, and whose failure entailed certain disaster on the country." Furthermore, he added, "the few who liked it not, feared to appear unpatriotic . . . and so kept quiet."[37]

Two incidents embody these changes in Athenian policy. The first consisted of a ruthless assault on the small island of Melos; the second entailed an ill-fated attack on the larger island of Sicily. Alcibiades was behind both incidents.

In 416 B.C.E., the Athenians led a force of approximately three thousand soldiers against Melos, a militarily insignificant poleis that wished to remain nonaligned during the war. Alcibiades recommended that if Melos did not agree to become an Athenian ally, it should be obliterated. The Melians argued that such a brutal attack would be unjust since they had not harmed Athens. Moreover, it was in Athens's self-interest to show restraint: destroying Melos would drive other neutral city-states into the Spartan bloc and set a precedent for how Athens might be treated if it lost the war. Finally, the Melians pointed out that it would be unreasonable to surrender while there was still hope of holding out against an Athenian siege and being rescued by the Spartans. Scornful of these appeals to justice, expedience, and reasonableness, the Athenians asserted that in interstate relations "the strong do what they can and the weak suffer what they must."[38] Regardless of the merits of the Melian argument, Athens had the strength to subjugate Melos if it so desired. The Melians chose to resist and were destroyed. The Athenians killed all adult men and sold the women and children into slavery.

Immediately following the destruction of Melos, Athens embarked upon a larger, more risky military expedition. Attracted by the possibility of acquiring grain, timber, and other resources, Alcibiades began planning an invasion of Syracuse, the most powerful Greek city on the island of Sicily. Opponents of the expedition complained that Athens should not divide its forces and seek new enemies before the military stalemate with the Spartans had been broken. Victory would prove difficult to achieve. The expeditionary force was deficient in cavalry; it did not entail a quick, decisive strike; and its command structure was divided among three rivals: Lamachus, who was killed in combat; Nicias, who opposed the expedition; and Alcibiades, who was soon relieved of his command.

Losing Alcibiades, the expeditionary force's most energetic leader, hurt morale and eventually brought Sparta into the conflict. In 415 B.C.E. just before the fleet departed, busts of the god Hermes, which stood before many Athenian houses and public buildings, were mysteriously disfigured. Alcibiades' opponents suspected he was to blame, so they recalled him from Sicily to stand trial. Instead of returning, he fled to Laconia and provided the Spartan general Gylippus with information that would be used to thwart the Athenian drive to conquer Syracuse. After two years of inconclusive campaigning far from home, the Athenian expeditionary force suffered a catastrophic defeat in a climactic battle fought in the Great Harbor of Syracuse. Estimates place the cost of the Sicilian expedition at approximately forty thousand soldiers and 240 war ships.[39]

Despite the antiwar protest in Athens, most famously demonstrated in 411 B.C.E. in Aristophanes's play *Lysistrata* in which Greek women withhold sex to force the men to negotiate peace, the war continued. Athens once again displayed amazing resilience, recovering enough strength to restore democracy, rein in wayward allies, and win several major battles against the Spartans. As late as 406 B.C.E., they won a decisive victory at Arginusae. Sparta offered peace terms, but was refused. The carnage finally ended the next year when Spartan commander Lysander defeated the Athenians at the battle of Aegospotami. The historian Xenophon described what happened when word of the fiasco reached Athens: "As the news of the disaster was told, one man passed it on to another, and a sound of wailing arose and extended . . . along the Long Walls until it reached the city. That night no one slept. They mourned for the lost, but more still for their own fate. They thought that they themselves would now be dealt with as they had dealt with others."[40] Fearing that Sparta would treat them just as they once treated the Melians, the citizens of Athens prepared for a siege, which arrived as they feared.

With Athens besieged and on the brink of starvation, Sparta convened a conference to decide how to deal with its defeated foe. Erianthus of Thebes proposed leveling the city and converting the land to pasture. Delegates from Corinth suggested enslaving the population. Neither of these punitive measures appealed to the Spartans, however. It is said that after listening to a recitation of poetry from Euripides they declared the city that produced such a writer should never be destroyed.[41] Furthermore, in recognition of what Athens had done for the Greeks during earlier wars against Persia, its people should not be enslaved. Sparta opted for a relatively lenient settlement. It was decreed that "The Long Walls and the fortifications of Piraeus must be destroyed; all ships except twelve surrendered; the exiles to be recalled; Athens to have the same enemies and the same friends as Sparta had and to follow Spartan leadership in any expedition Sparta might make either by land or sea."[42] Since the Spartans had little regard for democracy, they also backed an oligarchic government in Athens called the Thirty Tyrants. In addition, they established boards of supervisors over each of Athens's allies and stationed garrisons within their territories to maintain order.

As a lenient peace, the settlement of 404 B.C.E. did not destroy Athenian power, but neither did it moderate Athenian ambitions. Keeping Athens in check would require a level of cooperation the victors could not sustain. Although Sparta fought under the banner of liberating the Greeks from Athenian imperialism, it began encroaching on other states. Lacking a coherent grand strategy, the Spartans stumbled into confrontations with former coalition partners as well as with a resurgent Athens. And all the while, their population was gradually being depleted.

At the beginning of the Peloponnesian War, King Archidamus spoke about the Spartan virtue of *sophrosune,* a form of sobriety or prudence that induces "wise moderation" and prevents one from becoming "insolent with success."[43] After the war, however, its leaders fell victim to arrogant pride and overreaching, what the Greeks called *hubris* and *pleonexia.* Sparta's quest for empire resulted in years of fruitless skirmishing punctuated by untenable truces. Though they did not recognize it, the Spartans had emerged from the Peloponnesian War with a tarnished triumph. Little thought had been given to designing a political **grand strategy** for the post-war world. After the peace settlement was concluded, there was no guide for Spartan foreign policy. One mistake followed another until Sparta was prostrate. Perhaps the long-term prospects for Sparta would have been better if they had been more harsh with the Athenians. Unfortunately, for the decisionmaker who seeks a rough-and-ready answer to the question of how to deal with the defeated, punitive policies do not provide a simple solution. To illustrate the drawbacks of retribution, consider another well-known example from antiquity: Rome's victory over Carthage in a series of three successive wars during the third and second centuries B.C.E.

Rome and the Punic Wars

Two great empires, Rome and Carthage, collided between 264 and 146 B.C.E. (see Map 1.2). Growth in their respective power generated an intense rivalry, which turned violent with wars of twenty-three, eighteen, and three years duration interrupted by a period of peace lasting twenty-two years between the first and second wars and fifty-two years between the second and final wars. Enduring rivalries of this sort are common when bitter rivals experience different rates of growth. Sometimes the rising power uses newly acquired military might to muscle ahead of its opponent. On other occasions, the established power lashes out in the hope of arresting its competitor's growing strength.

While many factors contributed to Rome's growth, two were particularly important: a civic culture emphasizing duty, dignity, and virtue, and a military code that fostered discipline, valor, and tenaciousness. Nowhere was their patriotism and dauntless courage better exemplified than in the response of Gaius Mucius to the siege of Rome by Lars Porsinna, king of Clusium. According to the historian Livy, Mucius infiltrated the enemy camp but was captured after mistakenly stabbing someone other than the king. Upon hearing that his prisoner was just one of many determined assassins, Porsinna threatened to throw him into a nearby fire unless he revealed their names. Mucius retorted that his comrades would bear any hardship to slay Porsinna, whereupon he thrust his arm into the flames and held it steady without showing pain until his right hand was burned off. Shocked by this demonstration of resolve, the flustered king decided it would be prudent to end the siege and evacuate Roman territory. Gaius Mucius

MAP 1.2 Empires in the Mediterranean, about 240 B.C.E. The struggle for domination in the Mediterranean had shifted following the collapse of Alexander the Great's empire, which splintered into the Macedon, Egyptian, and Seleucid (Syrian) empires. In the West, the Roman Empire and the Carthaginian Empire were expanding. By the end of the Punic Wars (264–146 B.C.E.) the Roman Empire was dominant.

was subsequently honored for his bravery and given the name Scævola, or "lefty."[44]

The story of Gaius Mucius illustrates the Roman admiration for heroism. Eventually this martial spirit was combined with rigorous training and an outstanding logistical system to create an awesome fighting machine. Rome may have possessed an imposing military, but its rulers recognized the contribution defeated adversaries could make to their security. "Once victory has been secured," wrote the Roman philosopher Cicero, "those who were not cruel or savage in warfare should be spared."[45] To encourage the vanquished to accept Roman rule, conquered Latin cities that demonstrated their loyalty were given *civitas sine suffragio*—the same rights enjoyed by Roman citizens, except for the vote. Rome also rewarded these cities by exempting them from taxation and granting them a share in the plunder from subsequent conquests. Leniency paid handsome dividends, as defeated cities were systematically converted to allies.

Carthage presented the Romans with a greater challenge than the Latin cities of Italy. Founded just before 800 B.C.E. by a Phoenician queen known as Dido, Carthage encompassed most of what is today northern and central Tunisia. The city boasted an excellent harbor, a large market square bordered by rows of six-story houses, and surrounding lands planted with olive and fig trees. The entrepreneurial Carthaginians possessed a superb navy, and they deployed it to protect trade routes that stretched from Sierra Leone to the Brittany coast. Commercial issues underpinned the earliest diplomatic exchanges between Rome and Carthage. In the year 509 B.C.E., the two states signed a treaty, the text of which proclaimed that "there shall be friendship between the Romans and their allies, and the Carthaginians and their allies."[46] Under the terms of this treaty, two spheres of influence were established: The Romans were prohibited from trading in Africa or Sardinia without Carthaginian supervision, and Carthage accepted similar restrictions on the Italian peninsula. A new Romano-Punic Treaty in 348 B.C.E. expanded Carthaginian dominions while prohibiting Roman commerce in Spain.

Relations between the two powers deteriorated over the next century as Carthage gained control over Sicily. The Romans perceived their hold over this strategically important island as a threat to the heel and toe of Italy. In 264 B.C.E. the Roman Assembly voted to expel the Carthaginians from Sicily, and the First Punic War (264–241 B.C.E.; named after the Latin name for the Carthaginians, *Poeni*, a contracted form of Phoenician) began.

Rome was a continental power with a fearsome infantry but virtually no maritime forces.[47] To defeat the seemingly invincible Carthaginian navy, Rome copied and improved on Punic warships. Although inexperienced Roman sailors lost many fleets to storms, through daring and pure tenacity they took command of the sea and drove the leader of the Carthaginian armed forces, General Hamilcar Barca, into retreat. Relying upon their fabled tenacity and a larger population, the Romans wore the Carthaginians down in a grueling war of attrition.

The victorious Romans now faced the question of what kind of peace settlement to offer the Carthaginians. High principles were at stake, touching at the very core of the old Roman policy of generosity toward defeated foes. But the showdown with Carthage differed from Rome's earlier campaigns on the Italian peninsula: it was an exhausting ordeal that Rome did not wish to repeat. The Roman Consul G. Lutatius Catulus initially offered Hamilcar a generous peace. The Carthaginians were required to leave Sicily, return Roman prisoners, and to pay an indemnity of 2,200 silver talents. Hamilcar agreed, but the Roman Assembly, consumed by a zeal for revenge, replaced the offer with one that exacted heavy financial and territorial costs. The war indemnity was increased by a thousand talents and Carthage was required to evacuate the Lipari and Aegates islands that lie between Italy and Sicily.[48]

According to Polybius, the revised peace treaty "exasperated the anger of Hamilcar, [which] became one of the causes of the Second Punic War."[49]

Instead of removing the source of conflict, it fueled Carthaginian hostility, while at the same time leaving Carthage in a position from which it could avenge its sense of unjust injury. As historian Donald Kagan has written: "The peace [the Roman victors] finally imposed on Carthage in 238 was of the least stable kind: it embittered the losers without depriving them of the capacity for seeking revenge and without establishing a system able to restrain them."[50]

Boiling with resentment, Hamilcar Barca began planning for the day that Carthage would get even with Rome. Five years after the First Punic War ended, he fathered a son named Hannibal, who became the instrument for his revenge. Polybius claims that Hannibal swore an oath against Rome at the age of nine during a religious ceremony.[51] Seventeen years later, as Carthage's military leader during the Second Punic War, he developed a daring plan to extract revenge from the Romans. Hannibal's plan hinged on a series of assumptions: Roman maritime strength and control of the islands between Africa and Italy prevented Carthage from mounting a credible naval threat; speed and mobility could be used by the Carthaginian army to outflank, envelop, and destroy larger, slower Roman units; a string of dramatic victories over the Roman army on Italian soil would cause Rome's allies to unite with the Carthaginians; defections by its allies would deprive Rome of almost half of its manpower, thereby reducing its capacity to wage another war of attrition; because Carthage had a small fleet devoid of logistical support, troops and supplies for an assault on Italy could not be transported by sea; and the most promising invasion route extended overland from Carthage's resource base in Spain, through France, across the Alps, and down into the northern part of the Italian peninsula.

It was not long before Hannibal had the opportunity to implement his plan. The Second Punic War (219–201 B.C.E.) broke out following a dispute between the two powers over their respective spheres of influence in Spain. Hannibal quickly marched from Spain toward Italy over the treacherous, snow-covered Alps with his veteran army, an impressive cavalry, and trained war elephants. How he found enough food for his men and animals remains a mystery. Just as winter approached, Hannibal brought his half-starved and half-frozen army down into the Po River Valley, where he found support among Rome's ancient enemies, the Gauls.

Alarmed that their cunning adversary had reached northern Italy in 218 B.C.E., the Roman Senate sent forces to block the Carthaginian advance. Using speed and deception masterfully, Hannibal inflicted two humiliating defeats on the Romans, who lost some thirty thousand troops in a battle along the Trebia River and another twenty-five thousand soldiers near Lake Trasimene.

Emboldened by his lopsided victories, Hannibal marched on southern Italy, expecting Rome's allies to revolt and join him. Although many Italian cities were sympathetic to the Carthaginian cause, Hannibal's hopes were unfulfilled. No significant defections occured after the Carthaginian victories in the north. Convinced that just one more stunning victory would induce Rome's allies to defect, Hannibal sought an opportunity to deliver a decisive blow.

The showdown came in 216 B.C.E. near the village of Cannae, a Roman supply depot on the Aufidus River in southeastern Italy. Vastly outnumbered,

Hannibal deployed his troops in a convex formation with the apex facing the Romans. When the Romans surged forward, the Carthaginians fell back into a concave formation whose outer cavalry wings encircled the surprised legionaries. By encouraging the Romans to advance against what seemed to be the most vulnerable point in his unorthodox alignment, Hannibal had duped them into expending their energy in the wrong place, thus turning a fake retreat into a double envelopment of the charging Roman infantry. With cunning, Hannibal had strategically nullified his opponent's numerical superiority, because only those legionaries along the perimeter of the densely packed mass of soldiers could reach the Carthaginians with their swords. Of the roughly eighty thousand Romans who took the field that day, some fifty thousand were killed. Hannibal, on the other hand, lost less than six thousand of his thirty-five thousand troops. Yet, despite his magnificent victory at Cannae, few major cities on the Italian peninsula were willing to join him, and the disappointed Hannibal never acquired adequate strength to capture Rome itself.

Finally recognizing Hannibal's brilliance as a field commander, the Romans henceforth avoided set-piece battles. Under the leadership of Fabius Maximus, they adopted a defensive strategy: Roman legions would harass Hannibal's forces, deny them access to supplies, and ruthlessly punish any Italian city that defected to Hannibal's side. Although the Romans did not win any morale-boosting victories, their strategy of exhausting the Punic army had two important effects: (1) because Hannibal's men could not disperse and plunder on a large scale, Hannibal was unable to raise the funds needed to purchase additional mercenaries; and (2) because Hannibal's army remained relatively small and lacked a powerful siege train, it remained unable to coerce Rome's allies into defecting.[52]

At the same time, Rome continued to control the seas. Lacking an offensive naval capability, Hannibal watched helplessly as Rome took the offensive in Spain, drove the Carthaginians out of the Sicilian stronghold of Syracuse, and recaptured Tarentum in southern Italy. Soon, behind the talented general Cornelius Scipio, they threatened Carthage itself.

In 204 B.C.E., Scipio marshaled a huge expeditionary force for an invasion of north Africa, which included many of the disgraced soldiers who survived the battle of Cannae. Prior to setting sail, Scipio prayed to the gods of land and sea for "the power of vengeance" and requested the "means to inflict upon the Carthaginian state the sufferings which the Carthaginians have labored to inflict on ours."[53]

The clash between Hannibal and Scipio occurred near Zama two years later. After nearly a day of fighting, the veterans of Cannae regained their honor. Hannibal suffered the first major defeat of his military career, losing approximately twenty-five thousand soldiers compared to only two thousand for the Romans.[54] Given Hannibal's losses, Carthage had no choice but to surrender.

Following the rout at Zama, the triumphant Scipio rejected the argument that Carthage's annihilation was necessary. He wished to avoid weakening the Punic economy so much that it could not contribute to the richness and glory of Rome. Thus, while the peace treaty of 201 B.C.E. destroyed Carthage's capacity to threaten Rome again, it did not leave Carthage in ruins. After disarming the Punic army, Rome imposed an indemnity of ten thousand silver talents, forced Carthage to relinquish all of its overseas territories, and forbid it to ever again make war without Roman consent.

Though reduced to the status of a Roman protectorate, Carthage nonetheless recovered economically and was able to pay off the war indemnity within ten years. Alarmed by Carthage's revival, Marcus Porcius Cato, a powerful politician who had fought the Carthaginians at the decisive battle of Zama, became consumed with the fear that renewed Punic rivalry with Rome would occur unless drastic steps were taken. He concluded each of his public speeches by proclaiming: "As for the rest, I am of the opinion that Carthage must be destroyed."[55]

Rome heeded Cato's advice. Claiming that Carthage had breached the peace treaty of 201 B.C.E. by resisting the territorial encroachments of a neighboring king, Rome declared war in 149 B.C.E. and blockaded the city. Compared to the two previous wars between Rome and Carthage, the Third Punic War (149–146 B.C.E.) ended quickly. Not only was Carthaginian power destroyed, but the city of Carthage itself was annihilated. After the slaughter of nearly a half-million Carthaginian citizens, the remaining 10 percent who survived were sold into slavery, and the territory of Carthage was absorbed by Rome.

Rome was changed by its act of genocide as well. The prudence that had previously converted conquered peoples to willing allies of the Roman Empire was replaced by a creed that put the worship of power above honor. The Romans had substituted annihilation for assimilation.

Without the threat of Carthage to bind the Romans together, politics within Rome deteriorated. According to the historian Diodorus Siculus,

> once the rival city was destroyed, it was only too evident that there would be civil war at home, and that hatred for the governing power would spring up among all the allies because of the rapacity and lawlessness to which the Roman magistrates would subject them. All this did indeed happen to Rome after the destruction of Carthage, which brought in its wake the following: dangerous demagoguery, the redistribution of land, major revolts among allies, [and] prolonged and frightful civil wars.[56]

The Punic Wars placed an enormous strain on the Roman Republic. Fighting for almost a century without respite, the Romans financed warfare on a scale never before attempted. Not only did the sheer magnitude of the Punic Wars transform the Roman economy, but it ultimately shattered the political structure of the republic.

Hannibal's campaign ravaged the agricultural infrastructure of southern Italy. Small, rural landowners who had been conscripted into the Roman army could not tend their fields. When the Punic Wars ended, soldiers mustered out of the army returned to devastated, debt-ridden farms. Wealthy

aristocrats, enriched by the spoils of war, purchased these farms and combined them into vast estates *(latifundia)* worked by slave labor. Whereas
hardy, independent subsistence farmers had once been a central component
of the Roman citizenry, now resentful, landless army veterans began crowd-
ing into the city from the countryside.

Rome suffered through a prolonged period of revolutionary strife after
the Punic Wars. Political life degenerated into a class conflict between the
masses and the wealthy. Each side had its own military champion. Gaius
Marius, who distinguished himself in wars against King Jugurtha of
Numidia (112–105 B.C.E.), stood with the masses. Lucius Cornelius Sulla,
Marius's former lieutenant in the Jugurthine War, sided with the wealthy.
These generals led a gruesome civil war that ended with Sulla coercing the
Senate in 82 B.C.E. to declare him dictator for life. Once in control, he terrorized Rome by posting lists of enemies and offering rewards to those killing
anyone on the lists. Upon Sulla's death in 78 B.C.E., the question was not
whether the republic would be supplanted by imperial rule, but which ambitious military commander would use the army to inaugurate that rule. The
answer came several tumultuous decades later, when Julius Caesar vanquished his rival, Pompey, and assumed absolute power.

Thinking Strategically about War Termination

In retrospect, our two examples from antiquity suggest that there is no simple
answer to the question of how victors should treat the vanquished. Both
Sparta's leniency and Rome's ruthlessness had drawbacks. Since no stock formula exists for constructing peace settlements, serious attention must be given
to the political context surrounding the belligerents. If leaders "concentrate
exclusively on victory, with no thought for the after-effect," insists Liddell
Hart, "it is almost certain that the peace will be a bad one, containing the
germs of another war."[57] As the postwar difficulties encountered by Sparta and
Rome reveal, states need an overarching grand strategy under which warfare is
conducted with unremitting attention to the kind of peace that is desired.

At minimum, such a grand strategy should contain three elements. It
should (1) identify the goals that must be achieved to produce security, (2)
describe the military and nonmilitary actions that will result in these goals
being attained, and (3) specify how scarce human and material resources will
be coordinated to support those actions. Simply put, a grand strategy sets
forth a "means-ends chain" of contingent predictions: if we do *A*, *B*, and *C*,
the desired results *X*, *Y*, and *Z* will follow.[58] Unfortunately, rather than crafting a comprehensive, integrated strategy for shaping the contours of the
postwar world, most victors simply substitute a defense posture for a comprehensive plan for responding to unfolding events. Whether victors should
be magnanimous may seem insignificant as one revels in the applause of a
victory parade. Yet the wrong choice can breed the very problem that the
war was fought to resolve.

To be sure, it is not easy to keep long-term political goals in mind during the heat of battle. Leaders often find themselves defining and redefining their goals incrementally as a war unfolds. Over the course of the fighting, they come to think of grand strategy in the narrow terms of a military mission designed to coerce the enemy into submission and surrender. Rarely do they articulate the political goals that military missions ultimately serve.

Why decisionmakers frequently find themselves a lap behind is one of the subjects of the next seven chapters in this book. In Part II, we open by examining in chronological order three armed conflicts from the classical European state system: (1) the Thirty Years' War and the Peace of Westphalia, (2) the Napoleonic Wars and the peace settlement reached at the Congress of Vienna, and (3) the Wars of German Unification. In Part III, we turn our attention to the epic struggles that marked the transition from the classical European state system to the contemporary global system: World War I and the Treaty of Versailles, and World War II and the series of conferences that occurred in its aftermath. In Part IV, we look at two conflicts that many analysts believe foreshadow the hi-tech wars of the future: the Persian Gulf War and the war in Kosovo. These cases allow us to compare the various approaches that victors have taken in an effort to construct a durable peace. As we progress through these historical case studies, our focus will be on the following questions:

- Did the victors seek reconciliation or retribution?
- Was their attempt at engineering either a lenient or a harsh peace supported by a coherent grand strategy?
- If so, what were the elements of that strategy?
- How successful was the strategy?
- What lessons, practical and ethical, do these individual cases suggest about the most productive and moral paths winners should take to peacemaking with defeated enemies?

Each case tells a different tale and illustrates different aspects of the problems in making rational and ethical decisions about a set of very difficult problems. By asking similar questions about different historical episodes and comparing the choices made by the victors after a series of wars and their consequences, insights can be sharpened about the boundaries of prudent and just choice when nations attempt to make peace. These structured, focused comparisons will facilitate the formation of some policy prescriptions for leaders to follow in the wake of future wars.

WHAT TO LOOK FOR WHEN COMPARING CASES

To understand why states go to war and how they make peace, it is necessary to think like detectives, looking for clues left by the choices political leaders made from the onset through the conclusion of the fighting. Putting the pieces of this puzzle together is difficult because evidence can be ambiguous and easily misread. Nor is it easy to undertake **counterfactual analysis** and imagine the alternative course of events that would have occurred if different war and peace decisions were made.[59]

To meet this investigative challenge, it is helpful to identify the various factors that influence decisionmakers when wars start and as they wind down, with attention to how the causes and conduct of war influence the type of peace settlement that is eventually reached. What were the obstacles to finding a workable settlement? How were they overcome? As each case is explored, it is important to dig deeper than the choice itself and search for the roots of success and failure.

As a guide to inquiry, we offer the following framework that groups the factors most likely to affect peacemaking success or failure into three master categories. Based on the well-known **levels-of-analysis** distinction in the study of international relations,[60] this framework identifies three categories of variables that can be treated as clusters of causal agents which act together to shape postwar policy making: (1) the international environment, (2) the domestic setting within the warring countries, and (3) the individual characteristics of national leaders. Inasmuch as these general categories or levels operate collectively and are nested within one another, Figure 1.4 depicts them as the layers of a "causal funnel," with each subsequent layer located closer to the center of decision making where critical peacemaking choices are made.

International Conditions and Problem Definition

When a war concludes, political leaders in the triumphant state do not formulate policies strictly in terms of their sentiments about the defeated enemy. Often, their approach is conditioned by their perceptions of the opportunities and constraints created by changes the war may have caused in the structure of the international system. Radical shifts in the distribution of military capabilities and in the composition of military alliances may alter the victor's assessment of how to realize key foreign policy objectives. In effect, the state of the world at the time a war ends rules out certain otherwise attractive options and makes other choices possible.[61]

Examples throughout history demonstrate the need to consider how changes at the international level affected the victor's assessment of objectives and options. Take, for instance, the position of Sparta following the Peloponnesian War. Despite pledging to uphold the autonomy and independence of other Greek states, Sparta began intervening in their affairs. Sparta's brusque, dictatorial behavior alarmed so many states that it ultimately faced an unlikely coalition led by its former allies. In the Corinthian War of 395–387 B.C.E., Corinth and Thebes joined with a resurgent Athens to block Sparta's imperial ambitions. Even after the King's Peace of 386 B.C.E. brought the war to a conclusion, Thebes foresaw the need to prepare for future con-

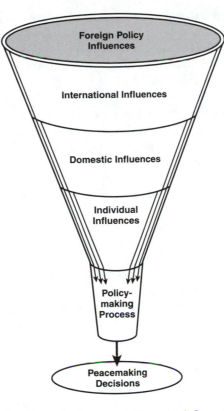

FIGURE 1.4 Making Decisions for Peace: A Funnel of Causality. The factors that influence states' capacity to make peace settlements can be classified according to three basic levels: international, domestic, and individual. Any and potentially all three levels of influence can modify peacemaking decisions.

frontations with Sparta. At the battle of Leuctra in 371 B.C.E., the brilliant Theban general Epaminondas routed the Spartan army. Nine years later, at the battle of Mantinea, he dealt them another crushing defeat. This reversal of great military alliances illustrates how changes in the state system's configuration after a war can modify the political landscape of victory.

Many theorists of world politics maintain that the international environment determines foreign policy behavior—that changes in the international system's configuration after a war can drive both victors and the vanquished to reassess their vital interests. Because the international system consists of multiple concurrent variables, and because how the winning side perceives the external environment can be as influential as the actual environment, it is difficult to generalize about which of many potentially important global dimensions will most influence the choices and behavior of victors and the defeated. In comparing the cases in this book, it is important to identify the aspects of the international environment that were most influential in shaping the peace policies of the victors. When evaluating individual cases, we recommend asking a series of questions about the conditions that might have affected how the peacemakers perceived their options. How policymakers perceived such questions usually influences their decisions about peace settlements. It is instructive, therefore, to assess in each case which of these concerns entered their calculations.

- *Polarity*   What was the balance of military capabilities when victors attempted to make peace? As the strength of some states rose and others fell after the war, were military capabilities distributed among several roughly equal great powers in a **multipolar** pattern, were they divided between two great powers in a **bipolar** pattern, or were they concentrated in the hands of one dominate state in a **unipolar** pattern?[62]
- *Polarization*   How were states aligned before and after the war? Were there flexible alliances with states frequently shifting partners? Or were alliances petrified in rigid **blocs** with various minor powers clustered around the great powers?
- *Contiguity*   What was the geographical location of the warring parties? Did they share common borders? Did the proximity of the belligerents prompt the victor to seek a harsh peace as a security guarantee against its next-door rival? Were territorial disputes and claims a source of war between neighbors and a factor influencing the durability of a peace settlement?[63] What other kinds of issues were prominent on the postwar political agenda?
- *Commerce*   Were economic issues prominent on the postwar agenda?[64] Did the victors refrain from harsh settlements that might hurt future trade relations? Were vanquished states that held resources important to the victor treated differently than states that did not?
- *Norms*   Did shared understandings exist about rules for a peaceful postwar order? Did international legal **norms** permit or prohibit particular kinds of peacemaking strategies? Were there precedents for the peace settlement sanctioned by the international community?

Of course, many other systemic factors can modify the international setting for choice and the willingness to abide by peace settlements.[65] To analyze why some peace settlements succeed and others fail, therefore, we need to consider the existing international system and if and how it influenced victors to make either wise or foolish peace agreements.

Domestic Pressures and Goal Selection

Moving down the funnel of causality from the international level to internal or domestic influences on postwar policies, we encounter such factors as the value orientation of the winning side and the attitudes held by the general public toward the vanquished. Peacemaking has rarely been above domestic politics.

Consider domestic politics in Rome following victory over the Carthaginians in the Second Punic War. Though humbled into client status by its military defeat, Carthage recovered economically within a decade. With the resurgence of Carthaginian prosperity, some Romans feared that Punic imperial ambitions might also resurface. Many Romans had acquired fertile land along the north African coast and worried about Carthaginian attempts to avenge their territorial losses. Other Romans were irritated at the prospect of competing once again with Carthaginian merchants. Although Carthage posed no real threat to Rome, calls for the destruction of Carthage by Marcus Porcius Cato struck a responsive chord among wealthy Romans who urged their government to declare war on Carthage. As the role of domestic Roman politics in the outbreak of the Third Punic War illustrates, the chambers of government where policies regarding war and peace are made have at times been swayed by strong societal influences.

Domestic Constraints and Policy Choice

When it comes to peacemaking, politics does not stop at the water's edge. Leaders are forced to confront the national circumstances that prevail as war ends. Faced with the task of charting their nations' destiny in a new milieu, political leaders are tempted to ask themselves several questions: What are the likely domestic repercussions of reconciliation or retribution? Will the option selected increase or erode my public approval? Might the choice I make convert, perhaps overnight, partisan backers into rabid opponents? Especially in democracies, heads of government entertain countless questions such as these when wars draw to a close. The record of their memoirs underscores the importance leaders give to the likely domestic reactions to any prewar or postwar strategy they formulate.

The decisions for war and for peace settlements presented in this book require us to question if settlement decisions are based primarily on an almost obsessive concern about the reactions they would provoke at home. Leaders' preoccupation with their public standing, and their natural desire to be admired, can easily encourage them to make peace in ways that will evoke a positive response domestically. It might even be said that when it comes to peacemaking, theater on the domestic stage can substitute for rational peacemaking choices, with image management an overriding concern. We need to identify when peacemakers have decided to take the popular approach rather than what they really thought was right or wrong for their country in order to estimate the extent to which decisions were influenced by leaders' fear that an unpopular war settlement might cause them to lose a bid for reelection.

This is not to suggest that leaders only make foreign policy decisions designed to curry domestic favor or to divert attention from their failures. That would be an exaggeration. Nonetheless, how often in the past history of peacemaking have leaders been inclined to approach the task primarily concerned with how their decisions would be evaluated by their constituents and recorded by future historians? In examining the cases, we recommend that you look at the extent to which peacemaking decisions were shaped by domestic factors, including:

- *Political Culture* Did deep-seated and widely shared values circumscribe the boundary of choice for leaders, preventing them from pursuing a peace strategy that deviated from the ideals held by the nation? How did beliefs about fair play and human rights affect the peace settlement?
- *Public Opinion* Did public enthusiasm for a vindictive peace settlement drive leaders toward punitive policies, even though they had moral reservations about the wisdom of a harsh settlement? What role did the mass media play in influencing public attitudes about the vanquished?
- *Interest Groups* Were there groups within either nation that aroused hatreds by demonizing the enemy? Did their activities modify peacemaking strategies? Were self-serving demands made by powerful business interests that would allow them to make large commercial profits in the postwar era?

There are many variations on the hypothesis that victors make peace in response to domestic pressures. In addition to the factors already suggested, the activities of political parties and lobbying by trade unions and professional associations can also mold the details of a peace settlement.

Societal pressures that singly or in combination shaped decisionmakers' peace policies should be evaluated also in terms of their dependence on conditioning factors. Two such intervening variables deserve particular attention. The first is the state's level of national prosperity, because the economic health of the state before and after a war can affect the overall influence of domestic pressures on national security decisions such as treatment of the vanquished, with good times conducive to a compassionate settlement and recession chilling that prospect. A second background factor that can modify the state's domestic environment and, in turn, influence prewar and postwar peace plans is the level of domestic stability. If a state benefits from the existence of a patriotic, united public, for example, it is likely the peace settlement that leaders craft will be accepted by the wider citizenry. However, conflict at home can easily undermine the success of strategies for international security by diverting leaders' attention from international affairs.

Institutional Impediments and Narrowed Options

A related cluster of internal factors that influence postwar policy making pertains to the institutional structure of government. Leaders do not make decisions about war and peace uninhibited by the organizational constraints of the governments they head. Presidents, prime ministers, kings, and emperors must all rely on vast administrative networks, and they can become prisoners of those networks when agencies within them equate their own organizational interests with those of the country.

Institutional influences on national security decisions include a plethora of variables. One of the most important is the degree to which a state's government is organized in a way that concentrates or divides authority over decisions. Does the winning side speak with one or many voices? To what extent do administrative procedures interfere with the capacity of leaders to rule? Who really makes policy?

Policy making is a turbulent process, one that involves complex problems, a chronic lack of information, and a multiplicity of conflicting departments, ministries, and agencies swept up in **bureaucratic politics.** Owing to differences in background and training, members of various foreign policy bureaucracies may disagree on how to deal with a particular policy problem. In addition, because they seek to advance organizational self-interests, bureaucracies and administrative departments may ignore directives they oppose, leak information to sabotage peace proposals from rival organizations, or take stands on issues that are designed to increase their budget, personnel, and functional responsibilities.[66] Because of this highly competitive environment, national leaders must cope with two institutional problems. On the one hand, they may be flooded with narrow, biased analyses from several fiercely competitive agencies. On the other hand, they may obtain a single analysis that is actually a "concealed compromise" produced by a series of lateral agreements among agencies quietly working in tandem to protect their own parochial interests. In neither situation will the leaders receive the full, balanced information they need to formulate a sound peace policy.

The impact of large institutions — complex organizations employing thousands or even millions in a maze of channels through which ideas must pass before they become policies — suggests some disturbing propositions worthy of analyses. Although foreign policy bureaucracies were created to increase administrative efficiency, does their size actually reduce the capacity for **rationality** — for making peace policies that are based on a thorough, dispassionate search of the best information available?[67] Did peacemaking emerge as the end product of a logical chain of reasoning, in which the costs and benefits of reconciliation versus retribution were weighed carefully to pick the strategy most likely to maximize the victor's desired goals? Although many official histories make the circumstances of events sound rational, the participants in the decision-making process have often described something quite different. To participants, as well as to many who subsequently have probed the record of events, postwar policy making is not clear-headed, coherent, and calculated.

Thus, it is fruitful to consider whether certain institutional conditions lead to counterproductive choices. As you read, look for symptoms of dysfunction. Was the victorious government a finely tuned machine or an inefficient bureaucracy? Was the outcome of the

> "You know, one of the hardest things in a government this size is to know that down there, underneath, is the permanent structure that's resisting everything you're doing."
>
> — RONALD REAGAN

policy process a product of rational choice or the result of **muddling through** in a process of trial and error?[68] Were peace policies formulated according to a vision of the future, or were they the result of inertia and grudging incremental adjustments?

The sheer size of modern governments is only one variable within the cluster of institutional factors within states that can affect peacemaking. Among the others to consider are:

- *Regime Type*   Democracies are organized institutionally in a way that usually makes it difficult for heads of government to implement foreign policies according to their personal desires (as leaders in authoritarian states can). Did constitutional limitations influence the postwar peace policies of democratic regimes? In presidential systems of separated institutions and shared powers, to what degree did a political struggle between the executive and legislative branches affect policy outcomes? Was the settlement made by a democratic regime different from what would have been reached by an authoritarian regime? Does the size of government exert the same impact on the policy-making process of democracies and nondemocracies?

- *Decision Rules*   Large organizations normally handle issues by means of **standard operating procedures** rather than by inventing a new way to deal with each issue that arises.[69] Did bureaucrats defer to precedents established in past peace settlements? If so, did this reliance on past policy prevent leaders from shifting course when a different strategy had a better chance of working?

- *Advisory Groups*   When small, homogeneous groups in stressful situations lack impartial leadership and are insulated from outside criticism, social pressures for conformity may lead to **groupthink**,[70] the propensity of the desire for consensus to replace critical thinking. Did the advisers on whom national leaders relied for guidance and emotional support show any of the symptoms of groupthink? Did they discount warnings, take extreme risks, or suppress personal reservations about the moral consequences of the policy recommendations they received?

While it is useful to assess whether peacemaking is handicapped by government departments that resist control from above while perfecting it from within, it is likewise advisable to evaluate the counterhypothesis that sound postwar policies may be impossible to formulate and implement without a professional bureaucracy and the kind of organizational support that it alone can provide. It is the division of large governments into separate agencies that encourages **multiple advocacy**[71] as leaders hear recommendations by different agencies and, as a result, consider a wide range of options. Moreover, it is only through the assistance of a large administrative staff that leaders can successfully manage a peace policy. While we need to be aware of the problems innate to bureaucratic organizations, we also need to be mindful of how to operate these organizations more efficiently and shape their power to national purposes and worthy ideals. For that, leadership is required. Let us turn, then, to consider our final element in the equation for determining success and failure in making peace: individual leaders.

Individual Obstacles to Successful Strategies

The last of the three levels or clusters of variables that should be evaluated when identifying the sources of postwar decisions pertains to the individual decisionmaker. National leaders deserve our attention because all foreign policies are filtered through and thus affected by these decisionmakers. Only by observing the motives of the key policymakers can we fully appreciate how peacemaking decisions are made. Theoretically, there is a clear need to evaluate decisions about peacemaking by focusing on the leaders who make decisions, because the impact of individual leaders is especially noticeable at the end of a successful war, when the time for deliberation is short and the public demands decisive action to ensure that a peace treaty produces sufficient rewards to justify the costs it has borne. If they can take credit for engineering the victory, leaders can sometimes govern without significant restraint. Triumphant leaders, of democracies or dictatorships, often enjoy a honeymoon period during which they can disregard the constraints that normally would restrict their decision making. Victory gives them a momentary mandate. So it is instructive to observe how their ideas and ideals directed the ways defeated enemies were treated after a decisive victory.[72]

Regardless of the popular adoration leaders experience in the glow of military triumph, they can make grave errors that undermine their nations' long-term security. As historian Barbara Tuchman notes, victorious governments have often pursued peace policies that were contrary to their self-interest, in part because "leaders in government do not learn beyond the convictions they bring with them" and in part because they are "ordinary men walking into water over their heads, acting unwisely or foolishly or perversely as people in ordinary circumstances frequently do."[73] Leaders basking in their achievements can become overconfident and rely too heavily on superficial lessons they have drawn from the immediate past. As one historian has put it, leaders "ordinarily use history badly."[74] They tend to inflate the meaning of their recent successes, embrace information that buttresses their beliefs, and deny or rationalize troublesome facts that contradict their convictions. In short, there is always a danger that the postwar policies promoted by overconfident leaders have been compromised by premature cognitive closure. When examining the cases provided in this text, inspect the material for evidence of the following decision-making pathologies:

- *Satisficing* Did the rational choice model of decision making describe the procedures by which leaders made choices about war and peace? Did they engage in a pure cost analysis of the relative merits of all possible options? Or is **bounded rationality** a better description of what occurred because of the need to take shortcuts in calculating decision costs that encouraged the acceptance of satisfactory rather than maximal options?[75] What role did leaders' emotions and biases play in the decision-making process?

- *Trade-Offs* Did leaders select less-than-optimal policy options because they did not feel they could build an international consensus around what they believed were the best possible options? Did some leaders benefit by sacrificing the options they preferred to placate powerful domestic interests?

- *Policy Momentum* Peace planning often evolves from the cumulative impact of a large number of decisions built up over time. Did principles for action become legitimized by many choices before, during, and after the war and create inertia for a retributive or conciliatory peace settlement that could not be overturned? Unpleasant surprise is a stern teacher. Did any of the leaders exhibit experiential learning after costly mistakes during the course of the war and the peacemaking process? Or were leaders preoccupied with sunk costs? Having made a commitment to a particular kind of peace settlement, did they refuse to reconsider their decision even though the chance of it working no longer appeared hopeful?

To summarize, the three clusters of factors that influence how states make peace — the structure of the international system, the victorious country's societal characteristics and domestic institutions, and its leadership — comprise an analytical framework that organizes the central questions for examining the success or failure of peacemaking decisions. No one cluster of factors, by itself, is likely to provide sufficient insight into why peace settlements last or collapse. And while the psychological characteristics of national leaders are crucial to explanations of why states make war and peace, they are not the only important variables in the equation. The task is to weigh the evidence in each case, and estimate the relative influence each factor had on the choices made between war and peace.

SUGGESTED READING

Doran, Charles F. *The Politics of Assimilation: Hegemony and Its Aftermath.* Baltimore, Md.: Johns Hopkins University Press, 1971.

Doyle, Michael W. *Ways of War and Peace.* New York: Norton, 1997.

Holsti, Kalevi J. *Peace and War: Armed Conflicts and International Order, 1648–1989.* Cambridge: Cambridge University Press, 1991.

Ikenberry, G. John. *After Victory.* Princeton, N.J.: Princeton University Press, 2001.

Kagan, Donald. *On the Origins of War and the Preservation of Peace.* New York: Doubleday, 1995.

Randle, Robert F. *The Origins of Peace.* New York: Free Press, 1973.

Rock, Stephen R. *Why Peace Breaks Out: Great Power Rapprochement in Historical Perspective.* Chapel Hill: University of North Carolina Press, 1989.

Vasquez, John, ed. *What Do We Know about War?* Lanham, Md.: Rowman & Littlefield, 2000.

Wapner, Paul, and Lester J. Ruiz, eds. *Principled World Politics: The Challenge of Normative International Relations*. Boulder, Colo.: Rowman & Littlefield, 2000.

Welch, David A. *Justice and the Genesis of War*. Cambridge: Cambridge University Press, 1993.

Woodhouse, Tom, Robert Bruce, and Malcolm Dando, eds. *Peacekeeping and Peacemaking*. London: Macmillan, 1998.

NOTES

1. Morgenthau, 1985, p. 52.
2. Gilbert, 1966, p. 23.
3. See Fox, 1970a; Goldstein, 1991; Hampson, 1996; Iklé, 1991; and Pillar, 1983.
4. For an extended discussion, see Solomon, 1976. Other relevant literature includes De Sousa, 1987; Gibbard, 1990; Lyons, 1980; and Rorty, 1980.
5. Welch, 1993, p. 3.
6. See Liberman, 1996.
7. Aron, 1968, p. 257. See also Rosecrance, 1986.
8. Organski and Kugler, 1980, pp. 144–145.
9. For synthesis and summaries of the divergent ideas associated with liberal and realist accounts of the international causes of international war and the conditions of peace, see Doyle, 1997.
10. Keohane, 1992, p. 174.
11. For a discussion of the differences among a suspension of hostilities, a cease-fire, a truce, and an armistice, see Smith, 1995, pp. 265–270.
12. Of course, the relative importance given to these arguments varies among national leaders as influenced by the myriad possible factors that condition such fateful calculations and choices. Some decisionmakers might be highly concerned about lost resources, while others might be driven by fears about the deterioration of their domestic support. Even among those motivated by the same kind of argument, different perceptions may exist over which warring state is stronger, and whether the balance of military capability is likely to disadvantageously wane in the immediate future, and if so, how fast that erosion will occur. Hence the decision calculus that encourages state *A* to disengage may not convince state *B* that the moment is ripe to stop fighting. Considerations that generate strong incentives for leaders with particular personal characteristics operating within certain types of political systems may not have the same impact on their counterparts.
13. Kent, 1866, p. 420. For a discussion of international treaty norms, see Kegley and Raymond, 1990.
14. Schelling, 1966, p. 7.
15. Hersch Lauterpacht, following Felix Oppenheim, as cited in von Glahn, 1996, p. 609.
16. Liberman, 1996.
17. See Hall, 1917, p. 31; Hershey, 1930, p. 276; Phillimore, 1879–1888, vol. I, pp. 222–225; and Westlake, 1910–1913, vol. I, pp. 86–118.
18. Vitoria, 1917. See also O'Donovan and O'Donovan, 1999, pp. 609–637.
19. See O'Donovan and O'Donovan, 1999, pp. 609–637.
20. Abbé Gabriel Bonnot de Mably, in McMahon, 1940, p. 43. See also Sagey, 1972, p. 58, and Korman, 1996.
21. Jacobini, 1962, p. 70.
22. Schwebel, 1994, p. 523.
23. In Montross, 1960, p. 145.
24. Jayatilleke, 1968, p. 552.
25. Pavithran, 1965, p. 619.
26. Blainey, 1968, p. 267.
27. Sengupta, 1925, p. 13.
28. Jayatillike, 1968, p. 550.

29. Liddell Hart, 1967, p. 357.
30. Churchill, 1951, pp. 373–374.
31. Thucydides, 1951, pp. 14–15.
32. Sylvan, 1995, pp. 94–95.
33. Herodotus, 1920, p. 101.
34. Thucydides, 1951, pp. 80, 82.
35. King Archidamus, a friend of Pericles, counseled against an immediate declaration of war. He recognized that Sparta could not defeat Athens at sea and, without adequate power projection capability, its heavy infantry could not attack Athens's island allies. "Let us never be elated by the fatal hope of the war being quickly ended by the devastation of their lands," he cautioned. "I fear rather that we may leave it as a legacy to our children." Thucydides, 1951, p. 47.
36. Andocides, 1941. pp. 549, 551.
37. Thucydides, 1951, pp. 120, 352.
38. Ibid., p. 331. In contrast to Callicles in Plato's *Gorgias* or Thrasymachus in *The Republic*, the Athenians are not simply saying that it is right for the strong to prevail over the weak or that justice is merely what is in the interest of the mighty. Instead, they submit that questions of justice are only relevant when both sides are "equals in power."
39. Woodruff, 1993, p. 153n.
40. Xenophon, 1979, p. 104.
41. Hamilton, 1942, p. 74.
42. Xenophon, 1979, p. 107.
43. Thucydides, 1951, p. 48.
44. Livy, 1919, pp. 255–261.
45. Cicero, 1991, p. 15. To emphasize this point, Cicero mentions the granting of citizenship to the Tusculani, Aequi, Volsci, and the Hernici after they had been defeated by Rome.
46. Picard and Picard, 1968, p. 72.
47. With the exception of Brindisi, Naples, and a few other ports, Italy lacked natural harbors. Rome itself was built at the first ford of the Tiber River, some fifteen miles from the sea, and thus did not possess the maritime tradition of Carthage. Consequently, when Gaius Duilius unexpectedly defeated the Carthaginians in the naval battle of Mylae in 260 B.C.E., a triumphal column was erected in honor of Rome's first victory at sea and a flutist played whenever Duilius dined in public. Soren et al., 1990, p. 95.
48. Kagan, 1995, p. 252.
49. Ibid., p. 254.
50. Ibid., p. 225.
51. Soren et al., 1990, p. 101.
52. Strauss and Ober, 1990, pp. 148–149.
53. Livy, 1965, p. 601. Despite Scipio's rhetoric of vengeance, it is said that the peace terms he offered defeated states would place him "on a pinnacle among the world's greatest conquerors — his entire absence of vindictiveness, his masterly insurance of military security with a minimum of hardship on the conquered, his strict avoidance of annexation of any civilised State. They left no festering sores of revenge or injury and so prepared the way for the conversion of enemies into real allies." Liddell Hart, 1994, p. 278.
54. Caven, 1980, p. 252.
55. Adcock, 1970, p. 77.
56. Diodorus of Sicily, 1967, p. 131.
57. Liddell Hart, 1967, p. 353.
58. Posen, 1984, p. 13; Walt, 1989, p. 6.
59. See Ferguson, 1997, for a discussion of counterfactuals in historical interpretation.
60. A multilayered analysis is needed because many of the determinants of peacemaking performance are located within an ever larger set of variables, all of which may be operating simultaneously. For a theoretical discussion of the logic behind distinguishing among different levels of analysis, see Singer, 1961; for an alternative statement applied to war and

peace, see Waltz, 1954; for a framework widely used in the comparative study of determinants of states' general foreign policy making, see Rosenau, 1966 and 1984.

61. This interpretation is most forcefully developed in the neorealist "structural" approach of Kenneth N. Waltz, 1979.

62. The assumption that military parity promotes peace is a core belief of many balance-of-power theorists. In contrast, proponents of hegemonic stability theory argue that the concentration of military power in one leading state increases the chances of peace because that superpower has the capability to prevent aggression through punishment; see Thompson, 1988. For a structural interpretation, see Kaplan, 1957.

63. For studies demonstrating the importance of territorial issues as a factor influencing the probability of war and durability of peace settlements, see Vasquez, 1995 and 1996, and Goertz and Diehl, 1992b.

64. For syntheses and reinterpretations of the impact of international economic conditions on war and peacemaking, see the "hierarchical equilibrium" theory of Midlarsky, 1989; the "world system" theory of Wallerstein, 1974; and the analysis of economic conditions on peace policies as reflected in such studies as those of Rock, 1989, and Rosecrance, 1986.

65. For example, the proportion of democracies in the system strongly influences the prospects for peace, with increases associated with the declining probability of war. For discussions of the "democratic peace" proposition, see Doyle, 1997; Ray, 1995; and Russett, 1993.

66. For a pioneering definition of the bureaucratic politics and organizational process models of the institutional barriers to rational peacemaking, see Allison, 1969 and 1971, and Allison and Halperin, 1989. Discussions of the impact of government type on foreign policy decisions are provided in most texts in the comparative study of foreign policy; see, for example, Ray, 1995; Rosenau, 1966; and Russett, 1993.

67. Rational choice models of decision making emphasize purposeful, goal-directed behavior guided by careful consideration of the costs and benefits of alternative options. Verba, 1969, pictures rationality as the effort by decisionmakers to use the best information and to choose from all potential responses to a problem the means most likely to maximize national goals. See Bueno de Mesquita and Lalman, 1992, for an application to war.

68. For a description of muddling through as a process by which rational decision making is compromised, see Lindblom, 1959.

69. See George, 1969; and Kegley, 1987.

70. This concept originated in the research of Janis, 1972, 1982, and 1989; for recent empirical elaborations, see 't Hart, 1990, and 't Hart et al., 1997.

71. A democratic victor will be forced to consider the full range of possible peacemaking options, because such polities tend to produce multiple advocacy: leaders hear advice on behalf of almost every viable peace-building approach. Autocracies do not; few advisers will dare to question the wisdom of authoritarian leaders about the consequences of their peace policy preferences, even if their decisions are doomed to failure. For this reason there is much virtue in reaching wise peacemaking decisions through democratic channels of communication that permit, even encourage by their very structure, consideration of all possible strategies. For an innovative rationale for why peacemaking is more productive when advocates of differing approaches are able to voice their recommendations, see George, 1972.

72. Peacemaking decisions have been influenced strongly by whether the victor's government was headed by a crusader or pragmatist; see Stoessinger, 1985. The more ideological the leaders, the less likely they have been to perceive constraints in peacemaking choices; the more pragmatic the leaders, the more responsive they have usually been to the impact of peacemaking policies on the defeated.

73. Tuchman, 1984, pp. 383 and 23.

74. May, 1973, p. xi. See also Neustadt and May, 1986.

75. For elaboration of the concept of satisficing and the theory of bounded rationality in decision making, see Simon 1982 and 1957.

PART II

War and Peace in the Classical European State System

The three chapters in Part II survey fateful decisions about war and peace-making that were undertaken during what many scholars call the classical European state system. It was an age of empire building by the great powers, whose competition was restrained primarily through balance-of-power diplomacy. Europe's monarchs were frequently linked by family ties during this period, which facilitated the creation of strategic alliances to contain one another's imperial designs. Together, these chapters provide detailed information about how national interests and ethical values framed the foreign policy options that political leaders entertained at the end of wars fought during the early modern period of international history.

When wars end, political leaders have an opportunity to think anew about the principles and practices of statecraft that may prevent a relapse into the terrifying ordeal they have just experienced. This is especially true following history's great wars — the largest, deadliest, and longest that alter the very structure of the international system. It is because of the system-transforming potential of some wars that Part II begins with a case study of the Thirty Years' War and the Peace of Westphalia in Chapter 2.

Although historians differ over the best point in time to date the advent of the modern era of world politics, most see it beginning in 1648 at the end of the Thirty Years' War, when the Peace of Westphalia dismantled the vertical structure of the medieval world order and introduced a new set of organizing principles that still color our view of international politics. Foremost among the system-transforming effects attributed to Westphalia is its creation of a horizontal world order, composed of sovereign territorial states with no higher authority above them to manage their relations. Chapter 2 tells the story of how a long, grinding war to counter the Hapsburg bid for hegemony contributed to the rise of the modern territorial state ruled by centralized governments.

The history of the Thirty Years' War provokes inquiry into the question of why it lasted so long, and provides a springboard for examining why the brutal practices in this protracted conflict became so widespread. When the participants finally convened in Westphalia to construct a peace settlement, they took to the bargaining tables lessons extracted from the battlefield. In presenting these lessons, this case develops the thesis that the sources and conduct of wars shape the conclusions the victors reach about the rules needed to sustain a new world order. In effect, the rules *of* warfare became rules *for* statecraft.

The case in Chapter 3 involves another complex war that ended with an elaborate peace process. Beginning in the last decade of the eighteenth century, Europe once again faced an aspiring hegemon, and only a coalition of great powers was able to block its ambitions. Buoyed by a rising tide of nationalism, the armies of Napoleonic France poured across the continent threatening to place authority for the management of interstate relations under hierarchical control. Following Napoleon's defeat, the delegates to the Congress of Vienna in 1815 restored the Westphalian system of sovereign equals and made a series of territorial adjustments to prevent any single state from commanding sufficient resources to threaten the rest. In addition, they established the Concert of Europe, a collaborative security mechanism for great-power consultation and policy coordination that included defeated France among its members. When compared to the previous case of the Thirty Years' War, Chapter 3 illustrates how victors can go beyond relying on laissez-faire competition to maintain postwar peace, and build new international organizations that incorporate the vanquished within a wider, more inclusive security architecture.

To balance these cases, Chapter 4 expands the coverage of types of wars and peace settlements by focusing on the notorious Wars of German Unification in the second half of the nineteenth century. Although the three wars fought by Prussia between 1862 and 1871 did not reach the magnitude or severity of either the Thirty Years' or Napoleonic wars, they raise equally important questions about the determinants of successful and failed peace strategies.

· 2 ·

THE THIRTY YEARS' WAR AND THE PEACE OF WESTPHALIA: VIOLENCE AS A WAY OF LIFE

Dangers, surprises, devastations—
*   The war takes hold and will not quit,*
But it lasts three generations
*   We shall get nothing out of it.*
Starvation, filth, and cold enslave us.
*   The army robs us of our pay.*
Only a miracle can save us
*   And miracles have had their day.*
*   —*BERTOLT BRECHT, *Mother Courage*

PREVIEW

For the student of war and peace, history provides few more exemplary cases about the connection between choice and consequence than does the Thirty Years' War. Most historians regard this war—and the Peace of Westphalia that ended it—as a paragon of the kinds of moral dilemmas that surround decision making in the realm of national and international security, when leaders are required to assess the probable consequences of alternative policy options under conditions of uncertainty. The choices made between the war's beginning in 1618 and its end in 1648 force the observer to think in terms of multiple causality at multiple levels of analysis in interpreting the mixed motives and cross-purposes that animate the making of decisions about war and peace.

The Thirty Years' War also has been a popular case for students of international politics because it profoundly transformed the conduct of international diplomacy. The choices made during the war

47

and at its conclusion gave rise to the contemporary international system. War is inherently a decision-making phenomenon, requiring fateful choices that force a confrontation between competing values. Throughout the Thirty Years' War rulers were forced to sort out their values and set priorities while acutely aware of the trade-offs involved in these fateful choices. In particular, they had to weigh the importance of their professed religious convictions against their allegiance to secular political authority. The story of the Thirty Years' War is the story of the passage from a predominantly religious to a primarily secular worldview, during which the medieval goal of a united Christendom gave way to acceptance of a society of independent and competitive sovereign territorial states.

The Thirty Years' War was a product of profound long-term changes ignited by the cultural Renaissance and religious Reformation that swept Europe in the twilight of the medieval period, provoking intense controversies about religious beliefs, institutions of governance, and political ideologies. From this clash of values, a realpolitik outlook on statecraft took root, in which consensual support was given to the assumptions that states were the dominant actors in world politics; that foreign policy should be guided by national interests according to the logic of *raison d'etat* (reason of state); and that in an anarchic environment the acquisition of power was the foremost foreign policy priority.

To inspect the context in which choices were made to create this political consensus, it is necessary to consider the larger background in which the Thirty Years' War erupted. In this regard, a word of caution is in order because even the true defining character of this war is a subject of considerable dispute. What really was the Thirty Years' War? The very name is ambiguous because historians do not agree about what it should describe. Some historians refer to the Thirty Years' War as a way of identifying the most intense and destructive period of a series of wars that swept across Europe in the century between 1559, when Spain's war to retain possession of the Netherlands began, and 1659, when France and Spain signed the Treaty of the Pyrenees. Other historians fix the onset of the Thirty Years' War with the March 1609 War of the Jülich Succession. Still other historians identify the starting and ending dates with the series of wars fought primarily in Germany and Bohemia, but engulfing most of Europe, that began in 1618 and ended three decades later in 1648.

Regardless of how the Thirty Years' War is dated, it has a lasting reputation as one of the most violent and revolutionary periods of European history. It occurred in an era historians have variously called "the crisis of the seventeenth century," "the age of religious wars," and "the era of a revolution in military affairs," and is universally regarded as putting into place an entirely new set of norms and institutions for international politics.

In tracing the mix of motives that led to decisions to wage war and, eventually, make equally fateful decisions about the preconditions for peace, a congeries of issues must be considered: What were the participants' objectives? Was there a hierarchy to their values that set priorities? If so, which preferences and ideals took precedence? Did the warring parties care most about religion, nationality, or wealth? How did the participants reconcile these values when they collided? By asking these questions, we ask our readers to explore a wider set of theoretical and moral issues. Lessons gleaned from the choices made in this case should enable many of the general properties of international decision making under conditions of crisis and uncertainty to be identified.

In evaluating the causes, character, and consequences of the Thirty Years' War, it is important to take into account the ways in which this period generated some of the most important concepts in the theoretical analysis of war and peace. The basic vocabulary for discussing international relations today, and the key theoretical concepts for interpreting world politics, evolved out of the turbulent and troubled Thirty Years' War. In this gestation period we find early expression of many of the core concepts in international relations theory, including:

- sovereignty
- state autonomy in international anarchy
- the national interest
- war profiteers and mercenary soldiers
- just war
- the balance of power
- collective security
- the security dilemma
- military intervention
- the revolution in military affairs
- international law
- the nonintervention norm
- hegemony

This case of a tragic war and a patchwork peace settlement negotiated between the winning coalition and its exhausted adversaries presents a treasure chest of insights into the underlying conditions that foment general, system-transforming wars. In this opening case study, consider how the quest for power, security, and wealth in a rapidly changing international system tore at the traditional value of global unity. Also look at the rules of modern statecraft that emerged in the wake of Wesphalia, and ask whether these rules helped cement a just and durable peace settlement.

In 1618 a conflict originated in the territory of the Holy Roman Empire that eventually spread to engulf almost all of Europe. In the early 1600s, the region of Bohemia was in the midst of a national and religious revival under the leadership of a strongly Protestant and fiercely patriotic local nobility, which resented domination by the ruling Catholic Hapsburg dynasty of the Holy Roman Empire. The Bohemians resisted the Hapsburg demand that they elect Catholic Ferdinand of Austria to the throne, and offered it instead to the Calvinist Count Frederick of the Palatine. When the Hapsburgs responded with force, the European tinderbox was ignited in a war that would not be extinguished for three decades.

With the outbreak of war, every great European power was forced to struggle not only with finding a solution to the widening split between Catholics and Protestants, but also to the growing rivalry between the entrenched Hapsburg dynasty and an ascending Bourbon France. Was the Thirty Years' War a religious conflict? Was it a political conflict? Or was it a product of multiple forces acting simultaneously? Most historians agree that the Thirty Years' War originated from a welter of crosscurrents: religious, political, intellectual, and economic issues combined to generate a multifaceted armed conflict. To better grasp the extent to which these factors animated the belligerents, it is helpful to review the preconditions that made the seventeenth-century European landscape ripe for war.

FAITH, FATHERLAND, OR FINANCE?
PRECONDITIONS FOR WAR IN SIXTEENTH-CENTURY EUROPE

A clash of cultures occurred in the sixteenth century that set the stage for the cataclysm which erupted in 1618 that resulted in a "loss of people . . . proportionately greater than World War II."[1] To place the Thirty Years' War into a historical context, it is important to take into consideration the underlying contestation between church and state that was brewing alongside two more deeply embedded influences that arose in the twilight of the medieval age: (1) the intellectual impact of the Renaissance and Reformation, and (2) gyrating cycles of economic growth and decline.

The rebirth of learning during the Renaissance engendered remarkable achievements in science and technology. In this "age of discovery," a rising middle class began to revolt against the stagnant medieval feudal hierarchy. At the same time, the forces of the Reformation began to challenge the vertical structure of Christianity, with the pope and the Holy Roman Emperor at the apex of power. Europeans now faced a choice between rival models of world order, one based on an all-powerful **hegemon** (the Hapsburg empire), and the other on a decentralized system of relatively independent actors. Vested ecclesiastical interests sought to resist the currents of intellectual change, and their opposition explains why the sixteenth century has been characterized as "an age of intolerance."[2] According to Henry Kissinger, this was a period "still dominated by religious zeal and ideological fanaticism" when "the Hapsburg Holy Roman Emperor Ferdinand II was attempting to revive Catholic universality" and "came to be perceived in Protestant lands less an agent of God than as a Viennese warlord tied to a decadent pope."[3] Sadly, much of the bloodletting that ensued from this era of intellectual turmoil was precipitated by the willingness of princes to exploit intra-Christian sectarian conflicts for their own political purposes

Economic factors also contributed to the growing level of civil strife. One scholar suggests that the Thirty Years' War "might be seen as an economic phenomenon intimately linked with the cycle of economic expansion and contraction."[4] Through mismanagement of the resources it obtained from colonies overseas, the Spanish branch of the Hapsburg dynasty began to suffer financially, and an income gap began to develop between the increasingly prosperous Protestant principalities in northern Europe and the increasingly debt-ridden Catholic principalities in many parts of the Holy Roman Empire. Encouraged by changes in relative economic strength, the Bourbons in France clashed with the Spanish and Austrian branches of the Hapsburg family dynasty. Contending that great power politics transcended religious conflict, **structural realists** note that with this power transition, war and counterbalancing alliances increasingly came to be seen as instruments to prevent the domination of the continent by any aspiring hegemon.[5]

At the core of European politics since the late 1400s stood the Holy Roman Empire, a territory composed of many small principalities united through marriages under the rule of the Catholic Hapsburgs (see Map 2.1 on p. 68). The empire at first consisted mainly of Germans centered in Vienna, but the family dynasty harbored wider ambitions and gradually extended its imperial reach over territories that stretched from France on the west to Poland and Hungary on the east. The Hapsburgs pledged to propagate the Catholic religion through a Counter-Reformation. In particular, the Spanish branch of the family launched a Catholic counteroffensive against Protestant and Muslim forces in Europe and the Mediterranean. Understandably, neighboring France viewed the possibility of Hapsburg expansion as a serious threat.

Thus, in the twilight of the sixteenth century the European continent split into opposed centers of power. The European geopolitical chessboard was complex, with numerous crosscutting alliances and percolating national rivalries. However, a polarized system was emerging on the eve of the Thirty Years' War. On one side stood the Austrian and Spanish branches of the House of Hapsburg; on the other, an anti-Hapsburg coalition composed of various Protestant states and, eventually, Catholic France.

THE INSTABILITY OF THE SEVENTEENTH-CENTURY BIPOLAR WORLD

In the emerging **bipolar** division of Europe, religious differences overlaid a growing political- military conflict. The first confrontation between the contending blocs occurred in 1608 when the Catholic Duke of Bavaria put down a Protestant uprising. Angry Protestants then joined forces to form the Protestant (or Evangelical) Union as a network of allied princes and towns in southern Austria under the Elector Frederick of the Palatine, the first Calvinist prince in the Empire.[6] In addition to its efforts at **collective security,** the Protestant Union attempted preemptive actions against the Hapsburgs because they believed Protestantism could not be secure without the overthrow of the German branch of the House of Austria.[7] Duke Maximilian of Bavaria promptly responded by creating the Catholic League, which proclaimed the same allegedly defensive purposes as those articulated by the Protestant Union. As measures to prepare for war by one coalition provoked countermeasures by the opposing coalition, a **security dilemma** was created with the result that both alliances' sense of security declined as their military preparations increased.

At roughly the same time that the Protestant Union and Catholic League were facing off in central Europe, Spain and Holland began to mobilize troops in preparation for war. Whereas Spain sought to repress the rebellious Dutch and recover their wealthiest European province, the Dutch wanted formal recognition of their independence from Spain. The Holy Roman Emperor made a compact, agreeing to expand the Austrian Hapsburgs' military efforts to control Germany while concurrently providing military assistance to the Hapsburg rulers in Madrid as they attempted to restore the northern part of the Spanish Netherlands to the Empire.

In many respects, the Thirty Years' War began as a clash of polarized alliances nested within the longer and larger epic religious struggles of the age. Seen from this perspective, it was the product of twin forces — the final effort by the House of Hapsburg to reestablish unity under Catholicism and the Emperor's universal power, and the first effort of the Protestant princes to free themselves from Hapsburg dominion. Together, religious strife and geopolitical struggle proved to be a deadly combination. Beginning with the Bohemian rebellion against the Hapsburgs in 1618, the Thirty Years' War widened through a series of consecutive phases. Historians conventionally divide the war into five sequential periods: the Bohemian (1618–1620), the Palatinate (1620–1624), the Danish (1625–1629), the Swedish (1630–1635), and the Franco-Swedish (1635–1648). Table 2.1 provides a chronology that summarizes the major events in each stage of the war.

REPRESSION AND REBELLION DURING THE BOHEMIAN PERIOD

Bohemia was the wealthiest of the Austrian Hapsburg regions of the Holy Roman Empire. Despite competition among Utraquist, Lutheran, and Calvinist Protestants, and strife between the nobility and the peasants, the Czech-speaking Bohemian kingdom had remained relatively stable until the 1547 Schmalkaldic War, when Hapsburg Catholic rule was more firmly established.

TABLE 2.1
A Chronology of the Thirty Years' War

Prelude to the War (1517–1617)

1517	Publication of Martin Luther's Ninety-five Theses sparks the Protestant Reformation.
1546–1555	Civil wars break out in the Holy Roman Empire.
1555	The Peace of Augsburg puts an end to years of sporadic conventional warfare in Germany between Catholics and Protestants, giving secular rulers the right to dictate whether their subjects' religion was to be Lutheran or Catholic.
1559	War breaks out in the Netherlands between Spain and Dutch rebels who seek to establish a republic.
1608	In May, the Protestant (or Evangelical) Union is formed.
1609	On July 9, Holy Roman Emperor Rudolf II signs the *Letter of Majesty (Majestätsbrief)* granting full toleration to Protestants. On July 10, Duke Maximilian of Bavaria forms the Catholic League. A truce of twelve years brings the war between Spain and the Dutch Republic to a temporary close.
1613	The Protestant Union signs a defensive treaty with the Dutch Republic.
1617	Both Bohemia and Hungary recognize Catholic Hapsburg heir Archduke Ferdinand as designated King of Bohemia.

The Bohemian Period of the War (1618–1620)

1618	In May, Protestants revolt against suspension of their right to worship in the event known as the Defenestration of Prague which touches off the beginning of the war.
1619	Ferdinand is crowned Holy Roman Emperor Ferdinand II. The Bohemian nobility deposes Ferdinand and offers the crown to Calvinist Frederick V who, after entering Prague, is crowned king by the Protestant rebels. In May, the Protestant rebel army lays siege to Ferdinand's supporters in Vienna; within weeks the Protestants are forced to withdraw when a large Spanish army, partly financed by the pope, invades Bohemia.
1620	Spanish Imperial Army commanded by General Spinola crosses from the Netherlands and occupies the Rhine Palatinate. *On November 3, the first significant battle of the war takes place at the White Mountain on the outskirts of Prague, where the victorious Hapsburg army ends the Bohemian rebellion and positions itself for conquest of the Palatinate.**

The Palatinate Period of the War (1620–1624)

1621	War between Spain and the Dutch Republic resumes.
1624	Following Henry IV's death, Cardinal Richelieu (Armand-Jean du Plessis) becomes the chief minister of France. *(cont.)*

(Table 2.1 cont.)
The Danish Period of the War (1625–1629)

1625	King Christian of Denmark intervenes in the war. Ferdinand authorizes Albrecht von Wallenstein to raise a new imperial army of 25,000 men to subdue the Danish threat.
1626	*On August 26, the Danes are routed at the Battle of Lütter, compelling the withdrawal of Denmark from the war; the imperial army advances northward.*
1629	On March 28, the Edict of Restitution is issued. Calvinist rebels are defeated in France, making it possible for the king to deploy troops in Italy to aid the Duke of Nevers. To meet this threat, Philip IV of Spain asks the emperor to send his troops to Italy rather than to the Netherlands.

The Swedish Period of the War (1630–1635)

1630	Louis XIII of France launches a second invasion of Italy; 50,000 imperial troops are brought south from Spain to oppose them, releasing the Dutch Republic from immediate danger and weakening the emperor's hold on Germany. In July, Gustavus Adolphus leads a Swedish interventionary force ashore in Germany. In August, Emperor Ferdinand II dismisses Wallenstein, his most capable commander, and appoints Tilly.
1631	In May, Tilly's army sacks Magdeburg. In June, Brandenburg signs a mutual defense treaty with Sweden, and in September Saxony, Bremen, and Hense-Kassel also ally with Sweden. *On September 17, in a turning point in the war, Gustavus Adolphus defeats Tilly at the Battle of Breitenfeld, just outside Leipzig in Saxony, and Swedish forces begin to overrun most of central Germany and Bohemia.*
1632	In April, Wallenstein is restored as imperial commander-in-chief. *On November 1, Wallenstein's army fights Swedish forces at Lützen, and Gustavus Adolphus dies in battle.*
1634	In February, Wallenstein is assassinated by his own officers by command of the emperor. *On September 6, Spain sends a large army across the Alps from Lombardy to join the Imperial forces at the Battle of Nördlingen; the Swedes are decisively beaten and obliged to withdraw their forces from most of southern Germany.*
1635	French troops begin to mass along the borders of Germany, preparing to enter the war on the side of the Protestants in order to prevent Hapsburg hegemony; France increases its subsidies to the Dutch fighting the Spanish Hapsburgs, and signs an offensive and defensive alliance with the Dutch Republic (February 8), with Sweden (April 28), and with Savoy (July 11). On May 19, France declares war on Spain. On May 30, the Peace of Prague is signed between the Catholic Holy Roman Emperor and the Lutheran Saxons; within a year most other German Lutherans shift their political allegiance from Stockholm to Vienna.

The Franco-Swedish Period of the War (1635–1648)

1636	In March, France declares war on the Hapsburg Emperor Ferdinand II; the Treaty of Wismar strengthens the Franco-Swedish alliance.
1637	On February 15, Ferdinand II dies; Ferdinand III becomes Holy Roman Emperor.
1639	Swedish army invades Bohemia following the Treaty of Hamburg between France and Sweden.
1642	On November 2, the Hapsburg imperial army is routed in Saxony at the second battle of Breitenfeld. Brandenburg and Brunswick strike a separate peace agreement with Sweden.
1644	Peace negotiations commence in the Westphalian towns of Münster and Osnabrück.
1645	In March, the Swedish armies reenter Bohemia, and totally destroy an imperial army at Jankov. In August, Maximilian's forces are decisively defeated at Allerheim. The Elector of Saxony makes a separate peace with Sweden and withdraws from the war.
1646	French forces occupy Bavaria.
1647	Cardinal Mazarin of France, despite a preliminary agreement with the emperor in September 1646 which conveyed parts of Alsace and Lorraine to France, starts a new military campaign in Germany to secure more territory.
1648	In January, Philip IV of Spain signs a peace treaty that recognizes the Dutch Republic as independent. In May, another Bavarian army is destroyed at Zusmarshausen. On October 24, the terms of the Peace of Westphalia are accepted between the Holy Roman Emperor Ferdinand III, the other German princes, France, and Sweden.

* The five major battles that most altered the course of the war are highlighted in bold italics.

In Bohemia, the threat posed to the material and spiritual interests of Protestant Czechs by the political repression under the Catholic rule of the Holy Roman Emperors became the trigger for revolt. Czech nationalism combined with Bohemian Protestantism to oppose Emperor Rudolf II and his intolerant policies.[8] The Protestants sought to counterbalance the Catholic Hapsburgs' plan to institutionalize absolute control over the entire empire, particularly after the reigning Holy Roman Emperor Matthias impetuously issued decrees withdrawing the charters of Protestant churches, ending appointments of non-Catholics, and banning Protestant meetings. "Tension increased until flash-point was reached" when Emperor Matthias named in 1617 his cousin, the crusading Catholic and Jesuit-trained Ferdinand, as the successor to the Bohemian throne.[9] These actions were widely interpreted as an intolerant effort to impose a version of

Catholic fundamentalism on the population by force. This fractious religious dispute ultimately sparked an outburst of civil strife that would eventually engulf much of Europe.

The Defenestration of Prague

The revolt began in Prague on May 21, 1618, in a dramatic act of defiance that was to become known as the Defenestration of Prague. Delegates to an assembly denouncing anti-Protestant policies threw two Catholic Hapsburg governors and their secretary from a high window in the Hradschin Castle into a dunghill below. Protestant members of the Bohemian Diet saw the defenestration as a justifiable response to Archduke Ferdinand's abrogation of the July 9, 1609, *Letter of Majesty* that had guaranteed religious freedom. This dramatic act of rebellion marked the beginning of a war that was to last thirty years.

Quickly seizing control of Bohemia and deposing king-elect and Hapsburg heir Archduke Ferdinand, the rebellious Bohemian nobles at first considered the possibility of creating an independent republic inspired by the hope that this would elicit the support of the Dutch, who shared their ideological interests in self-rule and religious freedom. Instead, they appointed a directorate of thirty deputies and named Wenceslas Ruppa its president.

Besides expelling the Jesuits and arming self-defense corps in towns throughout Bohemia, the new Bohemian Directorate made what proved to be a fateful and fatal decision: it elected as king the youthful, staunch Calvinist Elector Frederick of the strategically critical Rhineland Palatinate. Twenty-one-year-old Frederick V was ill-prepared to make and implement policy.[10] The assignment ruptured any hope of conciliation with the Holy Roman Emperor, because Frederick destroyed his legitimacy by using military intervention to achieve his political aims.

The Empire Strikes Back

The Hapsburgs reacted quickly to news of the latest revolt in Bohemia against their rule. The new emperor, Ferdinand II, saw no choice but to regain Bohemia because it was an important source of imperial revenues, and its elector held one of the seven imperial electoral votes. The self-righteous Ferdinand II firmly believed that as Holy Roman Emperor he had a divine calling to preserve Christianity under Catholicism. To this end, Emperor Ferdinand II called on the Catholic League for assistance, and in May 1619, the Spanish dispatched an interventionary force from their army in Flanders to suppress the rebellion, and the reinforcements grew when additional financial subsidies were provided by the papacy. With all of this external support, the Hapsburgs were confident they could crush the defiant Bohemians. After Frederick V and his wife arrived in Prague for his coronation late in 1619, the Jesuits predicted, "He will be a winter king. When summer comes he will be driven from the field."[11]

The first significant military encounter took place at the battle of White Mountain near Prague. Backed by the twenty-five thousand soldiers of the imperial army of the Catholic League commanded by Count Johann von Tilly, the superior imperial army confronted the Bohemians near Prague on November 8, 1620. When Frederick failed to receive hoped-for military assistance from the Dutch, the princes in the Protestant Union, or from his English father-in-law, King James I, his fate was sealed. The Bohemian revolt ended, and with it Frederick's brief rule. Ferdinand's troops recaptured Prague, and Bohemia's native nobility was suppressed so that the country could systematically be Catholicized.

TORMENT IN THE PALATINATE

Ferdinand II's victory over Frederick whetted his appetite to expand Hapsburg power elsewhere. The lands in the Palatinate region of Germany formerly held by the emperor were invaded from the Spanish Netherlands and eventually seized by the Bavarians, which rekindled the fighting as the Protestant princes grew determined to intervene in Germany before the Hapsburgs could consolidate their position. Other threatened principalities soon joined the conflict, thus making Germany the central front of the Thirty Years' War.

Count Ernst von Mansfeld and Christian of Brunswick led the Protestant resistance to Hapsburg rule in the Palatinate. Frederick had gained the support of the Dutch who, following the expiration of their Twelve-Year Truce with Spain in 1621, entered the Rhineland to counter Spanish Hapsburg occupation armies. They also confronted Spanish forces in the Palatinate.

Opposing the Protestant forces was the commander of the mercenary troops of the Catholic League, Imperial Austrian General Tilly. His brutal tactics of mass annihilation terrorized cities that stood in his line of attack. In 1622 he joined with elements of the Spanish military and began a savage campaign in northern Germany. Together with the Spanish forces, Tilly led the Imperialists to overwhelming victories in May and June 1622. In September, Tilly took Heidelberg by assault and laid siege to Frankenthal, therein consolidating the emperor's control of the Rhineland.

Unwilling to yield the lands Tilly's troops had subjugated, the emperor refused to negotiate a peace settlement at the Brussels peace conference organized by England. Tilly's victory at Stadtlohn in August 1623 over Christian of Brunswick ended this phase of the war, with the Hapsburgs in ascendancy. The emperor now controlled Austria and Bohemia, with Duke Maximilian of Bohemia given the title of elector to rule southern and northwestern Germany. The Spanish Hapsburgs gained control of the Palatinate, and Frederick became a landless exile surviving in sanctuary on the welfare of Dutch supporters. Throughout Germany the situation had become increasingly desperate for the Protestants.

ENTER THE DANES

Fearing Hapsburg control of northern Germany, in 1625 King Christian IV of Denmark and Norway became the first Protestant neutral to intervene in the fighting. Christian sought to champion the beleaguered Lutherans in Germany, but his motives were not entirely religious because he saw military intervention as a means to strengthen the Danish position in Germany.

Christian entered the fray with twenty thousand mercenaries and a belief that his intervention would be supported by other Protestants. However, the English and the Dutch, who had pledged substantial subsidies on behalf of Denmark's military intervention, did not fulfill their promises. The emerging norms of the age had begun to accept the expedient breaking of commitments when national interests were not served by faithful compliance with previous promises. Nonetheless, these allies did form the Hague Coalition to funnel subsidies so that Christian IV could challenge the imperial army. What Christian did not anticipate was that the emperor would choose to create a new army, assigning supreme command to Albrecht von Waldstein (known everywhere as simply "Wallenstein"), whose managerial and strategic skills would shift the tide of battle.

Wallenstein's Long Shadow

An ambitious, entrepreneurial Bohemian general and Catholic convert, Wallenstein was more interested in increasing his fame and fortune than fighting for a particular faith.[12] He began military service under Emperor Ferdinand in 1606 and immediately grasped the potential rewards of serving as a **war profiteer**.[13] During the Bohemian rebellion against the emperor, Wallenstein had remained loyal to Ferdinand and lent the Emperor huge sums of money. In 1625 the emperor was forced to repay his debt by rewarding Wallenstein with an appointment to head all imperial troops.

The anti-Hapsburg coalition undertook what appeared to be a coordinated strategic plan: Christian IV of Denmark was to engage Tilly and conquer Lower Saxony; Christian of Brunswick was to take the Wittelsbach bishoprics in Westphalia and the lower Rhineland; General Ernst von Mansfeld was to lead the alliance into Bohemia, passing Silesia and Moravia; and Prince Bethlen Gabor was to march his Hungarian troops from Transylvania to join with Count von Mansfeld's army in Bohemia. However, the plan had several drawbacks. Positioned to fight from the interior and able to confront one enemy at a time, Tilly and Wallenstein possessed the geostrategic advantage. Wallenstein won a battle in April 1626 for the Bridge of Dessau on the Elbe River. But the Protestants rebounded and penetrated Germany elsewhere. Count von Mansfeld's troops pulled Wallenstein's forces away from support of Tilly's army and, to compound the empire's problems, a widespread peasant revolt in Upper Austria could only be repressed with the deployment of needed imperial Bavarian forces. Perceiving a clear path to the Imperial nerve center in Vienna, Christian and von Mansfeld advanced from different directions, forging ahead in an effort to carry out their strategy to link with their Transylvanian allies in the south.

As the Protestant Union forces reached the Danube River through Silesia, Wallenstein's powerful imperial army countered by sweeping through most of the Protestant stronghold in northern Germany. With their morale crushed, the Duke of Mecklenburg and several other Protestant princes began to advocate reconciliation with the Empire.

The Hapsburgs were at the peak of their power. When Denmark withdrew from the war in 1629, the Hapsburgs appeared poised to reassert control over a unified German state and institutionalize their hold as far north as the Baltic Sea.

The Edict of Restitution

Intoxicated by their battlefield victories, the Hapsburgs transformed the war into an enterprise for making their rule absolute in Germany.[14] On March 6, 1629, Ferdinand II issued the Edict of Restitution in an attempt to enforce the ecclesiastical reservation of the 1555 Peace of Augsburg that had granted rulers the right to control their region's religion.[15] The triumphant emperor declared void previous Protestant titles to lands secularized after 1551, and sought to revise the empire's constitution, in order to secure control over both religious and political policy. His decision to issue the Edict of Restitution was counterproductive, however. Formerly neutral German princes were enraged; they were quick to recognize that the edict signaled the Hapsburg intention to eradicate both Protestantism and their independence.

A revolt ensued at the 1630 Electoral Diet of Regensburg, led by Lutheran Saxony and Catholic Bavaria. Suspicious Catholic princes refused to proclaim Ferdinand's son as "King of the Romans," the title traditionally given to the heir-apparent. When Wallenstein sought to mediate the conflict, Ferdinand ill-advisedly consented to the Catholic princes' demands to dismiss Wallenstein, his best general, and dissolve his army. This second fateful decision left the empire seriously weakened.

As the war unfolded, expediency was being elevated from a fact of political and military life to an international norm, under which it was becoming acceptable to disregard loyalty to allies or to religious causes when opportunities for individual gain presented themselves. The next stage of the war would further dramatize the extent to which raw power politics driven by myopic self-interest would underlie international behavior.

SWEDEN INTO THE BREACH

With the likelihood of a Hapsburg triumph now appearing strong, the formerly neutral Protestant ruler Gustavus Adolphus of Sweden stepped forward as the champion of Protestant interests. A pious Lutheran, Gustavus's main interests were to gain greater control of the Baltic and to establish Swedish influence over northern Germany. The fearless, self-confident king known as the "Lion of the North" felt compelled to enter the war when General Tilly defeated Denmark and Wallenstein's forces arrived on the Baltic coast, threatening Swedish trade.

Gustavus is considered by many military historians as "the father of modern warfare" because he engineered a **revolution in military affairs.** He demonstrated how well-disciplined, trained, and paid troops in uniform reporting through a clear chain of command to professional officers could defeat the massive formations relied upon by the imperial forces. Among other innovations, he introduced platoons firing continuous salvos, the use of light cannon and artillery, and coordinated shock-action attacks by combat teams. In short, the Swedish army set the standard for all other national armies to emulate.

Unlike the Hapsburg mercenary army, Gustavus's army was efficient and inspired by a sense of justice in fighting to liberate the oppressed (see Box 2.1). Swedish intervention transformed the conflict by giving the unorganized and leaderless Protestant coalition military discipline and renewed hope. When Wallenstein laid siege to the port of Stralsund in May 1628, Gustavus intervened. In what he claimed was a preemptive strike, his army of thirty thousand occupied Pomerania and retook Wallenstein's Duchy of Mecklenburg in June 1630. But the imperial army stopped Gustavus's advance, forcing him to seek allies before he could continue. The Swedish king eventually found assistance from an unlikely source — Catholic France.

Cardinal Richelieu Engineers French Involvement

French foreign policy by now was under the calculating **realpolitik** leadership of Cardinal Richelieu. Italian by birth and not particularly fluent in French, Cardinal Richelieu was thoroughly dedicated to the regeneration of France as a means of preventing domination by the House of Hapsburg. Although France was a predominately Catholic state, the Catholic cardinal's goal was primarily practical rather than spiritual — to halt the growing Hapsburg power by forging strategic alliances with all powers hostile to Hapsburg hegemony, whether they be Protestant or Catholic. "If Germany is lost," Richelieu reasoned, "France cannot exist."[16] What mattered to Richelieu was not how a potential ally stood on religious matters, but its ability to contribute to French security.

By this point in the war, "the choice between Catholic and Protestant had lost its meaning," the historian C. V. Wedgwood observes. "Hapsburg aggression had driven the papacy and Catholic France, the one into sympathy the other into alliance, with the Protestants, and Europe no longer presented even the approximate outline of a religious cleavage. The political aspect of the conflict had destroyed the spiritual."[17] In January 1631, Cardi-

BOX 2.1
THE *MEISTERTRUNK*

To illustrate the conditions that prevailed in the war's later stages, consider this infamous episode. In 1631 the imperial army attacked the town of Rothenburg-ob-der-Tauber along Bavaria's "Romantic Road." According to that feudal town's celebrated legend, General Tilly followed the accepted practice toward those who did not surrender unconditionally by ordering his soldiers to sack the town. The citizens begged for mercy, and Tilly agreed to spare the town providing a citizen would accept his dare to consume an unspeakably enormous tankard of wine. The *Bürgermeister*, Heinrich Toppler, accepted the challenge and saved the entire town by chugging the entire flagon of wine; but he passed out from intoxication and died. The mayor's brave feat is commemorated in a play, *Der Meistertrunk*, which by tradition is performed every Whit Monday in the town hall.

nal Richelieu signed the Treaty of Bärwalde to carry out his strategy, promising French financial support for Sweden to resist the Hapsburgs.

In August 1630, Emperor Ferdinand had been prevailed upon at the Regensburg Electoral meeting to dismiss Wallenstein from command of the imperial army. The mercurial Wallenstein had acquired many powerful enemies who feared that he was maneuvering to become the ruler of Germany. His dismissal was unwise, for the appointment of the seventy-three-year-old General Count Tilly to head all the imperial forces, assisted by his second in command, Count Goffried Heinrich Pappenheim (a militant soldier driven by vengeance), proved to be a serious military mistake.

On May 30, 1631, a second miscalculation occurred. Hoping to replenish his starving troops' supplies, General Tilly ruthlessly sacked Magdeburg, ignoring the prosperous Lutheran city's offer to surrender. Word spread of the brutal rapes, murders, and robberies under Tilly's command, sending a shock wave through Europe that ultimately worked to Gustavus's political advantage.

As news of Tilly's slaughter of all but five thousand of Madgeburg's thirty thousand inhabitants spread across Europe, Saxony and Brandenburg signed a military alliance with Sweden, and Gustavus was now able to move the Swedish army forward into the Palatinate. When combined with French assistance, these alliances expanded the Thirty Years' War. What had started as a civil war over religion in the German states now became a truly international fight over the redistribution of territorial possessions. As Gustavus explained, "All the wars of Europe are now blended into one."[18]

Surging with the confidence of allied support, the Swedish king, now joined by John George's Saxon army of eighteen thousand reinforcements, confronted Tilly's imperial army at Breitensfeld on September 17, 1631. The imperial army was dealt a crushing defeat by the small but efficient Protestant army—the first major breakthrough for the Protestants in the war. Two-thirds of the imperial army was destroyed and Tilly was fatally wounded. Gustavus's smashing defeat of the imperial army "marks the turn in the tide of the Counter-Reformation. The whole Empire now laid at the feet of the Swedish King."[19]

Gustavus now began a daring march north, devastating the emperor's best troops in a winter campaign. Following the November 1631 Saxon conquest of Prague by Hans George von Arnim, southern Germany stood exposed, and Gustavus advanced from the Rhineland west toward the very center of the Catholic bishoprics in Bavaria in a drive directed at Munich and Vienna. Ferdinand II's desperate "appeals to Rome brought only the cold answer that the Pope did not consider the war to be one of religion,"[20] and requests to Madrid went unanswered. The exhausted Spanish were unable to provide relief as they fought the Dutch, who took advantage of the eroding strength of the Hapsburg armies to end Spain's rule over the Netherlands.

The Empire's Fortunes Restored

In April 1632, the desperate emperor offered Wallenstein very generous financial incentives to reenter the war and lead the imperial troops. The experienced but controversial commander was the emperor's only hope to repel the Swedish troops. In May, Wallenstein regained control of Prague and blocked Gustavus's march on Vienna. By August, Wallenstein had built a barrier around the outnumbered Swedish forces, which were in dire need of supplies and reinforcements. A month later Gustavus offered to make peace with Wallenstein. Gustavus's terms—the unconditional revocation of the Edict of Restitution—were deemed unacceptable, so the two armies prepared to settle the matter on the field of battle.

On November 1, 1632, Wallenstein masterminded the first major defeat that Gustavus experienced, which allowed the Empire to recover much of Bavaria, Silesia, and Saxony. Although demoralized, the Swedes remained a significant fighting force composed of nearly 150,000 soldiers. Two weeks later, on November 16, 1632, the Swedes took on and withstood Wallenstein's army in the fog-shrouded Battle of Lützen, but the cost was immeasurable—Gustavus Adolphus was killed in the battle.

> "Know, my son,
> with how little
> wisdom the world is
> governed."
> — COUNT AXEL OXENSTERNA

Gustavus's death set back the Protestant cause as the relative power of the belligerents again shifted because the dispirited anti-Hapsburg coalition was left without a skilled, seasoned leader. The inscrutable Wallenstein attempted to take full advantage of the situation. In order to pacify the lands under his own control and exact revenge against the emperor for his dismissal in 1630, Wallenstein began his own secret peace negotiations with Sweden, France, Saxony, and Brandenburg. Wallenstein's arrogant personality and excessive wealth had won him few friends. Emperor Ferdinand declared Wallenstein guilty of high treason and secretly granted permission for his assassination. On February 27, 1634, Wallenstein's entourage was murdered at a banquet by imperial conspirators, who then killed the defenseless Wallenstein in his bedroom. After Wallenstein's death, the emperor promoted his son Ferdinand, the king of Hungary, to the position of supreme commander, and named General Matthias Gallas as imperial commander.

The Peace of Prague

By the mid-1630s, Germany was in economic ruin. Public opinion was strongly opposed to the continuing presence of foreign soldiers on their blood-soaked soil, and divisions within the Protestant ranks led to the 1635 Peace of Prague that drastically modified the Edict of Restitution, therein reducing tensions between Protestant and Catholic princes. Peace seemed imminent, especially following the September 1634 imperial victory of General Gallas's forces over those of General Bernhard of Saxe-Weimer at Nördlingen. In addition to retaking nearly all of Sweden's former conquests, the victory precipitated the collapse of the fragile Protestant League as war-weary German princes led by Saxony withdrew their soldiers from the Swedish army. Moreover, the Hapsburg victory at Nördlingen gave the Empire courage to pursue **total war** over the subdued Protestants. In the words of one historian, "It looked like the end for the Protestant cause."[21]

FRENCH REALPOLITIK AND ALLIANCE WITH SWEDEN

With the prospects for a Hapsburg triumph once again on the rise, it was not difficult for Cardinal Richelieu to convince King Louis XIII to fully engage French troops in the war. The French ruler believed that preemptive military action was required to prevent a Spanish invasion. In August 1634, Louis XIII ordered his defense ministers to prepare for a vigorous war against Spain in order to secure a general peace settlement that favored French **national interests.**

Richelieu and the Ascendance of Raison d'Etat

As a Catholic clergyman, Cardinal Richelieu had no affection for Protestantism. As a seasoned practitioner of realpolitik, however, he put French national interests above his religion. The glorification of French power was valued as an end in itself, justified by the necessity of ensuring national self-preservation even if war was required. The cardinal perceived not only grave danger for France in the shifting **balance of power** but also an opportunity to defeat the Spanish and Austrian Hapsburgs, the traditional enemies of France. The French decision to enter the war represented the culminating step in the transition of the Thirty Years' War from primarily a war of religion to a dynastic struggle between Bourbon France on one side and Hapsburg Austria and Spain on the other.

Alliances figured prominently in the new French strategy. Richelieu moved quickly to align France with other states whose national interests converged with those of the French throne. In February 1635, Richelieu signed an offensive and defensive alliance with the United Provinces of the Netherlands when Swedish Chancellor Count Axel Oxenstierna, anxious to protect Sweden's interests in Germany, offered Richelieu support. Two months later, the French and Swedish allies cemented their coalition with the Treaty of Compiègne, aimed at preventing the Swedes from surrendering after being decimated in the battle of Nördlingen. With the Franco-Swedish alliance in place, Richelieu forged an alliance with Savoy and Parma, negotiated a twenty-year truce between Sweden and Poland-Lithuania, and hired the experienced Lutheran general, Bernhard of Saxe-Weimar, to lead the French interventionary forces. In May 1635, "the unscrupulous Richelieu, who had long been intriguing with both Bavaria and Sweden at the same time, scented the opportunity of making significant gains for France," and declared war on the other throne of the Hapsburg dynasty, Spain.[22]

The thirteen-year Franco-Spanish final phase of the Thirty Years' War was purely political. The French decision to enter the conflict was motivated by a **rational choice** based on an estimate of projected costs and benefits. French involvement in the war had been carefully calculated,[23] and the timing of the decision for war occurred not coincidentally when the balance of power had most required it—"at the lowest point in the fortunes of the Protestant cause in Germany."[24]

For Cardinal Richelieu national survival meant pursuing three goals. First, he was determined to weaken the two branches of the House of Hapsburg and reduce their threat to French security. Second, he sought to expand French borders to include territories controlled by the Holy Roman Empire's armies. Third, he deliberately planned to delay the entrance of French troops into the war, subsidizing Hapsburg enemies such as Sweden in the hope that exhaustion would lead to an easy and profitable win once France intervened militarily.

The Long Road to Peace

With the French decision to intervene in the Thirty Years' War, the conflict became a general, system-wide war: "Practically all the petty wars and disputes of continental Europe were thus united into one grand holocaust."[25]

The final phase of the Thirty Years' War was a long, drawn-out, highly destructive series of inconclusive battles, and its brutality energized the cry for peace. Pope Urban VIII is credited with taking "the first steps toward the organization of peace talks to bring the war to an end [when] a papal legate arrived at Cologne in October 1636 and invited all interested powers to send representatives to a general peace congress. But his efforts at mediation failed: neither France nor Spain trusted the pope to be impartial and the Protestants rejected papal mediation altogether."[26]

In general, the closing phases of the war proved disastrous for the Holy Roman Empire. As the prospects for the Protestant coalition's subjugation of the Hapsburgs appeared in sight, the feeble Emperor Ferdinand II died on February 15, 1637, and was succeeded by his son Ferdinand III. The two most capable French commanders, the viscount of Turenne and the youthful but ingenious prince de Condé, proved to be more than a match for the emperor's troops. Bernhard of Saxe-Weimar conducted a series of masterful campaigns that culminated in the 1638 capture of Breisach, and Swedish General Johan Banér also won important battles in Germany, including a major victory over Imperial General Melchior von Hatzfeld at Wittstock. The Austro-Spanish Imperial army's last victory occurred at Thionville in June 1639.

The Stumbling Path to Negotiations

Endless rounds of combat steadily eroded whatever enthusiasm for war remained. Yet the belligerents continued fighting to achieve peace on advantageous terms. Ever more blood was spilled to guarantee that no power would find itself in a poor position at the bargaining table. The realist maxim "always negotiate from a position of strength" compelled both sides to keep their war-weary forces on the battlefield. Only after the devout Bernhard of Saxe-Weimer died from fever at the age of thirty-five in 1639 and Johan Banér died in 1640 did the ensuing stalemate enable earnest peace negotiations to finally begin.

A window of opportunity in this horrible war of attrition finally opened following the onset in 1640 of revolutions in both Catalonia and Portugal that forced the Spanish to concentrate their military efforts on the Iberian peninsula. When the Arras stronghold surrendered to the French during August, the Spanish position in the Netherlands was exposed, thus increasing Madrid's interest in a negotiated settlement. With the artery between Madrid and Amsterdam severed, "the Spanish Netherlands were left a rudderless ship drifting before the gale."[27]

Prospects for a peace settlement were also affected by the deaths of Cardinal Richelieu in December 1642 and King Louis XIII of France five months later. The papal nuncio to the French throne, Cardinal Jules Mazarin, succeeded Richelieu as chief minister of the French crown and continued to pursue French alignment with the Protestant coalition. Trained by Richelieu, Mazarin also placed French national interests ahead of his Catholic faith — a choice that outraged Pope Urban VIII, who resented Mazarin's opposition to his appointment as pope. The pope wished to end the war before the depopulation of Europe left Christendom with few souls to save, and he condemned French and Hapsburg intransigence and power politics as responsible for creating obstacles to peacemaking.

Although new proposals for peace negotiations continued to be voiced, progress proceeded haltingly through ad hoc, trial-and-error diplomacy while the fighting continued. A breakthrough did not come until the imperial coalition began to crumble in northeast Germany. Key electoral members of the empire forged separate peace agreements that enabled them to withdraw as neutrals from the war. Losing ground, the new Holy Roman Emperor, Ferdinand III, had to abandon all hope of driving the Protestant anti-Hapsburgs out of the empire and subjugating the French. When the Spanish were defeated at Rocroi in May 1643, Emperor Ferdinand III authorized peace negotiations with France and Sweden.

The Austrian Hapsburgs had been stripped of all their previous conquests, Bavaria was overrun, and enemy forces were approaching Vienna. With prostrate Spain no longer capable of fielding a significant military force, Ferdinand III was forced to bargain for the best peace terms possible. Though exhausted by the rigors of three decades of warfare, neither side trusted the other. The belligerent rulers had become hardened by a culture of death, equating expedience with wisdom and ruthlessness with virtue. Horrific actions bred militant attitudes. Now, at war's end, the warrior's philosophy had become the diplomat's creed.

THE PEACE OF WESTPHALIA

The moods of the diplomats negotiating separately in the two Westphalian towns of Münster and Osnabrück cannot be understood without recognizing that the brutality of the Thirty Years' War had destroyed the medieval ideals of European Christian unity. By any measure, the Thirty Years' War was a human tragedy of epic proportions. Estimates vary, but perhaps a third of Europe's population died as a result of the savagery.[28] As raw political advantage and financial gain became a way of life, basic **human rights** were habitually violated by despotic rulers who forced hundreds of thousands of refugees to seek sanctuary outside their homeland. What had begun as primarily a religious conflict over confessional rights and liberties became in time a war of political, military, and mercenary considerations without regard for the ethical just war constraints of Christian teachings. As the war became secular, the belligerents appealed to expedience and abandoned serious attempts to adhere to higher moral principles. **Military necessity** became the rationale for doing whatever would deliver an advantage on the battlefield.[29]

Decisions about terminating lengthy, system-wide wars force peacemakers to confront rival ideas, for which there seldom exist obvious solutions or universally applicable ethical principles. Those gathered around the bargaining tables in 1648 faced hard choices about incompatible courses of action. The political leaders of the belligerent states were caught between ineradicable competing aspirations, one for justice and the other for self-advantage, that required weighing difficult trade-offs between competing values. As they inched their way toward a political settlement, the tired, confused, and disorganized army of negotiators and the multitude of advising lawyers struggled to find a blueprint for international stability.

The Terms of the Peace Settlement

The delegates meeting at the Westphalian towns of Münster and Osnabrück faced two basic types of decisions, the first pragmatic and the second philosophical. The former dealt with questions of reallocating territory, resources, and titles in a way that could settle the material issues underlying the brutal armed conflict. The latter was more ambitious: to establish among the belligerents a "universal peace, and a perpetual, true, and sincere amity" (Article I of the Treaty of Münster) in order to construct rules of statecraft to peacefully govern postwar European diplomacy. The philosophical decisions were more challenging, but their results were more permanent.

Decisions on Material Issues

The Peace of Westphalia contained two interlocking treaties that ended the fighting in central Europe, one drawn up by envoys of the Catholic princes and states at Münster and the other by the envoys of the Protestant princes and states at Osnabrück. Both treaties converged on principles for international order that were celebrated throughout Europe as the springboard to a peaceful future. Signed on October 24, 1648, and ratified the following February, the details of their execution were worked out at a conference held in Nuremberg between April 1649 and June 1651. According to the military provisions of these treaties, a cease-fire suspending hostilities would be declared, prisoners released, and troops returned home. Furthermore, an **amnesty** was granted "of all that has been committed since the beginning of these Troubles" (Article 2). The material terms of the treaties were complex and profoundly affected the members of the new international order.

France. The French became the dominant power on the European continent, occupying the leadership position that Spain had previously held. France was now bordered by weak, fragmented states (see Map 2.1), and acquired almost all of Alsace in addition to its earlier gains in Lorraine. By acquiring German possessions, the French also gained a voice in German affairs when the new French territories became electors of the Holy Roman Empire.

Austria. In exchange for the county of Hawenstein, the Austrians received from France the Black Forest region, Upper and Lower Brisgaw, and four other strategically important regions (Articles 87–88). Fortifications on the

MAP 2.1 The Thirty Years' War and the Peace of Westphalia The Peace of Westphalia redistributed lands to newly created states in an innovative effort to sharply
define borders and erect a fluid balance-of-power system. Norms prohibiting military
intervention sought to safeguard rulers from external interference in their states'
internal affairs.

right bank of the Rhine River were to be dismantled (Articles 73–74) and
free navigation was restored (Article 79). Restitution was promised (Articles
6–7), and all contracts, exchanges, debts, and obligations extorted by threats
were annulled (Article 37–39).

Sweden.   Territorial transfers to Sweden rewarded this victor for its
wartime sacrifices. The north German Baltic coast, the western part of
Pomerania, and control over the mouths of the Elbe, Oder, and Weser Rivers
strengthened Sweden's strategic position, as did monetary **reparations** from
the Holy Roman Empire and Sweden's newly created right to send representative to the Imperial Diet. The peace settlement confirmed Sweden as the
dominant power in northern Europe.

United Provinces of the Netherlands.   Although the Netherlands had
enjoyed partial de facto independent status since the 1609 Treaty of
Antwerp, the general Westphalian peace settlement gave the Netherlands de
jure recognition as a sovereign state. Spain destroyed its forts in the Low
Countries, and the two countries agreed to cooperate in efforts to control

piracy, keep waterways navigable, and make restitution to those who had lost property during the war. Liberated from the threat of Spanish occupation, the Netherlands was free to concentrate on economic competition with its greatest mercantile rival, the Portuguese colonial empire.

Spain.   The government in Madrid was a clear loser. It was forced by necessity to make peace with the Dutch early in 1648 to deprive France of an ally in the Franco-Spanish war which continued until 1659. Because of these continuing hostilities, Spain was excluded from the terms of the Treaty of Münster, and under Article 3 of the treaty Austrian Emperor Ferdinand III was prohibited from assisting Hapsburg Spain in its conflict with France. Generally humiliated at the Westphalian peace conferences, Spain still held the Spanish Netherlands (Belgium) and a large part of Italy, but it slipped into bankruptcy and was slowly isolated. By the time it signed the 1659 Treaty of the Pyrenees ending the war with France, Spain was finished as an aspirant to European hegemony.[30]

The Holy Roman Empire.   The Westphalian settlement reduced the empire to "purely nominal existence"[31] in order to create a balance of power that limited its **sphere of influence** to parts of Austria and Germany. Although the Holy Roman Empire continued to exist until French Emperor Napoleon's conquests in 1806, "its authority was little more than parchment."[32] With the demise of the Madrid-Vienna axis, no emperor after 1648 had the means to reestablish central authority over all German territories. Indeed, the former empire was reduced to a loose federation of diverse Christian religions (with Lutherans prevailing in the north, Catholics in the south, and Calvinists along the Rhine and in the Netherlands). The emperor had to obtain the consent of the Imperial Diet of the 350 princedoms and bishoprics to issue laws, levy taxes, or recruit soldiers in the name of the Empire. Because the jealousies and ambitions of free cities in Germany "made agreement on such matters impossible, these provisions ended any possibility of Imperial control over Germany and doomed German unification."[33] Forced to allow separate states to be involved in the negotiations, the Emperor lost what little power he had retained over the German princes. "The disintegration of the Holy Roman Empire, which had been advanced by the drawing of internal religious frontiers in the days of Luther, was now confirmed in politics, and international law."[34]

The Papacy.   The Thirty Years' War cost the Roman Catholic Church politically. Formerly, the pope had exercised enormous influence over the secular relations of European states,[35] but in the wake of Westphalia this authority and jurisdiction plummeted. To end the religious wars that had plagued the continent for over a hundred years, the Westphalian settlement (Article 64) authorized each state to choose its own religion, secularized international diplomacy, and further specified that no supranational authority such as the

Catholic Church hereafter could "make or negate alliances made between sovereigns for the purpose of protecting respective nation's security" (Article 65). These provisions enraged Pope Innocent X who refused to acknowledge the treaty's clauses on sovereignty that effectively ended his dominion over Europe. The famous November 1650 *Zelo Domus Dei* bull reiterated the Vatican's protest claims, but to no avail. The Peace of Westphalia ended ecclesiastical tutelage over secular affairs. Instead of the pope orchestrating political affairs on the continent, states became the highest recognized level of governance as well as objects of patriotic worship in their own right. After the Peace of Westphalia, "people who could no longer bear to talk of 'Christendom' began to talk instead of 'Europe'."[36]

> [The Westphalian treaties are] "null, void, invalid, iniquitous, unjust, damnable, reprobate, inane, empty of meaning and effect for all time."
>
> — POPE INNOCENT X

Germany. Although the peace treaties enabled the Protestant princes in the north to conduct their own foreign and domestic policies without external interference, it should be remembered that Westphalia was an imposed peace. Territorial gains and losses were determined by the French, Swedish, and Austrian crowns, who regarded their weaker German allies as pawns to be shifted when required to keep the postwar balance of power in equilibrium. The absence of a strong German voice at Münster and Osnabrück was made transparent by Westphalia's provisos, which subdivided Germany into weak, divided jurisdictions. The peace settlement "recognized 343 sovereign states in Germany, of which 158 were secular states, 123 were ecclesiastical principalities, and 62 were Imperial cities."[37] As the main battlefield of the Thirty Years' War, Germany lay in ruins. The French now held the middle Rhine, and the mouths of Germany's three great rivers — Rhine, Elbe, and Oder — were held respectively by the Dutch, the Danes, and the Swedes. Destitution accompanied humiliation. "Broken, divided, economically weak, and lacking any sense of national unity, Germany became virtually a French protectorate."[38]

Other Relevant States.   States on the periphery of the fighting at war's end had little influence over the peace negotiations. Denmark, for instance, lost its status as a major European power after the 1629 Peace of Lübeck ratified its withdrawal from the conflict. Having not been a formal belligerent because of the outbreak in 1640 of the English civil war, England could exercise little clout in the peacemaking process. These nonparticipants were excluded from the deliberations, without influence over the decisions that established the principles that underpinned the Westphalian peace plan.[39]

The decisions made at Westphalia may have been reached by negotiation, but the parties were not equal in bargaining power. Some benefited at the expense of others. There were both winners and losers. The consequences were long lasting, solving some conflicts, and setting the stage for new rivalries. The fragile basis for international order can be assessed best by looking at the norms embodied in the peace treaties.

Decisions on the Rules of Statecraft

The negotiators drafting the Westphalian Peace did more than reach decisions about the reallocation of territory and resources. They made philosophical choices over competing values about how states in the future should seek to survive in the anarchical world that emerged from the Thirty Years' War. The articles of the treaties comprising the Peace of Westphalia defined new norms to "serve as a perpetual law" (Article 120), defended by all signatory parties (Article 123). Working like engineers, the envoys to the peace conferences could draw from two contending sets of ideas: **realism,** as subsequently espoused by Thomas Hobbes, and **liberalism** as pioneered by humanists such as Hugo Grotius. The former theorist insisted that peace could be best preserved by concentrating power in the hands of a strong central authority; the latter scholar averred that peace could be fostered by building a society of states around a shared moral consensus. In making philosophical choices about which plans should guide the construction of a new world order, the envoys gravitated toward the decentralized vision of Grotius rather than toward a more centralized architecture, while at the same time they embraced Hobbes's realist view of statecraft as a perpetual "war of all against all." The plenipotentiaries creatively fused diverse ideas to put international order on a new footing. The terms of the settlement contained ten philosophical tenets that still influence world politics today.

(1) Retributive Justice.   The negotiators at Münster and Osnabrück were embittered by the brutality of the war, and had powerful incentives to draft a punitive peace treaty. "Under the conventions of the day victors could require the enemy to pay for the costs of the war."[40] However, wanton vindictiveness had the potential to degenerate into an endless blood feud. Aware of the problems that could arise from spiteful, measureless retaliation, the peacemakers substituted retributive justice for outright revenge. **Retribution** offered several important benefits over revenge. First, it defused the possibility that all of the defeated powers would be collectively condemned. Second, avoiding collective condemnation facilitated the normalization of relations between the belligerents after the war. Finally, by eschewing revenge, reconciliation and the pursuit of restorative justice became possible. The scars of war could begin to heal, the victors reasoned, by giving the defeated a stake in the postwar order.

(2) Assimilating Losers into the Postwar System.   In an effort to avoid a new wave of armed struggle, the victors at Westphalia set a precedent for

collective bargaining in peace settlements by involving the losers in the post-war processes of collective governance. Showing disrespect to an adversary by excluding it from the discussion over the peace terms was deemed risky because such insulting treatment was believed likely to evoke future efforts to vindicate a wounded sense of honor. To this end, the Catholic parties were allowed to convene separately in the nearby town of Münster and participate on an equal footing in the negotiations through procedures that encouraged voluntary consent. The principle was also reflected in the treatment of the Austrian Hapsburgs, who retained their dignity in defeat. "Largely purged of dissidents and cut off from Spain, the compact private territories of the Austrian Hapsburgs were still large enough to guarantee them a place among the foremost rulers of Europe, and to perpetuate their hold on the Imperial title until the Empire was abolished in 1806."[41] The peace treaties looked forward rather than backward. Shared interests were not immediately obvious, but the negotiators found common ground so that the winners could satisfy some of their opponents' interests without compromising their own. The victors believed that the success of a multilateral peace conference depended on everyone's capacity to transcend the desire for short-term relative gains and support the new rules regulating the postwar system.

(3) The Secularization of International Politics. As we have seen, one of the searing problems in Europe at the onset of the Thirty Years' War was religious struggle. After the Reformation widened, the 1555 Peace of Augsburg attempted to resolve the conflict by adopting the principle *cuius regio, eius religio* ("Whose the region, his the religion") so as to permit each prince to regulate religious practices within his territory. Rulers could choose their religion, and that of their subjects. The Peace of Westphalia reaffirmed the Augsburg solution with amendments aimed at rectifying much of the religious intolerance that had formerly plagued Europe. To protect religious minorities, Westphalia made Protestant and Catholic states equal and for the first time ensured subjects within the northern Protestants' states of the right to worship as they preferred. In addition, to enhance the prospects for maintaining peace and equal treatment among Catholics, Lutherans, and Calvinists, the Treaty of Osnabrück created a supreme court for the empire staffed by twenty-six Catholics and twenty-four Protestants. The treaty strengthened the sovereignty of the German princes by allowing them to make treaties without the pope's approval, and "following the Peace of Westphalia, states only rarely forcibly interfered in the religious affairs of other states."[42]

(4) State Sovereignty. After Westphalia, no concept was more central to international law than state **sovereignty.** In international affairs, sovereignty means that no authority stands above the state, except that which the state voluntarily confers on any organizations it may join. Nearly every legal doctrine in the aftermath of Westphalia supported the principle that **states** were the primary subjects of international law, holding "a complete freedom of action" to preserve their independence.[43] Article 65 of the Westphalian set-

tlement marks the birth of the **nation-state.** For the first time, territorial states were legally permitted to interact with each other without interference by a higher authority; rulers could now freely manage their diplomatic relationships and their domestic affairs.

(5) The Equality of States.   The Peace of Westphalia closed one era and opened another when it overturned the preexisting vertical order of centralized authority and replaced it with a horizontal order of independent units. Hereafter, all states were equal under the law irrespective of religion and form of government, equally able to make the laws that would govern international society, and equally independent from any higher supranational authority to manage their relations. All states possessed the same rights and responsibilities, though they were obligated to adhere to only those laws to which they gave their consent.

Whether this set of rules served justice is debatable, however. Like all compromises, the sovereign equality of states was a regime of, by, and for heads of states; it sought justice for them, not their subjects. The regime fell short of protecting the equal rights of individuals or ensuring them of equal protection under international law, as Westphalia assigned monarchs the right to control domestic affairs within their territories. Westphalia protected rulers against people, not people against the human rights abuses of rulers. When taken to the extreme, the state became a kind of secular deity.

(6) The Balance of Power.   The Westphalian peace settlement redistributed power to compensate winners for wartime losses without rewarding them with gains that would heighten fears of their future expansionism. Territorial redistributions were designed to empower states to counter any future hegemonial threat. All states were encouraged to unite against any aggressor state, and France was empowered with the capability to perform the role of **balancer** to intervene unilaterally or with allies to prevent the domination of Europe by any single power. By exalting the autonomous state at the expense of a universal empire, Westphalia paved the way for acceptance of the balance of power as the primary mechanism for deterring a would-be hegemon from subjugating the other states. Autonomy meant that states were "free to do what they wish."[44] The logic of the Westphalian peace settlement assumed that from the unrestrained competition of rivals an equilibrium capable of maintaining the status quo would emerge.

(7) Collective Security and Multilateral Diplomacy.   The major security threat faced by the victors of the Thirty Years' War was the emergence of another catastrophic system-wide war. The Hapsburg empire was still viewed as a danger, so the victors in the Thirty Years' War encircled it with a ring of alliances and tried to institutionalize their **containment** strategy by building a rudimentary **concert** of great powers. This plan followed the thinking of Cardinal Richelieu, who advocated "a continental system of collective security."[45]

For unity to emerge from the fragmented landscape of national power, the architects of the Westphalian settlement envisioned the eventual creation of a European society, with a shared understanding of the need for collective security and pacific methods of dispute settlement. "The Peace of Westphalia was notable for inculcating the idea of a society of states, a type of body politic with communitarian characteristics, including reciprocal delegations based on equality, that falls midway between a structure of hierarchical authority and a system of pure anarchy."[46] This vision of a society of states drew inspiration from the writings of Hugo Grotius, who called for the resolution of interstate conflicts by judicial procedures and specified a body of legal principles to encourage cooperation, peace, and more humane treatment of people. However, the Westphalian settlement rejected the argument that for a peace system to function effectively, *organized* collective security was required. Instead, Westphalia supported the use of ad hoc collective defense alliances to maintain peace.

(8) Selective Nonintervention.   The delegates at Osnabrück and Münster had to face the problem of enforcing the rules of the settlement, including the norm of the now-sacred principle of state sovereignty. Sanctions were required to back the treaties' provisions, but no formal collective security institutions were created to punish violations of those rules. As a substitute, the Peace of Westphalia reluctantly acknowledged the possible need for intervention to defend the political goals expressed by the treaties' others provisions. For example, some provisions "gave France a right to intervene when necessary in order to vindicate the principle of the sanctity of treaties."[47]

Yet nonintervention was a corollary of the sovereignty principle. It defended states against the threat of interference in their internal affairs, under the rationale that "sovereignty guarantees that no one on that side of the border can interfere with what is done on this side. . . . We don't worry about your practices if you don't worry about ours. Live and let live is a relatively easy maxim when living is done on the opposite sides of a clearly marked line."[48] Thus, the Westphalian treaties took an ambivalent posture toward nonintervention, prohibiting it for the purpose of modifying religious practices within other states but permitting states to intervene for military purposes to promote their national security, protect their independence, and preserve established international law. "The signers of the Münster treaty had clearly struck a balance," observes Charles Doran, in adopting the nonintervention norm to prohibit intervention motivated to prevent religious persecution, while at the same time legalizing intervention for geostrategic purposes. Westphalia "circumscribed rather than unrestrained rights of intervention."[49] The use of force was not prohibited, and the pursuit of national power through foreign activism was seen as a natural and necessary priority that was believed a prerequisite for the functioning of the balance of power.

(9) Legitimizing Realpolitik.   Westphalia made a covenant with the use of armed force, in part because it was written by diplomats schooled in the ways

of realpolitik during the Thirty Years' War. Power was seen as a product of military capability, and preparing for war was understood as the best way of keeping peace. The mood at the peace conferences seemed to accept Cardinal Richelieu's warning that "many princes have lost their countries, and ruined their subjects by failing to maintain sufficient military force for their protection, fearing to tax them too heavily."[50] Not only did the peacemakers reject proposals to disarm in order to restrain the competition of states, but they refused to impose many legal restrictions on the use of military force. In short, protection provided for weak states was provisional and precarious, requiring the aid of stronger allies willing to offer military assistance.

The transformation of international society from one responsible to the dictates of morality to one that worshiped expediency was reached by people who regarded themselves as preservers of the practices that became habits during the Thirty Years' War. There is substantial evidence that the mission the peacemakers defined for themselves was primarily to confirm earlier proclamations and pronouncements.[51] How states had begun to routinely behave during three decades of fighting reinforced realpolitik conceptions about how states should act; war making that was frequent became legal, and what the most powerful did established norms for what others should do. In this sense, Westphalia ratified and licensed the expedient **self-help** practices in statecraft that had become customary in the first half of the seventeenth century. Indeed, after Westphalia "international law in the three centuries which followed . . . rejected the distinction between just and unjust wars. War became the supreme right of sovereign states and the very hallmark of their sovereignty."[52]

(10) The Demise of Moral Constraints.   The diplomats meeting in Münster and Osnabrück had to make fateful moral choices. Building peace requires weighing competing values and contending visions, all of which inextricably involve defining the place of morality in international statecraft. They found their answer in realist thought. Looking askance at the applicability of noble ideals to international affairs, the diplomats abandoned any notion of grounding the search for peace in a philosophy guided by religious or moral precepts. As Henry Kissinger observes, the negotiators replaced morality with the principle of ***raison d'état*** (reason of state), which "asserted that the well-being of the state justified whatever means were employed to further it." In the world of power politics countenanced by *raison d'état,* states do not receive credit "for doing what is right, they are only rewarded for being strong enough to do what is necessary."[53]

In making the principle of *raison d'état* paramount, Westphalia endorsed a norm that was already gaining popularity during the course of the Thirty Years' War, one that protected the unrestrained right of rulers to pursue expansionist policies for their state's aggrandizement. It was a principle predicated on the assumption that all political action should be "constantly directed towards one major, comprehensive end: state building."[54]

Having made glorification of the state acceptable, Westphalia paved the way for the beliefs that "the end justifies the means" and "might makes right" that were to later rationalize the use of war as a tool of foreign policy. What mattered was the expedient pursuit of national self interest, not lofty ideals, absolute moral values, or unbending religious principles. Realism substituted *raison d'état* for morality and pushed it outside the realm of religion. *Raison d'état* and the doctrine of the balance of power were "deeply offensive to the universalist tradition founded on the primacy of moral law" because they cut foreign policy loose from all ethical moorings.[55] As one critic complained shortly after the signing of the Treaties of Münster and Osnabrück, "Reason of state is a wonderful beast, for it chases away all other reason."[56]

Contending Interpretations of the Peace Settlement

It might appear that the Westphalian settlement of the Thirty Years' War was visionary and constructive. This was the enthusiastic endorsement that the French philosopher, Jean Jacques Rousseau, was to pen in 1761 when he wrote:

> What really upholds the European state system is the constant interplay of nego-
> tiations, which nearly always maintains an overall balance. But this system rests
> on an even more solid foundation, namely the German Empire, which from its
> position at the heart of Europe keeps all powers in check and thereby maintains
> the security of others even more, perhaps, than its own. The Empire wins uni-
> versal respect for its size and for the number and virtues of its peoples; its consti-
> tution, which takes from conquerors the means and the will to conquer, is of
> benefit to all and makes it a perilous reef to the invader. Despite its imperfec-
> tions, this Imperial constitution will certainly, while it lasts, maintain the bal-
> ance in Europe; no prince need fear lest another dethrone him. The Peace of
> Westphalia may well remain the foundation of our political system for ever.[57]

Other observers take a different position: the mixture of incompatible tenets within the Westphalian settlement made it seem to them as little more than a mixture of meaningless platitudes.[58] To these critics, the Peace of Westphalia was ineffectual in resolving the deep-seated problems of Europe. The view of one historian captures this negative interpretation well:

> The peace, which had settled the disputes of Germany with comparative suc-
> cess because passions had cooled, was totally ineffectual in settling the prob-
> lems of Europe. The inconclusive and highly unpopular cession of Alsace led
> direct to war; the seizure of half Pomerania by the Swedish Crown was only
> less disastrous because the Swedish Crown was palpably too weak to hold it.
> The insidious growth of Bourbon influence on the Rhine, and Mazarin's delib-
> erate policy of seizing good strategic points on the frontier, vitiated the settle-
> ment. The Peace of Westphalia was like most peace treaties, a rearrangement of
> the European map ready for the next war.[59]

Controversy continues to this day over the consequences of the Peace of Westphalia (see Box 2.2). Was it a visionary plan to usher in a new international order? Or was it a flawed scheme that did little more than serve the

---

BOX 2.2
THE NORMATIVE LEGACY OF THE PEACE OF WESTPHALIA

In retrospect, the postwar record of the Westphalian settlement presents a mixed picture of achievement and failure. On the *positive* side of the ledger, Westphalia can be credited with:

- Providing more religious freedom for Protestant and Catholic princes
- Terminating wars bred by religious conflict
- Repressing the threat of hegemonic domination in Europe
- Defining legally the concept of sovereign power, which prohibited interference from any authority above the state
- Creating a system for mediating international disputes and for making peace treaties after wars under the rule of law
- Creating the basis for the modern state system

On the *negative* side of the ledger, however, Westphalia may be said to have failed in a number of important respects to provide an adequate blueprint for international relations. It is blamed for:

- Failing to secure complete religious freedom
- Fomenting nationalist sentiments, especially in Germany, that were later to arouse public pressure to redress perceived injustices within the settlement
- Guaranteeing hegemonic rivalry by legitimating the race for predominant power
- Placing the maintenance of international peace on the precarious footing of a great power balance

---

immediate interests of the victors? Spirited arguments have been made on both sides. On the one hand, the period "is significant for the political analyst because, for all its apparent futility and lack of perfect or final settlement, it represented a new ordering of relationships."[60] On the other hand, the war and its settlement seem to have decided nothing: France and Spain continued fighting, and Bourbons and Hapsburgs remained on their respective monarchical thrones, subverting democracy and preparing for war.

Amidst these rival images of the Westphalian settlement, there is strong agreement that it dramatically changed the face of Europe through a multilateral process unprecedented in procedures and objectives. By introducing these far-reaching changes, Westphalia unquestionably transformed the normative order of world politics. Although the newly emerging sovereign states were not accountable to the judicial authority of others, this does not mean that Westphalia bred anomie. European states voluntarily accepted the nor-

CONTROVERSIES TO CONTEMPLATE

- Why did the Thirty Years' War last as long as it did? What motives and incentives caused the belligerents to accept the necessity of a cease-fire and armistice so that a peace conference could be convened in Westphalia?
- How did the origins and character of the Thirty Years' War influence the formation of a new diplomatic code of conduct that sanctioned warfare as a way of life?
- Was the Westphalian settlement more expressive, on balance, of the assumptions of realism or liberalism? What philosophies guided the peacemakers most? What experiences colored their outlook about war and peace? Should the Peace of Westphalia be interpreted as embracing a compassionate, forgiving outlook toward the defeated or a harsh, retributive posture to punish the warring states with the greatest losses?
- Why did the peace conference convene in two separate Westphalian cities, Münster and Osnabrück? Did the size of the number of participants help or hinder the building of a consensus about compromises for the final terms of the treaties? How did the number of participants affect decision making about peace?
- The Westphalian settlement is said to have "secularized" international politics by removing religion from international diplomacy. Was this beneficial? Does religion serve as a source of war or peace? What were the advantages and disadvantages of abandoning religion's moral codes for conduct as standards for behavior between states?
- Did the Westphalian settlement kill the medieval quest for a single, unified, European culture and polity sharing supranational institutions for governance and common ideals? If so, why? What benefits were ascribed to the division of Europe into separate, independent territorial states? Is the current international system Westphalian?

mative standards that developed after the Thirty Years' War, even in the absence of centralized mechanisms to articulate a code of conduct and enforce compliance.

It should also be noted that almost every social system emerges from controversies and debates over the rules and laws which will govern subsequent behavior. The system that came into being in 1648 was a product of an intense controversy about future rules. Moreover, it was a controversy that would reappear at all of the great peace congresses that followed Westphalia. Ever since the end of the Thirty Years' War, historians and social scientists have debated the costs and benefits of the international **norms** engendered by the Peace of Westphalia.[61] Emerging from a complex, multilateral war fought over three decades, the settlement was a product of mixed motives and clashing ambitions. The question persists: What is Westphalia's lasting legacy?

SUGGESTED READING

Asch, Ronald G. *The Thirty Years' War, The Holy Roman Empire and Europe, 1618–1648.* New York: St. Martin's Press, 1997.

Bueno de Mesquita, Bruce. "Popes, Kings, and Endogenous Institutions: The Concordat of Worms and the Origins of Sovereignty," *International Studies Review* 2 (Summer 2000): 93–118.

Caporaso, James A. "Changes in the Westphalian Order: Territory, Public Authority, and Sovereignty," *International Studies Review* 2 (Summer 2000): 1–28.

Falk, Richard A. *Law in an Emerging Global Village: A Post-Westphalian Perspective.* Ardsley, N.Y.: Transnational Publishers, 1998.

Gross, Leo. "The Peace of Westphalia, 1648–1948," In *International Law in the Twentieth Century,* edited by Leo Gross, 25–46. New York: Appleton-Century-Crofts, 1969.

Gutman, Myron P. "The Origins of the Thirty Years' War," *Journal of Interdisciplinary History* 18 (Spring 1988): 749–770.

Kegley, Charles W., Jr. and Gregory A. Raymond. *Exorcising the Ghost of Westphalia: Building World Order in the New Millenium.* Upper Saddle River, N.J.: Prentice-Hall, 2002.

Krasner, Stephen D. *Sovereignty: Organized Hypocrisy.* Princeton, N.J.: Princeton University Press, 1999.

Langer, Herbert. *The Thirty Years' War.* New York: Hippocrene Books, 1980.

Wedgwood, C. Veronica. *The Thirty Years' War.* London: Jonathan Cape, 1944.

NOTES

1. Blaney and Inayatullah, 2000, p. 36, citing Geoffrey Parker, 1998, pp. 192–193.
2. Albrecht-Carrié, 1964, p. 67.
3. Kissinger, 1994, pp. 62, 59, 58.
4. Parker, 1984, p. 214, citing Heiner Haan.
5. On structural realism, see Waltz, 1979 and 2000; on the balance of power, see Butterfield, 1968; Dehio, 1962, and Gulick, 1955.
6. Lee, 1986, p. 97.
7. Gardiner, 1895, p. 21.
8. Lee, 1986, p. 105.
9. Chandler, 1998, p. 24.
10. Wedgwood, 1938, p. 84.
11. Blum, et al., 1970, p. 220.
12. Parker, 1984, p. 76, illustrates Wallenstein's primal values by noting that Wallenstein "made enormous profits from the sale of confiscated lands in Bohemia" and raised his army by extorting contributions from his own troops. Wallenstein displayed, in the character assessment of Wedgwood, 1938, pp. 170–173, "a peculiar mixture of weakness and strength, vice and virtue."
13. "Wallenstein regarded war simply as a business proposition," Ogg, 1948, p. 139, observes, adding that "it is evident of Ferdinand's destitution that he decided to accept the services of a man so little influenced by religious motives."
14. Ogg, 1948, p. 141.
15. Parker, 1984, pp. 101–102. The Hapsburgs beleived what was good for the Roman Catholic Church was automatically good for the empire. Nonetheless, the Hapsburg worldview did

not find consistent favor in Rome. Pope Urban VII, for example, ended subsidies to Ferdinand and the Catholic League, "preferring to concentrate on what he perceived as the interests of the papal states in Italy—a task which he believed required the neutralization of Hapsburg influence in the peninsula." Parker, 1984, p. 86.

16. In Blum et al., 1970, p. 222.
17. Wedgwood, 1938, pp. 279–280.
18. In Holsti, 1991, p. 28, citing Roberts, 1967, p. 202.
19. Ogg, 1948, p. 156.
20. Wedgwood, 1938, p. 307.
21. Wedgwood, 1938, p. 377.
22. Chandler, 1998, p. 26.
23. Lee, 1986, p. 103.
24. Parker, 1984, p. 149.
25. Ogg, 1948, p. 163.
26. Parker, 1984, p. 160.
27. Wedgwood, 1938, pp. 431, 435.
28. Holsti, 1991, p. 29.
29. See Raymond, 1998–1999, for an analysis of arguments from necessity in foreign policy.
30. Limm, 1984, p. 42.
31. Albrecht-Carrié, 1953, p. 99.
32. Philpott, 1995, p. 356.
33. Blum et al., 1970, p. 225.
34. Palmer and Colton, 1984, p. 144.
35. Bueno de Mesquita, 2000, p. 96, observes that "the power and authority of the pope reached its high point roughly from the papacy of Innocent III (1198–1216) to that of Boniface VIII (1295–1303)." Although he once was no more than the bishop of Rome, during this period the pope "had become essential to the coronation and legitimation of the Catholic kings of Europe."
36. Davies, 1996, p. 568.
37. Strong, 1945, p. 161.
38. Barraclough, 1946, p. 384.
39. Polish and Russian influence at the peace conferences was also limited. Russia's refusal to become directly involved in Germany when it fought the War of Smolensk (1632–1634) with Poland compromised its bargaining power. Following the Peace of Polyanov, which ended the war with Russia, Poland's resumption of hostilities with Sweden that contributed to the disastrous Swedish defeat at Nördingen essentially deprived Poland of a voice in the Westphalian negotiations.
40. Holsti, 1991, p. 36.
41. Parker, 1984, p. 217.
42. Philpott, 1995, p. 359.
43. Parry, 1968.
44. Sørensen, 1968, p. 4.
45. Doran, 1971, p. 82.
46. Holsti, 1991, p. 39.
47. Gross, 1969, p. 26.
48. Walzer, 1977, pp. 19–20.
49. Doran, 1971, pp. 101–102.
50. Porter, 1994, p. 64.
51. Gay and Webb, 1973.
52. Lauterpacht, 1985, p. 24.
53. Kissinger, 1994, pp. 58, 61.
54. Church, 1972, p. 173.
55. Kissinger, 1994, p. 63.
56. In Parker, 1984, p. 219.
57. Ibid., p. 216.

58. This is the verdict of Wedgwood (1938, p. 39), who argues that "the war solved no problem. . . . Morally subversive, economically destructive, socially degrading, confused in its causes, devious in its course, futile in its result, it is the outstanding example in European history of meaningless conflict."
59. Wedgwood, 1944, p. 525.
60. Doran, 1971, p. 70.
61. See Kegley and Raymond, 2002, for a detailed evaluation of the consequences of the Westphalian rules for diplomacy over the past 350 years.

· 3 ·

THE NAPOLEONIC WARS AND THE CONGRESS OF VIENNA: BUILDING PEACE WITH A CONCERT OF POWER

For great evils, drastic remedies are necessary, and whoever has to treat them should not be afraid to use the instrument that cuts the best.

— PRINCE KLEMENS VON METTERNICH

PREVIEW

This chapter looks at one of history's turning points — between 1792 and 1815 — when Napoleonic France waged wars to spread its influence, ideals, and institutions throughout Europe. That bid to overturn the Westphalian order marks the beginning of the modern era. The Napoleonic Wars were revolutionary in three of the major ways by which international systems are transformed, because they were fought (1) in pursuit of revolutionary ideological objectives, (2) by a new type of national actor mobilizing nationalism in a fight to overthrow monarchies and dynasties, and (3) with huge military forces armed with highly destructive weapons.

This is the story of the reaction that an imperial power with hegemonic ambitions provoked. The response of the other great powers threatened by the revolutionary aspirations of France is traced from the outbreak of war to its dramatic climax at the Congress of Vienna, when the victors convened to create new rules for managing the postwar peace.

The terms of that settlement stand as a paragon of leniency toward the vanquished. But, as shall be seen, the peace treaty that emerged was guided less by sentiments of compassion than by realpolitik thinking about the balance of power. This chapter also

82

inspects the consequences in the nineteenth century of the rules that were created and the ways the Concert of Europe sought to act on them to police the system. It illuminates how states conceived of their interests and ideals as they wrestled with the competing values and moral principles that colored their thinking about prudent, expedient, and practical approaches to maintaining international stability. The narrative touches on many core concepts in contemporary world politics, including

- alliances and coalition formation
- the balance of power
- multipolar distributions of power
- nationalism
- popular sovereignty and liberal convictions about democratic governance
- a concert of the great powers to manage international affairs

These and other concepts within realist and liberal theories about international security are prominent in this chapter, in which we will pursue questions about the capacity of those theories to explain foreign policy choices before, during, and after wars.

Durable peace settlements are not neatly packaged by history. The past is cluttered with numerous treaties, some which lasted a long time and some which were quickly broken as the signatories prepared for a new war with one another. In order to fit the various pieces of historical evidence together, it is useful to first figure out how the big pieces are positioned, and to then surround them with the smaller details that fill out and complete the picture. In this chapter we inspect one of the largest pieces in the war-termination puzzle by inspecting the Napoleonic Wars, which set the stage for the Congress of Vienna that, like the 1648 Peace of Westphalia more than 150 years earlier, crafted a template from which the victors of subsequent wars drew lessons about whether their defeated enemies should be treated with compassion or with vengeance.

EUROPE'S CRUMBLING DYNASTIC SYSTEM

The seventeenth and eighteenth centuries were an age of dynasties. Monarchs ruled over territories that often resembled confederations of provinces tied together through crisscrossing marriages among noble families. Religion played a waning role in the politics among increasingly strong centralized states. In its place stood *raison d'état*, the realist notion that any act advancing state security interests was warranted no matter how morally repugnant it might seem. To realist theoreticians at the time, royal power was absolute — as expressed by French King Louis XIV, "L'etat, c'est moi" [I am the state].

Widespread agreement existed among this small, homogeneous group of monarchs over how the game of international politics ought to be played. They shared common experiences and held the same basic values and thus tended to feel more comfortable with fellow rulers than with lower-class citizens from their own states. In this aristocratic environment foreign policy was "a sport of kings, not to be taken more seriously than games and gambles, played for strictly limited stakes, and utterly devoid of transcendent principles of any kind. Since such was the nature of international politics, [all strategies and actions] were executed according to the rules of the game, which all players recognized as binding."[1] These monarchs understood that they were competitors with one another for power and believed that national survival frequently depended on forming flexible alliances with any nation in order to maintain a rough balance of power. They agreed on the divine right of all kings to rule at home as they saw fit and to follow a transnational code of conduct when dealing with one another. Reputation and personal honor precluded doing unseemly things to others who held the same station in life.

This **multipolar** system of many contending great powers survived until the French Revolution. To be sure, during its previous history Europe had experienced numerous wars, some of which dismembered once powerful states.[2] Yet the ebb and flow of countervailing alliances prevented any single power from conquering the rest. When an aspiring **hegemon** appeared within reach of military preponderance, other states coalesced to block its designs. The tacit rules of this balance-of-power game neither eliminated human rapacity nor prevented the collision of contending national interests; they merely prevented competition from degenerating into pure bedlam by specifying how the rivalry among dynastic states would be conducted.

The pillars of this laissez-faire, **self-help** system began to crumble in the late 1700s from a weakness that the ruling monarchs did not fully appreciate. Dynastic power declined more from internal causes than from external aggression. Nowhere was this more apparent than in France. Located at the center of the intellectual movement of the Enlightenment, and benefiting from the growing industry, commerce, and capital that its reform-minded and expanding middle class was generating, France was the most advanced country on the Continent. Yet its despotic government was reeling under the pressure generated by an inefficient system of taxation. As King Louis XV, who held power from 1715 until 1774, predicted: *"Après moi le déluge"* [after me the deluge].

THE FRENCH REVOLUTION

In eighteenth-century France, everyone belonged to an estate, or social order, that defined his or her legal rights. The First Estate consisted of the clergy, the Second Estate the nobility, and the Third Estate included the remainder of the population. Whereas the first two estates were privileged, the third was not and remained subject to a land tax called the *taille*.[3] Dividing French society into three categories, with the third combining such disparate groups as peasants, urban workers, merchants, financiers, physicians, and attorneys, aroused serious tensions. On the one hand, the wealthy commercial and professional classes in the Third Estate resented being classified together with impoverished laborers and lashed out at feudal privileges retained by the nobility. On the other hand, the nobility bemoaned what they saw as the pretensions of a rising bourgeoisie and sought to protect their long-standing social and political privileges.

Meanwhile, peasants throughout the French countryside and proletarians working at menial jobs in the cities harbored economic grievances. Heavily taxed by an inefficient government, they suffered without hope of relief. As Victor Hugo's moving historic novel *Les Miserables* captured it, the daily struggle for survival for the common person was extremely difficult, especially if he or she relied upon wages rather than selling handicrafts or agricultural products at market prices. Not only was income unevenly distributed, but the classes with the least wealth paid the bulk of the taxes.

The financial collapse of the French government precipitated a mass rebellion that became the French Revolution. King Louis XVI's intervention in the 1778–1783 War of American Independence had exhausted the French treasury, and to replenish it the king required tax burdens to be shouldered by the entire nation. When the well-to-do resisted, the king called for a convocation of the Estates General in May 1789 at Versailles, the first such assembly since 1614. The initial plan was to have representatives from each of the three estates sit in different chambers and cast votes separately; however, the Third Estate, possessing as many representatives as the other two estates combined, shrewdly called for all delegates to be combined in a single legislative house where they would hold the majority. The nobility refused and pressured Louis XVI to close the building where the Third Estate had been meeting. In response, representatives of the Third Estate gathered in a nearby indoor tennis court, where on June 20 they swore an oath proclaiming themselves to be the National Constituent Assembly charged with drafting a constitution.

> "The outcome of the greatest events is always determined by a trifle."
> — NAPOLEON BONAPARTE

For those who had taken the "Oath of the Tennis Court," the king's actions revealed he was siding with the hated nobility against the commoners. As a result, many of them argued for a constitution that kept the monarchy weak. Louis considered dissolving the Assembly, but eventually ordered the two other estates to join this new legislative body, though he never reconciled himself to the role of a constitutional monarch and continued working to undermine the Assembly. Indignant over their loss of privilege, many of the nobility emigrated to neighboring countries where they urged their hosts to overthrow the new regime.

Compounding the political problems now facing the monarchy were the wrenching economic consequences of a poor harvest and a decline in foreign trade. Unemployment, rising food prices, and labor unrest staggered French society: waves of panic swept across the country. On July 14, 1789, a Parisian mob stormed the royal fortress and prison, the Bastille, and organized a revolutionary municipal government. Outside of Paris, manors were looted, private estates occupied, and landlords murdered. Some revolutionaries were appalled by the violence; others insisted on even more extreme actions. Internal resistance among many clergy to sweeping reform combined with the threat of foreign intervention to push the revolution along a more radical, nationalist course.

On August 26, 1789, the Assembly issued the Declaration of the Rights of Man and Citizen as a guide to the new political system it was creating. "Men are born, and always continue, free and equal in respect of their rights," asserted Article I. According to Article II, these rights were "liberty, property, security, and resistance of oppression." "The nation is essentially the source of all sovereignty," continued Article III, "nor can any individual, or any body of men, be entitled to any authority which is not expressly derived from it." Inspired by the liberal ideas of the eighteenth-century philosophes,[4] the authors of the declaration had articulated a set of principles that would replace the last vestiges of feudalism in France with a political order based on *liberté, égalité, fraternité* (liberty, equality, fraternity).

The Society of Friends of the Constitution, known as the Jacobin Club because they met in a Jacobin monastery, were among the most militant of the French revolutionaries. The Girondins, then the dominant faction within the club, believed the Revolution would not be secure at home until it was exported abroad. Arguing that the French army would find allies among the oppressed populations of adjacent countries, they envisioned war as a crusade against monarchy. Ironically, the king and many of his conservative supporters also expected war to deliver them from their political problems. If revolutionary France lost, the powers of the Bourbon dynasty would be restored. By 1792, various royal courts across the Continent began preparations to prevent the spread of revolution to their own territories. As international tensions mounted, Franco-Austrian relations rapidly deteriorated, leading the National Assembly to approve a declaration of war on April 20 with only seven dissenting votes.

THE RISE AND FALL OF NAPOLEON

Contrary to Girondin predictions, the war began badly for France. Prussia joined the Austrian side, French defenses were weakened by the desertion of officers drawn from the nobility, and within a year the British joined this first coalition against France. When the duke of Brunswick, commander of the Austrian and Prussian forces, issued a manifesto threatening retribution against anyone who harmed the French royal family, rumors circulated throughout

Paris that King Louis XVI was assisting the invaders. On August 10, 1792, an armed mob attacked the Tuileries Palace and forced the royal family to flee. A revolutionary "commune" assumed control of the government in Paris and ordered the election of a new legislative body, the National Convention.

Authority now passed from the Girondins to more violent men. A Committee of Public Safety was established in 1793 to secure the home front by executing counterrevolutionaries. Under Maximilien Robespierre, a fanatical Jacobin who had once served as a small-town lawyer in northern France, it unleashed the Reign of Terror that sent Louis XVI and his queen, Marie Antoinette, to the guillotine. Over the next fourteen months, hundreds of thousands of people were arrested and approximately forty thousand were killed. The strength of popular government lies in virtue, Robespierre thundered in a speech to the Convention on February 5, 1794. But, he continued, virtue is powerless without terror. The campaign to uproot domestic conspiracies against the Revolution eventually devoured Robespierre. He was executed five months later, along with several of his closest associates.

To deal with foreign threats, the Committee of Public Safety ordered a *levée en masse* (universal conscription). By the spring of 1794, it had raised 800,000 troops. Unlike other armies of the day, this was a national armed force composed of enthusiastic citizen-soldiers who marched to battle singing, "To arms, to arms, ye brave," the rousing lyrics to "La Marsellaise," which later became the French national anthem. Commanded by officers who had risen through the ranks according to merit, France now possessed a formidable military machine.

Napoleon Bonaparte was one of the most talented officers in this machine. A short, temperamental man from the Mediterranean island of Corsica, he gained the attention of the Jacobins by brilliantly expelling British forces from Toulon in 1793. Napoleon claimed that his mind was like an ordered chest of drawers: Each drawer contained a vast amount of information on a particular topic, and he could open any of them whenever necessary to inspect their contents without missing a single detail. On October 5, 1795, when some twenty thousand royalists marched against the Convention, the twenty-six-year-old officer dispersed the crowd by firing at it with grapeshot from a cannon. Less than two weeks later he was appointed to the rank of brigadier general.

The following year, Napoleon received command of an army. He forced the Austrians out of Italy, and, in the 1797 Treaty of Campo Formio, he obtained the Austrian Netherlands and the Ionian Islands. From there, Napoleon's armies pursued an expansionist policy that sought to surround France with dependent countries modeled after Republican France. These actions precipitated a Second Coalition against France in 1798, composed of Great Britain, Austria, and Russia. Building on his popular support and rising national pride after the intervening "triumvirate" period, Napoleon seized control of the government in 1799 in a coup d'état that secured his position as supreme military commander. On December 4, 1804, his personal power increased even more when he assumed the title "Napoleon I, Emperor of the French." The French Republic was now a personal dictatorship.

Napoleon Bonaparte had come to power on the heels of a revolution inspired by the twin forces of **liberalism** and **nationalism**. The Napoleonic Wars, which ravaged Europe from 1803 to 1815, were undertaken to establish a new international order, one that would impose political unity on the Continent and reform the way European leaders ruled their tributary states. Napoleon sought to establish a single code of law, a public school system, and to implant liberal ideals in constitutions of the countries he conquered. His reforms generated several movements for national unification and republican administration. However, his methods were at times ruthless, and victory on the battlefield sometimes led him to violate many of the liberal principles that he espoused. Occasionally he installed members of his own family as the rulers of subjugated lands.[5]

Napoleon's Grand Empire reached its zenith in 1810 (see Map 3.1). Beyond France (which included Belgium and lands on the left bank of the Rhine) were layers of dependent states and political allies. The former encompassed what is today the Netherlands, Spain, Switzerland, western and southern Germany, most of Italy, and parts of Poland. The latter included Austria, Prussia, Denmark, Sweden, and Russia. All of these countries were part of Napoleon's Continental System, a mechanism designed to crush Great Britain by prohibiting the importation of British goods into Europe. By interrupting this trade flow, Napoleon hoped to dry up a major source of London's revenues and establish France as the economic hub of Europe. Since its naval victory over the French in the 1805 Battle of Trafalgar, Britain had been able to retain control of the seaborne commerce, thwarting Napoleon's military ambitions outside of Europe.

Napoleon's pursuit of hegemony stalled after 1811. The economic sacrifices demanded by the Continental System bred resentment from Zeeland on the North Sea to the distant shores of the Baltic Sea. Simultaneously, France began to suffer serious military setbacks. Although Napoleon had sent military units to Spain several years earlier to suppress a revolt against French rule, his forces were unable to defeat or pacify the country. As savage fighting with local guerrillas continued, he committed over 250,000 troops to what he called his "Spanish ulcer." Yet the French never tasted victory in this Peninsular War, despite the vast resources they hurled at their opponent.

More resources were drained by the June 1812 invasion of Russia. Determined to punish Czar Alexander I for withdrawing from the Continental System two years earlier, Napoleon assembled an enormous multinational force for the campaign. Despite defeating the Russians at Borodino and occupying Moscow on September 14, he could not compel them to surrender. Overextended, with limited supplies, and facing an opponent who engaged in scorched earth tactics, Napoleon confronted the unsavory prospect of being isolated in the smoldering ruins of Moscow as cold, harsh weather arrived. Realizing it would be difficult to feed and equip his Grande Armée under these conditions, he ordered a withdrawal. Relentlessly harassed by the Cossack

MAP 3.1 Napoleon's Europe in 1812. In 1812, Napoleon had subdued continental Europe and the occupying French armies aroused nationalism in the territories they occupied.

cavalry, the Grande Armée retreated slowly through the snow, icy wind, and seemingly eternal darkness of the Russian winter. Of the 611,000 troops who invaded Russia, roughly 400,000 died from exposure, starvation, and battle wounds. Another 100,000 men were taken prisoner. When the frozen tatters of what remained of the Grande Armée crossed back into Poland, it was no longer a disciplined fighting force.

With Europe no longer in awe of Napoleon, another coalition consisting of Great Britain, Russia, Prussia, and Austria was forged against French expansionism (see Table 3.1). Napoleon's empire finally collapsed after the Waterloo Campaign of June 12–18, 1815, but its fate had been sealed in defeats France suffered in the preceding three years. Following a series of treaties and armistice agreements, the victors met in Vienna to craft a peace settlement with France.

TABLE 3.1

A Chronology of the Napoleonic Wars and Peace Settlement

Date	Event
1800	French forces inflict crushing defeat on the Second Coalition in Italy and southern Germany, and Austria sues for peace.
1801	The 1801 Treaty of Lunéville terminates the provisions of the Campo Formio armistice.
1802	In March Great Britain and France sign the Treaty of Amiens, which accepts the Lunéville Treaty settlement and adds a British promise to restore all the colonial conquests engineered during the war (with the exception of Ceylon and Trinidad).
1803	In May Great Britain renews hostilities in response to the French refusal to cease its interventionary pursuits in Italy, Switzerland, and the Netherlands.
1805	Great Britain, Austria, Russia, and Sweden form the Third Coalition to overthrow Napoleonic France. In December, Napoleon's victories at Ulm and Austerlitz force Austria to abandon the Third Coalition, and the Treaty of Pressburg gives Venetia to Italy and recognizes Napoleon as its king.
1806	Prussia declares war on France, but Napoleon's armies inflict disastrous defeats in the battles of Jena and Auerstädt. Napoleon occupies and takes possession of most of Prussia.
1807	In June Napoleon defeats the Russians at Friedland, and Czar Alexander sues for peace. In the Treaty of Tilsit, Napoleon unexpectedly offers Alexander magnanimous terms, asking for no Russian territory in exchange for Alexander's pledge to help prevent British trade on the Continent. However, this treaty extracts from Prussia half of the territory it controlled in Poland and requires Prussia to pay France a large indemnity — a provision that destroys the Third Coalition, with the effect that opposition to French dominion on the European continent is provided only by Great Britain and Sweden.
1809	In April Austria launches a war of national liberation, but at the battle of Wagram in October, Napoleon forces the Austrians to accept the harsh terms of the Treaty of Vienna (or Peace of Schönbrunn), which costs Austria 4.5 million subjects, a forced disarmament of 150,000 soldiers, heavy indemnities, and a pledge not to trade with Great Britain.
1812	Napoleon's forces cross the Niemen River on June 24, and begin the invasion of Russia. In September, Napoleon takes possession of Moscow, but the lack of supplies in the burning city forces Napoleon to evacuate Moscow on October 22 and retrace his tracks toward the Niemen, where a mere remnant of his army crosses the river on December 13. Czar Alexander I proclaims the liberation of Europe, and Prussian and Swedish forces join Russia in a new allied effort to vanquish the French.

Date	Event
1813	In May Austrian chief minister Klemens von Metternich mediates an armistice and proposes a general European peace settlement between the faltering French and the allied armies, with territorial transfers and the reconstruction of Prussia. Seeking a decisive victory with expected French and Italian reinforcements, Napoleon stalls, and on August 12, Austria formally joins the coalition against him.
	An unofficial offer of peace is sent on November 9 to Napoleon from Frankfurt, asking France to withdraw behind the natural frontiers of the Rhine, the Alps, and the Pyrenees. Napoleon conveys his consent to this agreement, but the outbreak of a rebellion in Holland means that France can no longer control the mouth of the Rhine. The allies change their thinking about the terms they should request from France, and on December 5 the members of the Quadruple Alliance promulgate the Declaration of Frankfurt, which withdraws their previous offer in regard to the frontiers, and the Alliance begins instead to aid the revolt of Holland and pursue a policy of alienating Napoleon's friends in France and abroad. The allied armies cross the Rhine into France on December 21, and the main allied army invades from Switzerland through Lorraine.
1814	By the terms of the January 14 Treaty of Kiel, Denmark, which had been an ally of France, is forced to cede Norway to Sweden. The Norwegians refuse to accept the Treaty of Kiel, declare themselves independent, establish a liberal constitution, and offer the Norwegian throne to the Danish crown prince Christian Frederick, who holds the Norwegian throne only from May 17 to August 14.
	The Treaty of Chaumont, signed March 9 by Great Britain, Russia, Prussia, and Austria, strengthens the allied offensive against France and establishes a unified effort to police European politics. The combined allied armies deal Napoleon a decisive defeat at Laon, northeast of Paris.
	Austrian, Prussian, and Russian troops enter Paris on March 30. On April 1 Charles-Maurice de Talleyrand convokes the Senate, which until then had been a tool under the control of Napoleon. On April 2 the invading armies demand Napoleon's abdication, but the emperor continues to resist.
	French troops are defeated on April 10 by the Duke of Wellington at Toulouse, France, in the last battle of the Peninsular War (1808–1814). On April 11 Napoleon signs the Treaty of Fontainebleau and abdicates his title as Emperor of France; in exchange the allies grant Napoleon sovereignty over the island of Elba off the coast of Italy.
	The First Treaty of Paris, signed on May 30 between France and the Quadruple Alliance, establishes a preliminary peace in Europe. French Minister of Foreign Affairs Talleyrand receives extraordinary leniency in exchange for the pledge to restore the Bourbon monarchy to the throne in a limited rather than absolute monarchy: French boundaries *(cont.)*

(Table 3.1 cont.)

Date	Event

1814	are to be kept to those of 1792, and France is not required to pay any reparations. France also is allowed to keep the colonial possessions taken by Great Britain, except for Mauritius and the Seychelle Islands in the Indian Ocean and the West Indian islands of St. Lucia and Tobago. The treaty confirms Great Britain's possession of Malta.
	Louis XVIII is restored to the French throne June 4 as a result of the negotiations of Talleyrand and the acquiescence of the allies.
	The Congress of Vienna convenes in September. Representatives from all European states in existence prior to the Napoleonic Wars gather to settle territorial disputes and establish a perpetual balance of power in Europe to be overseen by the members of the Quadruple Alliance. The congress remains in session until June 9, when the Final Act of the Congress of Vienna is signed.
1815	On February 26 Napoleon escapes from Elba and is warmly received by the French people who join his bodyguards to recreate an army, Napoleon claims, to "save France from the outrages of the returning nobles [and] to secure to the peasant the possession of his land and to uphold the rights won in 1789. . . ." The monarchies then debating treaty provisions in Vienna put aside their disputes and renew their alliance.
	On June 18 Napoleon wages his final battle and is dealt a crushing defeat in the Battle of Waterloo. Three days later he abdicates his power for the final time to the French provisional government. On July 7 the allies' armies reoccupy Paris and restore the Bourbons by putting Louis XVIII at the head of the French government. Napoleon surrenders to the commander of a British warship on July 15 and is sent to a prison on St. Helena, where he lives for the next five and a half years.
	On September 15 Austria, Prussia, and Russia sign the Treaty of the Holy Alliance in which they vow to "remain united by the bonds of a true and indissoluble fraternity" and "on all occasions and in all places, lend each other aid and assistance. . . ."
	Less than a month later, the alliance expands to include Great Britain in postwar planning and reaffirm the pledge of cooperation that all four had previously made to repel French aggression. They resolve to hold periodic congresses "for the purpose of consulting upon their common interests. . . ." This agreement thus stipulates the goal of creating a league among the great powers to collectively maintain European peace through a concert system for collective security.
	On November 20 the Second Treaty of Paris is signed. It renews the Quadruple Alliance for twenty years to prepare the way for the members to jointly manage international relations, and it increases the penalties to France. Article 6 of this treaty provides for future conferences to promote peace and lays the groundwork for the postwar Concert of Europe.

EUROPE'S QUEST FOR PEACE

Napoleon's defeat at Waterloo concluded a period that had battered Europe for almost a quarter century and left over 2.5 million combatants dead. When measured by battle deaths per population, the toll exceeded all previous wars fought during the preceding three centuries.[6] The carnage inspired pity in people of compassion and horror in people of prudence. It galvanized a consensus among the victors who met at the Congress of Vienna about the need to prevent another great-power death struggle from again erupting.

The Congress of Vienna

Vienna was famed for its charm and beauty. As the site for the peace deliberations, it played host to a dazzling assemblage of people: monarchs and their servants, diplomats and their deputies, generals and their aides, as well as wives, mistresses, spies, pickpockets, and hangers-on. Numerous banquets, teas, and balls were organized to delight the city's guests. Despite being almost bankrupt, the Austrians spent over 15 million dollars providing entertainment. Among the cultural events was the first performance by the German musician Beethoven of his Seventh Symphony.[7]

While the festivities went on, statesmen toiled over more than just ending the roar of artillery. As the Austrian chancellor Prince Klemens von Metternich proclaimed in an opening session, the Congress of Vienna had as its mission goals beyond those of previous peace congresses.

> It does not require any great political insight to see that this Congress could not model itself on any predecessor. Previous meetings which have been called congresses have confined themselves to making treaties of peace between parties which were either at war or ready to go to war. This time the treaty of peace is already made, and the parties are meeting as friends, not necessarily having the same interests, who wish to work together to complete and affirm the existing Treaty. The matters to be negotiated are a multifarious list of questions, in some cases partly settled by previous discussions, in other cases, as yet untouched. The Powers which made the Treaty of Paris will determine the meaning which they wish to attach to the word Congress, and will also decide the form which would seem most appropriate for reaching the goals they have set themselves. They will use this right of determination equally to the advantage of the interested parties, and thus, to the good of Europe as a whole, and the plenipotentiaries at Vienna will deal with matters in the most efficient, prompt and confidential way. Thus the Congress is brought into being of itself, without having received any formal authority, there being no source which could have given any.[8]

The victors in the Napoleonic Wars operated from an unusually high level of agreement about the rules that should govern their future relations. The world they restored was a conservative world defined with an unusual clarity of purpose and consistency of vision. Napoleon's quest for hegemony had challenged not only the existing distribution of power on the European continent, but also

> "One must, if one can, kill one's opponent, but never rouse him by contempt and the whiplash."
>
> — KLEMENS VON METTERNICH

the self-help system of legitimized competition among sovereign great-power equals that policymakers inspired by realist theory advocated. Napoleon embraced an imperial vision of international order with himself at the apex of authority; he had tried to recreate the quasi-world government that had operated throughout the medieval system prior to the 1648 Peace of Westphalia.[9] But with the defeat of Napoleon came the defeat of his vision for a new international order. Metternich, backed by Russian czar Alexander I, Prussian king Frederick William III, and British foreign minister Castlereagh, tried to restore as much of the pre-Napoleonic map of Europe as possible and return to the laissez-faire rules so that the old Westphalian game could be played again.

The bargains struck among the victorious powers about territorial matters reflected the **realpolitik** belief that conflict was a natural component of interstate interaction. Disputes were bound to arise just as friction results from objects in contact. Whereas they might not be able to prevent future disputes, realist leaders assumed that they could reduce the likelihood of such disputes escalating to war by preserving an equilibrium among the **great powers.** In effect, the final act of the peace settlement of the Congress of Vienna redrew the map of Europe, guided not just by the goal of rewarding the victors for their sacrifices, but, more importantly, of making Austria, Russia, Prussia, Great Britain, and France approximately equal in their capacity to wage war. A stable **balance of power** was sought, with territorial boundaries altered so that no single state would be in a position to threaten the rest.

To attain this goal, the negotiators bargained long and hard to delineate a new set of borders that would allow the invisible hand of the balance of power to work. The biggest prize went to Russia, as Poland was again partitioned with the czar gaining the largest slice. Russia also received Finland from Sweden, which had gained Norway from Denmark. To build a counterweight to France, Prussia gained a portion of Saxony, all the German territories Napoleon had taken from it, as well as land in Westphalia and the Rhineland. For similar reasons, Austria regained the Tyrol and other formerly held land, including territories in wealthy and strategically important regions of Italy, as compensation for its willingness to accept the suspension of claims on the southern Netherlands. The Vienna settlement also permitted the Vatican's recovery of its former possessions in central Italy, and Switzerland was made a neutral state. In addition to these and other changes in Europe, modifications were made in colonial possessions, again with the aim of fine-tuning the overall equilibrium. For example, Great Britain returned to the Netherlands all the overseas territories seized in 1806, except for Ceylon, the Cape Colony in Africa, and part of the Guyana coast of South America east of Venezuela. In compensation, the various settlements on the Atlantic coast (including the colonies of the Essequibo River, Berbice, and Demerara) were united in 1831 to form the Crown Colony of British Guiana, the only British colony in South America.

The Bourbon Restoration

The most memorable aspect of the peace settlement was its resuscitative policy toward the defeated power, France, which had tried to establish universal dominion. Article 32 of the first Treaty of Paris provided for French representation at Vienna, but a secret clause excluded France from the actual decision making. However, Charles-Maurice de Talleyrand, who represented France at the congress, was able to use discord among the victors to leverage French participation in the negotiations. France, it was finally concluded, would be needed as a **balancer** to help police the new order, and its exclusion, partition, or forced demise could easily become the seed of a subsequent war. A conciliatory attitude toward France was seen as prudent because a Bourbon government in Paris could help shore up monarchical rule elsewhere in Europe.

Talleyrand's appeals to the "sacred principle of monarchical legitimacy" helped to prevent his nation from remaining a pariah. The former bishop of Auteuil, who had forsaken the Catholic Church during the Revolution only to abandon the Revolution for Napoleon, was famous for his caustic wit and cleverness. It was said that he had both the laughers and the thinkers on his side.[10] Upon arriving in Vienna, he insisted that with Napoleon gone, the victors had no right to exclude Bourbon France from the deliberations. His reiteration of the mantra of legitimacy eventually resonated with conservatives, who feared the Continent might suffer a relapse into revolutionary turmoil. As Metternich put it, what Europe wanted was not liberty but peace.

The Concert of Europe

To maintain peace after the congress ended, the diplomats in Vienna established the Concert of Europe, an oligarchic system of great-power consultation and policy coordination. The assumption behind the **concert** was that discussion and consensus building among those at the apex of the global hierarchy would produce multilateral decision making on divisive issues. Compromise and collaboration, rather than the thrust and parry of unbridled competition, would yield outcomes acceptable to all of the great powers. Not only would rule by this self-appointed coalition help control rivalries among the mighty, but it would provide a vehicle for enforcing peace among the smaller states, whose conflicts and civil wars could draw the great powers into combat.

Although theorists had in earlier times advocated various organizational schemes for orchestrating such collective responses to common problems, none were ever implemented. What made the climate of early-nineteenth-century opinion different was shared great-power fear of the strife unleashed by the French Revolution. Democratic ideals had taken root in a political landscape populated by monarchies adhering to strict realist conceptions of rules for peacekeeping. The consequences for European royalty were profound:

> Decision makers no longer felt more loyalty to each other than to their own people. Fewer social and cultural ties united decision makers of different countries, and correspondingly more social and cultural ties grew between each country's decision makers and its general populace. The willingness to use more force and less restraint against other states increased as members of the system became geographically dispersed and culturally heterogeneous. Increases in speed of transportation and communication did more to tie nations together internally than promoting cooperation among states. Xenophobia, the fear and hatred of foreign states, became a force . . . in almost every state. Where [before the French Revolution] the classical decision maker had difficulty in engendering patriotism among nations, the decision maker [after the French Revolution] had difficulty in controlling patriotism in order to follow a flexible foreign policy.[11]

From this setting emerged a set of rules that took a different posture toward the use of force than had existed in the seventeenth century. Intervention in the internal affairs of states, for example, was uncommon in the eighteenth century; but since revolutionary France had overturned the constitutions of conservative states, reactionary statesmen like Metternich and Friedrich Gentz now proclaimed the right to use forcible methods to suppress revolutionary uprisings within other nations' borders.[12] United in a common cause to combat rebellion from within, the victors experimented with the idea of collective intervention. For instance, at the Congress of Aix-la-Chapelle in 1818, Czar Alexander I of Russia proposed an alliance to intervene on behalf of rulers who were threatened by insurrection.

However, great-power unanimity proved to be elusive. While the British were willing to help the three Eastern monarchies stem military aggression aimed at overturning the post-Napoleonic balance of power, they did not countenance **military intervention** to prop up tottering autocrats. Foreign Minister Castlereagh, for example, refused Metternich's invitation in 1819 to approve the Carlsbad Decree and in 1829 rejected the Protocol of Troppau. In the first instance, the burning of conservative books and the murder of a conservative journalist by members of the German nationalist student movement prompted Metternich to convene a meeting of the larger German states at Carlsbad, where he coerced those leaders to promulgate measures he had drafted in order to suppress liberal nationalist ideas.[13] In the second instance, revolts in Spain and Naples led the three Eastern courts to agree at the Congress of Troppau that force could be used against states that had been transformed by internal upheaval and were threatening to their neighbors. Although Castlereagh was sympathetic to the fears held by his counterparts across the Channel, he resisted the use of the congress system to regulate other states' domestic affairs. Castlereagh, observed the Austrian ambassador in London, "is like a great lover of music who is at church; he wishes to applaud but he dares not."[14]

Despite British refusal to police sociopolitical disturbances, Austria, Prussia, and Russia were determined to use the Concert of Europe to prevent revolution. Therefore, at the Congress of Laibach the three conservative powers sanctioned Austria's intervention into Naples and Piedmont to suppress liberal revolts, and the following year at Verona they agreed to a French proposal to crush rebels in Spain.

METTERNICH'S LEGACY

Metternich's dexterity at guiding events during this turbulent period earned him the title "Coachman of Europe." For him, no lasting peace was possible "with a revolutionary system, whether with a Robespierre who declares war on chateaux or a Napoleon who declares war on Powers."[15] Leery of **popular sovereignty** (the belief that citizens should have a voice in governmental policies and governments should be accountable to the public), Metternich preferred discipline and social order. The story is told that having observed an eclipse of the sun from the garden of his castle on the Rhine, a "great sense of relief came over him when the moon finally completed its path across the sun and the temporary darkness was dispelled. There was 'order' again in the world."[16]

Still, despite Metternich's best efforts, popular attacks on absolute monarchy occurred after the Vienna settlement. On July 29, 1830, after an unsuccessful attempt to exert royal control over the French press and legislature, Charles X lost his throne to Louis Philippe, who had fought in the republican army of 1792. Shock waves reverberated across the Continent: the Belgians revolted against King William I of Holland; the Polish diet declared their country independent of Russian control; and the rulers of Brunswick, Hesse-Cassel, and Saxony were forced to abdicate their thrones. In response, the Austrian and Russian emperors and the crown prince of Prussia met at Münchengratz in 1833 to voice support for collective great-power cooperation and to exercise the declared right to use force to contain civil rebellion.[17]

Successive congresses of the Concert of Europe were convened over the next five decades (see Table 3.2), and additional proposals were advanced to coordinate a collective great-power response to the threat of the moment. These conferences also sought to amend the understanding reached at the Congress of Vienna in order to accommodate it to changing international circumstances.

Though Britain's insular position sometimes led it to differ with Austria, Prussia, and Russia over the peacekeeping rules of the Concert of Europe, at critical junctures the great powers were able to agree on a normative framework that prevented serious disputes from escalating into wars. To be sure, many conflicts later arose as the great-power struggle for influence continued, and mutual suspicions eroded confidence in what has been called "the

TABLE 3.2
Significant Great-Power Conferences, 1815–1870

Date	Location	Issues on the Agenda
Concert Period		
1814–1815	Vienna and Paris	Peace Treaty, Quadruple Alliance
1818	Aix-la-Chapelle	France, Quadruple Alliance
1820	Troppau	Naples revolution
1821	Laibach	Naples revolution
1822	Verona	Italy, Spain, "the Eastern question"
1830–1832	London	Belgian independence
1831–1832	Rome	Papal States government
1838–1839	London	Belgium (implementation of Treaty of London)
1839	Vienna	Egyptian insurrection
1840–1841	London	Egypt and the Straits
Postconcert Period		
1850–1852	London	Schleswig-Holstein
1853	Vienna	Turkey
1855	Vienna	Crimean War settlement
1856	Paris	Crimean War peace treaty
1858	Paris	The Principalities (implementation of Paris Treaty)
1860–1861	Paris	Syrian revolution
1864	London	Schleswig-Holstein, the Ionian islands
1866	Paris	Navigation on the Danube
1867	London	Luxembourg
1869	Paris	Cretan revolution

scheme for the continuous management of the international system."[18] However, these fears were generally overcome, as the spirit of cooperation instilled at the Congress of Vienna went a long way in preserving peace.[19]

The fragile normative consensus underlying the Vienna settlement managed to persist for three decades—an extraordinary achievement, given the past record of common purpose vanishing after a common enemy was defeated.

Nonetheless, it was eventually challenged. The liberal revolutions that swept Europe in 1848 undermined both the governments and the rules for international conduct that the victors had advocated when the Napoleonic Wars ended. The outbreak of the Crimean War in 1854 signaled the ultimate demise of the accords struck at the Congress of Vienna, which had required constant lobbying for them to work. That in itself is symptomatic of the inherent fragility of any peace program, however creative in design and durable its initial application.

The intellectual climate following the collapse of the Metternichean concert to collectively manage international affairs elevated national self-interest far above the old ideal of a common European interest. Instead of promoting collective action, it led the great powers to return to a security strategy based on flexible, short-term countervailing alliances.[20] The consensus that had constrained international rivalry in the first three decades after the Battle of Waterloo dissipated, bringing to a close a remarkable experiment in peacemaking.

To place the achievements of the Vienna settlement in their proper perspective, it is useful to compare the concert period of 1815–1848 with the postconcert period of 1849–1870. The concert period witnessed roughly the same number of serious interstate disputes as did the postconcert period, but between 1815 and 1848 there were fewer disputes between great powers and none escalated into wars. This is especially noteworthy given the greater frequency of interventions and reciprocated military actions during the reign of the concert system. In contrast, during the postconcert era between 1849 and 1870, no less than half the serious great-power disputes resulted in war, and, as we will see in the next chapter, some of these drastically altered the European balance of power.[21] The ostensible harmony at the congresses in London (1850, 1864, 1867), Paris (1856, 1858, 1860, 1869), and Vienna (1853, 1855) masked the unraveling of Metternich's security regime. The conservative solidarity that provided the normative underpinning for the Concert of Europe had collapsed. By the end of the Crimean War, no major power remained committed to preserving the rules emanating from the Vienna settlement. On

> "Eternal peace lasts only until next year."
> — RUSSIAN PROVERB

the contrary, various political leaders actively sought to replace the agreement of the great powers to act collectively with a new set of rules that permitted each to act unilaterally in pursuit of its own perceived interests. As rivalries intensified, the consensus for cooperative peacekeeping in the Concert of Europe broke down and balance-of-power politics reemerged.

THE POWER OF PRINCIPLE IN PRESERVING PEACE

The Vienna settlement stands in history as a paragon of a conciliatory peace that produced large dividends for the victors. It suggests that the prospects for a durable peace settlement can be enhanced by giving the vanquished enemy a stake in preserving the new order. To quote one famous contemporary realist theoretician on policy making, Henry Kissinger,

> In dealing with the defeated enemy, the victors designing a peace settlement must navigate the transition from the intransigence vital to victory to the conciliation needed to achieve a lasting peace. A punitive peace mortgages the international order because it saddles the victors, drained by their wartime exertions, with the task of holding down a country determined to undermine the settlement. Any country with a grievance is assured of finding nearly automatic support from the disaffected defeated party.[22]

Minimizing potential resentment requires a statesmanship of self-restraint. Defeated powers, this exceptional case suggests, must not be humiliated; neither should they be denied their legitimate rights, nor have their honor impugned.[23] Yet even with a conciliatory peace, a proud nation "sustains a deep wound from which there is no full recovery. . . . However much resilience the nation may retain outside the field of politics, a spring has been broken which cannot be welded together again."[24]

Offering a conciliatory peace, however, should not be confused with being ambivalent about whether the settlement will be vigorously upheld. A generous peace, realpolitik counsels, must still be a firm peace. By itself, a conciliatory settlement is no guarantee against revisionism. Victors must be capable of marshaling the military resources needed to convince the vanquished that efforts to overturn the status quo carry grave risks.

In 1807 Napoleon Bonaparte observed, prophetically, "If they want peace, nations should avoid the pin pricks that precede common shots."[25] One of the most difficult tasks in statecraft is anticipating the issues that potential adversaries will likely see as so important that they will take up arms, if necessary, to resolve them to their own satisfaction. As adept as the negotiators at the Congress of Vienna were in preventing the rapid onset of another major war, deficiencies marred the final peace settlement and led, over time, to the gradual erosion of the foundation on which the Concert of Europe rested. As one student of the period notes,

> the Vienna peace settlement was backward-looking. The problem of the future was assumed to be the problem of the past: French revolutionary expansionism. . . . The drafters created a successful system to cope with the problem of hegemony-seeking. That is not an insignificant accomplishment, but the threat of hegemony was not to arise for many more decades. In the meantime, the problems of national liberation, national unification, and liberal institutionalism were already on the horizon. They would become the most important sources of war throughout the nineteenth century, but the 1814–1815 settlements ignored them. The statesmen of the great powers created a static system for a world of change . . . and a peace system that anticipated for the future little more than a recurrence of a problem they had already resolved.[26]

Peace treaties are not self-enacting; all parties must work energetically to guarantee that their provisions are carried out, and they must address divi-

CONTROVERSIES TO CONTEMPLATE

- Did Republican France's effort to spread liberal ideals in national governance and international affairs create the modern world system?
- Why did France under Napoleon pursue an imperial policy of expansionism that ravaged Europe? What were the ideas, ideals, and interests behind this quest for hegemony?
- What motives united the alliances that opposed each other in the European balance-of-power system?
- What national interests and ideals were uppermost in the minds of the leaders of the victors when they convened at Vienna and Paris to negotiate the terms of a peace treaty and devise new rules for the maintenance of world order? What was the prevailing philosophy of the victors?
- Was the consensus of the victors at Vienna about peacemaking principles morally just? Why? What are the criteria by which such evaluations are best judged?
- How did nationalism and ascendant liberal values such as popular sovereignty influence international relations in the late eighteenth century?
- Why did realists at the Congress of Vienna create the Concert of Europe and endorse conciliation and compassion toward a vanquished expansionist power, France, as a prudent and practical peace policy?
- Did the Congress of Vienna settlement succeed? What are the preconditions for successful peacemaking?

sive issues that may later arise. As prescient as it was, the Vienna settlement still failed to identify two "pin-prick" issues that would precede the cannon shots fired during the second half of the nineteenth century: liberal reform movements and hypernationalism.

Controversies remain about the transferability of lessons derived from this historical episode. What do the events of 1814–1815 tell us about the viability of future peace settlements? For some nations, the Congress of Vienna laid the groundwork for a lengthy peace; for others, it stifled democracy and national self-determination and thus sowed the seeds of subsequent trouble. To draw lessons about the most effective means of achieving durable peace settlements, we need to broaden our focus and look at other cases for additional evidence. In Chapter 4 we take up this challenge by examining the Wars of German Unification.

SUGGESTED READING

Asprey, Robert. *The Rise of Napoleon Bonaparte.* New York: Basic Books, 2001.

Blanning, T. C. W. *The Origins of the French Revolutionary Wars.* New York: Longman, 1986.

Dehio, Ludwig. *The Precarious Balance*. New York: Knopf, 1962.

Drayton, Richard. "Themes in Modern European History 1780–1830," *History: The Journal of the Historical Association* 81 (1996): 685–686.

Fregosi, Paul. *Dreams of Empire*. New York: Carol, 1989.

Gulick, Edward Vose. *Europe's Classical Balance of Power*. Ithaca, N.Y.: Cornell University Press, 1955.

Kissinger, Henry. *A World Restored: Mettternich, Castlereagh, and the Problems of Peace, 1812–22*. Boston: Houghton Mifflin, 1973.

Lyons, Martyn. *Napoleon Bonaparte and the Legacy of the French Revolution*. New York: St. Martin's Press, 1994.

Nicolson, Harold. *The Congress of Vienna: A Study in Allied Unity: 1812–1822*. New York: Harcourt Brace Jovanovich, 1946.

Schroeder, Paul W. "Did the Vienna Settlement Rest on a Balance of Power?" *American Historical Review* 3 (1992): 683–706.

Sofka, James R. "Metternich's Theory of European Order: A Political Agenda for Perpetual Peace," *The Review of Politics* 59 (1998): 115–150.

NOTES

1. Morgenthau, 1985, p. 210.
2. Poland, for example, was partitioned three times (1772, 1793, and 1795) and ultimately disappeared as an autonomous state, until reconstituted at the end of World War I.
3. Because the bourgeoisie generally found ways to avoid paying this tax, most of the revenues were collected from the peasantry.
4. The philosophes were men of letters who popularized the ideas of the Enlightenment. Drawing upon the previous work of Francis Bacon, Rene Descartes, John Locke, and Isaac Newton, they were confident in the power of reason to discover the laws of nature and promote human progress. Within France, the center of this intellectual movement, Condorcet, Diderot, Helvétius, Montesquieu, Quesnay, Rousseau, Turgot, and Voltaire were the most renowned figures.
5. For example, his brother Joseph was made king of Spain, Louis served as king of Holland, and Jerome became king of Westphalia, an artificial state cobbled together from Prussian and Hanoverian territories. Napoleon's sister Caroline was named the queen of Naples, and his stepson became viceroy of the Kingdom of Italy.
6. Levy, 1983, p. 58.
7. Lane et al., 1959, p. 341.
8. Langhorne, 1986, p. 318.
9. Miller, 1985, p. 31.
10. Kissinger, 1973, p. 148.
11. Coplin, 1971, p. 305.
12. Rosecrance, 1963, p. 29.
13. Nicolson, 1946, p. 265.
14. Kissinger, 1973, p. 275.
15. Kissinger, 1973, p. 12.
16. Pinson, 1966, p. 56. Metternich's last words in 1859 revealingly were, "I was a rock of order." In Green, 1982, p. 25.
17. The right to intervene in lesser powers' internal affairs was also rationalized by goals other than the conservative purpose of preserving monarchies and the status quo. Under Castlereagh's successor, George Canning, the threat of British sea power was used to support the independence movement in Spanish America; later, under Lord Palmerston, the British supported constitutionalist causes in Spain and Portugal. Intervention and forcible procedures, in other words, also had become tools of liberal statecraft, as progressive thinkers like Stratford de Redcliffe and John Stuart Mill advocated their use to liberate

oppressed peoples and engender democratic reform. For a history of the rise and decline of the nonintervention principle in international law since 1816, see Kegley, Raymond, and Hermann, 1998.

18. Langhorne, 1986, p. 317.
19. For example, when peace was threatened by an uprising in Belgium in 1830, the great powers were able to resolve their differences despite King William's plea to the conservative states for help, a plea which threatened to expand to war when Russia responded with an offer of sixty thousand troops to assist in restoring him to his throne.
20. Hinsley, 1963, p. 238.
21. See Schroeder, 1986; Wallace, 1979.
22. Kissinger, 1994, p. 81. Schroeder, 1994b, p. 477, elaborates, characterizing the peace that the victors launched as testimony to the capacity to achieve, "or at least approach, consensus on a sane, practical concept of peace. This was the product of learning, of changing previous concepts of peace and victory to fit reality."
23. Elrod, 1976, p. 166.
24. Dehio, 1962, p. 173.
25. Seldes, 1985, p. 305.
26. Holsti, 1991, pp. 136–137.

· 4 ·

THE WARS OF GERMAN UNIFICATION: THE DIPLOMACY OF IRON AND BLOOD

The statesman is like a man wandering in a forest who knows
his general direction, but not the exact point at which he will
emerge from the wood.

— OTTO VON BISMARCK

PREVIEW

The Thirty Years' War and the Napoleonic Wars were system-transforming struggles that pitted the most powerful states of the day against one another to determine whose vision of international order would prevail. To place these hegemonic wars in perspective, we turn our attention in this chapter to the Wars of German Unification — a set of shorter, less destructive clashes that helped pave the way for World War I, history's next system-transforming war. Fought early in the second half of the nineteenth century, they were an important link in the chain of events that led the victors of World War I to design a peace treaty that was far more harsh than the settlement crafted a century earlier at the Congress of Vienna.

The Wars of German Unification were dominated by the towering personality of Otto von Bismarck. His realist approach to statecraft accepted military force as a tool of foreign policy to be unleashed whenever the value of what could be won exceeded the costs of fighting. In wars against Denmark (1864), Austria (1866), and France (1870–1871), he skillfully used military force to achieve his political goals. Once these wars were over, he sought to preserve their cumulative outcome by building a network of alliances that would solidify the new balance of power in Europe. A study of the

104

Wars of German Unification thus gives us an avenue for exploring how war and peacemaking are influenced by:

- nationalism
- power politics
- technology that rewards taking the offensive
- irredentism
- secret diplomacy
- alliances

When reading this chapter, note how Bismarck deftly isolated an opponent before hostilities were initiated and how each victory positioned him to undertake another war against a different opponent. In addition, contrast his settlement of the war with Austria with the settlement that terminated the war with France.

On September 24, 1862, Count Otto Eduard Leopold von Bismarck-Schönhausen was appointed minister-president of Prussia by King William I. The king was desperate. His decision to undertake a comprehensive reform of the Prussian military had precipitated a constitutional crisis, pitting the crown against liberal members of parliament. The proposed reforms would expand the officer corps and double the size of the army, both costly undertakings that required the legislature to authorize a substantial tax increase. When liberal legislators balked at providing the necessary appropriation, a somber William briefly considered abdicating, but he turned instead to his new minister in the hope that this self-proclaimed man of action could break the political deadlock over funding the military reforms.

Bismarck was a tall, broad-shouldered man with deep loyalty to the Prussian state. For him, domestic politics were subordinate to questions of foreign policy. Like Karl von Clausewitz, the Prussian general who had fought against Napoleon half a century earlier, Bismarck saw war as an instrument in the conduct of foreign policy.[1] Without a modern, effective military force, Prussian foreign policy would lack an essential tool. A practitioner of **realpolitik,** during his first appearance before the legislative budget committee on September 30, he declared, "The position of Prussia in Germany will be determined not by its liberalism but by its power." In his opinion, "Prussia must concentrate its strength and hold it for a favorable moment." "Not through speeches and majority decisions are the great questions of the day decided," he concluded, "but through iron and blood."[2]

During Bismarck's era at the helm of Prussian foreign policy, his policy of iron and blood resulted in a series of wars, collectively known as the Wars of German Unification. In this chapter we will examine the character of these wars, compare the peace settlements that were constructed in their aftermath, and evaluate the consequences that resulted from the philosophies of state-craft that shaped the policies of the victors.

THE RISE OF BRANDENBURG-PRUSSIA

The first German empire, or *Reich,* had its origins in the vast lands once controlled by Charlemagne, the Frankish king who conquered much of western Europe during the ninth century. Following his death in 814, these lands were inherited by his only surviving son, Louis the Pious, who spent half of his life trying to figure out how to distribute the territory among his own sons. Following a series of civil wars, Louis's holdings were subdivided: one son took the west, another took the east, and the third received a corridor stretching from the North Sea to Rome (including modern Belgium, Alsace, Lorraine, the Rhineland, Switzerland, and the Po valley). Much of European history ever since has involved a struggle between the west (contemporary France) and east (contemporary Germany) for control of this middle kingdom.

The Holy Roman Empire

The eastern Frankish region came to be known as the Holy Roman Empire of the German nation. A conglomeration of many different tribes speaking various dialects, this First Reich suffered from an ever-growing tension between central authority and the power of local princes. As central control gradually decayed, a feudal structure took its place. What we today call Germany was a mosaic of political units: duchies, free cities, bishoprics ruled by churchmen, and minuscule fiefdoms controlled by an assortment of counts and barons, each nominally the vassal of some higher lord. Certain frontier principalities called *Marken* (or marchlands) were given special privileges for defending the borders of the empire. The most important of these were Brandenburg in the northeast and Austria in the southeast (see Map 4.1).

In a drive to the east, Brandenburg accumulated territory largely at the expense of the neighboring Slavs. In 1618, it inherited the duchy of Prussia when the male line of the dukes died out. An area along the coast of the Baltic Sea, Prussia had been colonized by the Knights of the Teutonic Order in the thirteenth and fourteenth centuries,[3] but was acquired by Poland after the order was defeated twice during the fifteenth century. When the Hohenzollern dynasty of Brandenburg inherited Prussia, it initially recognized the overlordship of Poland. But due to warfare between Poland and Sweden, the House of Hohenzollern was able to gain complete **sovereignty** over the duchy of Prussia and ultimately renamed it the Kingdom of Prussia. Before long, all of the Hohenzollern possessions throughout Germany were referred to as Prussia.

Under Hohenzollern rule, Prussia developed an efficient bureaucratic machine that turned landed aristocrats into administrators. Though rela-

MAP 4.1 The Medieval German Empire. Following the death of Frederick II in 1250, the Holy Roman Empire was a mosaic of hundreds of small, quasi-autonomous principalities. German territory remained fragmented politically until the nineteenth century.

tively poor and lacking in natural resources, Prussia was fortunate to have been led by several skilled monarchs, most notably Frederick William (1640–1688) and Frederick the Great (1744–1786). The Hohenzollerns demanded discipline and sacrifice from their subjects. Through their leadership, Prussia emerged in the eighteenth century as "a new state prototype in Europe, a state with a drillmaster administration based on principles of unquestioning obedience and total regimentation, directed toward the development of unbridled and unlimited military power."[4] It became "not so much a State which possessed an army as an army which possessed a State."[5]

While many Germans living to the west and south of the Prussian capital of Berlin had misgivings about this upstart kingdom, they faced a greater threat in Napoleonic France. As discussed in the previous chapter, Napoleon Bonaparte invaded German territory in 1806 and replaced the region's kaleidoscope of petty principalities with larger units of government (see Table 4.1). Prussia, too, was overwhelmed by the French juggernaut. At the Battle of Jena, it suffered a catastrophic defeat, resulting in the loss of roughly half of its territory. Over the next decade, a group of Prussian reformers headed by Baron Karl Freiherr vom Stein and General Gerhard von Scharnhorst began planning a war of revenge. From their perspective, future military success depended on mobilizing the entire population as a citizens' army in service of the state. This emphasis on strong, centralized bureaucratic government took precedence over all other concerns.[6] It led to the creation of a general staff within the military, various social and educational reforms, and a ministerial system designed to advise the king on issues of foreign and public policy, the very system that Bismarck would someday head as minister-president.

The German Confederation

After Napoleon's defeat in 1815, the units of government he had established were consolidated into a loose-knit confederation of thirty-eight states known as the German Confederation.[7] The diet of the confederation was located in Frankfurt and functioned like a standing conference, with permanent emissaries representing their respective states. Because the confederation required unanimous approval of any significant policy initiative, it was not an active organization. Nevertheless, it provided a stage where the drama of German national unification would soon be performed.

The liberal ideas of liberty, fraternity, and equality that crossed the Rhine River with Napoleon's armies took root in the fertile soil of German **nationalism.** So long as Germany was splintered into more than three dozen small states, Germans would be at the mercy of their larger neighbors.[8] "We Germans have never lacked natural strength," noted the eminent historian Ludwig Dehio:

> But if German power at times towered up like a cloud bank, it also dissolved again in rolling mists. Unformed in formless territory, our power was without core or sequence, always developing, never developed. Its forces boiled over across our frontiers, and at the same time turned against one another within them.[9]

According to German liberal nationalists, the remedy was to unite under a constitutional monarchy that would provide security against external attack and protect civil rights against the capricious acts of petty princes. As advocates of citizen participation in policy making, the liberal nationalists were distrusted by the conservative aristocrats leading Prussia. When the liberals meeting in Frankfurt during 1849 petitioned King Frederick William IV of Prussia to become the head of a new unified German state governed by a

TABLE 4.1
A Chronology of the Wars of German Unification

Date	Event
1806	Dissolution of the Holy Roman Empire following Napoleon's invasion of central Europe; Prussia defeated at the Battles of Jena and Auerstädt and loses its western territories under the Treaty of Tilsit
1813	Napoleon defeated in the Battle of Leipzig, marking the end of French control over German territory
1814	Convocation of the Congress of Vienna, which established the German Confederation under the presidency of Austria
1834	Creation of the *Zollverein,* a Prussian-sponsored customs union that excluded Austria
1848	Political uprisings throughout Europe, including liberal revolts in Berlin, Frankfurt, and Vienna
1850	The "humiliation" of Olmütz: the Prussian attempt to establish a political union of German states blocked by Austria and Russia; Prussian constitution revised
1852	London Protocol gives international recognition to the Danish position on the provinces of Schleswig and Holstein
1861	William I crowned King of Prussia
1862	Otto von Bismarck appointed minister-president of Prussia
1863	Alvensleben Convention between Russia and Prussia regarding the Polish question
1864	War waged by Austria and Prussia against Denmark
1865	Gastein Convention provides for Austrian administration over Holstein and Prussian administration of Schleswig
1866	The Seven Weeks' War of Austria against Prussia
1867	Establishment of the North German Confederation
1870–1871	Franco-Prussian War; creation of the Second Reich

parliamentary monarchy, he refused because he saw it as an offer "molded out of the dirt and dregs of revolution, disloyalty, and treason."[10] Still, efforts to forge a German national spirit continued. Glee clubs, debating societies, and various professional associations were organized across regional lines, all for the purpose of building solidarity among people whose political loyalties had long been to their local princes.

Prussia and Austria were the two major powers within the German Confederation. Rivalry between them had festered since Frederick the Great wrested the resource-rich province of Silesia from the Austrians in a series of wars (1740–1742, 1744–1745, 1756–1763). Perhaps nowhere could the intensity of this rivalry be shown more starkly than in a letter Bismarck wrote in 1856:

> Germany is clearly too small for us both [Austria and Prussia] . . . Austria will remain the only state to whom we can permanently lose or from whom we can permanently gain.
>   For a thousand years intermittently . . . the German dualism has regularly adjusted the reciprocal relations [of Austria and Prussia] by a thorough internal war; and in this century also no other means than this can set the clock of evolution at the right hour.
>   I wish only to express my conviction that, in the not too distant future, we shall have to fight for our existence against Austria and that it is not within our power to avoid that, since the course of events in Germany has no other solution.[11]

Bismarck's prediction highlighted the tension between two schools of thought about German unification. Whereas advocates of "Great Germany" hoped to forge strong ties between Austria and the other German states, those calling for "Little Germany" argued that Austria should be excluded from the unification process. Well before this debate was settled on the battlefield, Prussia took the initiative by establishing a **customs union** with the states of Little Germany. By giving more favorable trade status to member states, the customs union fostered economic interdependence within Little Germany while undermining Austria's position in central Europe.

WAR WITH DENMARK

By 1862, when Bismarck became Prussian minister-president, the economic influence of Prussia had become so great that many of the smaller German states began to see Austria's Hapsburg dynasty as a counterweight to the growing power of the house of Hohenzollern. To capitalize on these fears of Prussia, the Austrians proposed a series of changes in the German Confederation that would have weakened Prussian influence within the organization. Their plan was thwarted, however, when Bismarck persuaded King William to boycott the 1863 Frankfurt Congress of Princes, where the Austrian reforms were to have been proposed.

Unlike the Austrians, who as early as 1850 had proposed a union of the northern German states, Bismarck had no preconceived plan to unify Germany. For him, unification remained less important than advancing Prussian power in the face of Austrian opposition. Bismarck might not have been a liberal nationalist, but he recognized the wave of nationalism sweeping across German lands as a potent source of political power that could be mobilized to achieve his policy goals.

Bismarck was a master of bluffing, intrigue, and alliances of convenience. A loyal servant of his king, Bismarck believed in duty and order. To his critics, however, he appeared obstinate, arrogant, and an unscrupulous reactionary. Indeed, during his tenure, Bismarck undertook many actions that inspired this reputation.

In addition to his assertive and often abrasive style, Bismarck had an uncanny ability to isolate his opponents and defeat them one at a time. No better illustration of this ability can be found than in the prelude to the 1864 war with Denmark, ostensibly fought over the duchies of Schleswig and Holstein. The status of the duchies was extraordinarily complicated. Lord Palmerston, the British prime minister, once claimed only three people understood its intricacies: one had died, another had gone crazy, and he himself, the third, had forgotten it all.[12] Though neither duchy was part of Denmark proper, both were possessions of the Danish crown and had been politically united for centuries. Schleswig, the province immediately south of Denmark, was inhabited by both Danes and Germans; Holstein, adjoining Schleswig, was predominantly German and held membership in the German Confederation. Although neither duchy had much economic importance, their geographic locations each had strategic significance.

On November 13, 1863, a new constitution was promulgated for Denmark that included provisions which would lead toward the eventual incorporation of Schleswig into that country. Just over a decade earlier, hostilities had arisen over this very issue. In 1848 the duchies erupted in revolt when the Danes tried to make Schleswig a part of Denmark. Whereas Danish nationalists maintained that the Eider River dividing Schleswig from Holstein was Denmark's natural frontier, German nationalists responded by identifying the more northern Königsau (or Kongeaa) River separating Schleswig from Sonderjylland as the appropriate boundary. Ultimately thirty thousand troops from Prussia and other members of the German Confederation poured into the duchies to support the German nationalists. Denmark appealed to the **great powers,** and pressure from England and Sweden soon prompted a Prussian withdrawal. The Convention of Malmö appeared to settle the matter, but this peace treaty proved to be a brief truce as hostilities flared up again during the following spring. After the British and Russians exerted further pressure, the 1850 Treaty of Berlin and the London Protocol of 1852 gave international recognition to the political conditions that had existed prior to the fighting. In exchange, Denmark promised not to annex Schleswig.

When King Frederick VII died on November 15, 1863, two days after the Danish parliament had approved the new constitution, his successor, Christian IX, signed the document. Austria and Prussia then protested that this action violated the 1852 agreement and thereupon issued an ultimatum for Denmark to rescind those terms of the November constitution that affected Schleswig and Holstein. The Danes refused, and on February 1, 1864, Austro-Prussian forces swarmed into Denmark.

"Great crises," Bismarck once observed, "represent the weather which is conducive to Prussia's growth, when we use them without fear and perhaps very ruthlessly."[13] Although Danish troops mounted a stout defense, Denmark was vastly outnumbered by the combined Austro-Prussian forces.

> "Pointed bullets are better
> than pointed speeches."
>
> — OTTO VON BISMARCK

After a brief truce did not yield a peace settlement, the fighting resumed. By July 20, King Christian had acknowledged his cause was hopeless and agreed to a new truce. Five days later a peace conference began in Vienna. A preliminary agreement was reached on August 1, and a final peace treaty was signed on October 30. Under the Treaty of Vienna, Denmark renounced all rights to Schleswig and Holstein.

Once Denmark relinquished its control over the two duchies, the question arose over their future disposition. On August 14, 1865, Austria and Prussia concluded the Gastein Convention by which Austria would administer Holstein while Prussia took Schleswig. This formula portended problems between the victors because Holstein was surrounded by Prussian territory. Soon tensions mounted over passage rights and Prussian encroachments in Holstein. While feigning a willingness to negotiate, Bismarck felt content to let the dispute escalate to armed conflict. More had been at stake in the war with Denmark than the future of the duchies. The design of the Treaty of Vienna and the Gastein Convention gave Prussia an opportunity to create a diplomatic incident over the occupation of Schleswig and Holstein, discredit the Austrians, and settle old scores on the battlefield without appearing to be the aggressor. As Bismarck later put it, "One must always have two irons in the fire."[14]

THE SEVEN WEEKS' WAR

Because Bismarck doubted that Austria's influence among the German states could be curtailed without unsheathing the sword,[15] he sought to isolate the Austrians so military action could be taken without worrying whether another state might come to their aid. In October 1865, Bismarck offered Napoleon III vague promises of territorial "compensation" in western Germany if France remained neutral during a war between Austria and Prussia. Bismarck also gained the support of Italy by concluding a secret agreement that would permit the Italians to annex the Austrian-ruled region of Venetia if Prussia was victorious. Russia was expected to remain on the sidelines owing to earlier Prussian support for the czar's repression of a Polish uprising in 1863. Finally, England was not expected to interfere due to trade concessions granted by Prussia.

Meanwhile, Austria reacted to growing Prussian influence in Holstein by unilaterally appealing to the diet of the German Confederation, where it hoped to gain support from the other German states. Declaring that this violated the Gastein Convention, which called for the two powers to decide all issues pertaining to Schleswig and Holstein by common consent, Bismarck accused the Austrians of aggression and sent troops into Holstein on June 7, 1866. The Hapsburgs responded by calling upon the diet to assemble an army and punish the Prussians.

Prussia, a state of 18 million people, now faced conflict with an empire almost twice as large. Despite this, Prussia won a resounding victory on July 3 at Königgrätz (also known as Sadowa), with the Austrians suffering 42,812 casualties among their officers and troops to just 9,153 for the Prussians.[16] The Prussian breech-loading needle gun gave their troops superior firepower over the Austrians, who relied upon antiquated muzzle-loading rifles and outmoded shock tactics. Breech-loading rifles revolutionized infantry tactics by allowing soldiers to reload on the move or in a prone position rather than only while standing.[17]

An Italian attack on Austria's southern border aided Prussia's war effort. Nevertheless, the Austrians defeated the Italian army at Custozza on June 24 and might have been able to move additional forces north if they had more time. If the Hapsburgs had rebounded from their losses at Königgrätz and continued fighting, France or Russia might have intervened on their behalf. Bismarck moved swiftly to foreclose either possibility. He persuaded King William to relinquish any possibility of further battlefield triumphs and offer Austria lenient peace terms, even though the king and many of his generals had hoped to march in triumph through the streets of Vienna. In his memoirs, Bismarck wrote:

> We had to avoid wounding Austria too severely; we had to avoid leaving behind in her any unnecessary bitterness of feeling or desire for revenge; we ought rather to reserve the possibility of becoming friends again with our adversary of the moment, and in any case to regard the Austrian state as a piece on the European chessboard and the renewal of friendly relations with her as a move open to us. If Austria were severely injured, she would become the ally of France and every other opponent of ours; she would even sacrifice her anti-Russian interests for the sake of revenge on Prussia.[18]

An armistice was reached on July 22 and a preliminary peace agreement was signed four days later. Under the terms of the final peace treaty, signed in Prague on August 23, Austria agreed to pay an indemnity of 40 million Prussian talers, but its territorial integrity was respected.

Additional treaties were signed in Berlin during August and September of 1866 with the southern German states who had supported the Austrians. Prussia solidified its boundaries by annexing those states which lay between its territories along the Rhine and Elbe Rivers. Hanover, Hesse-Cassel, Nassau, and Frankfurt were all absorbed, and an indemnity was imposed on the remaining defeated states.

The Italians received Venetia despite their defeat at Custozza and a naval defeat at Lissa. Counting on a protracted war, Napoleon III of France was unable to respond to the rapid movement of events. The German Confederation was dissolved and Austria was excluded from Germany. All states north of the Main River joined a North German Confederation under Prussian leadership while the south German states remained independent. When Napoleon III insisted upon compensation for staying neutral, and his ambassador indiscreetly put his demands in writing, Bismarck touted this request as proof of Napoleon's aggressive intent. More fearful of France than of Prussia, the southern German states of Bavaria, Baden, and Würtemberg responded by forming military alliances with Prussia.

THE FRANCO-PRUSSIAN WAR

The creation of the North German Confederation in 1867 increased Prussian military strength. Together with the political unification of Italy (1859–1861), this league presented new risks for France since previously there had been only divided minor powers on its borders. To make matters worse, French intervention in Mexico proved disastrous. French troops, which were part of a larger European force sent to Vera Cruz in 1861 to collect debts owed to European bondholders, failed in an ill-conceived attempt to make Mexico a French satellite. Napoleon III was called the "Sphinx of the Tuileries" because many people believed he had been working in secret to devise an elaborate scheme aimed at restoring French domination in Europe. In truth, his foreign policy was foundering; he needed a resounding diplomatic triumph to quell a rising tide of criticism.

Public apprehension over Germany soared after the Luxembourg crisis of 1867. The Grand Duchy of Luxembourg had been given to the Netherlands after the Napoleonic Wars as part of the Vienna peace settlement discussed in Chapter 3. Though not part of Bismarck's North German Confederation, the Grand Duchy was garrisoned by Prussian troops. When the French approached King William III of the Netherlands to purchase Luxembourg, the king replied that the sale would be contingent upon Prussian approval. Bismarck rejected the French request, and hostilities between Prussia and France were only avoided when the Grand Duchy was **neutralized.**

Although the Luxembourg crisis had been defused, people in both countries anticipated war. During the summer of 1870, the Spanish government invited a German prince, Leopold of Hohenzollern-Sigmaringen, to assume the vacant Spanish throne. Two years earlier, an insurrection had driven Queen Isabella II into exile. Finding it difficult to obtain a suitable replacement, the Spanish turned to Leopold, a Roman Catholic married to a Portuguese princess. Leopold's candidacy spoke to the dream of someday uniting the Iberian peninsula. Yet when news of the invitation reached Paris, it prompted fears of a Prussian-Spanish alliance because Leopold was a member of the Prussian ruling family.[19] Just as Charles V, the Hapsburg Holy Roman Emperor, had ruled over Austria, Germany, and Spain during the sixteenth century, many feared that Bismarck would encircle France once again.

The French statesman Adolphe Thiers once remarked that "the highest principle of European politics is that Germany shall be composed of independent states connected only by a slender federative thread."[20] In line with this principle, the French ambassador to Berlin, Vincente Benedetti, was instructed to insist that Leopold should decline the crown. The withdrawal of the prince's candidacy failed to placate the French, however. During an interview at the resort of Bad Ems, Benedetti pressed King William I of Prussia for an apology and future guarantees. The king politely declined and sent a report of the conversation to Bismarck. Seeing the chance, as he put it, to wave a "red flag to the Gallic bull,"[21] Bismarck published an account of the interview that gave the false impression of a rude encounter, which led to further antagonism between Paris and Berlin.

With national honor and pride now at stake, the French declared war on Prussia. The Franco-Prussian War lasted six months and ended with a shattering defeat for the French. Once again, Bismarck was able to isolate an adversary.[22] Rather than side with Paris, the Italians used the opportunity created by the withdrawal of French troops from Rome to occupy the Eternal City. The Russians maintained neutrality and used the distraction created by the war to refortify their Black Sea bases. The British declined to act as well. Annoyed with Napoleon III's policies, they were satisfied with promises from Prussia that Belgian neutrality would be respected. Finally, Bismarck published the 1866 French demands for territorial compensation in the Rhineland to rally the southern German states to the Prussian cause.

Devoid of allies, the French marched on to inevitable defeat. By September 2, 1870, Napoleon III himself was captured at Sedan with 39 of his generals, 2,700 officers, and over 80,000 troops. A second French army of 173,000 under Marshal Bazaine surrendered at Metz on October 27. Although the minister of war had claimed his country was ready down to the last detail, the French were woefully unprepared. Mobilization was chaotic, commanders disagreed on strategic questions, and the Prussians made innovative use of technology. Although the French possessed the *mitrailleuse,* a thirty-seven barrel machine gun, and their *chassepot* rifle was superior to the Prussian needle gun, the Prussians were better trained, had more artillery, and were able to use the railroad to give their troops speed and mobility.

Prussia's victory has been described as "a triumph of planning."[23] For years, Prussian officers disguised as tourists painting the French landscape had studied the sites of probable battles.[24] Rather than fight a protracted war of position, the Prussians devised a war of movement aimed at encircling a stunned opponent. So important were the Prussian railroads for military operations that as early as 1860 half of them were owned by the state. During the 1866 war with Austria, the benefits of speedy troop deployment through rail transportation became obvious. Railroads thus presented commanders with new strategic opportunities. By relying on the railroad, Prussian forces from multiple locations could mobilize rapidly, move to the front from opposite directions, and converge upon a slower-moving opponent with numerical superiority at the point of attack. Within the first two weeks of fighting, the Prussians mobilized 1,180,000 troops, compared to only 330,000 for the French.[25]

The news of the defeat at Sedan toppled the French government. Napoleon III was dethroned and republican leaders, headed by Léon Gambetta, proclaimed a Government of National Defense. The republican government desperately tried to raise new armies to reverse their fortunes on the battle-field. The French simply could not believe they had been beaten. Refusing to credit the Prussians with any virtues whatsoever, they insisted that their losses were due to trickery and to Prussia's substitution of technology for courage.[26] German forces laid siege to Paris on September 19, forcing the city to surrender four months later. As a result, a newly elected French National Assembly met in Bordeaux and voted for peace. On January 22, 1871, the French asked for an armistice. It was implemented six days later and peace negotiations began. On February 26 a preliminary agreement was reached, and on March 3 the final Peace of Frankfurt was signed.

Parisians were more resistant to making peace than were most other French citizens. Radical leaders in Paris denounced the Bordeaux Assembly and, in a gesture of defiance, the Parisian National Guard refused to surrender its weapons. An independent government, called the Commune of Paris, was declared. With many of the streets of Paris barricaded by insurgents and the city inflamed by insurrection, the assembly decided to subdue the rebellion. In June, after weeks of bloody fighting, rebel resistance was broken. Estimates place the number of people killed at over twenty thousand.

The emotions unleashed in Germany by victory over France were overwhelming. Rather than crafting the kind of lenient peace that had been implemented following the Seven Weeks' War with Austria, the triumphant Prussians took a series of actions humiliating to their prostrate opponents, including holding a victory parade that entered Paris by way of the Pont de Neuilly, proceeded to the Arc de Triomphe, and continued down the Champs Élysées. Convinced that hostility between the two countries was inescapable, Bismarck acceded to demands to weaken France. "An enemy, whose honest friendship can never be won," he agreed, "must at least be rendered somewhat less harmful."[27]

Under the terms of the Peace of Frankfurt, France ceded Alsace and part of Lorraine to Germany. From a military point of view, control of the Vosges mountains and the fortress of Metz were critical for German defenses. But whereas Alsace had been under German control prior to the 1648 Treaty of Westphalia and contained a substantial German-speaking population, the people of Lorraine spoke French. The loss of Alsace and Lorraine embittered the French for years to come. France, as one government official put it, "could forget a military disaster; she could not forget the wrong done to the liberty of her nationals."[28]

In addition to accepting the annexation of two provinces, France pledged to pay Germany an indemnity of five billion francs. The first billion was to be paid in 1871 and the remainder over the next three years. Most German occupation forces would be withdrawn after the initial two billion francs were paid, with the remainder withdrawn once the total indemnity was discharged.

Deputies in the French National Assembly called the terms of the peace treaty a "sentence of death."[29] The terms were harsh, but not nearly as harsh as those the French had imposed on the Prussians in 1807. France retained control over its internal affairs, no limits were placed on its military, and its overseas colonies remained intact. Bismarck's adroit diplomacy and General von Moltke's peerless armies brought the fragmented German lands together and shaped them into a centralized state (see Map 4.2). On January 18, 1871, leading German princes acclaimed William I of Prussia German kaiser or emperor in the Hall of Mirrors in the Palace of Versailles. In structure, the new empire became an extension of the North German Confederation, with the southern German states of Bavaria, Württemberg, Baden, and Hesse-Darmstadt added. With approximately 41 million inhabitants, the Second Reich, as the new German empire was called, possessed a dynamic, growing economy and the most powerful army in Europe. Yet something was amiss. Writing in his diary, Crown Prince Frederick William III lamented, "We are no longer looked upon as the innocent victims of wrongs, but rather as arrogant victors, no longer content with the conquest of the foe, but determined to bring about his utter ruin."[30]

> "What our sword has won in half a year, our sword must guard for half a century."
>
> — HELMUTH VON MOLTKE

Bismarck was quickly appointed the imperial chancellor for the Second Reich. Having accomplished his foreign policy goals, Bismarck turned his attention to internal politics, where he tried under the so-called *Kulturkampf* to reduce the influence of Catholic orders and clergy, especially in education. As socialism gained ground, it too was repressed. Within less than a decade, the new German Reich was an industrialized, authoritarian state in which powerful conservative groups could steer policy behind a facade of representative government.

GERMANY'S FRAGILE PEACE

Bismarck's genius resided in his ability to entertain multiple courses of action, explore all of their permutations, and move on several fronts simultaneously. No single move was an end in itself; each positioned him to advance in another direction. "One cannot play chess," he insisted, "if from the outset sixteen of the sixty-four squares are out of bounds."[31] A tenacious advocate of Prussian interests, he could see the opportunities presented by different configurations on the diplomatic chessboard. To exploit them, he was willing to be disingenuous and, at times, even ruthless. "If it hadn't been for me, there wouldn't have been three great wars, 80,000 men would not have died, and parents, brothers, sisters, and widows would not be in mourning," he once admitted. "But that I have to settle with God."[32]

Before the Wars of German Unification, Prussia was the smallest of Europe's great powers; afterward, it held a semi-hegemony over the continent. With an excellent educational system, skilled labor, and unparalleled electrical, chemical, and steel industries, the new united Germany was an

MAP 4.2 The Unification of Germany, 1815–1871. Following the Napoleonic Wars, the German Confederation (or Bund) replaced the old Holy Roman Empire. After Prussia's victory over Austria in 1866, the states north of the river Main joined Prussia in the North German Confederation. Once France was defeated in 1871, all non-Hapsburg southern German states merged with the North German Confederation to create the Prussian-led Second Reich.

economic powerhouse. To be sure, it had liabilities. Located in the center of Europe, Germany lacked abundant resources and the natural protection of formidable mountains or vast oceans. In other words, it was "too weak to go it alone, too strong to be left alone; with enough muscle to best any single comer, but too exposed to defy them all at once."[33] To make matters worse, the manner in which the Second Reich was created produced both enemies bent on revenge and bystanders wary of its military might. On the one hand, France still felt humiliated and sought to avenge the loss of Alsace and Lorraine. On the other hand, Russia became suspicious of Berlin's territorial aims and worried about possible expansion to the east. While Bismarck went on to build an intricate network of secret alliances to keep France and Russia from making common cause against Germany, his successors lacked the vision and skills to prevent a protracted two-front war that would divide German forces.

A resentful France would now bide its time for an opportunity to reverse its fortunes on the battlefield. In the words of a popular slogan of the day, "Never speak of it, always think of it." In a symbolic gesture, the statue of Strassburg on the Place de la Concorde was draped in black. Expressing the emotions of a wounded nation, the novelist Victor Hugo told the National Assembly "the day would come when France would rise again invincible and take back not only Alsace and Lorraine but the Rhineland."[34] The Reverend W. Gibson, an English Methodist working in France at the time, anticipated what would come from the demand for vengeance he witnessed among Parisians. "Germany," he wrote, "when within the next few years she again encounters France in arms, will find a very different foe from the France of 1870; and who knows but that before the end of this century there may be a similar triumph in Paris to that which is now being celebrated in Berlin?"[35]

The Gospel of Offensive Power

Flush with victory, most Germans saw a different future. "We Germans today are in a happy position," wrote Field Marshal von der Goltz. "The star of the young Empire has only just risen on the horizon; its full course lies still before it."[36] The writer Friedrich Naumann agreed. The German nation, he proclaimed, "feels the spring-time juices in its organs."[37] This heady atmosphere even intoxicated German liberals. Heinrich von Treitschke, once a prominent liberal spokesman, turned to **realism** and reveled in the glory brought by Prussian militarism. Writing about the provinces of Alsace and Lorraine, he boasted:

> These provinces are ours by the right of the sword, and we shall dispose of them by a higher right — the right of the German nation. . . . With joyful wonder, we have watched the immortal progress of these moral forces of history.[38]

The Wars of German Unification and the peace settlements they produced transformed the political landscape of Europe. Bismarck subsequently installed a huge statue of Germania on a hill above the vineyards of Assmannshausen and Rüdesheim in the Rheingau to commemorate this transformation. Few people scanning the horizon on the day the monument was dedicated could see the storm clouds building in the distance. Bismarck's wars had fostered the belief that modern technology gave an advantage to the attacking side by increasing the speed and maneuverability of combat units. Offense, in other words, was thought to be the best defense. Lured by the presumed superiority of offensive doctrines and fearing that an adversary might move first and capture the battlefield initiative, commanders across the continent formulated meticulous plans that required rapid mobilization at the instant a conflict began. The relentless pressure of these rigid, intricate military timetables produced an atmosphere of urgency whose deleterious effect on foreign-policy decisionmakers was magnified by the assumption that future wars would be won by whoever possessed an army massive enough to make a decisive thrust in the shortest possible time. By the end of the century, German spending on arms had risen some 80 percent and its war establishment had grown to 3.4 million personnel. Similar trends unfolded elsewhere. Russian spending climbed at a rate approximating the German increase, to support roughly 4 million men under arms. French military expenditures expanded by 45 percent, and troop strength was doubled to 3.5 million.[39] As Winston Churchill later summarized the situation, "when mighty populations are impelled on each other . . . when the resources of science and civilization sweep away everything that might mitigate their fury, a European war can only end in the ruin of the vanquished and scarcely less fatal dislocation and exhaustion of the conquerors."[40]

The Departure of the Iron Chancellor

The way peace was made after the wars of 1866 and 1870 had serious consequences for Europe's future. By forging a lenient settlement at the end of the Seven Weeks' War, Prussia was able to cultivate a working relationship with an Austro-Hungarian Empire worried about future conflict with Russia. Alternatively, the harsh settlement imposed upon the French crippled relations between Paris and Berlin. **Irredentism** became the cornerstone of French foreign policy toward Germany. Although the 1871 Peace of Frankfurt was punitive, it did not weaken France enough to eliminate it from the ranks of the great powers and thus from the heart of German defense plans. French willingness to stand alone in a war for the lost provinces would ebb with the passage of time, but Germany could still count on France throwing its weight on the side of any great power who might someday confront German troops on the battlefield.

No political order is self-maintaining. At the end of the Wars of German Unification, Bismarck assured his contemporaries that Germany was a satisfied power, willing to play the role of an "honest broker" in mediating threats to the international status quo. By following this pragmatic policy of moderation and restraint for the next twenty years, Bismarck became "one of the rare leaders of mighty states who chose to limit his ambitions."[41] With France isolated due to Germany's secret arrangements with Austria and Russia, Bismarck believed the danger of war was remote.

But the structure of the Bismarckian order did not long outlive its architect. Following the death of William I in 1888, and the death of his son Frederick III shortly thereafter, Frederick's son William II became the new German emperor. Impulsive, insecure, and insistent on being his own chancellor, the young kaiser dismissed Bismarck and unveiled a "new course" of *weltpolitik* (world policy), under which power projection capabilities were

---

CONTROVERSIES TO CONTEMPLATE

- Both Otto von Bismarck and Austrian chancellor Prince Klemens von Metternich (see Chapter 3) were guided by political realism. Were there any significant differences between Bismarck and Metternich in their strategies for dealing with defeated adversaries? Does realism offer national leaders clear guidelines on how victors should design a peace settlement?

- Despite Bismarck's belief that Austria should be excluded from the process of German unification, he offered a lenient peace settlement to the Austrians after they were defeated in the Seven Weeks' War. On the other hand, a harsh settlement was imposed upon the French after the Franco-Prussian War. What accounts for the differences in Prussian policy at the end of these two wars?

- Realist theory advises political leaders to heed strategic necessities when formulating their foreign policies. They must do whatever they can to advance national interests, regardless of whether their actions contravene the moral values that guide people in everyday lives. Was the goal of German unification justified? Did Bismarck violate any moral standards by employing the means that he used to attain the goal of unification? Under what specific circumstances do which kinds of foreign policy goals justify which means?

- Prussia defeated its adversaries in the Wars of German Unification by engaging in thorough planning and by harnessing modern technology to give their forces speed, mobility, and firepower. How did the manner in which the Prussians won these striking battlefield victories create new problems for maintaining peace following the Wars of German Unification?

---

expanded and colonies sought. Germany now saw itself as more than a continental power. Demanding a redivision of great-power **spheres of influence** around the globe, Germany became a dissatisfied, expansionist state, bent on changing the international status quo. As friction between Germany and other great powers mounted, the linchpin of Bismarck's **grand strategy** — the isolation of France — fell to the wayside. When William II allowed Germany's secret reinsurance treaty with Russia to lapse, the Russians formed a military alliance with the French. Similarly, Great Britain responded to Berlin's heavy-handed behavior by jettisoning the long-standing policy of "splendid isolation" and reconciling its differences with both France and Russia. While not an immediate cause of World War I, the harsh peace settlement embodied in the Peace of Frankfurt set the parameters within which Bismarck had to work. Owing to the outcome of the Franco-Prussian War, all efforts to build a lasting peace were impaired by a feud over lost territory.

Moreover, the punitive, humiliating peace of 1871 would provoke French retaliation when the tables were turned after World War I. It is for this reason that one historian has said the annexation of Alsace and Lorraine "was worse than a crime, it was a blunder."[42]

SUGGESTED READING

Carr, William. *The Origins of the Wars of German Unification*. London: Longman, 1991.

Feuchtanger, E. J. *Imperial Germany, 1850–1918*. London: Routledge, 2001.

Foster, Stig and Jorg Nagler, eds. *On the Road to Total War: The American Civil War and the German Wars of Unification, 1861–1871*. Cambridge: Cambridge University Press, 1997.

Grenville, J. A. S. *Europe Reshaped, 1848–1878*. Oxford: Blackwell, 2000.

Howard, Michael. *The Franco-Prussian War: The German Invasion of France, 1870–1871*. New York: Macmillan, 1962.

Pflanze, Otto. *Bismarck and the Development of Germany*. Princeton, N.J.: Princeton University Press, 1963.

Steefel, Lawrence D. *Bismarck, the Hohenzollern Candidacy, and the Origins of the Franco-German War of 1870*. Cambridge: Harvard University Press, 1962.

Taylor, A. J. P. *The Struggle for Mastery in Europe, 1848–1918*. Oxford: Clarendon Press, 1971.

Tilly, Charles, ed. *The Formation of Nation States in Western Europe*. Princeton, N.J.: Princeton University Press, 1975.

Wawro, Geoffrey. *The Austro-Prussian War: Austria's War with Prussia and Italy in 1866*. Cambridge: Cambridge University Press, 1997.

NOTES

1. To underscore this point, he wrote in his memoirs that fixing the objectives in warfare is "a political function" which "cannot be without influence on the method of conducting the war." Bismarck, 1966, p. 106.
2. Pinson, 1966, p. 128.
3. During the crusades of the twelfth and thirteenth centuries, the popes bestowed privileges on various religio-military orders. The Knights Templars were dedicated to the protection of pilgrims. The Knights Hospitallers were devoted to the care of the sick.
4. Manuel, 1951, p. 105.
5. Howard, 1991, p. 52.
6. Gillis, 1978, pp. 320–323.
7. The membership of the German Confederation rose to thirty-nine in 1817 with the addition of Hesse-Hamburg.
8. As noted in Chapter 2, The Thirty Years' War (1618–1648) provides a horrifying example of the devastation that occurred on German land. Once one of the most prosperous regions of Europe, German territory was ravaged by religious warfare that ultimately resulted in troops from France, Denmark, Spain, and Sweden fighting on German soil. For a fuller account of the heavy human toll of this protracted war and its consequences, see Kegley and Raymond, 2002.
9. Dehio, 1962, p. 210.
10. Detwiler, 1976, p. 113.
11. Bismarck, 1948, p. 220.
12. Pinson, 1966, p. 133.
13. In Carr, 1991, p. 70.

14. In Pflanze, 1963, p. 91.

15. Pinson, 1966, p. 135.

16. Craig, 1964, p. 166.

17. Hammond, 1993, p. 82. Increased firepower made old shock tactics obsolete. "Close order, with advance of the line ending up with the bayonet charge became suicidal. . . . So also did frontal attacks." Finer, 1975, p. 159.

18. He also commented that it would be a political mistake "to endanger everything that has been achieved by trying to get from Austria a few square miles of territory or a few million more indemnity." Friedjung, 1966, p. 287.

19. Prince Leopold belonged to the Sigmaringen branch of the Hohenzollern family and was actually more closely related to Emperor Napoleon III of France than to King William I of Prussia.

20. Craig, 1982, p. 21.

21. Carr, 1991, p. 196.

22. Bismarck had previously hinted that it would be possible to create the image that the Prussians were on the defensive: "Mobilization, national manifestations in Germany and Italy, over relations with Belgium or even with Spain, would give us the opportunity of a diversion which would bring us into the war without giving the appearance of an aggressive . . . war." Steefel, 1962, p. 10.

23. Taylor, 1962b, p. 114. The Prussians were aided by the "inferiority of force and stupidity of mind" of their opponents, adds British military strategist B. H. Liddell Hart. "In preparation for war, any strategist would be rash to base his plans on the supposition that his enemy would be as weak in brain and body as the Austrians of 1866 and the French in 1870." Liddell Hart, 1967, p. 137.

24. Mann, 1968, p. 190.

25. Ziegler, 1993, p. 26. Trains had become such an important element in military mobilization that German staff officers once watched the visiting Ringling Brothers circus load its railway cars to learn more efficient ways of moving troops and supplies to the front. Quester, 1977, p. 79.

26. Kranzberg, 1950, p. 15.

27. Pflanze, 1963, p. 479.

28. Raymond Poincaré, as cited in Welch, 1993, p. 102.

29. Giesberg, 1966, p. 119.

30. Crankshaw, 1981, p. 299.

31. Carr, 1991, p. 59.

32. Craig and George, 1995, p. 279.

33. Joffe, 1995, p. 101.

34. Pinson, 1966, p. 148.

35. Horne, 1965, p. 427.

36. Von der Glotz, 1992, p. 252.

37. Kennedy, 1987, p. 211.

38. Treitschke, 1948, p. 226.

39. Bartlett, 1984, pp. 6–7.

40. Ibid, p. 88.

41. Kagan, 1995, p. 101.

42. Fay, 1966, p. 51.

PART III

The Quest for Peace in a Century of Global War

On the eve of the twentieth century, rising prosperity, international economic interdependence, two disarmament conferences, and thirty uninterrupted years of peace among the great powers fueled expectations that war was becoming obsolete. Few observers in the early 1900s expected a large-scale war to erupt.

But to the surprise of nearly everyone, 1914 unleashed a truly global war that wreaked havoc on three continents — Europe, Asia, and Africa. So devastating was this war that leaders geared their postwar foreign policies against the threat of another such catastrophe.

Despite this common concern, in 1939 the world once again faced a devastating global war. The political destiny of much of humanity hung in the balance, because the goal of the Axis powers (Germany, Japan, and Italy) was world conquest, animated by an ideology that glorified war as an inherent right in the struggle for power. Even more than its predecessor, this second global war was a struggle over the ideas, values, and institutions that would govern interstate interaction.

Juxtaposing these two global wars in chronological order helps to provide a basis for assessing how past wars, and the ways in which they are settled, may sow the seeds of either a durable peace or a new, and possibly expanded confrontation. Moreover, comparing these epic struggles highlights the different policy prescriptions emanating from the realist and liberal theoretical traditions, and for evaluating the adequacy of their alternative ethical visions about justice.

The efforts to forge a lasting peace after both world wars in the twentieth century redefined both realist and liberal thought. A comparison of these rival theoretical traditions forces evaluation of important questions. Which theory best accounts for the outcome of each war? Are there moral principles that these two cases suggest that apply across historical periods and geographic circumstances? Or do the two cases illustrate the contingent nature of policy prescriptions, forcing us to conclude that the applicability of any lessons about peacemaking must be restricted to particular international conditions?

The two cases in Part III represent a transition in the history of war and peace, for World Wars I and II were not the contests between rulers and their small, professional armies that characterized the classical European state system. They involved fully mobilized societies and weapons of frightening destructive capability that threatened national annihilation. In the wake of World Wars I and II, many people began to rethink the traditional distinction between victory and defeat. Would it be possible to win a war fought with weapons of mass destruction? What did the concept of "winning" mean in a nuclear age?

In presenting these two wars and their peace settlements, Chapters 5 and 6 tell the story of a series of fateful decisions made during the first half of the twentieth century that ultimately shaped the second half of the century. In presenting the available evidence, we have attempted to capture in simple terms the key controversies in the scholarly debate over the causes and consequences of these two wars. We ask our readers to dig into the details and fit together the clues from the historical data to discover the moral and policy lessons that can be learned about the passage from war to peace.

· 5 ·

WORLD WAR I AND THE TREATY OF VERSAILLES: A WAR TO END ALL WARS?

It must be a peace without victory. . . .
Only a peace between equals can last.
— WOODROW WILSON

PREVIEW

The assassination of Archduke Franz Ferdinand in 1914 touched off a series of actions that ultimately embroiled the world's most powerful states in a gruesome war of attrition. There are numerous explanations for why this happened. Many scholars emphasize how certain underlying conditions made the world ripe for a violent flare-up. Virulent nationalism, ethnic conflict, intense military and economic competition among the great powers, a polarized system of alliances, and offensive strategic doctrines built around rigid mobilization schedules created a volatile international environment that would have eventually ignited a war regardless of whether the archduke was assassinated. Other scholars stress more immediate causes, pointing to the inability of political leaders in Berlin, London, Paris, and St. Petersburg to douse the flames of war before they spread beyond Austria-Hungary and Serbia. According to this view, misperceptions about the capabilities and intentions of rival states prevented these leaders from extinguishing the crisis sparked by the assassination.

In retrospect, various factors contributed to the outbreak of the First World War. Remembering the short, decisive wars fought by Bismarck to achieve German unification, few people believed it would last very long. But by the time what came to be called the "Great War" ended four years later, Europe was devastated. France, which had sought revenge for its humiliating loss to Germany in 1871, was particularly hard hit since most of the major battles on the western front occurred on its soil. Not only were the French staggered by a frightening number of casualties, but national reconstruction was hampered by the need to service the enormous foreign debt incurred to finance the war effort. Recalling the harsh peace treaty imposed upon them by the Germans following the Franco-Prussian War in 1871, the French under Premier Georges Clemenceau pushed for a peace settlement that would weaken Germany so it no longer posed a military threat.

The French demand for ironclad security guarantees to keep Germany at bay collided with the liberal idealism of Woodrow Wilson. The American president's exhortations for a new international order were initially received with enthusiasm by the traumatized, war-weary population of Europe. People hoped their suffering had not been in vain. Democracy, open diplomacy, national self-determination, and a League of Nations would allegedly usher in an era of perpetual peace.

France's enthusiasm for dismembering Germany also clashed with the interests of Great Britain, its other major wartime partner. With the German navy no longer menacing the sea lanes that sustained the British empire, policymakers in London declined the French request for a formal military alliance aimed at Germany and returned to their traditional policy of promoting a balance of power on the Continent. Germany, they calculated, would once again become an important market for British manufactured goods as well as a potential counterweight against any land power that might seek to dominate Europe.

Thus, despite the euphoria surrounding the opening of the Versailles Peace Conference in January 1919, there were serious differences among the victors about how to deal with Germany. As you read this case, think about how the following issues drove a wedge between the French and their Anglo-American allies:

- territorial boundaries
- reparations payments
- disarmament
- collective security
- self-determination for nationalities seeking statehood

In addition to examining the cleavages that divided the victors, consider the reaction of the vanquished to the 1919 Treaty of Versailles. Since Germany had routed the Russian army in the east and relinquished its position in the west without having lost territory to the Allies, how would the German population respond to a harsh peace settlement? How could demagogues within Germany use this response to their political advantage? What were the consequences of creating a group of weak, unstable states on Germany's eastern border? Marshal Ferdinand Foch of France once said the Treaty of Versailles was not a peace settlement; it was merely an armistice for twenty years. Was he correct?

The activities of the 1899 International Peace Conference began at a small Orthodox chapel on the edge of the Scheveningen Woods. Attired in ceremonial uniforms and accompanied by a magnificent escort, the Russians attended mass before proceeding to the opening ceremony held on May 18 at a splendid chateau on the outskirts of The Hague. They were joined that afternoon by representatives from more than two dozen other countries. With colorful flags rustling against an azure sky, the delegates began grappling with such issues as **disarmament, arbitration,** and the law of war. According to one delegate, it was "a place in which to forget old passions and prejudices and the grosser forms of selfishness; a place for good consideration, courtesy, patience, and the philosophic mind."[1] When the conference concluded at the end of July, those in attendance believed they had taken an important step toward regulating interstate violence.

Optimism ran high at the beginning of the twentieth century. The marriage of science and industry spawned one technological innovation after another, international commerce generated extraordinary wealth in trading countries, and at The Hague conference of 1899 the world community developed new rules to control the use of force. Europe had avoided a military showdown between major powers since the end of the Wars of German Unification. Now almost everyone thought it would continue to enjoy peace throughout the new century.

Global optimism was nourished by faith in progress, including progress toward maintaining peace. Andrew Carnegie, a wealthy industrialist and philanthropist who had emigrated in his youth from Scotland to the United States, gave much of his fortune to educational programs aimed at abolishing war, which he saw as "the foulest blot upon our civilization."[2] Maintaining that the ancient dream of perpetual peace was now within reach, he provided funds to build a "Peace Palace" in The Hague that would house a court for the pacific settlement of international disputes. The British writer Norman Angell also saw a bright future: In *The Great Illusion*, he asserted that economic development made preventing war mandatory, because its costs were prohibitive.[3] To Carnegie, Angell, and many others, progress had bestowed peace and prosperity upon the twentieth century.

In just over a decade, however, Europe was engulfed by the flames of war. The conflict ignited in the Bosnian city of Sarajevo on June 28, 1914, when a Serbian nationalist assassinated Archduke Franz Ferdinand, a successor to the throne of Austria-Hungary. Seeking to punish Serbia, the Austrians delivered an ultimatum on July 23 that was deliberately worded so Belgrade would reject it. Five days later Austria declared war, setting in motion a series of moves by other states who distrusted one another's intentions. Before the assassination at Sarajevo two hostile alliances had already existed, pitting Germany, Austria-Hungary, and the Ottoman Empire against France, Great Britain, and Russia. When Russia mobilized against Austria to support fellow Slavs in Serbia, Germany attacked France, and Britain entered the fray to counter the Germans. Like a chain reaction, the dispute between Austria and Serbia rapidly expanded across the Continent to involve every major power.

By the time World War I ended, nearly 20 million people were dead, empires had crumbled, and new states were born. It was hardly the buoyant future that had been predicted for the twentieth century. What caused this unanticipated spasm of carnage? Could a durable peace be built on its ashes? Would this titanic struggle serve as a war to end all wars?

THE EUROPEAN TINDERBOX

How can such a catastrophic war be explained? Although the answers appear numerous, many converge around psychological explanations regarding the motives and emotions of the major players in this tragedy. Some historians maintain that World War I was an **inadvertent war,** inspired by passions, hatreds, and misperceptions, and not the result of anyone's master plan. It was a war bred primarily by the participants' fearful confusion and their inability to overlook insults — a war that none wanted or expected, but one which resulted from their failure to recognize how others would react to their own retaliatory actions. A review of the steps taken prior to the war suggests just how uncoordinated are the processes through which states often stumble in their efforts to make and keep peace (see Table 5.1).

Many historians believe that the great powers' prior rearmament efforts also played a major role in the onset of World War I. It might seem obvious, on the surface, that one state's acquisition of arms would make others feel frightened and less secure, but few of the actors engaged in the European **arms race** appeared to take that psychological reaction into account. The Europeans proceeded by assuming that their own armaments would gain them respect rather than arouse suspicions about their expansionist motives. This belief was espoused most by France and Germany, which raced against each other in establishing superior schools for officers, requiring peacetime compulsory military training for development of military engineering and supply capabilities, and manufacturing improved cannons, rifles, and machine guns. Whenever one made an advance in military preparedness, the other

"Till the world comes to an end, the ultimate decision will rest with the sword."

— KAISER WILLIAM II

TABLE 5.1
Major Peace Treaties and Peace-Disrupting Events, 1899–1914

Date	Settlement/Event
1899	First Hague Peace Conference
1901	Peace of Peking ends Boxer Rebellion
1902	Triple Alliance between Germany, Austria, and Italy renewed
1903	Britain and France sign "Entente Cordiale"
1905	William II of Germany and Nicolas II of Russia sign Treaty of Bjorko pledging mutual security pact in Europe
	Anglo-Japanese alliance renewed for ten years
1906	Algeciras Conference grants France and Spain control of Morocco
1907	Second Hague Peace Conference
1908	Austria and Russia agree to Austria's occupation of Bosnia and Herzegovina
1910	Japan annexes Korea
1911	Kaiser William II's Hamburg speech asserts Germany's "Place in the Sun"
1912	Montenegro declares war on Turkey; armistice signed also by Bulgaria and Serbia ends crisis
	Italy and France sign Treaty of Lausanne
	German-Austrian-Italian alliance renewed
1913	Balkan War ends with signing of London Peace Treaty between Turkey and Balkan states; Second Balkan War ends with armistice signed at Bucharest
1914	Archduke Franz Ferdinand and his wife are assassinated in Sarajevo on June 28

country felt it had to follow — unaware of the possibility that disarmament and **arms control** agreements to alleviate fears might produce greater security for both.

By 1914, Germany had taken the lead in developing its armed forces, building military roads and railroads, and planning future campaigns down to the smallest detail. But other powers besides the Franco-German rivals were also participants in the armaments race. At the turn of the century, Great Britain could still proudly sing "Britannia rules the waves." Command of the seas had long been necessary to feed the people and the industries of the British Isles and to protect the distant parts of the British Empire. To counter Great Britain's maritime preeminence, Germany began to build a navy that could challenge the British. France, Italy, the United States, and Japan also built powerful navies, but the British navy continued to be the largest, and to Germany, Great Britain justifiably appeared to be the biggest obstacle to its desire for status, for what the kaiser called its deserved "place in the sun." In short, the quest for ever more arms had transformed Europe into a tinderbox that would be ignited by the Austro-Serbian confrontation.

Another key argument about the origins of World War I assigns blame for the outbreak of the war to the anxieties that coalition formation unleashed. Many historians contend that, in addition to an unrestrained arms race, the **polarization** of **alliances** and counteralliances (the Triple Alliance of Germany, Austria-Hungary, and Italy versus the Triple Entente of Russia, Britain, and France) engendered a chain reaction following the 1914 Austrian reprisal against the Sarajevo assassination, where prior commitments pulled one European state after another into a continental war.

A key factor in the outbreak of the First World War was Germany's challenge to British strength in the overall geostrategic **balance of power** and the fears this action aroused. Although Germany did not become a unified country until 1871, the German Reich had prospered and used its growing wealth to build a formidable military machine. As the predominant military and industrial power on the European continent, Germany sought to compete for international position and status; as Kaiser William II put it in 1898, Germany had "great tasks . . . outside the narrow boundaries of old Europe."

The Germans attempted to expand their empire under Kaiser William II, who reigned between 1888 and 1918 and whose ambitious plan for the expansion of German power and prestige superceded the policies of Otto von Bismarck. Under the kaiser's concept of *weltpolitik* (world policy), Germany began building a strong navy that would command respect for the German flag around the globe. Fearing that Great Britain, Russia, and France were encircling Germany, William II insisted that a larger military was necessary to protect German interests.

Germany was not the only newly emergent power at the turn of the century, however. Russia was also expanding, and becoming a threat to Germany. The decline in power of the Austro-Hungarian Empire, Germany's only ally, heightened that threat. Russian nationalists glorified the distinctiveness of their country; they hailed "Holy Russia" as the rightful inheritor of the old Byzantine religion and culture. Consistent with this haughty patriotism, and governed by their "endemic refusal to forget a slight,"[4] the Russian czars dedicated themselves to expanding their empire's power and prestige. Germany responded with apprehension and looked for an opportunity to block the Russian drive for preeminence. For William II, the opportunity came with the assassination of Archduke Ferdinand. He was convinced that a short, localized, and victorious Balkan war was possible and feared that an unfavorable shift in the balance of power would occur in the event of a long war. Austria-Hungary had to be preserved, because the disintegration of this neighboring empire would have left Germany isolated, without an ally. As a result, Germany gave Austria-Hungary a blank check to crush Serbia, so that it could undercut Russia's ally and thereby weaken Russian influence in Europe.

Germany's unconditional support proved, however, to be a serious miscalculation, as it provoked an unexpected reaction from France and Russia, the two allied powers on Germany's western and eastern borders.

In the so-called Schlieffen Plan, Germany's generals had long based their military preparations on the premise that in the event of German war with both Russia and France, German troops would first quickly defeat the French and then turn against the larger but slower-moving Russians. The quickest way into France was through neutral Belgium. When the Germans marched into Belgium, Britain declared war, thus joining France and Russia in opposing Germany.

Although Britain's immediate objective was to defend Belgian neutrality, the war later expanded across the globe when on August 23 Japan complied with its alliance commitment to Britain by declaring war on Germany (taking advantage of the situation by seizing some important German colonial possessions in Asia). The war's enlargement proceeded in October when the Ottoman Empire in Turkey and, later, Bulgaria, joined Germany and Austria-Hungary. These four nations became known as the Central Powers. Although a member of the Triple Alliance, Italy decided not to join Germany and Austria-Hungary in the war. Italy declared its neutrality, and later allied itself with the Triple Entente alliance composed of Russia, France, and Great Britain. Japan, Rumania, and many other countries also joined this expanding coalition to form a partnership referred to as the Allies. On April 6, 1917, the war expanded further when the United States entered the conflict. Outside Europe, Britain remained supported by its vast empire. In time, China and some South American countries joined the Allies. Before World War I ended, thirty-two countries on six continents were at war. For the first time ever, war had become truly global in scope.

WAR BECOMES TOTAL

World War I differed from any previous war in several ways other than the number of participants and its geographic scope. Science and technology made the conflict a war of machinery: old weapons were improved and produced in great quantities, new and far more deadly weapons were rapidly developed and deployed. Widespread universal military conscription drew soldiers from nearly every family and touched the lives of every citizen. Huge armies had to be fed, and therefore agricultural production was a necessary part of national efforts to wage war. Equipping the armies with machine guns, cannons, and shells made factories vital to victory. Thus, whole national populations, including women and children, became part of the war effort, with the result that mass mobilization and communication made public opinion and nationalistic sentiments a potent factor in the way warring nations approached one another.

The hatreds incited by wartime propaganda must also be considered in this mix. The adversarial governments expended great effort attempting to persuade their populations of the righteousness of their cause and the malev-olence of their enemies. The Central Powers' propaganda emphasized that the Allies had been trying for years to deprive them of their just share of the world's trade and colonies. The Allies' propaganda claimed that the Ger-mans, assisted by their allies, were trying to conquer the world and that the authoritarian government in Berlin was hostile to Western democracy and international law. Allied propaganda vehemently condemned the German march through Belgium in violation of prior treaty provisions and alleged that the Germans had committed terrible atrocities against the Belgian popu-lation. Both sides told their populations that the enemy had started the war, and both sides distorted facts in their propaganda. "In war," said one Allied statesman, "the first casualty is the truth."[5]

The U.S. publicist Henry Adams noted in 1907, "Politics as a practice has always been the systematic organization of hatreds."[6] This statement may be an exaggeration in times of peace, but in wartime it is accurate. Demonization of the adversary would prove instrumental in the conduct of the war as well as its conclusion. Passions of hatred rationalize the sacrifice of life and property in an exhaustive, protracted war. But by vilifying the entire population of enemy nations, a compromise settlement became difficult. In effect, the war was total: Doing whatever was necessary for victory became permissible, surrender unthinkable. What was expected to be a short war contin-ued mercilessly, with no end in sight and no willingness on either side to terminate the slaughter at the bargaining table.

> "We must dictate the peace and I am determined to continue the war until the Central Powers are destroyed. . . . No Congress or mediation for me!"
>
> — CZAR NICHOLAS II

By the third year of the war, soldiers were dying by the thousands on the western front without a hope of breaching enemy lines. The Allies were demoralized and angry. Russia was ripped apart by the Bolshevik revolution which, during the next year, forced it to withdraw from the war. In the Treaty of Brest-Litovsk (March 3, 1918), Germany annexed one-third of Russia's European territory and established a protectorate over the Ukraine. Germany was disinclined to treat its vanquished foe charitably; it saw in Russia's partition a just and deserved dividend for the cost of warfare, to which it was entitled. Having defeated its foe in the east, Germany was free to turn all of its forces westward. As the war continued, mutiny began to spread in the French army — to such an extent that at one point only two French divisions between Soissons and Paris were considered reliable enough to continue the struggle. But the Germans, outnumbered to begin with, were also in desperate straits. Huge losses on the western front undermined the German commanders' confidence. To worsen the situation, the British naval blockade was exerting a devastating effect on German morale. Despite strict rationing and the ingenuity of German scientists, ammunition shortages developed and long lines of people waited for dwindling stocks of food.

Worried German leaders observed that, for the first time, Allied propaganda was beginning to weaken the German army's spirit.

Early in 1917, desperate German leaders announced the resumption of unrestricted submarine warfare. Like other Americans, President Woodrow Wilson had been drifting toward the conviction that war with Germany was necessary to protect American interests. The toll that Germany's return to submarine warfare would take on American shipping led the United States to declare war on Germany in April 1917. The United States' entry into the war gave the weary Allies an enormous boost at the very time Germany was fighting without additional reserves and with allies whose armies were disintegrating. By the end of 1917, a fresh, well-equipped American army of almost 3 million soldiers was expected to join the fight. Meanwhile, the German population neared starvation. Revolution began to sweep through the land, and groups within Germany started lobbying for peace.

Germany's leading general, Prussian Paul von Hindenburg, felt it necessary to end the state of belligerency and asked President Wilson for an armistice. General Hindenburg's willingness to agree to a truce settlement was shaped by his awareness that, as Napoleon Bonaparte put it in 1802, "to negotiate is not to do as one likes."[7] Hindenburg had incentives beyond military necessity for surrendering. He expected the offer to result in fair treatment for Germany, as a bargain struck between equals, based on principles of equity and **reciprocity**. Hindenburg approached his grim task, therefore, with a sense of remorse but also with hope and spoke on behalf of the country for which he had fought (the kaiser had fled to Holland, and Hindenburg was the appointed defender of German national interests). Aboard French general Foch's special train in the forest of Compiégne, early in the morning of November 11, 1918, Hindenburg consented to a prearmistice agreement. In the very same car in which the Franco-Prussian armistice was negotiated in 1871, Hindenburg's order to "cease fire" ended a war that had killed 13 million soldiers and sailors, approximately the same number of civilians, and injured some 30 million people.

The prearmistice contract had been signed under duress, but the cease-fire agreement was accepted primarily because of Germany's expectations of accommodation: "The Germans had laid down their arms after receiving solemn assurances that they could be granted a peace of justice based on Wilson's Fourteen Points."[8] Those principles, first sketched in Wilson's Senate address in 1917 (see Box 5.1) and later elaborated in his Fourteen Points speech in January 1918, outlined a framework for a lasting and just peace on which the Germans felt they could rely. As events unfolded, that expectation would be dashed by the angry emotions unleashed after years of bitter fighting.

PLANNING FOR PEACE

The document signed on November 11, 1918, was only a preliminary armistice. It nonetheless set the stage for the peace conference that would eventually follow and explicitly established the ambitious goals that would

BOX 5.1
PRESIDENT WOODROW WILSON'S PLAN
FOR A LASTING PEACE
(ADDRESS TO THE U.S. SENATE, JANUARY 22, 1917)

In every discussion of the peace that must end this war it is taken for granted that the peace must be followed by some definite concert of power which will make it virtually impossible that any such catastrophe should ever overwhelm us again. Every lover of mankind, every sane and thoughtful man must take that for granted.

. . . It will be absolutely necessary that a force be created as a guarantor of the permanency of the settlement so much greater than the force of any nation now engaged or any alliance hitherto formed or projected that no nation, no probable combination of nations, could face or withstand it. If the peace presently to be made is to endure, it must be a peace made secure by the organized major force of mankind.

. . . The equality of nations upon which peace must be founded if it is to last must be an equality of rights; the guarantees exchanged must neither recognize nor imply a difference between big nations and small, between those that are powerful and those that are weak. Right must be based upon the common strength, not upon the individual strength, of the nations upon whose concert peace will depend. . . . Mankind is looking now for freedom of life, not for equipoises of power.

. . . I am proposing, as it were, that the nations should with one accord adopt the doctrine of President [James] Monroe as the doctrine of the world: that no nation should seek to extend its polity over any other nation or people, but that every people should be left free to determine its own polity, as its own way of development, unhindered, unthreatened, unafraid, the little along with the great and powerful.

I am proposing that all nations henceforth avoid entangling alliances which would draw them into competitions of power, catch them in a net of intrigue and selfish rivalry, and disturb their own affairs with influences intruded from without. There is no entangling alliance in a concert of power. When all unite to act in the same sense and with the same purpose all act in the common interest and are free to live their own lives under a common protection.

I am proposing government by the consent of the governed, that freedom of the seas which in international conference after conference representatives of the United States have urged with the eloquence of those who are the convinced disciples of liberty, and that moderation of armaments which makes of armies and navies a power for order merely, not an instrument of aggression or of selfish violence.

> These are American principles, American policies. We could stand for
> no others. And they are also the principles and policies of forward-looking
> men and women everywhere, of every modern nation, of every enlightened
> community. They are the principles of mankind and must prevail.

be pursued. As David Lloyd George, the British prime minister, announced,
"I hope that we may say that thus, this fateful morning, come to an end all
wars."[9] The British prime minister shared Woodrow Wilson's vision of
World War I as "the culminating and final war for human liberty"[10] and perceived the rules for international conduct that would emerge from the peace
negotiations as the dawning of a new age.

To craft the final peace terms, a conference assembled in Versailles, outside Paris, a couple of months later in January 1919 with representatives
from twenty-seven allied states, accompanied by hundreds of advisors and
clerks. In addition to the official delegates, representatives from a host of dissatisfied peoples who wished to place their claims before the world also
attended, including the Irish, the Ukrainians, the Finns, the Albanians, the
Armenians, and the Koreans. The result was by far the largest, most widely
reported peace conference ever convened. After four years of carnage, the
attention of people throughout the world was riveted on Paris, where they
hoped the participants would find a formula to keep such destruction from
ever occurring again.

> For most Europeans, the Great War had been a source of disillusionment. . . .
> When it was all over, few remained to be convinced that such a war must never
> happen again. Among vast populations there was a strong conviction that this
> time the parties had to plan a peace that could not just terminate a war, but a
> peace that could change attitudes and build a new type of international
> order. . . .
>
> For the first time in history, broad publics and the peacemakers shared a
> conviction that war was a central problem in international relations. Previ-
> ously, hegemony, the aggressive activities of a particular state, or revolution
> had been the problem. In 1648, 1713, and 1815, the peacemakers had tried to
> resolve issues of the past and to construct orders that would preclude their
> reappearance. But in 1919 expectations ran higher. The sources of war were
> less important than the war itself. There was a necessity to look more to the
> future than to the past. The problem was not just to build a peace, but to con-
> struct a peaceful international order that would successfully manage all inter-
> national conflicts of the future.[11]

The war's destructiveness prompted many people to question the **realpolitik** philosophy that had rationalized weapons acquisition, secret alliances,
and power politics. The time was ripe for a different approach to building
world order. Instead of establishing a new balance of power, the American

president Woodrow Wilson preached the need for a peace plan rooted in the idealism of **liberal** international relations theory.

Wilsonianism Ascendant

President Woodrow Wilson personally led the American delegation to the Paris peace conference. Many people regarded Wilson as the architect of a better world. In Italy, along Wilson's route to the conference, people threw flowers at his feet. When he arrived in France, bands escorted him down the broad boulevards of Paris and a palace was put at his disposal. From Eastern Europe to the Far East, war-weary and impoverished peasants placed Wilson's picture beside their religious symbols.

Many months before the war ended, Wilson had urged in eloquent speeches that World War I must be "the war to end all wars," that the peace must benefit all and hurt none. He had put his ideals into specifics earlier in his widely proclaimed Fourteen Points speech of January 22, 1917. Some of these points concerned boundary lines or other specific arrangements, but seven key points heralded bold new principles for making peace: (1) "open covenants openly arrived at" — that is, the end of secret treaties; (2) a settlement of all territorial claims on the basis of **self-determination** to permit each nationality to determine the flag under which it wanted to live; (3) disarmament to reduce war-breeding weaponry in all nations; (4) the cutting of protective tariff barriers to free trade, barriers which had encouraged imperialistic rivalries and inhibited economic growth; (5) the promotion of democratic governance within states, based on the belief that democracies would resolve their disputes through **mediation** rather than war; (6) strengthening international law; and (7) creating a League of Nations to guarantee the independence and territorial integrity of all states. These seven principles shaped the thinking of states during debate among the participants at the peace conference.

Before substantive issues could be debated, however, it was necessary to settle various procedural matters. Because no formal agenda had been established prior to the conference, on January 12, 1919, meetings began to hammer out organizational issues. Ultimately it was decided that the key decision-making body would be a Council of Ten, composed of the foreign ministers and heads of state from France, Great Britain, the United States, Italy, and Japan. Not long thereafter, the foreign ministers were dropped, thus leaving a Council of Five. Since Japan only participated when the council dealt with a topic pertaining to the Pacific region, most of the decisions were made by a Council of Four (which became a council of France, Great Britain, and the United States when Italy withdrew at the end of April). Because council members lacked detailed information about most substantive issues they addressed, fifty-eight commissions of experts were established to study specific problems and make recommendations. Council deliberations over these recommendations were held in secret, and only eight plenary sessions involving all delegates to the peace conference were held.

TABLE 5.2
A Chronology of World War I and the Restoration of Peace

Date	Event
1914	World War I erupts with assassination of Archduke Franz Ferdinand and his wife, June 28
1917	Czar Nicholas II of Russia abdicates throne, March 16
	United States declares war on Germany in response to submarine attacks in violation of its neutral status
	German-Russian armistice signed at Brest-Litovsk
1918	Woodrow Wilson proposes Fourteen Points for world peace
	Brest-Litovsk Treaty between Russia and Central Powers; Soviet government assumes power in Moscow, cedes large portions of Russian territory
	Rumania signs peace treaty with Central Powers
	Pittsburgh Agreement signed between Czechs and Slovaks
	Germany and Austria agree to Wilson's demand that their soldiers retreat to their own territory before an armistice is signed
	Allies agree to truce suspending fighting with Austria-Hungary, November 3
	Prearmistice agreement signed between Allies and Germany, November 11, to end the fighting and begin negotiations for a peace settlement based on Fourteen Points
	Allies agree at Versailles on peace terms for Germany; Germany consents to establish an electorally based republic
	Polish republic proclaimed
	Austria becomes an elective republic
	Montenegro united with Serbia
	Serbo-Croatian-Slovene kingdom of Yugoslovia proclaimed
	Woodrow Wilson arrives in Paris for Versailles Peace Conference
1919	Peace conference opens at Versailles, convenes between January and June
	President Wilson presides over first League of Nations meeting in Paris
	Hapsburg dynasty exiled from Austria
	Finnish-Soviet War erupts
	Treaty of Versailles signed, June 28
	Treaty of St. Germain forces Austria to surrender 73 percent of its territory, pay reparations, and limit its army to thirty thousand, September 10

(cont.)

(Table 5.2 cont.)

Date	Event
	Treaty of Neuilly cedes Bulgarian territories to Yugoslavia and Greece, November 27
1920	After Greece invades Asia Minor in May 1919, the abortive Sévres Peace Treaty of August 10, 1920 wrests control of Thrace and Asia Minor from the Ottoman Empire and internationalizes the Straits to shipping
	U.S. Senate votes against joining the new League of Nations, leaving the fledgling international organization without its most enthusiastic advocate
	Treaty of Trianon forces Hungary to accept huge territorial losses and heavy reparations payments, June 4
1921	Paris conference of Allies sets schedule for German reparation payments
	Treaty of Riga moves the resurrected state of Poland to the east of the Curzon Line established at the Paris Peace Conference following the Polish-Soviet war, March 18
	London Imperial Conference
	Washington Conference produces Four Power Treaty committing the United States, Great Britain, France, and Japan to consultations in the event of any threat of aggressive action against the rest, November; the Five-Power Treaty establishes disarmament to maintain naval parity; Nine-Power Treaty pledges respect of China's independence, November
1922	Treaty of Rapallo between Germany and the Soviet Union provides for mutual diplomatic recognition, reciprocal trade and cancellation of prior financial claims and permits Germany to train its army in the Soviet Union in violation of the Versailles Treaty, April 16; Germany cedes Upper Silesia to Poland
	Austria denounces Anschluss in Geneva Protocol
1923	Hitler's "Beer Hall Putsch" attempt to overthrow democratic institutions in Germany and acquire power for Nazis fails
	Treaty of Lausanne revises the Treaty of Sévres, July 24
	U.S. Senate votes to withdraw American occupation forces from the Rhineland
1924	Pan-American Treaty, to prevent international conflicts, signed
	London Conference approves Dawes Report to resolve controversies about German reparations following Germany's default on its payments and French occupation of the Ruhr, April
1925	Locarno Conference seeks to cooperatively amend Versailles agreements to keep the peace, guarantee Germany's western frontiers, December 1
1927	Inter-Allied military control of Germany ends
	Geneva economic conference of fifty-two nations fails to reach agreement
	Germany's economy collapses on "Black Friday"

Idealism versus National Self-Interest

As the delegates to the conference approached their historic mission, they were also influenced by the fact that the Germans had asked for a peace grounded in Wilson's Fourteen Points. The Germans believed such a peace would be based on reconciliation rather than recrimination because Wilson had preached that "only a peace between equals can last."[12] However, once the Allies began their work, the knives of national interest began to whittle away at the liberal internationalist philosophy underpinning the Fourteen Points. Although many were moved by the Wilsonian program, each state expected their leaders to pursue their own parochial concerns.

Many European politicians believed the Fourteen Points were merely utopian dreams built on illusions about human nature and the willingness of nations to sacrifice for the larger collective good. These leaders remembered that during the war the Allies had made many secret (and occasionally conflicting) agreements concerning territories they hoped to obtain. Not ideals, but the quest for land, defensible frontiers, ports, and supplies of raw materials shaped the bargaining. Statesmen grounded in realpolitik remained reluctant to accept Wilson's idealism and were offended by the pontificating American president and his preaching style. "God was content with Ten Commandments," growled Georges Clemenceau, the cynical French prime minister. "Wilson must have fourteen."[13] Statesmen's behavior at the bargaining table showed that they were only willing to support those particular principles of the Fourteen Points that served their national interests.

Clemenceau, a disciple of the **realist** premise that wars were inevitable, evaluated all proposals for a peace settlement on the basis of how much they strengthened France and weakened Germany. Great Britain's policy was guided by Prime Minister David Lloyd George, who, like Woodrow Wilson, was himself something of a reformer; nonetheless, Lloyd George believed in the necessity of preserving Britain's freedom of decision and had his ear attuned to the public's cry for a peace treaty that would put British interests ahead of grand global ideals. Lloyd George did not see the need for charity toward external enemies, having campaigned in the 1918 election with the slogan "We will squeeze the orange till the pips squeak."[14]

> "I wish to be buried standing, facing Germany."
>
> — GEORGES CLEMENCEAU

As negotiations at the conference proceeded, Clemenceau's stark realpolitik thinking prevailed. His philosophy was rooted in the politics of revenge, although he gave his consent to Wilson's fourteenth point—the need to create the League of Nations to keep the peace through **collective security** instead of the discredited balance-of-power process, which had shown itself unreliable. If the League were established, Wilson believed, it would allow the victors to deal with serious flaws in the final peace settlement, help nations become accustomed to resolving their disagreements peacefully, and provide the machinery by which future disputes could be settled without war.

How the League would be structured remained an issue of vigorous debate, however. Should it be designed in accordance with the theory of collective security, or should it have a permanent staff and an international army? What roles and responsibilities would the great powers have in comparison to small- and medium-sized countries? Although Wilson had asked his trusted adviser Colonel E. M. House to prepare a blueprint for the new organization, other countries advanced their own ideas. Lord Phillimore of Great Britain, Léon Bourgeois of France, V. E. Orlando of Italy, and Jan Christiaan Smuts of South Africa all offered different proposals. The American president may have commanded enormous popular attention on the topic of a League of Nations, but the organization would only emerge through a patchwork of compromises with allies striving to protect their competing national interests. After considerable wrangling among the victors, a combined Anglo-American draft was issued by Cecil Hurst and David Hunter Miller, which then served as the basis for the Covenant of the League.

Wilsonianism in Decline

The League of Nations that had been advocated so vigorously by Woodrow Wilson was written into the peace treaty with Germany as the first of 440 articles. The rest of the settlement became largely a compromise among the ambitious, self-interested demands of the other victors. Agreements were not openly arrived at because the important decisions were made behind closed doors. The central issues of the final settlement were settled through bargaining among the victors, with the vanquished and the other affected states excluded from full representation. Furthermore, no agreements were reached to lower tariffs or reduce armaments. As the pursuit of self-advantage dominated the debate, the Versailles peace conference increasingly began to resemble a victor's peace instead of the "peace without victory" that Wilson had championed.

In thinking about the ways the Germans should be treated in defeat, the Allies could not help but to take into consideration how, had Germany won the war, it probably would have treated its victims. The victors shuddered over the March 13, 1918, Treaty of Brest-Litovsk between Germany and Russia. Its terms were so exploitative that the Russian negotiator, Leon Trotsky, at first refused to sign the armistice, in reaction to the German demand that would deprive Russia of 26 percent of its population, 27 percent of its arable land, and 33 percent of its manufacturing industries. Trotsky was overruled by his comrade, Vladimir Lenin, who was willing to accept these enormous Russian losses in order to allow the Bolsheviks the opportunity to consolidate their control within Russia. The Allies concluded that, if victorious, the Germans would have imposed the same kind of harsh terms against them. These fears undermined sympathy for the surrendering Germans and made it difficult for the Allies to contemplate treating the Germans in a manner the Germans were unlikely to have treated them if the outcome were reversed. As a result, the Allied powers responded with a vindictive settlement that mirrored the punitive policy of Germany toward Russia after Russia's surrender. Lloyd George, for example, publicly demanded in his November 1918 "Khaki" campaign for office that Germany pay for the entire cost of the war.

The settlement finally reached is known as the Treaty of Versailles because it was signed in the glittering Versailles palace — the same hall in which Louis XVI had held court during his reign as king prior to the French Revolution and where Prussian chancellor Otto von Bismarck had imposed terms on France in 1871 after the Franco-Prussian War. The newly created republican German government headed by its socialist president, Friedrich Ebert, submitted to the agreement on June 28, 1919. The final draft departed from the approach Woodrow Wilson had originally recommended. It was a punitive peace settlement best known not for what it created, but for what it destroyed: the spirit of **conciliation** that the belligerents had pledged to respect when the prearmistice pact on November 11, 1918, had been signed in the celebrated "boxcar" truce.

The treaties that ended World War I ratified the end of the kaiser's rule in Germany, as well as the dissolution of the Austro-Hungarian and Ottoman empires. Inspired by revenge, the settlement was an act of retaliation rather than reconciliation. "No quarrel ought ever to be converted into a policy," David Lloyd George had once admonished,[15] but this sentiment was ignored at Versailles as the victors redrew the map of Europe to prevent Germany's recovery. As Maps 5.1 and 5.2 show, in the follow-up Treaty of St. Germain (September 10, 1919), Austria was allowed to retain only 27 percent of its former territory (ceding South Tyrol, South Styria, and the Sudetenland). Its army was limited to thirty thousand soldiers, and Austria had to pay a large indemnity. Likewise, the Treaty of Neuilly (November 27, 1919) forced Bulgaria to cede four strategically important areas to Yugoslavia and its Aegean coastline to Greece. The Treaty of Trianon (June 4, 1920) required Hungary to surrender 71 percent of its territory, pay reparations to the Allies, and reduce its armed forces to thirty-five thousand soldiers. Similarly, the Treaty of Sévres (August 10, 1920) dismantled the Ottoman Empire, with Greece gaining ground in Thrace and Asia Minor, and Arab provinces placed under League of Nations mandates. Beyond these territorial adjustments, the Versailles treaty forced Germany to relinquish various holdings. Specifically, it was required to give

- Alsace-Lorraine to France
- North Schleswig to Denmark
- West Prussia, Posen, portions of East Prussia, Outer Pomerania, and Upper Silesia to Poland
- Eupen and Malmedy to Belgium
- the Memel district to Lithuania

MAP 5.1 Empires and Competing Alliances on the Eve of World War I. Prior to the First World War, the major powers in Europe had separated into two opposed coalitions, the Triple Entente and the Central Powers, with only a handful of neutral states avoiding entanglement in these alliance networks. When the war erupted, this bipolarized balance-of-power distribution engulfed the entire continent.

Moreover, the Versailles peace treaty mandated the Saar region to the administrative control of the League of Nations and made Danzig a "free city" in which Germany had no jurisdiction. In addition, Germany was prohibited from uniting with Austria.

In addition to the boundary revisions, the Germans suffered the humiliating presence of military occupation forces on their territory and the forced reform of their governing institutions. The Versailles treaty called for a special tribunal to try Kaiser William II for offenses against international morality and the sanctity of treaties and obligated Germany to create a democratic government ruled by the consent of the governed. To make matters even more difficult,

MAP 5.2 The New Distribution of Power after the Versailles Treaty's Border Changes in 1919. When World War I came to an end, the winners redistributed territories at the expense of the defeated. Empires were reduced to shadows of their former selves, and the boundaries of Germany were stripped of territories to which German nationalities had long laid claim. The wisdom, or folly, of this settlement was to be shown by subsequent developments.

Germany was assessed an astronomical $33 billion (1,452,360 billion reichsmarks) indemnity by the Reparations Commission in 1921. In interpreting the fantastic level of this indemnity, and the improbability that Germany could ever hope to repay it, one should keep in mind that the German government's annual revenue at the time was less than 3 billion reichsmarks.

Many historians believe that this extreme approach might have been avoided if, as originally planned, the United States had taken its seat on the

Reparations Commission. This is not to argue that the victors were divided about the kind of peace that should be made once the conference got underway, with Wilson on one side and the other Allies in opposition. At the conference Wilson himself shifted from his prior light-handed position, keeping his options open concerning the provisions of a final settlement. In fact, from the start Wilson had viewed imperial Germany as "the epitome of evil in the modern world"[16] and had harbored no sympathy for its militarism and autocracy; his disdain for Germany helps to explain why "the salient feature of American diplomacy from April 1917 to October 1918 was Wilson's attempt to impose a moratorium on political consultation with the Allies"[17] about the way the Germans should be treated after victory.

As early as September 27, 1918, Wilson had begun to voice his support for a settlement among the Allies that would exclude the enemies' participation; instead of **negotiations,** Wilson insisted that the settlement should be imposed by the victors:

> We are all agreed that there can be no peace obtained by any kind of bargain or compromise with the governments of the Central Empires. . . . They have convinced us that they are without honor and do not intend justice. They observe no covenants, accept no principle but force and their own interest. We cannot "come to terms" with them . . . Germany will have to redeem her character, not by what happens at the peace table but by what follows.[18]

As a result of Wilson's posture, "the Paris Peace Conference became the first European multilateral war settlement that was not negotiated between all the belligerents. Whatever the pretensions of the peacemakers that their work represented leniency and justice and that it could serve as a basis for an enduring peace, it was a *diktat*—as most Germans were to claim from the day it was signed."[19]

Moreover, although there remained much disunity and even competition among the victorious allies at the bargaining table, Wilson was not "prepared to insist on a peace of reconciliation,"[20] and as a consequence the defeated powers were forced to accept the heavy burden that the victors imposed on them. There seemed little recognition of the possible rewards that might result from leniency, despite some professions by the peacemakers of the importance of treating the vanquished as equal members deserving of respect in the community of nations. "Germany and the other defeated belligerents would have to serve a probationary period, earning their way to membership through their foreign policy behavior, even though they otherwise met the only specific membership requirement in the Covenant, that a state be 'self-governing.'"[21]

The final terms of the lengthy text of the Versailles treaty made the victors' true intention—to strip Germany of its status as a great power—abundantly clear. Germany, though defeated, was allowed to remain an independent sovereign state, but the peace terms were intentionally so burdensome as to ensure Germany's decline and, with Poland created as an independent buffer state between Germany and Russia, to also guarantee that Germany's potential resurgence would be contained. As one historian summarizes:

> Germany's military and naval power was drastically curtailed; Allied soldiers could occupy the left bank of the Rhine for up to fifteen years; Alsace and Lorraine were returned to France; German colonies were divided among the victors; East Prussia was separated from Germany proper by the new Poland. The German government was obliged, moreover, to pay reparations for the physical and human suffering of the war, reparations that soon became a major political and economic stumbling block to Europe's recovery and stability.[22]

The harsh terms of the Treaty of Versailles provoked resentment in the Germans, who felt betrayed by the victors' refusal to honor their prior promise to grant Germany a voice during the deliberations. On learning of the provisions the Germans were told to accept, the exiled German kaiser is said to have declared that "the war to end wars has resulted in a peace to end peace."[23]

VENOMOUS VICTORY AND ITS CONSEQUENCES

The victors' mood after World War I was driven by the spirit of revenge. With nightmarish visions of trenches, poison gas, barbed wire, and mechanized slaughter fresh in their minds, the victors assembled at Versailles approached the task of making peace in a state of anger. They sought revenge against an enemy that, in the words of French foreign minister Georges Clemenceau, had "flung aside every scruple of conscience" to wage a brutal war "hoping for a peace of enslavement under the yoke of militarism destructive of all human dignity."[24]

At Versailles, the victors did not just blame the leaders of their defeated adversaries for their aggression. They blamed their entire populations, holding them collectively accountable for the crimes committed. "War guilt" was assigned to the German people and their allies: the famous Article 231 of the treaty the German authorities were forced to sign stipulated that "Germany accepts the responsibility of Germany and her allies for causing all the loss and damage to which the Allied and Associated Governments and their nationals have been subjected as a consequence of the war imposed upon them by the aggression of Germany and her allies."[25]

What were the consequences of the punitive peacekeeping strategy that the victors embraced at Versailles? Many feel it backfired, producing the very outcome it sought to prevent. In 1928 the Kellogg-Briand Pact (or Pact of Paris) outlawed the right of states to make war, but the Versailles peace settlement failed to extinguish Germany's hopes for global status and influence. On the contrary, some have argued that the vengeance of Versailles and the blame it assigned was the kindling that led to the global conflagration that erupted in 1939.

Germany's hegemonic ambitions were renewed in the helter-skelter atmosphere of the 1920s and 1930s. Incited by resurgent nationalism, **irredentist** calls for the recovery of lost territory focused on the plight of Germans living in Austria, Czechoslovakia, and Poland. The rise of fascism in Germany can be attributed, in part, to the angry emotions unleashed following the conclusion of the First World War. Adolf Hitler's meteoric rise to power, and subsequent German aggression under him, were fueled by many Germans' resentment over the harsh conditions imposed upon them after the war. "Hitler exploited the Versailles Treaty as a symbol of a vindictive Western policy designed to hold down a defeated Germany — rhetoric that pushed onto the Western allies the blame for Germany's domestic misery."[26] Since no foreign army had reached German soil during World War I, many felt that the German army had not been defeated; it was stabbed in the back by traitors within Germany itself.

Germany's armed forces were reduced by the peace settlement to 100,000 volunteers, the navy was cut to six cruisers, and it lost 13 percent of its prewar territory and colonies overseas. Yet Germany was also denied membership in the League of Nations until 1926. When Germany defaulted on the war reparations payments in 1922, France sent troops to occupy the German industrial area of the Ruhr Valley. In 1925, in response to the German delay in adhering to the disarmament provisions of the Versailles treaty, the French postponed the scheduled evacuation of their occupation troops. The crisis was momentarily defused by the efforts of German foreign minister Gustav Stresemann.

> He proposed a set of nonaggression and arbitration treaties, principally among France, Britain, Italy, and Germany. These countries, as well as Belgium, Czechoslovakia, and Poland, met in the Swiss town of Locarno in the fall of 1925 in an omnibus negotiation of a pact to remove the scourge of war from Europe. A treaty on the Rhineland provided for that region's full demilitarization, pledging France, Germany, and Belgium to refrain from resorting to war against each other, except for a flagrant breach of the Locarno Pact itself or as a part of a League of Nations action against an aggressor state. France also signed two special treaties of guarantee with Poland and Czechoslovakia providing for mutual assistance against Germany in case that country should violate her new obligations. Finally, Germany signed arbitration treaties with each of the other countries, agreeing to submit her disputes with them to a conciliation commission and then, if necessary, to the World Court and the Council of the League. As the icing on the cake of peace, Germany was admitted to the League of Nations.[27]

The so-called hopeful spirit of Locarno succeeded in adjusting the terms of the Treaty of Versailles, in large part because the government in Paris came to the reluctant conclusion that France's relative position was declining, which made reconciliation with Germany crucial for France's security. With France prepared to relax its punitive policies, a window of opportunity opened for a retreat from the Versailles provisions. On September 27, 1926,

France agreed to return the Saar coal region to Germany without the plebiscite that had been required in the Treaty of Versailles and removed its occupation forces from the Rhineland the next year.

This spirit of cooperation and conciliation did not last long, and further serious efforts to amend the Versailles peace treaty were not undertaken. The efforts by the great powers to work together, through the League of Nations, to collectively keep the peace, sputtered. Realpolitik returned, spawning the very behaviors that Wilson and others had sought to expunge at Versailles: unilateral initiatives and the struggle for national power and position through secret treaties pitting one set of states against another. Alliance formation became frantic and reached epidemic proportions as national leaders sought protection not through international organization but through arms and military alliances. As Hans J. Morgenthau observed, in the period after the First World War, "the principle of the balance of power was supposed to have been superseded by the League-of-Nations principle of collective security," but in fact that principle was put "under the sign of the balance of power by alliances and counteralliances."[28] France, for example, sought to buttress its security by forging alliances with Belgium, Poland, and the so-called Little Entente of Yugoslavia, Rumania, and Czechoslovakia. The frequency with which states entered into formal alliances between 1923 and 1933 warrants the label for this period: "the era of pacts."[29] The plan to make peace through concerted international cooperation was stillborn. Ironically, the United States, which had fathered collective security under Woodrow Wilson, refused to join the League of Nations.

War clouds gathered in a relatively short amount of time after the Versailles conference. Symptoms of the gathering storm included the failures of the global economic conferences in 1927 and 1933, as well as the inability of the League of Nations to respond effectively to the 1931 Japanese invasion of Manchuria, the Chaco War of 1932, and Italy's 1935 invasion of Ethiopia. By the late 1930s it appeared another great-power war was about to erupt. Not prepared themselves to enforce the peace, the victors in World War I responded to German rearmament with an **appeasement** policy aimed at pacifying potential aggressors with concessions. Adolf Hitler, the German dictator who came to power in 1933, pledged not to expand German territory by force, and this encouraged the democracies to withdraw from the challenge of peace maintenance in the false hope that war could be avoided without active engagement. Hitler betrayed his promise when in March 1938 he forced Austria into union with Germany in violation of the terms of the Versailles treaty. Shortly thereafter Hitler insisted upon the annexation of the German-populated area of Sudentenland in Czechoslovakia. The fears that German expansionism provoked led to the final Allied effort to prevent another European war. At the September 1938 Munich Conference, Britain, France, and Italy agreed to Hitler's territorial demands. Their decision was rationalized by noting that Hitler's request fell under the right of national self-determination and, once the Sudentenland was given to Germany, Berlin would issue no more territorial demands.

Rather than satisfying Germany, appeasement encouraged further efforts at overthrowing the international status quo.[30] Between September 1, 1939, when Germany invaded Poland, and December 7, 1941, when Japan launched a surprise assault on the United States at Pearl Harbor, the world slid back into a global war. Just two decades after the Versailles peace conference, the world was again in flames. If Versailles teaches us anything, it is the scope and complexities of the peacemaking endeavor. To succeed, the victors must tighten the bonds among themselves, cultivate a consensus on goals and strategies, and persevere in their efforts to implement and adjust the peace plan on which they agree. Ideally, allies should begin negotiations while the war is still being waged and mobilize public support for the plans they create to enable them to abide by the agreements they pledge. It is critical for the victors to adhere to the provisions they declare in the armistice so that the vanquished will not feel betrayed and be tempted to reverse the settlement by force at a later date. To be sure, as one scholar has put it, almost "every treaty which brings a war to an end is, in one sense, a dictated peace; for a defeated Power seldom accepts willingly the consequences of its defeat. But in the Treaty of Versailles the element of dictation was more apparent than in any previous peace treaty of modern times. . . . At the ceremony of signature, the two German signatories were not allowed to sit with the Allied delegates at the table but were escorted in and out of the hall in the manner of criminals conducted to and from the dock."[31] These humiliations linked the new Weimar Republic in Germany to a feeling of national disgrace and helped to create the belief that the provisions of the treaty were not morally binding.[32] Finally, the tragic case of Versailles illustrates the need for victorious states to distinguish realizable goals from unobtainable ideals. As Henry Kissinger concludes, the victors assembled in Paris felt so eager to avoid what they considered to be the mistakes of previous settlement plans that they embraced a set of terms that

> mortgaged the new international order instead of helping to create it. . . . What they finally produced was a fragile compromise between American utopianism and European paranoia—too conditional to fulfill the dreams of the former, too tentative to alleviate the fears of the latter. [The terms of the Treaty of Versailles] were too onerous for conciliation but not severe enough for permanent subjugation.[33]

It proved exceedingly difficult to strike a balance between satisfying and subjugating Germany. Ultimately, neither occurred.

Given the failure of the Allies to forge a durable peace settlement after World War I, renewed emphasis was placed on the issue of war termination by the Allies following World War II. In Chapter 6 we will examine what the victors did differently and whether they were any more successful than the delegates to the Versailles peace conference.

CONTROVERSIES TO CONTEMPLATE

- Was World War I inevitable? If not, what could policymakers have done to avoid war?
- How did wartime propaganda and electoral rhetoric of political leaders in the Allied states affect the provisions of the peace settlement?
- President Woodrow Wilson attended the Paris Peace Conference in person and, despite complaints from members of the U.S. Congress, remained in Europe for six months to negotiate the details of the final settlement. What are the drawbacks of having heads of state negotiate the details of peace settlements?
- Was the Treaty of Versailles a failure because of its inherent defects or because it was never fully implemented?
- What were the consequences of imposing a war indemnity on Germany but not specifying in the peace treaty the sum to be paid? What were the problems of having a Reparations Commission draw up the bill years later?
- Whatever the faults of the Treaty of Versailles, Woodrow Wilson believed they could be rectified by the League of Nations. Why was it problematic to expect the League to correct any flaws in the peace treaty?
- John Maynard Keynes, a British economist and former treasury official who attended the Paris Peace Conference, complained that French Premier Clemenceau saw international politics as a perpetual prize fight. Germany was victorious in 1871, now France had won in 1918, but this was not likely to be the final round. To what extent did the peace settlement after World War I contribute to the outbreak of World War II?
- After the initial feelings of righteous anger toward Germany faded, many British citizens expressed misgivings about the Treaty of Versailles. David Lloyd George, the British prime minister involved in negotiating the treaty, later commented that the war resulted from botched decisions by all sides, not from the master plan of the kaiser. How did second thoughts over the cause of the war and the harshness of the peace settlement influence British foreign policy toward Germany during the interwar years?

SUGGESTED READING

Carr, E. H. *The Twenty-Years' Crisis, 1919–1939*. London: Macmillan, 1939.

Ferguson, Niall. *The Pity of War: Explaining World War I*. New York: Basic Books, 1999.

Goemans, H. E. *War and Punishment: The Causes of War Termination and the First World War.* Princeton, N.J.: Princeton University Press, 2001.

Joll, James. *The Origins of the First World War.* London: Longman, 1984.

Knock, Thomas J. *To End All Wars: Woodrow Wilson and the Quest for a New World Order.* New York: Oxford University Press, 1992.

Ninkovich, Frank. *The Wilsonian Century.* Chicago: University of Chicago Press, 1999.

Pick, Daniel. *War Machine: The Rationalization of Slaughter in the Modern Age.* New Haven, Conn.: Yale University Press, 1993.

Ross, Graham. *The Great Powers and the Decline of the European States System, 1914–1945.* London: Longman, 1983.

Turner, L. C. F. *The Origins of World War I.* London: Edward Arnold, 1983.

Wilson, Keith. *Decisions for War, 1914.* New York: St. Martin's Press, 1995.

NOTES

1. In Eyffinger, 1988, p. 21.
2. Ibid., p. 52.
3. Angell, 1910.
4. Kissinger, 1994, p. 214.
5. Lane et al., 1959, p. 567.
6. In Green, 1982, p. 12.
7. Bailey, 1968, p. 144.
8. Ibid., p. 268. Wilson's Fourteen Points proposal was one of several peace plans that surfaced toward the end of the war. Prime Minister David Lloyd George of Britain issued a Declaration of Aims on January 5, 1918, which listed conditions his government saw as necessary for peace. In addition, numerous agreements had been reached among different allied states throughout 1916 and 1917 over how specific issues (such as the disposition of lands held by the Ottoman Empire) would be handled after the war.
9. Link, 1957, p. 100 ff.
10. Hunt, 1996, p. 22.
11. Holsti, 1991, pp. 175–176, 208–209.
12. Bailey, 1968, p. 268.
13. Lane et al., 1959, p. 571.
14. Craig and George, 1995, p. 45.
15. Bailey, 1968, p. 8.
16. Esposito, 1996, p. 5.
17. Fowler, 1969, p. 5.
18. Holsti, 1991, p. 198.
19. Ibid., p. 199.
20. Kissinger, 1994, p. 229.
21. Holsti, 1991, p. 199.
22. Williamson, 1993, p. 989. For a full account of the terms of the Versailles settlements and a highly critical realist assessment of the fallacious hopes on which the liberal-idealist peacemakers based their thinking, see Carr, 1947.
23. Bailey, 1968, p. 267.
24. Holsti, 1991, p. 191.
25. At the end of the war, public opinion in many of the victorious countries demanded a formal condemnation of Germany. The original intent of Article 231 was to indicate that while Germany was morally responsible for the war, it was only legally liable for more narrowly defined damages. By embracing collective guilt in asserting that the German nation was morally responsible, the victors "in the passion of the moment, failed to realize that this extorted admission of guilt could prove nothing, and must excite bitter resentment in German minds. German men of learning set to work to demonstrate the guiltlessness of their country, fondly believing that, if this could be established, the whole fabric of the treaty would collapse." Carr, 1947, p. 46.

26. Dean, 1996, p. 18.
27. Brown, 1994, p. 170.
28. Morgenthau, 1985, p. 212.
29. Langsam, 1954, p. 79.
30. Disillusioned with Western liberalism and the Paris settlements, and suffering economically from the effects of the Great Depression of the 1930s, Japan also embraced militarism. Inspired by Germany's imperialistic quest for national aggrandizement, Japanese nationalists took Japan on the path to imperialism and colonialism. When Japan invaded China in 1937 after subjugating Manchuria (1931–1935), this accelerated the momentum for still more aggression. Italy attacked Ethiopia in 1935 and absorbed Albania in 1939, and both Germany and Italy intervened in the 1936–1939 Spanish civil war on the side of the fascists headed by General Francisco Franco.
31. Carr, 1947, pp. 4–5.
32. Ibid., pp. 44–45.
33. Kissinger, 1994, pp. 240, 242.

· 6 ·

WORLD WAR II AND ITS AFTERMATH:
THE LONG, COLD PEACE

Too often in the past, each war only planted the seeds of the
next. We celebrate today the reconciliation . . . that has
liberated us from that cycle of destruction.

— JOHN F. KENNEDY

PREVIEW

In 1919 the victors, in what was then called the Great War, met in Paris to design a peace settlement that would prevent such a human tragedy from ever happening again. It was a war fought and rationalized as "a war to end all wars." Just twenty years later, the liberal idealist plan for lasting peace was shattered when the second global war of the twentieth century broke out. This chapter will examine the path to the outbreak of World War II and, in particular, the impact of the Versailles peace treaty on Germany's foreign policy. The chapter then reviews the conferences held by the Allies during the war to construct a new, more durable peace settlement. Next, the divergent interests among the Allies and growing distrust they had of one another are charted in order to explain the different ideas that surfaced regarding the treatment of the vanquished Axis powers, Germany and Japan. The chapter concludes by describing the forces that splintered the Allies into opposing blocs in what was to become a forty-year Cold War that postponed a final settlement to the Second World War until the collapse of communism in the period between 1989 and 1991. The material covered in this case highlights the following concepts from a structural realist approach to the study of war and peacemaking:

- hegemonic wars
- the balance of power

- arms races
- the security dilemma
- spheres of influence
- collective security

When reading this case, give particular consideration to how decisionmakers in 1945 tried to avoid what they saw as the mistakes of 1919. In what ways did the peace settlement of World War II differ from the settlement of World War I? Did those differences improve the prospects for a durable peace?

Germany's defeat in World War I did not extinguish its desire for global status and influence. On the contrary, defeat and humiliation became the soil from which sprouted an intensified desire for recovery and revenge. Beginning in the 1930s, Germany, joined by Japan and Italy, began pursuing an aggressive course, which resulted in the twentieth century's second worldwide conflict.

World War II personified a hegemonic struggle for power that pitted a fascist coalition striving for world supremacy—the Axis trio of Germany, Japan, and Italy—against the "grand alliance" of four great powers—Great Britain, France, the United States, and the Soviet Union. The Allies united although they espoused incompatible ideologies—communism in the case of the Soviet Union and democratic capitalism in the case of Britain, France, and the United States. Their victory was achieved over a six-year ordeal, but at a catastrophic human cost: Each

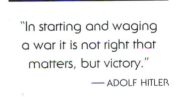

"In starting and waging a war it is not right that matters, but victory."

— ADOLF HITLER

day twenty-three thousand lives were lost, and the war resulted in the death of 60 million people worldwide.

To appreciate what the victors did at the end of World War II, one must first recall the atmosphere and attitudes that prevailed prior to the onset of what became the biggest and most destructive war in history. This atmosphere was to shape the thinking of the victors toward the vanquished after they repelled the Axis threat to conquer the world.

THE PATH TO WORLD WAR II

Germany's hegemonic ambitions were driven by hypernationalism, which stimulated that country's latent **irredentist** effort to recover provinces ceded to others after World War I and to expand its borders to absorb Germans living in Austria, Czechoslovakia, and Poland. The Nazi regime's fascist ideology championing race, flag, and fatherland preached the most extreme version of realism, *machtpolitik* (power politics), to justify the forceful aggrandizement of the state. What helped to make this political philosophy acceptable to many Germans was their resentment of the harsh terms imposed at the 1919 Paris peace conference. As described in Chapter 5, the settlement insisted on the destruction of Germany's armed forces, the sacrifice of territory (such as Alsace-Lorraine, which Germany had acquired following the Franco-Prussian War of 1870), and the imposition of heavy reparations to compensate the Allies for the damage exacted by the German military. Denied membership in the League of Nations until 1926, Germany was not accepted as an equal member of the state system. Affronted by this treatment, Berlin sought by force of arms to restore its perceived rightful status as a great power.

As German preparations for war gathered speed in the 1930s, the other **great powers** ignored the signs of danger. The United States retreated to isolationism and Britain and France each maneuvered to their advantage. Whereas France wanted to prevent Germany's revival, Britain, by contrast, saw Germany as a counterweight to balance growing Soviet power on the European continent. By viewing a revitalized Germany in these terms, London underestimated the threat posed by growing German strength and ambition.

A circumstance poisoning the prospects for international cooperation was the collapse of the international economic system during the 1930s. As a result of the costs of fighting World War I, a weakened Great Britain could not continue to perform leadership and regulatory roles in the world political economy. Although the United States appeared the logical successor to Britain as world economic leader, Washington refused to exercise leadership. The Depression of 1929–1931 was followed in 1933 by the abortive World Monetary and Economic Conference. This meeting failed to address the chain reaction of retaliatory trade protectionism and beggar-thy-neighbor tariff walls that were emerging. The advent of trade wars and the financial decline they precipitated worldwide contributed to interstate hostility and rivalry. In this depressed global environment, disgruntled countries sought a remedy in **imperial** expansion.

Acquiescence to German rearmament was justified in Great Britain by a policy of **appeasement,** designed to pacify dissatisfied countries with concessions. Adolf Hitler, the dictator who by this time controlled the German government, claimed to have limited territorial objectives that were supported by the principle of national **self-determination.** He betrayed that declaration in March 1938 by forcing Austria into a union with Germany. Shortly thereafter he began pressuring Czechoslovakia, which led to the September 1938 Munich Conference attended by Hitler, British prime minister Neville Chamberlain, and leaders from France and Italy (Czechoslovakia was not invited). Under the erroneous conviction that appeasement would halt further German expansionism, Chamberlain and the others agreed to Hitler's demands to annex the German-populated area of Sudetenland in Czechoslovakia.

Complacency followed by appeasement encouraged Hitler to press for further revisions in the international status quo. He was joined in this effort by Japan and Italy. The former invaded Manchuria in 1931 and China proper in 1937; the latter absorbed Abyssinia (Ethiopia) in 1935 and Albania in 1939. Furthermore, both Germany and Italy intervened in the 1936–1939 Spanish civil war on the side of the fascists, headed by General Francisco Franco. The failure of the League of Nations to mount an effective response to German, Japanese, and Italian acts of aggression revealed the hollow promise of **collective security.** International institutions were powerless to dispel the gathering war clouds.

THE EXPANDING WAR

These acts of aggression paved the way for the century's second massive war. After Germany occupied the previously unannexed area of Czechoslovakia in March 1939, Britain and France reacted by joining in an alliance to protect the next likely victim, Poland. They also opened negotiations in Moscow in hope of enticing the Soviet Union to join the alliance, but this attempt failed. Then, on August 23, 1939, Hitler and the Soviet leader Joseph Stalin shocked the world by announcing that they had signed a nonaggression pact.[1] Certain that the Western democracies would not intervene without Soviet assistance, Hitler promptly invaded Poland on September 1, 1939. Honoring their pledge to defend the Poles, Britain and France declared war on Germany two days later. World War II had begun.

The war expanded rapidly as Hitler turned his forces loose on the Balkans, North Africa, and westward. Powerful, mechanized German units invaded Norway and marched through Denmark, Belgium, Luxembourg, and the Netherlands. They swept around France's defensive barrier, the Maginot Line, and forced the British to evacuate a sizable expeditionary force from the French beaches at Dunkirk. Paris itself fell in June 1940, and in the months that followed, the German air force pounded Britain in an attempt to force it into submission as well. Instead of invading Britain, however, the Nazi troops turned against Hitler's former ally, attacking the Soviet Union in the surprise blitzkrieg operation known as Barbarossa in June 1941.

The next phase of the war's expansion was even more rapid. On October 17, 1941, the first American casualties were taken when a German torpedo hit the USS *Kearny;* this was followed by another German submarine attack on the USS *Reuben James,* even though the United States was still officially neutral. American neutrality ended on December 7, 1941, when the Japanese launched a surprise attack on the U.S. Pacific fleet anchored in Pearl Harbor, Hawaii. The next day President Roosevelt asked Congress for authorization to declare the existence of a state of war with Japan, and an angry Congress passed that resolution with only a single negative vote. Three days later Adolf Hitler mysteriously acted out of character and honored his promises to Japan by declaring war on the United States, and Italy followed suit. On that same day, the U.S. Congress passed a resolution recognizing that a state of war existed with Germany and Italy, thereby ending years of American **isolationism** and neutrality.

TABLE 6.1
A Chronology of Key Events Surrounding World War II and Its Aftermath

Date	Events
Prewar Phase	
1928	The Kellogg-Briand Pact, signed by sixty-five nations, outlaws war as an instrument of national policy
1932	The Stimson Doctrine protests the Japanese invasion of Manchuria and declares that the United States will hereafter not recognize territorial changes resulting from the use of armed force
1933	The Enabling Law gives Hitler dictatorial power in Germany; Nazi persecution of Jews intensifies
1935	The Nazi regime in Germany repudiates the Treaty of Versailles; Italy invades Ethiopia
1936	Hitler and Mussolini announce the formation of the Berlin Axis alliance
1937	Japan invades China; Italy withdraws from the League of Nations
1938	Germany occupies the Sudentenland of Czechoslovakia
World War II	
1939	Germany invades Poland on September 1; the Allied Powers of Britain and France declare war and World War II begins; the Soviet Union invades Poland in September and Finland in November; the Soviet Union is expelled from the League of Nations in December
1940	Germany attacks Denmark and Norway in April and overruns Belgium and the Netherlands in May; the Allies withdraw after a crushing defeat at Dunkirk; Italy enters the war against France and Britain; Canada declares war against Italy; France is invaded by Germany and signs an armistice on June 22; Italy invades Egypt and Greece; on September 27, Germany, Italy, and Japan sign the Tripartite (Axis) Pact; Hungary and Romania join the Axis in November; from 1940 to 1941 Britain fends off German bombers in the Battle of Britain
1941	The British invade Ethiopia and defeat the Italian occupation; Bulgaria joins the Axis; Germany invades Greece and Yugoslavia; Japan and the Soviet Union sign a nonaggression pact on April 13; Germany invades the Soviet Union on June 22; the Atlantic Charter between the United States and Britain is announced in August; Japan attacks Pearl Harbor on December 7 and the United States declares war on Japan; Germany and Italy declare war on the United States on December 11
1942	The Allies pledge not to make separate peace treaties with their enemies; Japan conquers Manila and Singapore; the Japanese

Date	Events
	advance is halted by Allied victories at Coral Sea and Midway; German forces enter Stalingrad
1943	U.S. President Roosevelt and British Prime Minister Churchill meet at Casablanca in January; German forces surrender Stalingrad and the Axis forces in North Africa surrender; the Allies invade Sicily, Mussolini falls from power, and Italy signs a secret armistice; Italy declares war on Germany; Churchill, Roosevelt, and Stalin hold a conference in Teheran
1944	The Soviet Union breaks the siege of Leningrad; in the D-Day invasion on June 6 the Allied forces land at Normandy, France; the United States wins the Battle of the Philippine Seas; Dumbarton Oaks Conference is held in Washington, D.C. in October; on December 16 the Germans strike back in the Battle of the Bulge, but the Allies halt the Germans on December 27
1945	Allied troops invade the Philippines; Churchill, Roosevelt, and Stalin meet at Yalta in February; Allies reach Berlin in April and the Germans surrender unconditionally on May 7, bringing an end to the European war; allied Control Commission divides Germany into four occupation zones; San Francisco conference organizes plans for the United Nations; three-power occupations of Berlin takes effect; Churchill, Truman, and Stalin confer at the Potsdam conference in July; United States drops atomic bombs on Hiroshima and Nagasaki on August 6 and 9; the Soviets declare war on Japan and invade Manchuria; on August 14 Japan surrenders and ends the war in the Pacific

The Cold War Aftermath

Date	Events
1946	The Paris conference of twenty-one states convenes
1947	U.S. President Harry Truman issues the Truman Doctrine which dictates the containment of the Soviet Union as the preeminent foreign policy of the United States
1949	United States and several western European powers sign the North Atlantic Treaty to protect western Europe from Soviet military threat; Communists take power in China; Nationalists retreat to Taiwan
1950–1953	Korean War is fought ending with communist rule North Korea
1951	Peace treaty with Japan is signed in San Francisco
1953	Soviet Union decrees an end to the war with Germany
1961–1962	United States clashes with communist Cuba in the failed invasion of the Bay of Pigs in 1961 and the Cuban Missile Crisis in 1962
1964	U.S. Congress passes the Gulf of Tonkin Resolution which effectively gives President Johnson the power to escalate to war against the North Vietnamese communists *(cont.)*

(Table 6.1 cont.)

Date	Events
1965–1972	United States openly participates in the war in Vietnam
1972	As part of the new U.S. policy of détente, President Richard Nixon visits communist China; the Strategic Arms Limitations Treaty (SALT) between the United States and the Soviet Union is signed;
1979	Soviet Union invades Afghanistan
1985	Soviet leader Mikhail Gorbachev loosens restrictions in the Soviet Union under the policy of *perestroika*
1989	The Berlin Wall falls; the Cold War ends

Under the claim of racial superiority, Hitler waged war to create an empire that could settle the historic competition among the great powers in Europe by eliminating all rivals. As political scientist Kalevi Holsti notes, the Nazi vision had few limits.

> The broad vision of the Thousand-Year Reich was . . . of a vastly expanded — and continually expanding — German core, extending deep into Russia, with a number of vassal states and regions, including France, the Low Countries, Scandinavia, central Europe and the Balkans, that would provide resources and labor for the core. There was to be no civilizing mission in German imperialism. On the contrary, the lesser peoples were to be taught only to do menial labor or, as Hitler once joked, educated sufficiently to read the road signs so they wouldn't get run over by German automobile traffic. The lowest of the low, the Poles and Jews, were to be exterminated. . . .
>
> To Hitler . . . the purpose of policy was to destroy the system and to reconstitute it on racial lines, with a vastly expanded Germany running a distinctly hierarchical and exploitative order. Vestiges of sovereignty might remain, but they would be fig leaves covering a monolithic order. German occupation policies during the war, whereby conquered nations were reduced to satellites, satrapies, and reservoirs of slave labor, were the practical application of Hitler's conception of the new world order. They were not improvised or planned for reasons of military necessity.[2]

Italy and Japan, intoxicated by dreams of glory, found the quest for empire equally irresistible. Their victims had reason to recognize the magnitude of the security threat but failed to do so until the Axis rush toward worldwide war was almost irreversible. The failure of the French, British, Russians, and Americans to recognize the danger is perplexing. All received ample signs of the looming threat; indeed, all had extensive evidence of German, Italian, and Japanese intentions, as conveyed by the words and deeds of those states. As shown in Box 6.1, the Allied powers had a clear basis for alarm about the conduct of the three members of the Axis coalition. This failure to recognize the danger, together with the brutality of the acts of violence committed by the Axis states when a full-scale state of war erupted, helps to account for the emotional calls for unconditional surrender. Once engaged, the Allies sought

BOX 6.1
ALLIED GRIEVANCES AGAINST THE AXIS POWERS
PRIOR TO WORLD WAR II

The acts that led the United States, France, Great Britain, and the Soviet Union to despise the Axis powers were varied. Among the steps that led the Allies to stereotype their adversaries as evil and undeserving of forgiveness were:

Germany

- Adolf Hitler's conversion of the German democracy into a military dictatorship after his 1933 election
- The Nazi regime's withdrawal from the League of Nations, suppression of trade unions, and persecution of the Jews (culminating in the Holocaust)
- Hitler's March 7, 1933, reoccupation of the demilitarized Rhineland, in violation of the Treaty of Versailles
- Germany's forced merger of Austria and annexation of the Sudetenland of Czechoslovakia
- The German attack of Poland on September 1, 1939
- To the Soviet Union, Germany's June 21, 1941, Operation Barbarossa invasion in violation of the von Ribbentrop pledge of nonaggression

Italy

- Benito Mussolini's establishment of a military dictatorship in 1922 after his Fascist Party came to power
- Italy's invasion in 1935 of Ethiopia without a declaration of war

Japan

- Japan's suspension of liberalizing democratic reforms, such as the introduction of universal male suffrage and governance by major party rule in the 1920s, and in the 1930s its dissolution of political parties and trade unions as Japanese leaders moved to create a militarized state
- The 1931 Japanese invasion of China's northeastern province of Manchuria, which the Japanese renamed Manchukuo
- The 1932 Japanese invasion of Shanghai
- The 1937 Japanese invasion of mainland China and siege of Nanking, the provisional capital of the Chinese leader Chiang Kai-shek (the conquest of that city became known as the Rape of Nanking because of its brutality)
- For the Soviet Union, Japan's defeat of Russia in the 1904–1905 war, its termination of the Neutrality Pact, and Japan's July 1938 and May 1939 attacks at the Manchukuo-Soviet border
- Japan's December 7, 1941, surprise attack on Pearl Harbor

not just defeat of the aggressors, but revenge, and each had psychologically powerful reasons to demonize their adversaries and to wage **total war.**

WARTIME PLANNING FOR A POSTWAR PEACE

Although they were far from confident of victory, at the onset of World War II the Allies almost immediately began to search for principles to underpin a stable postwar world order. Determined not to repeat the failure associated with the Treaty of Versailles, they concurred about the need for unity. Within less than a month of the Japanese attack on Pearl Harbor, on January 1, 1942, the United States, the Soviet Union, Great Britain, China, and twenty-two other states signed the United Nations Declaration, which pledged to proceed with a united front employing all available resources to defeat Germany, Italy, and Japan. The declaration also established the agreement for no signatory to make a separate armistice or peace. This convention, to which an additional twenty signatories later agreed, set the stage in the war's final days for the April 1945 conference of fifty states to draft the United Nations Charter in San Francisco.

A series of other agreements were negotiated during the war at various conferences. Operating under the strong conviction that they could not afford to wait until the war was over to plan for a postwar peace, the United States, Great Britain, and the Soviet Union also accepted the principle of mutual responsibility for maintaining world order. The two western democracies were especially cognizant of the need to work together. Four months prior to the United States' official entry in the war, President Roosevelt and Prime Minister Churchill agreed to the 1941 Atlantic Charter while meeting on a ship off the coast of Newfoundland. This vital document restated many of Wilson's principles, such as the right of self-determination, the illegality of military aggression, and a commitment to economic cooperation. In particular, the Atlantic Charter firmly established support for the view that competition among the allies should be eschewed; the Allies were to work in tandem to preserve world order in accordance with specific rules of conduct.

Particularly critical to the successful operation of such a **security regime** became the resolution of the troublesome issue of the governments the Allies would install in Germany, Italy, and Japan after the war. The Soviet Union especially dedicated itself to eradicating fascism since "Nazi hatred of Communists and Nazi racist definitions of Slavic peoples combined to turn the German war against the U.S.S.R. into an attempt at the annihilation of a society."[3] Although Britain and the United States found fascism equally repugnant, the Allies nonetheless found themselves mired in the sticky issue of whether fascism should be replaced by liberal democratic capitalism or communistic planned economies—a question that threatened to divide the United States and Great Britain from the Soviet Union. Agreement on a solution to this dilemma was reached, however, when the Allies decided to reaffirm the classic **noninterference principle** prohibiting external intervention in the internal affairs of states, which, since the Peace of Westphalia, under international law permitted all states to choose their own systems of government. The Atlantic Charter explicitly endorsed this "hands off" principle as a partial solution to the problem, proclaiming "the right of all peoples to choose the form of government under which they will live," even while it qualified that principle in spirit by accepting, in President Roosevelt's words of May 27, 1941, that the Allies would "not accept a world . . . in which the seeds of Hitlerism can again be planted and allowed to grow."[4] This posture led the Soviet Union on September 24, 1942, to notify "London and Washington that a consistent application of those principles will secure the most energetic support on the part of the Government and the Peoples of the Soviet Union."[5]

Acting largely in concert, the Allied powers established coordinating committees to refine and extend their understandings about unity, mutual responsibility, and **military intervention.** Table 6.2 describes a series of additional meetings that were designed to clarify these understandings.

These meetings produced a general consensus about the aims and preferred strategies for reconstructing a world destroyed by war. Yet beneath the surface uncertainties percolated about the best path for postwar peace. How should the Axis powers be treated? Should they be forgiven, so that their reconciliation and collaboration in postwar peacekeeping would be possible? Or was a vindictive peace prudent, to prevent their recovery and, with it, their possible resumption of forceful expansion?

Responses to these pressing questions varied from Washington to London to Moscow. As political scientist Hans Morgenthau notes, the Allies recognized that "as war is fought in order to make peace possible, foreign policy should be conducted in order to make peace permanent."[6] But which policy would best ensure a permanent peace — a compassionate or a punitive one?

THE POSTWAR BARGAINING PROCESS

On the threshold of victory, the Allies voiced enthusiasm for the doctrines and principles they had previously negotiated. Each Allied leader hoped the others would adhere to their prior agreements and act in concert after the war. For example, after the Yalta Conference, on March 1, 1945, President Roosevelt concluded that the meeting "was a successful effort by the three leading nations to find a common ground for peace. . . . It spells — and ought to spell — the end of the system of unilateral action, exclusive alliances and spheres of influence, and balances of power and all other expedients which have been tried for centuries and have always failed."[7]

A Vindictive Mood

At first, common ground appeared to exist in the American, British, and Soviet perceptions about the need to penalize the Axis for its offenses. Fighting had heightened hostility and resolve. As victory neared, the Allies insisted

TABLE 6.2
Postwar Planning during World War II: Declarations and Doctrines

Date	Conference/Declaration	Key Doctrinal Principle(s)
January 14–24, 1943	Casablanca Conference (French Morocco)	Roosevelt and Churchill pledge that the war would end only with the unconditional surrender of the Axis states
October 1943	Moscow Foreign Ministers Conference (Four Power Declaration)	Allied unity and establishment of a global organization to maintain peace and security
November 28–December 1, 1943	Teheran Conference	Allied unity to preserve order, with U.S. air and naval support for Soviet and British soldiers for peacekeeping in postwar Europe
July 1–22, 1944	Bretton Woods system (United Nations Monetary and Financial Conference in New Hampshire)	Rules and institutions created near the end of World War II to govern international economic relations; creation of the International Monetary Fund (IMF) and the International Bank for Reconstruction and Development
August–September 1944	Big Four Conference (including China) at Dumbarton Oaks (Washington, D.C.)	Draft for negotiations to create the United Nations
September 1944	Quebec Conference	Roosevelt and Churchill agree on goal of reducing Germany to an agricultural economy, without any "war-making industries"
February 4–11, 1945	Yalta Conference (Crimea, Soviet Union)	Confirms policy of unconditional surrender and complete demilitarization of Germany, division of Germany into four zones of occupation (U.S., British, French, Soviet) under unified control commission in Berlin, war crimes trials of Nazis, and study of reparation question; Soviet Union to enter the war against Japan within three months of Germany's surrender (with territorial concessions pledged to the Soviet Union for its participation)

Date	Conference/Declaration	Key Doctrinal Principle(s)
April 25–June 1945	San Francisco Conference	Design of United Nations Charter; Big Four responsibility for preserving postwar order, with China's inclusion; dismemberment and disarmament of Germany, which would be de-Nazified through occupation
July 17– August 2, 1945	Potsdam Conference/ Potsdam Declaration of July 26	Four powers discuss new procedures for disarming Germany and preventing its resurgence as a military power and encouraging free elections; all former German territory east of the Oder and Neisse Rivers transferred to Polish and Soviet administration; Council of Foreign Ministers created to evaluate a peace settlement, as well as the Allied Control Council to administer it; in addition, Japan given the ultimatum of unconditional surrender and the Soviet Union promises to enter the Pacific War once Germany was subjugated

that **war crimes** had to be punished; German and Japanese atrocities could not be overlooked. Indeed, as the war moved toward its climax, Allied behavior took on the characteristics of bloody revenge. The American and British firebombing of Dresden, an act that targeted city-center churches and palaces filled with refugees and scorched twenty-five thousand or more of its inhabitants in a notorious firestorm in a single night of bombardment[8] seemed more a product of vengeance than of military necessity. So too, did the March 1945, firebombing of Tokyo, which took some eighty thousand lives, as well as the American carpet bombing of thirty-six other Japanese cities, that killed an estimated four hundred thousand civilians.[9] Similarly, the Soviet Army zealously annihilated a despised enemy that had shown no compassion toward Russian prisoners of war and had slaughtered about 3.25 million Soviet soldiers in Nazi custody.[10] The mood of revenge had become so pronounced by the time the United States dropped atomic bombs on Hiroshima and Nagasaki that U.S. general

> "When you are winning a war almost everything that happens can be claimed to be right and wise."
>
> — WINSTON CHURCHILL

Omar N. Bradley observed that man had "grasped the mystery of the atom and rejected the Sermon on the Mount."[11]

The demand for revenge that colored Allied thinking during the closing phases of the war fed off a diabolical image of the enemy. Take, for example, the implicit assumption of **collective guilt** in the Morgenthau Plan for Germany, which Roosevelt and Churchill accepted in principle at the September 1944 Quebec postwar preparation conference. This plan called for "not just reparations, but Germany's return to its eighteenth-century 'agricultural and pastoral' economy, minus all 'war-making industry.'"[12] Germans, it was believed, were all warlike; hence they should be deprived of the tools for waging war.

Growing Discord among the Allies

On May 2, 1945, Berlin surrendered to the Russians, and on May 7 in Reims, France, the Germans agreed to the complete and unconditional surrender of all their forces. On August 14 the Japanese surrendered unconditionally following the devastating bombings of Hiroshima and Nagasaki on August 6 and 9, 1945.

At this point the victors faced a monumental challenge: how to overcome the exhilaration that followed the **strategic surrender** of their adversaries and begin to construct a postwar peace plan that all the Allies could accept. This challenge proved beyond the Allies' capacity, as their interests pushed them in divergent directions. Division rapidly replaced the harmony that had characterized the Allies' postwar peace discussions. As Winston Churchill lamented in his March 5, 1946, Iron Curtain speech in Fulton, Missouri, "a shadow [had] fallen upon the scene so lately lighted by Allied victory."[13]

That latent differences should emerge among the victors regarding the precise terms of the peace settlement is not surprising, because changes in global circumstances historically have preceded redefinitions of national interests, allegiances, and eventual realignments. However, at the end of the war there still remained a basis for the Allies' hope that they would continue to cooperate to build a stable world order: they had successfully overcome their differences during the war. This hope was exhibited in the high level of agreement that had attended the planning at various summit conferences for a new postwar structure of peace even as the war raged. As early as 1943, the Four Power Declaration advanced principles for Allied collaboration following the war. The Allies' determination to create a new international organization to manage the postwar international order—the United Nations (UN)—was conceived in this and other wartime agreements, to ward off any collapse of this cooperation. Consistent with the expectation that the great powers would collaborate to manage world affairs, China was promised a seat on the UN Security Council along with France. Recognizing the benefits of inclusiveness in an attempt to implement **collective security,** the purpose was to guarantee that all of the victorious great powers would share responsibility for keeping the peace.

In practice, the United States and the Soviet Union became most influential because they were the most powerful. However, their ideological differences about capitalism and communism undercut the prospects for their continued solidarity. Still, Franklin Roosevelt and Joseph Stalin had made repeated promises to work together. Upon returning to Washington from the summit conference in Teheran, for instance, President Roosevelt told a national radio audience: "I got along fine with Marshal Stalin. . . . I believe that we are going to get along very well with him and the Russian people — very well indeed."[14] At the Yalta Conference fourteen months later, Stalin echoed Roosevelt's optimism. According to James F. Byrnes, director of the Office of War Mobilization, Stalin had been lavish in his praise of the United States; in fact, "Joe was the life of the party."[15]

Yet the period between the 1943 Teheran and 1945 Yalta **summit conferences** would mark the apogee of Soviet-American cooperative relations. The vague promises of continued unity voiced in these summits concealed many problems, and history would show that the party would end in sobering gloom. When their armies met on April 25, 1945, at the Elbe River, the common military threat had been destroyed. Nonetheless, long-gestating mutual suspicions in Moscow and Washington began to harden almost immediately into policy disagreements over the future of the postwar world. Following the death of Roosevelt in April and Germany's unconditional surrender, the United States, now represented by Harry S Truman, met again with the Soviet Union and Great Britain at Potsdam in July 1945. The meeting ended without agreement over specifics or the larger issues beyond the transfer of territorial boundaries in Europe. The facade of Allied unity began to crumble.

Interallied problems notwithstanding, an air of accommodation prevailed when the victory celebrations commenced. The victors arrived at agreement on some preliminary principles after the truce, in part as a consequence of the thoroughness of the Allied victory. Surrender was unconditional, and the devastated Axis powers were in no position to bargain. Taking advantage of their position of strength, the victors decided to remove Germany and Japan from the ranks of the great powers. Germany was partitioned into four occupation zones that later were used as the basis for creating the Federal Republic of Germany (West Germany) and the German Democratic Republic (East Germany). Japan was occupied by the United States and divested of its conquests in Southeast Asia and Korea.

Partitioning Germany into separate states was not a part of the victors' original peace plan. They had agreed to treat Germany as a single state, with the Allied Control Council in charge. However, the decision to divide Germany into four zones of occupation, with the military commanders-in-chief of each victor given complete administrative authority, had the unintended consequence of preventing any treatment of Germany as a single unit. The Allies' peace policy was therefore not **rational** in the sense that it could be described as a logically consistent and coherent decision. The step-by-step formula did not link means to goals, and the agreement to permit each occupying power to control reparations in its respective zone contradicted the original aim of overseeing Germany as a whole. This inconsistency made the outcome almost a forgone conclusion, when four years later the United States, Great Britain, and France decided to combine their zones in the west to create a central democratic government, freeing the Soviet Union to impose a communist regime in its **sphere of influence** in the remaining zone in the east. Differences among the leaders and within their nations about the best way to make a lasting peace also undermined allied harmony and pushed decision making about a postwar settlement in divergent directions.

Nonetheless, all the victors shared a conception of justice—about what was prudent and moral with regard to suitable punishment of Germany for its aggression and war crimes. The victors agreed that Germany should pay for its sins, and they agreed on four principles to carry out a **retributive** policy. First, they would destroy the remnants of Nazi ideology; Nazi leaders were tried as war criminals for crimes against humanity at the special court established at Nuremburg, which condemned twelve of them to death. Second, the victors agreed to demilitarize Germany, insisting on complete disarmament. Third, the victors undertook a coordinated effort to control and dismantle German industry, under their conviction that deindustrialization was necessary to ensure that Germany's remarkable engineering and technological talents could not be used for weapons production. And finally, at the urging by the West, the Allies agreed to a program of building democratic institutions within Germany as a deterrent to the rise of another totalitarian government under a new autocrat like Hitler. Although in implementation these principles were compromised, they defined the major ideals of the victors.

Most problematic was the issue of territory—who would obtain and control what. A Council of Foreign Ministers was created at the Potsdam Conference for the purpose of working out the terms of surrender in a way that was mutually satisfactory to the victors, but to little avail. Mistrust and acrimony divided the winners, and as **zero-sum** thinking arose about which victors deserved to gain at the other victor's expense, disagreement over the German question led to a settlement that proved unacceptable to all. This division bred a fierce competition that paralyzed collective decision making for many decades. Allied discord and distrust became the seeds from which the Cold War was to grow, as international borders were redrawn across the Eurasian landmass. Out of this redistribution of territorial boundaries the Soviet Union gained nearly 600,000 square meters of territory in the west from the Baltic states of Estonia, Latvia, and Lithuania and from Finland, Czechoslovakia, Poland, and Romania—territorial changes that enabled the Soviet Union to recover what Russia had lost after World War I. Poland was compensated with land taken from Germany (see Map 6.1).

Italy, too, was targeted for punitive treatment, although the perpetrators of Italian aggression were no longer on the scene when the final major peacemaking decisions were taking place. Italy ceased to be a real player in the war after Sicily fell to Anglo-American forces. Fearing that Italy would defect to the Allies, Hitler had sent reinforcements to carry on the fight and watch over the king and Mussolini, whom Hitler restored as a puppet dictator. Mussolini

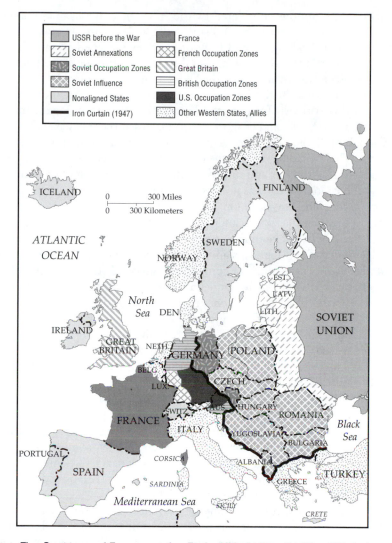

MAP 6.1 The Partitions of Europe at the End of World War II. The Allied victory in Europe shifted the European geostrategic landscape, as borders were redrawn and each of the victors dominated the zones their armies occupied when the fighting stopped. Discord among the winners over territorial issues led to the division between East and West as the so-called Iron Curtain separated the new rivals in the Cold War.

did not survive long enough to see his German ally go down to defeat; he was captured and executed by Italian partisans. This took the sting out of the debate about how to treat Italy and the other minor states that had aligned with the Axis powers. At Potsdam, the Council of Foreign Ministers was assigned the task of negotiating the peace settlement with Italy and the other states that had been aligned with the German-Japanese Axis (Romania, Bulgaria, Hungary, and Finland) when they surrendered. The border and territorial transfer options considered by the Allies quickly became wrapped up in the larger controversies that poisoned the relationship between Moscow and its allies in Washington and London, as they searched in vain for a bargain to safeguard their goodwill and make a satisfactory peace settlement.

Finally, pro-Soviet regimes with the USSR's support assumed power throughout Eastern Europe. In the Far East, the Soviet Union took the four Kurile Islands, or the Northern Territories as Japan calls them, from Japan, and Korea was divided into Soviet and U.S. occupation zones at the thirty-eighth parallel.

World War II thus produced a massive redistribution of power based on landmass. The United States was the only one of the great powers whose economy grew during the war and surged to equal that of the rest of the world combined — the United States was not just wealthier than anyone, it was wealthier than everyone. The Soviet Union, though economically exhausted, possessed the largest army in the world, and its annexation of the northern half of East Prussia, along with its expanding sphere of influence, catapulted it to the status of a superpower. The Americans and Russians now held in their hands the fates of half the world's populaton. In comparison, all other states were dwarfs.

All alliances are inherently fragile, and even wartime allies tend to quarrel despite the bond of a common enemy. In this regard, the victorious Grand Alliance was never altogether "grand" while it collectively sought to engineer victory. The United States, Great Britain, and the Soviet Union had interests that were not always convergent, and this became apparent at times even while the three Allies worked together to subdue Germany, Japan, and Italy. In fact, the hostility felt by the American and Soviet allies for one another, while glossed over during the war when the need to suppress the discord was overwhelming, was always recognized as a probable danger. Without a common goal to unite them, victory only magnified the growing distrust that each great power harbored about the others' motives.

It is important to inspect more closely how the peace settlements struck at the end of World War II influenced Soviet-American relations and international stability over the next fifty years. This was an era during which the **Cold War** unfolded, while Germany and Japan rose from the ashes of defeat to become prosperous economic powers without military ambitions. It is instructive to review the policy redirections that took place in Washington and Moscow at the end of World War II when the two major victorious powers struggled to find a formula for peacefully managing international affairs.

The Origins of a Forty-Year Peace Settlement Process

The preeminent status of the United States and the Soviet Union at the top of the international hierarchy at the end of World War II gave each superpower reason to be wary of the other. However, their collision was not predetermined. After victory had been achieved, new efforts were made by both superpowers to construct rules for continuing cooperative engagement. These efforts proceeded crabwise, with zigs and zags in different directions

TABLE 6.3
Major Postwar Peace Plans, 1945–1951

Date	Proposed Plan	Goals
June 14, 1946	Baruch Plan to create the new UN Atomic Energy Commission	An international authority is proposed to exercise monopoly control over all atomic energy production and use for war purposes (this proposal was not accepted unanimously, with the Soviet Union leading the opposition)
February 10, 1947	Treaties of Paris	Italy loses its colonial empire, which became UN mandates, and cedes territory on the Adriatic Sea to Yugoslavia and the Dodeconese Islands to Greece
1947–1952	Marshall Plan (European Recovery Program)	Massive $50 billion U.S. foreign assistance program to rebuild Europe's war-torn economy, in order not only to ensure a market for American exports but to strengthen Europe's capacity to resist communist subversion and Soviet domination
September 8, 1951	Treaty of San Francisco	In agreement with forty-eight allied states, Japan accepts the loss of all territory acquired in its past wars since 1895 and consents to an imposed constitution which declares that "the Japanese people forever renounce war as a sovereign right of the nation"

through a series of agreements (see Table 6.3). Unfortunately, they did not succeed in reaching agreements; many issues (such as the future of Germany) were simply postponed without resolution. A final settlement was not reached until the Cold War ended nearly a half-century later.

Why did the superpowers fail to reach a conclusive and permanent peace settlement that all the Allied victors could accept? To answer that question, we must put the problematic role of disagreements about how to treat the key defeated nations of Germany and Japan into the equation. The Soviets and Americans came to very different conclusions on this fundamental issue, and those differences became the primary source of the failure to arrive at a final peace settlement for another four decades.

DIVISION OVER THE TREATMENT OF GERMANY AND JAPAN

Despite their deep resentment of the German and Japanese aggressors, the United States and Great Britain began in the early postwar period to radically shift their thinking about the value of retribution. Recalling that the harsh terms of the Versailles treaty had contributed to the rise of fascism, Churchill and Roosevelt repudiated vengeance in favor of a policy guided by magnanimity, in the expectation that assistance with the restoration and reform of Germany and Japan could repair those prostrate states and permit them to play a constructive role in the new world order. Rather than require reparations for the costs of the war, the United States and Great Britain undertook steps to resuscitate their former enemies — much to the dismay of the Soviet Union, which clung tenaciously to the Allies' prior agreement to exact revenge.

Resuscitating Germany

Britain and the United States began to lose confidence in and patience with Joseph Stalin and against this background found it increasingly prudent to question the wisdom of a punitive approach to Germany and Japan. Given Russia's perceived intransigence, its prompt institutionalization of Russian regional hegemony over the eastern half of Europe (which had been liberated by the Red Army, with Roosevelt's tacit support[16]), and the heavy reparations it extracted in its zones of occupation, the United States began to rethink its prior punitive peace settlement philosophy toward Germany and Japan. At the same time, the United States was facing the reality of growing Soviet ambitions and the collapse of unity within the Allied Control Commission. The Soviets appeared intent on reaping the fruits of war and expanding their power, and, in light of this, U.S. leaders came to the conclusion that rising Russian influence needed to be balanced. That goal, in turn, required a different plan — one that replaced the impulse toward revenge with a policy seeking reconciliation with Germany and Japan. The spirit of Yalta and Potsdam quickly evaporated, and the interallied tension level escalated in the first few years after the surrender of Germany and Japan (see Box 6.2).

The signal of the U.S. change of heart was conveyed dramatically by U.S. Secretary of State James F. Byrnes. "The gamecock from South Carolina," as he was known, was in a fighting mood — not toward America's former enemy, but its former ally. In a major turning-point speech in Stuttgart on September 6, 1946, Byrnes drew a sword, which the Soviets promptly interpreted as not only an intentional breach in the Soviet-American relationship, but a declaration of enmity. In that speech Byrnes declared that a policy of reform, rehabilitation, resuscitation, and reconciliation would now define U.S. policy toward West Germany. Germany, he informed the audience, would be allowed to earn its way back into the international community, and the United States would assist the reconstruction and democratization program, backed by financial assistance and the promise of U.S. military protection.

In a repudiation to prior agreements, Byrnes refused to recognize the Oder-Neisse frontier between Germany and Poland, throwing American support behind the German people's wish for the restoration of the sizable

---

BOX 6.2
THE END OF THE SOVIET-AMERICAN WARTIME ALLIANCE:
KEY EVENTS IN THE SLIPPERY SLOPE TO THE COLD WAR

1945

- United States rejects Soviet request for $6 billion reconstruction loan
- Churchill, Roosevelt, and Stalin (the Big Three) sign Yalta agreement
- United States approves transfer of Kurile Islands to Soviet Union
- Moscow formally abrogates 1925 Turko-Soviet Friendship Treaty, makes territorial demands
- Allied Control Council establishes four-power occupation of Berlin and right to determine Germany's boundaries
- San Francisco Conference approves UN Charter
- Korea partitioned into Soviet and American occupation zones
- Churchill, Stalin, and Truman attend Potsdam Conference
- United States drops atomic bomb on Hiroshima
- Chiang Kai-shek and Molotov sign Sino-Soviet friendship treaty
- Soviet-Polish treaty recognizes Oder-Neisse line as Poland's western border
- Iranian rebellion, supported by Soviet arms, erupts; civil war resumes in China
- Big Three meet at Moscow Conference; Secretary of State James F. Byrnes agrees to recognize Romanian and Bulgarian satellite governments

1946

- Soviet Union protests British role in Greek civil war
- United States protests the continued presence of Soviet troops in Iran
- United States leads UN involvement in Iranian crisis over Soviet protest
- Stalin announces new Soviet Five-Year Plan making rearmament a priority for defense against foreign encroachment
- Churchill delivers militantly anti-Soviet Iron Curtain speech in Fulton, Missouri
- Council of Foreign Ministers convenes Paris Peace Conference
- General Lucius Clay stops reparations to Soviet zone of Germany
- Soviets reject Baruch Plan to destroy atomic weapons and place control of nuclear energy in international hands
- Japan's wartime leaders (including Emperor Hirohito) imprisoned or hanged following Tokyo war crimes trials
- United States signs treaty of friendship and commerce with China
- Iran crushes independence movement in Azerbaijan with U.S. aid
- Treaties at New York Foreign Ministers Conference confirm U.S. recognition of Soviet control in southeastern Europe
- War breaks out in Vietnam

(cont.)

(Box 6.2 cont.)
1947

- The United States and Great Britain merge their occupation zones in Germany, January 1
- United States charges violation of Yalta agreement following communist electoral victory in Poland
- Britain and France sign a fifty-year Treaty of Alliance and Mutual Assistance at Dunkirk
- Truman Doctrine pledges aid to Greece, Turkey, and others resisting communism
- Big Four Foreign Ministers Conference in Moscow concludes without agreement
- Communists smash Hungarian ruling party
- Secretary of State George C. Marshall announces European Recovery Program (Marshall Plan)
- Under Soviet pressure, Poland and Hungary decline Marshall Plan assistance
- George F. Kennan's "X" article proposing U.S. containment of Soviet communism, based on 1946 telegram sent from Moscow, published in *Foreign Affairs*
- NSC-68 blueprint moves U.S. foreign policy from containment to confrontational strategy against Soviets
- Soviet Union charges that the United States threatens war
- General Agreement on Tariffs and Trade (GATT) treaty signed by twenty-three countries
- Rio Pact for collective defense of Western Hemisphere commits the United States and Latin American republics to mutual assistance against aggression
- United States, Australia, and New Zealand conclude ANZUS tripartite security treaty
- Comintern revived by Soviet Union and greatly expanded as Cominform
- London Council of Foreign Ministers ends without agreement on mutual administration of occupation zones in Germany

1948

- Communist coup occurs in Czechoslovakia
- Soviet Union withdraws from the Allied Control Council, March 20
- Brussels Treaty calls for cooperation among Belgium, France, Luxembourg, the Netherlands and the United Kingdom; creates Brussels Pact military alliance to repel attack
- Soviet Union imposes a blockade on Berlin (from June 20, 1948, until May 1949) after the Western powers implement currency reform in their occupation sectors of Germany
- United States and Great Britain supply West Berlin with a massive airlift

- Organization of European Economic Cooperation (OEEC) established to disburse Marshall Plan funds
- Organization of American States (OAS) created to replace the Pan American Union
- Vandenberg Resolution pledges U.S. support for Brussels Treaty and defense agreements in Europe
- Brussels Treaty powers, Canada, and the United States meet in Washington to create North Atlantic defense treaty

1949

- "Point Four" of Truman's inaugural address promises aid to developing countries
- Council for Mutual Economic Assistance (Comecon) is created for Soviet assistance in Europe
- Negotiating powers invite Denmark, Iceland, Italy, Norway, and Portugal to adhere to the North Atlantic Treaty
- Soviet Union protests that prospective North Atlantic Treaty Organization (NATO) is contrary to UN Charter
- NATO formed with signing of North Atlantic Treaty
- London Ten-Power Agreement creates the Council of Europe
- Berlin blockade lifted; separate West and East German governments established when Western powers' occupation zones are merged to form the Federal Republic of Germany and the Soviets establish the German Democratic Republic in their zone (Berlin remains under four-power occupation until the reunification of Germany in 1990)
- Mao Ze-dong unifies mainland China and proclaims People's Republic of China
- Greek civil war ends in communist defeat
- Mutual Defense Assistance Act pledges U.S. aid to countries vulnerable to communist pressure

1950

- United States announces intention to build hydrogen bomb
- Soviet Union begins eight-month boycott of UN Security Council
- Soviet Union and Communist China sign thirty-year Mutual Aid Pact
- National Security Council issues Memorandum No. 68
- North Korean forces invade South Korea and capture Seoul; U.S. troops enter Korea with orders to defend Formosa and prevent Chiang's forces from attacking mainland China
- United States invades North Korea; South Korean troops cross thirty-eighth parallel
- U.S. proposes to British and French that German divisions be added to NATO, though Potsdam agreement had forbidden German participation in Western European defense   *(cont.)*

(Box 6.2 cont.)

- Greece and Turkey accept North Atlantic Council invitation to participate in Mediterranean defense planning
- East German-Polish treaty ends dispute over border
- UN General Assembly passes the Uniting for Peace Resolution

1951

- Secretary of State Marshall tells Senate that Chinese Nationalists were beaten by communists due to lack of public support and "the character of their government"
- San Francisco peace treaty ends state of war with Japan (Russia and China not included)
- Treaty establishing European Coal and Steel Community (ECSC) signed
- Mutual Security Act pledges U.S. military assistance throughout the world
- Korean truce line (thirty-eighth parallel) accepted at United Nations

---

territory Germany had been required to cede to Poland (to compensate Poland for the territory it had been forced to cede to the Soviet Union).

The message to the relieved and applauding Germans was one of compassion. America would live up to the most charitable liberal ideals in its heritage, treating all others as equals in the community of nations. However, parochial self-interest also appeared as a U.S. motive: "This was a straightforward message to the Soviet Union that the United States was not going to permit Germany to be completely absorbed into any communist sphere."[17] This balance-of-power realpolitik policy was geared toward a clear geostrategic objective: to remove the Soviet Union from the path of the peace process and clear the way for the recovery of Germany, and with it, the rest of Europe.

With this turnabout in U.S. policy toward a conciliatory approach to the Germans, U.S. policy toward the Soviets had also changed and become combative. The wartime Allies would now proceed separately, acting independently in their respective spheres of influence. With the breakup of this wartime partnership, the European geostrategic landscape shifted, and the way was paved for the division of Europe into two blocs, with the east controlled by Moscow and the west dominated by the United States.

Resuscitating Japan

The new U.S. policy of assisting in the recovery of Germany did not mean that a nonretributive peace philosophy would remain confined to the European continent. The United States also abandoned a vindictive approach for a conciliatory one in the Far East. General Douglas MacArthur, the commander of the U.S. occupation forces, built a recovery and reform program on the principle that, in a country in which "face" matters greatly, America's long-term interest did not sanction the humiliation of the Japanese. In August 1945 MacArthur stated his goals, and the liberal peacemaking philosophy that would define U.S. policy in postwar Japan, when he directed the occupation forces he commanded to destroy Japan's military power, punish its war criminals, build a representative government, establish a free press, and encourage an open economic system. Permitting the emperor to retain his position of prestige to facilitate Japanese compliance, the United States dismantled the country's feudal system and built new democratic institutions in its place. MacArthur's staff drafted a new constitution for Japan which went into effect May 3, 1947. Article IX of the Constitution pledged that Japan would "forever renounce . . . the threat or use of force as a means of settling disputes" and prohibited Japan's right to maintain "land, sea, and air forces, as well as other war potential." Similarly, U.S. reform policy redistributed land from baron families to tenant farmers, gave women rights equal to men, and encouraged the formation of powerful trade unions. The Constitution also established a parliamentary form of democratic government similar to the British system and instituted procedures to protect civil liberties such as a free press and free speech.

Consistent with this reform program, the U.S. occupation forces exercised respect for those the United States had vanquished. Japanese customs and courtesies were honored, and MacArthur encouraged his own troops (whom he disarmed to lessen Japanese anxieties and resentment) to fraternize with the Japanese people and educate them about the meaning of democracy.

Behind the ideals inspiring the United States' compassionate policy of revival and reconciliation was a stronger, ulterior motive. The United States had powerful geostrategic interests in assisting Japan's recovery because of the fear that a weakened Japan could fall prey to the expanding influence of the Soviet Union. With this in mind, the United States encouraged full economic recovery without restriction and with the help of U.S. financial assistance.

Reconciliation and resuscitation, in short, served U.S. interests as well as its ideals; the compassionate postwar peace plan emerged from a combination of American faith in liberal democracy and the United States' need for a strong Japan which could be shaped into a faithful American ally. The philosophy practiced by the United States — treat the former enemy forgivingly, in conformity with the Golden Rule — bred Japanese goodwill and appreciation that paid huge dividends to the future Japanese-American diplomatic relationship.

The Treaty of San Francisco that was signed on September 8, 1951 (without inclusion of the Soviet Union, which did not issue a declaration ending its state of war with Japan until October 19, 1956), terminated the state of war with the United States and forty-eight other states and allowed the American occupation force to exit Japan on April 28, 1952. The treaty contained no demands for reparations or restrictions on Japan's foreign policy. The treaty signaled the forceful conversion of Japan to a liberal democracy dedicated to peace. Japan's climb to the top of the global pyramid of economic power began. In addition, by reorganizing Japan's right to defend itself militarily, the Japanese peace settlement transformed the global **balance of power** and, by so doing, completed the break between the American and

Soviet wartime allies. In conjunction, the U.S. shift from retaliation against Germany and Japan to assistance of both countries produced changes of massive proportions. Both of these defeated foes soon became steadfast members of the community of liberal democratic and free-market capitalist states and the most reliable allies of the United States. Fed by vast sums of U.S. financial assistance under the shield of the U.S. nuclear umbrella, Germany and Japan also became economic giants. They were freed from the burden of heavy defense expenditures, and both were liberated from the legacy of their imperial traditions.

Germany's and Japan's active participation in the liberal economic order as U.S. allies undoubtedly contributed to the stability of the emerging **multipolar** system and its continuing prosperity in the free-trade regime among the industrialized democracies of the northern hemisphere. The achievement of the longest period of great-power peace in the past half-millennium in this part of the world testifies to the payoff that the compassionate reconstruction policies of the Western Allies provided. History has few cases of successful peace settlements that approximate this remarkable accomplishment — the most enduring **long peace.** By permitting Germany and Japan to reenter the liberal community of democratic nations, the United States allowed these states to build stable governments, provide leadership in the integration of a globalized political economy, and to participate in the defense of liberal values. Both former enemies became among the most faithful allies of the United States and major partners in trade, investment, and development-assistance ventures. In retrospect, the rewards and returns of this reconciliatory policy were remarkable and provided the basis for a **democratic peace** predicated on the principle that democratic governance, if it spreads, will be an antidote to war because democracies rarely wage war against each other.

This outcome of this resuscitative policy should not automatically lead to the conclusion that the rewards of reconciliation between the Western Allies and the Axis powers came without substantial costs. The schism that culminated in the Cold War between the East and West exacted an enormous toll and became a primary consequence of the goodwill that allowed Germany and Japan to become members of the Western bloc that united in solidarity throughout the Cold War.

That a compassionate peace settlement between Germany and Japan and the United States could cause a Cold War to break out between the United States and the Soviet Union presents a puzzle. Is intra-allied discord and disunity a likely price in the aftermath of victory? Was the Soviet-American conflict necessary? Did the differences in the postwar peace goals and philosophies of the victors produce this colossal hegemonic struggle between two titans and postpone final resolution of a post–World War II settlement for over forty years?

> "Peace, like war, can succeed only where there is a will to enforce it and where there is available power to enforce it."
>
> — FRANKLIN D. ROOSEVELT

THE ORIGINS OF THE COLD WAR

Lacking the glue of a common external threat, the Grand Alliance of World War II began to dissolve amidst distrust, apprehension, and recriminations. Stalin insisted in 1946 that the defeat of Germany did not eliminate the danger of foreign aggression, and his heir apparent, Andrei Zhdanov, in 1947 identified American expansionism as the major threat to world peace. On the other hand, W. Averell Harriman, U.S. ambassador to the Soviet Union, warned of a probable "barbarian invasion of Europe"[18] from America's former wartime ally.

The United States and the Soviet Union, former partners in war, ceased to remain allies and became foes. Each superpower acted in accordance with the realpolitik premise that the only language a recalcitrant rival understands is military might. President Truman, a staunch realist, for example, argued that "unless Russia is faced with an iron fist and strong language, another war is in the making."[19] U.S. Secretary of State James F. Byrnes agreed, maintaining, "The only way to negotiate with the Russians is to hit them hard."[20]

The Cold War originated in part because of the superpowers' mutual disdain for their rivals' political system and way of life. As James F. Byrnes argued at the conclusion of World War II, "There is too much difference in the ideologies of the United States and Russia to work out a long-term program of cooperation." Such assumptions were widely held in both Washington and Moscow, and these ideological differences converted the rivalry from a conflict of interests between two powerful states to a conflict between two opposed philosophies for organizing systems of governance and economics within states. Whether real or imagined, U.S. fears of Marxism stoked the flames of anticommunism at home and ignited a global crusade to remove the communist ideology from the face of the earth.[21] The rupture in U.S.-Soviet relations occurred bit by bit, ultimately producing a schism that would place the competitors for global hegemonic leadership in the throes of a classic **security dilemma** that reduced their sense of safety, and placed the rest of humanity on the edge of nuclear destruction. As UN Secretary-General Trygve Lie lamented on September 23, 1947, in his plea for a return to the spirit of Yalta and San Francisco, "The very cornerstone of the UN, Big Power cooperation and understanding, is being shaken."[22]

American leaders acted on the perception that the triumph of communism in one country would cause the fall of its neighbors, and still others in turn. This prediction, which became known as the **domino theory,** maintained that, like a row of falling dominoes, a chain reaction would bring the entire world under communist domination unless checked by the power of the United States and its allies. Similarly, Soviet policy was energized by the assumption that in the long run capitalism could not coexist with communism. "A funeral dirge will be sung either over the Soviet Republic or over world capitalism," Lenin once predicted.[23] Believing that their security would be enhanced if class struggle spread across the globe, Soviet leaders were dismayed by their former wartime allies' efforts to smother communist movements in Japan, Germany, and other states within their occupation zones.

Mistrustful states are prone to see in their own actions only virtue and in those of their adversaries only malice. When such **mirror images** exist, hostility becomes likely.[24] Each side imposes its definition of reality on events, and they then become captives to those nightmarish visions. George F. Kennan, the American ambassador to the Soviet Union in 1952, noted how misread signals, common to both sides, eroded the wartime allies' unity:

> The Marshall Plan, the preparations for the setting up of a West German government, and the first moves toward the establishment of NATO were taken in Moscow as the beginnings of a campaign to deprive the Soviet Union of the fruits of its victory over Germany. The Soviet crackdown on Czechoslovakia (1948) and the mounting of the Berlin blockade, both essentially defensive . . . reactions to these Western moves, were then similarly misread on the Western side. Shortly thereafter there came the crisis of the Korean War, where the Soviet attempt to employ a satellite military force in civil combat to its own advantage, by way of reaction to the American decision to establish a permanent military presence in Japan, was read in Washington as the beginning of the final Soviet push for world conquest; whereas the active American military response, provoked by this move, appeared in Moscow . . . as a threat to the Soviet position in both Manchuria and in eastern Siberia.[25]

Thus, in the Cold War's formative stage, U.S. leaders and their allies in the West saw the many crises that erupted as part of a Soviet plan for world domination. The Soviets viewed these same crises altogether differently — as tests of their resolve and as Western efforts to destroy their socialist experiment. Both states operated from the same "inherent bad faith" image of their rival's intentions, and this precluded their cooperation in postwar planning for peace.

Additional factors beyond those rooted in divergent interests, ideologies, and images undoubtedly combined to transform a wartime Soviet-American alliance into an explosive hegemonic rivalry. Whatever the relative influence of the individual factors that combined to produce it, the Cold War's rise was profoundly affected, in the last analysis, by the realignment of the vanquished World War II powers (Germany and Japan) with two of the victors (the United States and Great Britain). The great schism between the United States and the Soviet Union that converted former allies into Cold War antagonists was accelerated by the Western powers' conciliatory patterns toward Germany and Japan and the Soviet Union's belief that this move was designed to encircle the Soviet Union and smother the communist movement. "Nothing," Harry Truman had argued at the organizing conference of the United Nations in San Francisco, was "more essential to the future peace of the world than the continued cooperation of the nations which had to muster the force necessary to defeat the conspiracy of the Axis powers to dominate the world."[26] That cooperation, however, had collapsed. With its collapse came the collapse of the postwar peace settlement process.

THE LONG ROAD TO A POSTWAR PEACE SETTLEMENT

Once the wartime alliance had splintered into two competing factions, the challenge for the United States and the Soviet Union became that of developing rules to prevent their Cold War from turning hot. The postwar settlement with the Axis powers could not be finalized until this obstacle was overcome. During the treacherous course of the next forty years, the two superpowers struggled in their search to avoid war. Mutual recrimination often poisoned their efforts. However, the challenge was eventually met. A set of rules gradually emerged, through trial and error, and disputes between the Kremlin and the White House never escalated to war. Among the implicit rules in this security regime were an acceptance of separate spheres of influence, avoidance of direct military confrontations, maintenance of a sharp distinction between conventional and nuclear weapons, and forgoing the first use of the latter. Still, both sides paid a staggering price for their rivalry. The United States alone spent an estimated $10 trillion to contain the Soviet Union, an expenditure equivalent to "enough to buy everything in the United States except the land."[27] The costs of waging the Cold War were not just financial; both sides paid a heavy psychological price. They had to survive in the shadow of possible nuclear annihilation. Throughout the Cold War's long evolution, there were many periods when fears of nuclear war increased as tension mounted and the arms race escalated, interrupted by occasional periods of **détente** when confrontation was replaced by a relaxation of tension between the adversaries. Yet, over the troubled course of this global contest of will, the former allies during World War II managed to coexist peacefully without taking up arms against each other directly. Given a circumstance involving a choice between nonviolence and nonexistence, the enemies choose to peacefully coexist.

Exhausted economically, in the 1980s reform-minded Mikhail Gorbachev sought to reconcile his country's differences with the liberal democracies in the capitalist West in order to halt the Soviet Union's deteriorating global position. His pursuit of **rapprochement** — normalization of relations — paid a big and unexpected dividend: The Cold War — which began in Europe and had centered on Europe for over forty years — ended there in 1991, when the Soviet Union dissolved. All communist governments in the Soviet **bloc** in Eastern Europe permitted democratic elections in which Communist Party candidates routinely lost. Capitalist free markets replaced socialism and, astonishingly, the Soviet Union acquiesced in these revolutionary changes.

This momentous sea change allows us to appreciate how a true peace settlement of the scars of World War II was finally reached when the Berlin Wall

---

CONTROVERSIES TO CONTEMPLATE

- What issues were at stake when the victors in World War II began discussions to fulfill the mission described in December 9, 1941, by Franklin D. Roosevelt: "We are going to win the war and we are going to win the peace"?
- Did the victors learn lessons about how to build peace from the failures of the post–World War I settlement at Versailles a generation earlier? What were those perceived lessons? Were they accurate?
- Is it possible to plan for peace when a war is still being fought? What obstacles interfere with successful postwar planning? Was Winston Churchill wise when he advised, "It is a mistake to look too far ahead. Only one link in the chain of destiny can be handled at one time"?
- Can wartime alliances outlast the defeat of common enemies? What problems bred competition and conflict among the former Allies of World War II?
- Did the Grand Alliance of the victors disintegrate because of their divergent philosophies about lenient vis-à-vis punitive treatment of vanquished enemies? To what extent did the differences in the victors' types of political and economic systems cause them to part ways?
- Why did the United States (and Great Britain) treat Germany and Japan so leniently after World War II, considering the injustice of the aggressors' cause and criminality of their brutal wartime deeds?
- Was the post–World War II settlement successful or flawed? What are the best criteria for evaluating success or failure?
- What international, societal, institutional, and individual variables most influenced the victors' war-making and peacemaking decisions?
- Were the postwar peacekeeping approaches of the United States, Great Britain, and the Soviet Union inspired most by realist or liberal thought? What does this case say about the relative benefits and limitations of these two theories?

---

was torn down in 1989 and the Warsaw Pact began to disintegrate. It was not really until 1990, when the Soviet Union reversed its long-standing opposition to German reunification and agreed to withdraw its troops from Europe (in exchange for the promise that Germany would not rearm and that the United States would keep a military presence on German soil through NATO), that the Cold War ended and a final settlement of the disagreements that surfaced at the end of the Second World War was truly struck. On September 12, 1990, the Four Powers (the United States, the Soviet Union, Great Britain, and France) and the two Germanys (the "Two

> "Compromise does not mean cowardice."
>
> — JOHN F. KENNEDY

plus Four") signed the Treaty on the Final Settlement with Respect to Germany, which terminated the Four Powers' rights over Germany and made the reunification of Germany possible. German leaders agreed to make no territorial claims in Europe, including the territories in Poland that were annexed during and after World War II.[28] Moreover, German leaders pledged never to obtain nuclear, biological, or chemical weapons and to reduce their 670,000-person armed forces to 370,000 troops (in exchange for the removal of 370,000 Soviet soldiers from Germany). Afterward, Germany and the Soviet Union signed a bilateral treaty under which the two powers promised never to attack each other but instead to cooperate economically for the next twenty years.

The dramatic change these agreements produced was enshrined in the 1992 Camp David Declaration on New Relations, which proclaimed that "from now on the relationship [between Russia and the United States] will be characterized by friendship and partnership, founded on mutual trust." At long last, the Cold War was over, and with its collapse it was finally possible for the issues left unresolved since the end of World War II to be put to rest.

There is a possible lesson suggested by this exceptional case about the prospects for peacemaking, because the abrupt end of the Cold War suggested something quite different from the lesson of the two world wars: that **enduring rivalries** between great powers are doomed to end in armed conflict. The Cold War was different; it came to an end peacefully. This suggests that great powers with hegemonic aspirations are capable of settling their struggles without bloodshed and that it is sometimes possible for them to build enduring détentes to manage their competition and eventually resolve their disputes.

As we have seen in this chapter, military victory can easily breed conflict among victorious allies unless they manage their relationship carefully. It is important for them to reach a consensus on the terms of a postwar settlement before their guns fall silent. Victors must prepare for peace if they wish it to prevail, and preparations for constructing a satisfactory peace settlement should begin early in the war.

SUGGESTED READING

Bell, P. M. H. *The Origins of the Second World War in Europe.* London: Longman, 1986.

Churchill, Winston. *The Gathering Storm.* Boston: Houghton Mifflin, 1948.

Dower, John W. *Embracing Defeat: Japan in the Wake of World War II.* New York: Norton, 2000.

Feis, Herbert. *The Atomic Bomb and the End of World War II.* Princeton, N.J.: Princeton University Press, 1966.

Mitrany, David. *A Working Peace System.* Chicago: Quadrangle, 1966.

Murray, Williamson, and Allan R. Millett. *A War to Be Won: Fighting the Second World War.* Cambridge, Mass.: Harvard University Press, 2000.

Newhouse, John. *War and Peace in the Nuclear Age.* New York: Knopf, 1989.

Shirer, William L. *The Collapse of the Third Republic.* New York: Simon & Schuster, 1969.

Sigal, Leon V. *Fighting to a Finish: The Politics of War Termination in the United States and Japan, 1945.* Ithaca, N.Y.: Cornell University Press, 1988.

Yergin, Daniel. *Shattered Peace: The Origins of the Cold War and the National Security State.* Boston: Houghton Mifflin, 1977.

NOTES

1. Hitler is reported to have declared when he heard that the Soviet Union had agreed to the German-Soviet nonaggression treaty on August 23, 1939, "Now Europe is mine. The others can have Asia."
2. Holsti, 1991, pp. 224–225.
3. Shriver, 1996, p. 77.
4. Kissinger, 1994, p. 390.
5. Holsti, 1991, p. 243.
6. Morgenthau, 1985, p. 591.
7. Holsti, 1991, p. 243.
8. See Jenkins, 1995.
9. Shriver, 1995, p. 133.
10. Davies, 1994, p. 23.
11. In Green, 1982, p. 94, citing a speech Bradley delivered on Armistice Day in 1948.
12. Shriver, 1996, p. 79.
13. Cook, 1989, p. 53.
14. *Public Papers and Addresses of Franklin D. Roosevelt, 1943,* p. 558.
15. In Yergin, 1977, p. 67.
16. Keylor, 1996, p. 255.
17. Puchala, 1996, p. A9.
18. Truman, 1955, p. 71.
19. Ibid., p. 552.
20. Paterson, 1978, p. 314.
21. Commager, 1983; Morgenthau, 1985; Gardner, 1970.
22. Schuman, 1958, p. 235.
23. In Kegley and Wittkopf, 1997, p. 83.
24. See Bronfenbrenner, 1971.
25. Kennan, 1976, pp. 683–684.
26. Kissinger, 1994, p. 424.
27. Sagan, 1992, p. 24.
28. The German-Polish treaty of November 14, 1990, confirmed the continuation of the Oder-Neisse border as the permanent frontier between these two states.

PART IV

The Face of War and Peace on the Eve of the Twenty-First Century

The character of warfare has dramatically changed since the end of the Cold War in 1989. According to the Stockholm International Peace Research Institute (SIPRI), 110 armed conflicts broke out around the world in the period between 1989 and 1999. These included 7 that broke out between states and 103 that erupted within states, with 9 of the latter resulting in external military interventions. The civil wars that occurred within states took the international community by surprise, and led many people to ask what could be done to prevent or lessen the bloodletting. Sadly, these new wars have proven difficult to terminate. According to the same inventory, less than one-third of these armed conflicts have been terminated by formal peace agreements. War and peacemaking have taken on a new face.

In Part IV, we present two cases representative of the kinds of wars and troubled peace settlements that appear destined to dominate the twenty-first century. Together, the cases provide detailed information about how national interests and ethical values are woven into the process by which decisions about war and peacemaking are made. And in the blow-by-blow accounts of these two separate disputes, we can see the tangle of factors that condition the victors' decisions when war making ceases and peacemaking commences.

The Persian Gulf War of 1991 is the case of an armed conflict between contemporary enemies who are unequal in power. Looking at this multilateral effort by great powers to enforce peace in the post–Cold War era affords an opportunity to assess the practicality of collective security. The lasting controversies surrounding the Persian Gulf War, which failed to remove Iraqi dictator Saddam Hussein from power, indicate the extent to which military interventions into the internal affairs of independent states are successful. In this case, no peace settlement was achieved. Moreover, postwar economic sanctions proved ineffectual as an alternative to military enforcement because they brought suffering to the civilian population and strengthened the Iraqi political elite the sanctions were designed to punish.

The Persian Gulf War highlights the changing character of contemporary warfare, now fought more frequently through multilateral collective armed force than was common in previous periods of history. Accordingly, paths to peace for contemporary warfare differ in many respects from traditional approaches to peacemaking. Formerly diplomats could make the assumption that negotiations between victors and vanquished would unfold based on rational calculations of national geostrategic interests. Today other factors such as issues of history, culture, economics, and even religion and ethnicity need to be understood.

The next case adds yet another piece to this perplexing puzzle by examining a civil war within the failed state of Yugoslavia, where a government has committed acts of atrocity against an ethnic minority population, prompting outside humanitarian intervention. The case of the 1999 war in Kosovo hints at what may be the wave of the future and suggests how we might begin thinking about new ways to build durable peace settlements.

The triumph of democracy in Serbia in late 2000 following the U.S.-backed intervention in Kosovo and the earlier NATO intervention in Bosnia has inspired confidence in some quarters that humanitarian intervention can help protect human rights. However, critics are quick to point out the obstacles to using military force for moral purpose. When should states use or threaten the use of military force? Must core national interests be at stake for military action to be justified? What problems constitute real threats that warrant war as an instrument of statecraft? As these cases suggest, reaching agreement on the criteria for humanitarian intervention, even in the name of high ideals, is difficult.

The cases in Part IV reveal a great deal about the morality and practicality of waging war for high ideals. When reading, reflect on the views of UN Secretary-General Kofi Annan about when a military response is justified for humanitarian ends. The challenge, he submits, is finding "ways of deciding what action is necessary, and when, and by whom." The world cannot stand idly by while horror unfolds, he argues. However, to arrest the emerging threats to peace, it is imperative that the global community address some difficult questions: What is the common interest? Who shall define it? And under whose authority?

· 7 ·

THE PERSIAN GULF WAR:
A HOLLOW VICTORY

The end game: it was bad.
— MAJOR GENERAL BARRY McCAFFREY,
COMMANDER, 24TH U.S. MECHANIZED DIVISION

PREVIEW

World Wars I and II were complex global wars that radically altered the international distribution of military and economic power. Not every war involves such stupendous collisions between great powers. Many wars are asymmetrical: They involve contestants that are unequal in military capability and economic resources. While asymmetrical wars may have a significant impact on the belligerents and their immediate neighbors, they seldom have enormous long-term consequences for the structure and processes operating within the larger world system.

The case in this chapter highlights a new kind of war that marks a transition from the modern era in the twentieth century, as a prelude to the kinds of warfare likely in the twenty-first century: the Persian Gulf War of 1991, an asymmetrical conflict between Iraq and a large, diverse coalition led by the United States. Various asymmetrical wars could have been selected to compare with the system-transforming wars covered in previous chapters. We have selected the Persian Gulf War for several reasons. As the first war of the post–Cold War era, it provides an opportunity to probe the limits of multilateral peace enforcement under the auspices of the reinvigorated United Nations. Nothing like this had been approved by the UN Security Council during the previous four decades. Second, as the world's first electronic war —fought with stealth aircraft, infrared targeting systems, precision-guided weapons, and global positioning satellite devices—it gives us a glimpse of what warfare and the problems of peacemaking may be like in the twenty-first century. Finally, although the outcome of the Persian Gulf War did not transform the world system, it did have wider implications for regional security in the Middle East and for the energy policies of industrialized nations in Europe, Asia, and North America. The Persian Gulf War thus deserves attention because, although it was not a war fought to end all wars, it was a war that changed war: It was the first war in which ground forces were secondary, and it was the first post–Cold War test of the capacity of the victors to terminate war in a way that would bring a lasting peace.

As you read this case, think about the cross-pressures buffeting the United States, as it searched for an appropriate response to the Iraqi invasion of Kuwait. Policymakers in Washington realized they could not afford to conduct the war unilaterally; they had to persuade other states to share the financial costs. But to garner international support they would have to reconcile multiple conflicting interests. Not only did the first Bush administration need to be attentive to the mood of a public fixated on live reports from the war zone broadcast by the Cable News Network (CNN), it also had to balance myriad demands from Israel, numerous Arab states, Japan, NATO allies, and the Soviet Union. How could the United States hold its unwieldy coalition together during and after the war? How could it defeat Saddam Hussein without making him a martyr? How could a peace be constructed that did not provide opportunities for Iran or other dissatisfied states to increase their influence over the region? And how, ten years after the Persian Gulf War, should the new Bush administration deal with Saddam Hussein, who in 1991 was left in power with his elite Republican Guard intact, and who in 2001, with rising oil prices leaving Iraq awash in cash, was poised to pursue a policy of revenge? Should Saddam Hussein's Iraq be "contained" or "rolled-back," or is there a strategy that can open the door to a peaceful rapprochement?

Speaking from the Oval Office on February 27, 1991, President George Bush proclaimed a victory "for all mankind, for the rule of law, and for what is right." Kuwait had been liberated from Iraqi occupation. Reminding the nation of his promise that Iraq's aggression against the tiny, oil-rich emirate would not stand, the president announced that all military objectives had been achieved. After expressing pride in "the people whose strength and resolve made victory quick, decisive, and just," he concluded by highlighting the next challenge facing the United States: "We must now begin to look beyond victory in war. We must meet the challenge of securing the peace."

At the time of the invasion, Iraqi leader Saddam Hussein possessed the fourth largest army in the world. It was regarded as "a professionally competent, well-equipped, well-led, and well-trained force with considerable experience in combined arms warfare."[1] Seasoned by eight years of war with Iran, Hussein's military machine included an extensive chemical weapons arsenal, an array of medium-range ballistic missiles, and a proven ability to mount a tenacious defense. In view of these strengths, commentators as varied as Patrick Buchanan and Senator Edward Kennedy (D-MA) warned that any attempt by the United States to evict Iraq from Kuwait would cost thousands of Americans their lives.[2] According to conventional wisdom, liberating Kuwait by military means would "most likely be bloody and protracted."[3] Rumors had circulated in Washington that the Pentagon ordered sixteen thousand body bags in preparation for war. But instead of a long, grinding campaign with heavy U.S. casualties, Iraq was routed in one of the most one-sided military engagements in history. "By God," George Bush would later exclaim, "we've kicked the Vietnam syndrome once and for all."[4]

Yet Bush was worried about the future. Saddam Hussein's military forces—save the crack Republican Guard military units he had shielded from attack—had been crushed, but the Iraqi dictator was still in power. The president's trepidation about "screwing up" the war "with a sloppy muddled ending"[5] emerged during his first press conference after the fighting had ended. Responding to a reporter's question about his somber mood, Bush admitted: "I want to see an end. You mention World War II. There was a definite end to that conflict. And now we have Saddam Hussein still there, the man that wreaked the havoc upon his neighbors."[6]

If the military victory over Iraq appeared tainted by unfinished political business, at least the president's position at home looked secure. Buoyed by battlefield success, his approval rating among the American electorate climbed to 89 percent, the highest rating for any president during the five decades that the Gallup organization had been polling public opinion. In the words of the *Arkansas Democrat-Gazette*, George Bush stood over the "political horizon like a colossus."[7] Ironically, just twenty months later, Bush suffered a stunning defeat in the 1992 presidential election at the hands of Arkansas governor Bill Clinton. Meanwhile, Saddam Hussein's tyrannical rule in Baghdad remained as fierce as ever. More than ten years after Iraqi tanks rolled into Kuwait and provoked a crushing military counterattack upon his country, Hussein remained firmly in power, living in splendor while Iraqi citizens lived in crushing poverty without basic civil liberties. A decade after the fighting stopped, the political conflict continued, and Iraqi television was still celebrating "the victory of Baghdad" and praising the willingness of the Iraqi population to "sacrifice" themselves to defend Iraq.[8] "The Gulf War," lamented one commentator, "turned out to be a modest victory snatched from the jaws of triumph."[9] Added another critic: "So we have to face it, Saddam has triumphed. A decade after he lost the war, the fears that he would win the military and political fruits of peace now are realized as fact. His defiance of the U.S., and his rejection of the peace conditions make him stronger politically and in emotional appeal throughout the Muslim world than since he went to war by occupying Kuwait. He and his supporters everywhere are understandably contemptuous of a country that cannot enforce the conditions of peace on a militarily defeated dictator."[10]

This is a harsh verdict about a military triumph that in 1991 seemed as perfect as a war could be. To better understand the lessons of this war, it is important to first inspect the steps from a "perfect war" to an imperfect peace.

THE INVASION OF KUWAIT

Saddam Hussein was born on April 28, 1937, to a peasant family in the impoverished village of al-Auja. Raised by an abusive stepfather, he later moved to Baghdad to live with his maternal uncle, a fervent nationalist who cultivated the belief that Hussein was destined to follow in the footsteps of Nebuchadnezzar, the ancient Babylonian conqueror, and Saladin, the Arab warrior who defeated the Crusaders. In Baghdad, Hussein became immersed in political activism, joining the Baath Party and articulating its rallying cry that "the primary method of achieving [Arab unity] . . . is through armed struggle."[11] In 1956, he supported a failed coup attempt against King Faisal II, and a few years later he participated in an attack on the general who had assumed power after deposing the king. In Hussein's mind, he was the heir to Gamal Abdel Nasser, the Egyptian president seen by many during the 1950s and 1960s as the symbolic leader of the Arab world.

When the Baath Party seized control of Iraq in 1968, Saddam Hussein began his ascent to absolute power. Angered by rifts within the party, he created a secret-police apparatus loyal to himself alone. His reputation for ruthlessness and his alliance with the secret police combined to provide Hussein a foundation for achieving the presidency of Baathist Iraq in 1979. Ever suspicious of potential rivals, Hussein purged the party of many of its senior members and established a cult of personality around himself the "father/leader." Massive billboards, murals, and statues across the country depicted him as a triumphant field marshal, a devout Muslim in prayer, or as a simple peasant surrounded by children. Through religious symbolism, he cultivated his image as a fearless defender of the Muslim community who would not submit to anyone but God. In the cutthroat environment of Iraqi politics, Saddam Hussein was a shrewd tactician and savage competitor who demanded unconditional subservience. Underneath his lavish presidential palace sat a vast bunker constructed of steel and prestressed concrete. As one observer of the Iraqi leader has written, "The architecture of this complex is Saddam's psychological architecture: a defiant, grandiose facade resting on the well-fortified foundation of a siege mentality."[12]

It would be difficult to imagine two men from more different backgrounds than Saddam Hussein and George Herbert Walker Bush. The former, whose name in Arabic means "the one who confronts," had a modest education and little experience outside the Middle East. The latter came from elitist stock, attended Andover and Yale, and served as American envoy to China, U.S. ambassador to the United Nations, and director of the Central Intelligence Agency (CIA). Whereas Hussein was an opportunist who would eliminate anyone he perceived as an impediment no matter how loyal they might have been in the past, Bush, a self-avowed pragmatist, was a practitioner of consensual politics who valued the camaraderie of old friends. The Iraqi president's pursuit of personal power was boundless. The American president saw public service as a citizen's highest calling. Products of different worlds, neither man understood the personal motives and political calculations of the other. Yet their fates would soon become intertwined.

Early on the morning of August 2, 1990, columns of T-72 tanks from Saddam Hussein's elite Republican Guard crossed their country's southern border and raced down a six-lane superhighway toward Kuwait City (see Map 7.1). Allegedly his troops had been invited by revolutionaries to assist in liberating Kuwait from the rule of a corrupt minority, the al-Sabah family and their minions. Within hours, resistance to the invasion collapsed. Announcing that the new provisional government of Kuwait wanted to rejoin the "motherland" through an "eternal merger," Saddam Hussein issued a decree making the emirate the nineteenth province of Iraq and threatened to "turn Kuwait into a graveyard" if any foreign power intervened.[13]

Iraq's claim to Kuwait stretched back to the days of the Ottoman Empire, when Kuwait was an administrative subdivision of the Iraqi province of Basra. After the dismemberment of the Ottoman Empire following its defeat in World War I, the borders between Iraq and Kuwait were redrawn by the victorious British at the 1922 Uqair Conference. Iraqi dissatisfaction with these frontiers was voiced by King Ghazi ibn Faisal during the 1930s, and again in 1961 by President Abdul Karim Qassim. Seizing on this history of territorial frustration, Saddam Hussein asserted that his recovery of "lost" Iraqi land was just, because it redressed an old wrong. To ensure their petroleum interests, he argued, "Western colonialism divided and established weak states ruled by families . . . [that] kept the wealth away from the masses." Now "the branch had been returned to the tree trunk."[14]

In addition to this historical claim, Hussein spelled out more recent grievances to justify his blitzkrieg. Kuwait, he charged, was engaged in economic aggression against Iraq. Rather than behaving like Arab brothers, the al-Sabah family had thrust a poisoned dagger into the back of the Iraqi nation. On the one hand, it had exceeded the oil production quota set by the Organization of Petroleum Exporting Countries (OPEC), therein driving prices down at the very moment that Baghdad needed revenue to rebuild after its eight-year war with Iran. On the other hand, Kuwait purportedly had been drilling under Iraq's border in order to extract oil from the Rumalia field.

MAP 7.1 The Persian Gulf Region. Iraq is situated in the strategic center of the oil-rich and politically unstable Middle East — a region composed of states with a history of recurrent rivalries and episodic warfare. The Persian Gulf War erupted when Iraqi leader Saddam Hussein sent a powerful army into Kuwait to secure territory that he maintained was within the traditional boundaries of his country. Following his defeat, Iraqi war planes were banned from flying missions in the northern and southern regions of the country.

Prior to the invasion, Tariq Aziz, the Iraqi foreign minister, listed a series of demands to be met by Kuwait to avert war. Included among these were demands for $2.4 billion in compensation for the oil "stolen" from the Rumalia field; cancellation of the debt Iraq incurred to Kuwait during the war with Iran, estimated at $40 billion; $10 billion in aid to help Iraq recover from the war; and a long-term lease on Bubiyan and Warba, two strategically important islands guarding Iraq's access to the Persian Gulf. If these demands were not met, Saddam Hussein would take what he wanted: "If anyone tries to stop me," he threatened, "I will chop off his arm at the shoulder."[15]

PRESIDENT BUSH'S RESPONSE

Iraq's invasion caught the White House off guard. Throughout the previous decade, the United States and Iraq had coinciding interests: Each state saw Iran as a threat to its position in the region (see Table 7.1). The Ayatollah Ruholla Khomeini had denounced the United States as the "Great Satan" and called for a holy war against Saddam Hussein. When hostilities erupted between Iraq and Iran, the Reagan administration adopted one of the core tenets of **realpolitik**—the enemy of an enemy is a friend. In search of an ally, the United States removed Baghdad from its list of state sponsors of terrorism, thus making the country eligible for U.S. government–financed export credits as well as arms and technology sales. American officials proclaimed Iraq was changing and a prominent foreign policy consultant dismissed Hussein's "butcher of Baghdad" image as a stereotype.[16] Because Iraq was seen as a modernizing state seeking a respected position within the world community, almost everyone in the Bush White House believed that the threats against Kuwait were a bluff. Even Egyptian president Hosni Mubarak insisted that the dispute between Iraq and Kuwait was "a cloud that would pass with the wind."[17]

Prior to the invasion, the Bush presidency was foundering. Little headway had been made on resolving the problems of crime, poverty, and skyrocketing health care costs. Moreover, the President had reneged on his "no new taxes" pledge and was hounded by suspicions of his earlier involvement in the so-called Iran-Contra affair, in which the Reagan administration had secretly sold arms to Iran in order to fund a covert war against the Sandinista government of Nicaragua. A cautious, practical decisionmaker, George Bush valued patience and prudence over impulsiveness and improvisation. Reputed to be a "man of the moment" who tackled problems in an ad hoc fashion, Bush's foreign policy was widely criticized for lacking a "grand design."[18] His detractors scoffed, "He believes in doing nothing—but doing it well."[19]

In a stark departure from his record of temporizing, President Bush's response to the August invasion was strong and unequivocal. With personal ties to the emirate from his days with Zapata Petroleum, he defined the crisis in terms of good versus evil: Kuwait was the victim; Saddam Hussein, the villain. When Treasury Secretary Nicholas Brady spoke of adapting to the situation, Bush snapped: "Let's be clear about one thing: We are not here to talk about adapting. We are not going to plan how to live with this."[20]

George Bush responded to the invasion as if it were a personal affront. Though a patrician heritage encouraged his "kinder, gentler" side, he often lashed out at challengers, a trait satirized by Garry Trudeau when he gave

TABLE 7.1

A Chronology of Major Events Surrounding the Persian Gulf War

Date	Events
1979	The Shah of Iran relinquishes power in January; the Ayatollah Khomeini leads the new government, and the anti-American regime seizes the U.S. embassy personnel as hostages in November; on July 16, Saddam Hussein becomes president of Iraq and commander-in-chief of the country's armed forces
1980	The Iran-Iraq War begins
1982	U.S. forces are sent to Lebanon as part of a multinational peacekeeping force; Reagan administration initiates its opening to Saddam Hussein by removing Iraq from the list of states that sponsor terrorism
1983	Beirut bombing kills 241 U.S. Marines in October; the remaining marines withdraw from Lebanon the following February
1988	Iran and Iraq agree to a cease-fire of their brutal eight-year war
1990	On January 17, President Bush issues an executive order declaring that expanded U.S trade with Iraq, supported by the Export-Import Bank, is in the U.S national interest; on July 17, Saddam Hussein and United Arab Emirates accuse Kuwait of cooperating with a U.S. conspiracy to force oil overproduction to push down oil prices and undermine Arab security; on August 1, the U.S ambassador to Iraq meets with Saddam Hussein on instructions from the President to seek better relations with Iraq; Iraq invades Kuwait on August 2; on August 7, Saudi Arabia requests U.S. help and the next day President Bush orders deployment of U.S. troops to the Persian Gulf; UN Security Council Resolution 660 demands Iraq's withdrawal and Resolution 661 imposes a trade embargo on Iraq; Operation Desert Shield begins; in November, Resolution 678 authorizes member states to use all necessary means to evict Iraq from Kuwait
1991	U.S.-led coalition launches devastating air war on Iraq in Operation Desert Storm on January 17; on January 18 the first Iraqi SCUD missiles hit Israel; U.S. airstrikes are followed by a ground offensive on February 24; on February 26 Kuwait is liberated and on February 28 Baghdad accepts a cease-fire to end hostilities and begin peace talks; expecting western support, Kurds in northern Iraq and Shiite Muslims in southern Iraq revolt against Saddam Hussein in March; both rebellions are savagely crushed by the Iraqi military; on March 2, a day before scheduled peace talks, the U.S. Twenty-fourth Infantry Division claims it had come under attack, and launches a massive assault in which thousands of Iraqi soldiers, civilians, and children are killed; on April 3, UN Resolution 687 specifies terms for a permanent cease-fire with Iraq, which aims for a complete accounting and elimination of Iraqi weapons of mass destruction and all associated production capabilities; UN inspection teams begin work; UN accuses Iraq of hiding missiles and nuclear facilities; in May the United States, Britain and France declare northern

Date	Events

Iraq a "safe haven" for Kurds and impose a no-fly zone above the thirty-sixth parallel

1992 After Iraq launches renewed attacks on Shiite Muslim rebels, the United States backed by France and Britain declares a no-fly zone below the thirty-second parallel over southern Iraq; United States and its allies begin to patrol the no-fly zone; in December, U.S. planes intercept and shoot down an Iraqi MIG-25

1993 In January, the UN Security Council votes to maintain economic sanctions; United States accuses Saddam Hussein of moving missiles into southern Iraq; allied planes and ships attack suspected missile sites and a nuclear facility near Baghdad; in June, following the discovery of a plot to assassinate former President George Bush, U.S. ships fire twenty-four cruise missiles at intelligence headquarters in Baghdad

1994 Saddam Hussein moves Iraqi troops to the Kuwaiti border; the forces withdraw after the United States deploys a carrier group, warplanes, and 54,000 troops to the Persian Gulf region

1996 Iraqi armored forces violate the 1991 cease-fire agreement by entering the Kurdish city of Irbil; United States responds by attacking Iraqi targets with cruise missiles; in September, U.S. ships and airplanes attack Iraqi military targets and President Clinton extends the southern no-fly zone to just south of Baghdad; with widespread famine in Iraq, UN loosens the 1990 economic sanctions by starting its "Oil for Food" program

1997 Iraq bars UN inspection team from entering any sites, and attempts to determine the nationality of team members; on October 31, Saddam Hussein accuses U.S. members of being spies and expels the majority of U.S. participants; the UN Security Council threatens renewed economic sanctions; confrontation continues into November as Iraq expels the remaining six U.S. inspectors and the UN withdraws other inspectors in protest. Inspectors are readmitted after the United States and Great Britain begin a military build-up in the Persian Gulf and warn of possible military strikes; on November 14, within about twenty minutes of attack, Saddam Hussein agrees to allow UN monitors to return; later that month, Iraq announces it will not allow inspectors access to sites designated as "palaces and official residences"; UN officials protest, suspecting such sites conceal weapons of mass destruction; on December 8, chief UN weapons inspector Richard Butler reports that Iraq is still impeding inspections as UN teams begin departing Iraq; on December 15, a UN report accuses Iraq of a repeated pattern of obstructing weapons inspections; on December 16, the United States and Great Britain begin a massive air campaign against key military targets in Iraq

1998 In February, UN Secretary-General Kofi Annan negotiates an agreement with Iraq that resumes weapons inspections in exchange for a promise that the UN will consider removing economic sanctions; inspections continue into August, when Iraq cuts ties with weapons inspectors, claiming it has seen no UN move toward lifting sanctions;   *(cont.)*

(Table 7.1 cont.)

Date	Events
	Iraq moves air defense units in the northern and southern no-fly zones; United States immediately begins Operation Desert Fox to strike military and security targets in Iraq; in November, President Clinton signs the Iraq Liberation Act pledging financial and military assistance to the Iraqi opposition; on December 16, weapons inspectors are withdrawn from Iraq; hours later, a U.S.-British force begins four days of air and missile strikes on Baghdad
1999	Operation Desert Fox continues; on November 16, a pipeline connecting Iraq's oilfields with Syrian ports, closed since 1982, is reopened, and an estimated 150,000 barrels a day are exported to generate Iraqi revenue
2000	Pentagon releases investigation of possible causes of unexplained illnesses suffered by tens of thousands of U.S. veterans of the Gulf War, including the possibility that the diseases resulted from Iraqi chemical and biological weapons and exposure to nerve gas when the U.S. forces blew up an Iraqi weapons stockpile in 1991 at Khanislyah; in August, President Clinton authorizes the U.S. Air Force to bomb and strafe Iraq on slim provocation; on August 10, Venezuelan President Hugo Chauez becomes the first Western head of state to visit Iraq since the Gulf War; on September 22, a French charter flight becomes the first international flight into Baghdad to ignore the request from the UN sanctions committee to wait for clearance, starting a flood of flights from other states
2001	George W. Bush is inaugurated on January 20 as U.S. president, and shortly thereafter orders air strikes on Iraq; support for the UN economic sanctions against Iraq continues to crumble

Bush a mean-spirited twin called "Skippy" in his *Doonesbury* cartoon strip. It was this tougher, more aggressive George Bush who responded in 1988 to jokes about his wimpiness with one of the most negative presidential campaigns in years.

Iraq's annexation of Kuwait presented George Bush with a new mission. In a speech delivered on August 8, he seized the opportunity to dispel his image as a leader who lacked "vision" and starkly outlined the mission's objectives:

> First, we seek the immediate, unconditional, and complete withdrawal of all Iraqi forces from Kuwait. Second, Kuwait's legitimate government must be restored to replace the puppet regime. And third, my administration, as has been the case with every president from President Roosevelt to President Reagan, is committed to the security and stability of the Persian Gulf. And fourth, I am determined to protect the lives of American citizens abroad.[21]

A pilot whose aircraft had been shot down during battle in World War II, Bush saw the crisis in the Gulf through the lens of the 1930s. As he told the UN General Assembly, "Iraq's unprovoked aggression is a throwback to another era, a dark relic from a dark time."[22] In his eyes, Saddam Hussein was another Adolf Hitler, demagogic and maneuvering to conquer defense-less countries. Less than a month later, in a speech delivered before a joint session of Congress, the president added another objective to his mission:

> The crisis in the Persian Gulf, as grave as it is, also offers a rare opportunity to move toward a historic period of cooperation. Out of these troubled times, our fifth objective—a new world order—can emerge: a new era, freer from the threat of terror, stronger in the pursuit of justice, and more secure in the quest for peace.[23]

"We will succeed in the gulf," Bush promised in his 1991 State of the Union address. "And when we do, the world community will have sent an enduring warning to any dictator or despot, present or future, who contemplates outlaw aggression."[24]

From Bush's perspective, Britain and France failed to deter German aggression at the 1938 Munich Conference due to a series of miscalculations regarding Hitler's character. The Führer was not a prudent leader with limited territorial aims, such as Prussian Chancellor Otto von Bismarck, who had masterminded German unification over a half century earlier through shrewd diplomacy and the calculated exercise of military might. In contrast, Adolf Hitler was an avaricious and untrustworthy dictator. Anglo-French vacillation in the face of Hitler's remilitarization of the Rhineland, their acquiescence to his annexation of Austria, and their efforts to appease the Nazi leader were among the foreign policy mistakes Bush believed had led to World War II. If London and Paris had stood firm and communicated a credible threat to punish aggression, German expansion would have been contained. Each time the Western democracies failed to show resolve, Hitler was emboldened to make further encroachments on contiguous countries.

Vowing not to ignore the lessons of the 1930s, the Bush administration formulated a response based on three rules of **realist** statecraft:

1. Do not make unnecessary concessions to aggressive, deceitful opponents; they cannot be accommodated. If aggressors pocket an easily achieved concession, they will be encouraged to press for more. Expecting a cruel, rapacious opponent to foreswear expansion and adhere religiously to his promises invites more aggression. "A half century ago," the president told those attending the Ninety-first National Convention of the Veterans of Foreign Wars, "the world had the chance to stop a ruthless aggressor and missed it. I pledge to you: We will not make that mistake again."[25]

2. Negotiate with aggressive, deceitful opponents from a position of strength; the language of military might is the only language they understand. A preponderance of power was seen by the president and those around him as a prerequisite for making intransigent opponents bargain in

> "History teaches that wars begin when governments believe the price of aggression is cheap."
>
> — RONALD REAGAN

earnest. Conciliatory gestures made after unjustified demands would only be taken as a sign of weakness. As General Colin L. Powell, then-chairman of the Joint Chiefs of Staff, once put it, "A side that sees an easy victory will go after it."[26]

3. Counter every attempt by aggressive, deceitful opponents to amass more power; it is better to fight a small war now than a big war later. Adversaries such as Saddam Hussein, it was assumed, continually probe for soft spots. Any unchallenged extension of their influence into some new geographic area will produce a **domino effect** on neighboring countries. If these incremental increases in their power are not blocked, they will become progressively more difficult to defeat. As Secretary of State James Baker posed the matter to the House Foreign Affairs Committee: "Do we want to live in a world where aggression is made less likely because it is met with a powerful response, a world where civilized rules of conduct apply? Or are we willing to live in a world where aggression can go unchecked, where aggression succeeds because we cannot muster the collective will to challenge it?"[27]

Lurking beneath the president's lofty rhetoric about not appeasing aggressors was oil, a commodity on which daily life in industrialized countries had become so dependent that they have been referred to as "hydrocarbon societies."[28] While President Bush preferred to speak in terms of liberal principles such as fighting aggression and upholding the rule of law, he admitted in a speech to Pentagon employees on August 15 that access to energy resources was also important. Secretary of State Baker was more blunt: "The cause, in one word, is jobs."[29] As an advisor to the president put it, "If Kuwait's export [were] oranges . . . there would be no issue."[30] To add to the gravity of the situation, Saddam Hussein would control almost half of the world's proven petroleum reserves if he followed up his conquest of Kuwait by overrunning Saudi Arabia. In the words of Representative Stephen Solarz (D-NY), "It would be unthinkable for the United States to permit a rampaging dictator like Saddam to have his hands on the economic jugular of the world."[31]

TIGHTENING THE ECONOMIC SCREWS

From George Bush's inauguration to the eve of Saddam Hussein's invasion, U.S. policy rested on the premise that Iraq was a war-weary nation—the **war-weariness hypothesis**—that could be converted into a force for stability in the region. Sabers might be rattled in Baghdad from time to time, but pure exhaustion after eight years of war with Iran made any new military adventures unlikely. National Security Directive (NSD) 26 argued that the United States could promote peace in the Middle East by using "economic and political incentives for Iraq to moderate its behavior." Despite Iraq's abysmal human rights record, its pursuit of nuclear and binary chemical weapons, and its work on a "super gun" capable of launching huge projectiles over enormous distances, efforts to reassure Saddam Hussein of the American desire for better relations continued, and expectations were high that he would cooperate if given the proper incentives.

In Baghdad, Washington's reassurances sounded like equivocating. For example, on July 24, when evidence of suspicious troop movements opposite the Kuwaiti border raised questions about Saddam Hussein's intentions, State Department spokesperson Margaret Tutwiler answered: "We do not have any defense treaties with Kuwait, and there are no special defense or security commitments to Kuwait." The next day, in a conversation with the Iraqi leader, U.S. ambassador April Glaspie stated, "We have no opinion on Arab-Arab conflicts, like your border disagreement with Kuwait."[32] Similarly, in his testimony before a House Foreign Affairs subcommittee on July 31, Assistant Secretary of State for Near Eastern and South Asian Affairs John Kelley affirmed, "We have no defense treaty relationship with any Gulf country."[33] These statements signaled Baghdad that the United States was less fearful of Iraqi expansionism than it was hopeful that Iraq could serve as a bastion against the spread of Islamic fundamentalism in the Middle East.

The day after the invasion, President Bush flew to Colorado to fulfill a previously scheduled speaking engagement at the Aspen Institute and to have an informal meeting with British prime minister Margaret Thatcher. The two leaders compared Iraq's attack to Germany's aggression in the 1930s and agreed that Saddam Hussein had to be stopped. During a press conference held outside the elegant mountain home of Henry Catto, the American ambassador to the Court of St. James in London, Bush told reporters that he was not ruling any options out. Bush had already moved to freeze all Iraqi and Kuwaiti assets in the United States and had ordered his advisors to explore what other sanctions might be imposed. At a National Security Council meeting convened upon the president's return from Colorado, National Security Adviser Brent Scowcroft insisted: "There are lots of reasons why we can't do things [about the invasion], but it's our job."[34] Deputy Secretary of State Lawrence Eagleburger agreed: "It is absolutely essential that the U.S.—collectively, if possible, but individually, if necessary—not only put a stop to this aggression but roll it back."[35]

The initial strategy of the Bush administration, recalled a senior advisor, "was to deny Saddam a chance to expand his aggression . . . [and] to put in place the sanctions to tighten the screws."[36] To deter further aggression, then-Secretary of Defense Dick Cheney secured an invitation from King Fahd allowing elements of the U.S. Rapid Deployment Force (RDF) to be stationed in Saudi Arabia; meanwhile, President Bush began contacting world leaders by telephone in order to forge a multinational coalition against Iraq. Eventually thirty nations joined, including such traditional U.S. allies as Great Britain and France, as well as Arab states such as Egypt and Syria. To dislodge Iraq from Kuwait, the United States lobbied the United Nations to organize a global arms and economic embargo against Iraq. The UN Security Council had already unanimously adopted Resolution 660, which demanded

Iraq's immediate and unconditional withdrawal. On August 6 it spelled out a list of economic sanctions to be levied against Iraq (Resolution 661), and a few weeks later called upon member states with maritime forces in the region to enforce those sanctions by inspecting the cargoes of any ships thought to be assisting Iraq (Resolution 665). Operation Desert Shield was underway.

Iraq provided an ideal target for tightening the screw of **economic sanctions:** Its economy was vulnerable, Saddam Hussein was isolated, and the sanctions were applied decisively. Relying heavily on a single natural resource and highly dependent on foreign sources of finished goods and technical services, Iraq faced the prospect of growing disruptions and deprivation. William Webster, director of the CIA, testified before the Senate Armed Services Committee that the economic embargo had cut off more than 90 percent of Iraq's imports and more than 97 percent of its exports, depriving the country of approximately $1.5 billion of foreign exchange earnings monthly. At the current rate of depletion, Iraqi foreign exchange reserves would be drained within a few months.[37]

Yet there were drawbacks to a strategy of military **containment** and economic strangulation. The longer sanctions were applied, the greater the likelihood that the diverse military coalition so carefully assembled by George Bush would disintegrate. Friction from the ongoing Israeli-Palestinian dispute, Islamic fundamentalist resentment over the growing number of non-Arab soldiers in the region, and the staggering cost of maintaining troops in a distant and inhospitable environment were just some of the problems that threatened to weaken coalition resolve as the months wore on. Furthermore, because Saddam Hussein remained indifferent to hardships borne by his own people, there was no guarantee that Iraq's economic suffering would compel him to withdraw from Kuwait. Defiant as ever, the Iraqi leader tried one ploy after another in his attempt to erode the American-dominated coalition that encircled him. To dislodge Syria and other Arab states, he proposed to negotiate an end to the crisis if Israel vacated the Golan Heights, Gaza Strip, and the West Bank of the Jordan River. To shake loose popularly elected Western governments, he threatened to make "human shields" of the hundreds of European nationals captured in Kuwait. He even tried to curry the favor of Iran by returning territory previously captured from his old enemy.

By late fall, few in the White House retained hope that the economic vise around Iraq would pressure Saddam Hussein into giving up Kuwait. Reflecting on his gradual disenchantment with sanctions and his subsequent shift from guarding a line in the sand to an offensive strategy aimed at evicting Hussein from Kuwait, President Bush revealed: "I cannot pinpoint all of this to a certain date, but . . . as the military planners went forward, I was more and more convinced that we could use force and be successful."[38] By the end of October, the president told Secretary of Defense Dick Cheney that he was inclined to use his authority as commander in chief to allocate the wherewithal needed to undertake offensive operations, but nothing could be disclosed until after November 6 since any such announcement would be taken as an attempt to influence the upcoming congressional elections.[39]

On November 8 George Bush declared that he would double U.S. troop strength in the Persian Gulf. Two political steps would be necessary before these troops could be sent into battle. The first step was taken by the end of the month, when the UN Security Council passed Resolution 678 authorizing member states "to use all necessary means" to evict Iraq from Kuwait if it did not leave voluntarily by January 15, 1991. The second step occurred shortly thereafter, when a joint resolution was passed in the U.S. Senate by a vote of 52 to 47 and in the House of Representatives by 250 to 183 authorizing the president to wrest control of Kuwait from Iraq. With nearly 1 million heavily armed soldiers standing toe-to-toe astride the welter of failed peace proposals littering the diplomatic landscape, the forces of war were gaining momentum. "What is at issue," the American president wrote in a letter to his Iraqi counterpart, "is not the future of Kuwait . . . but rather the future of Iraq."[40]

OPERATION DESERT STORM

Early in the morning of January 17, 1991, the USS *Bunker Hill* and the USS *San Jacinto* fired Tomahawk cruise missiles at Baghdad from their respective locations in the Persian Gulf and the Red Sea. As the Tomahawks sped toward the Iraqi capital, a group of F-117A Stealth fighters and a task force of Apache AH-64 and MH-53J Pace Low helicopters were preparing to engage other targets. Their attack would be followed by waves of fighters, bombers, and electronic warfare aircraft, including B-52s, F-15E Strike Eagles, F-4G Wild Weasels, EF-111 Ravens, A-6 Prowlers, British and Saudi Tornados, and French Jaguars. What Saddam Hussein called the "mother of all battles" had begun.

The Doctrine of Invincible Force

Although Operation Desert Storm, the U.S. plan for liberating Kuwait, went through many iterations and was an amalgam of contending ideas, its roots reach back to what then-General Colin Powell called the doctrine of invincible force. Haunted by the ghost of Vietnam, a generation of American military officers was leery of the argument that political leaders in Washington could fine-tune a program of rising military pressure in a **limited war** to persuade an opponent to relinquish territory already won. Threats of further violence after a pause in escalation were supposed to induce enemy forces to withdraw and spare the United States the cost of slugging it out on the ground. This strategy failed. Hence, the Bush administration concluded that military gradualism was counterproductive; it amounted to fighting with one hand tied behind your back.

Rather than orchestrating an alternating pattern of incremental escalations and pauses, Powell advocated marshaling all of the resources necessary to overwhelm an adversary. By harnessing the latest technology, he maintained that U.S. forces could use mobility and firepower to win swift, decisive victories. "I don't believe in doing war on the basis of macroeconomic, marginal-analysis models," the general said. "I'm more of the mind-set of a New York street bully: 'Here's my bat, here's my gun, here's my knife, I'm wearing armor. I'm going to kick your ass . . .'"[41]

Whereas the U.S. military was geared to fight a fast and furious campaign, Saddam Hussein pinned his hopes on a war of attrition, believing he could exploit a fatal weakness in America's democratic policy-making process a lack of patience with protracted warfare. The United States "is a society that cannot accept 10,000 dead in one battle," he insisted.[42] If Iraq could lure U.S. troops into frontal assaults on heavily fortified "killing zones," Hussein assumed mounting casualties would prompt the Americans to yield. Just as they had done in their earlier war with Iran, the Iraqis constructed an elaborate system of minefields, bunkers, antitank guns, and fire trenches all surrounded by concertina wire. Slowed by these barriers, the American attack would come under a heavy artillery barrage, followed by a counterattack by armored and mechanized divisions of Saddam Hussein's Republican Guard. The key to the plan resided in Iraq's ability to ride out the preliminary strikes by coalition air power. "The U.S. may be able to destroy cities, factories, and to kill," Saddam Hussein once proclaimed, "but it will not be able to decide the war with its Air Force."[43]

Operation Desert Storm unfolded in two phases: a relentless air assault (January 17–February 24) followed by a devastating ground offensive (February 24–28). The objectives of the first phase were to achieve air superiority; cripple Iraq's ground forces; and destroy electric power grids, military facilities, bridges, and other strategic targets. By the end of the war, coalition aircraft had flown "52,000 air-to-ground sorties [that] delivered approximately 210,000 unguided bombs, 9,300 guided bombs, 5,400 guided air-to-surface missiles, and 2,000 anti-radar missiles; American forces also hurled more than 300 cruise missiles at the enemy."[44] In addition to pummeling Iraq's infrastructure, logistical network, and armored formations, the air campaign demoralized Hussein's troops. Americans watching tapes of the bombing runs with the lethal accuracy of heat-seeking sensors and laser-guided munitions likened the action to a computer video game.[45] In the words of reporters covering the air assault, it was a Nintendo war.

The second phase of Operation Desert Storm involved deceiving Saddam Hussein into thinking that the ground offensive would be aimed directly at Kuwait City. Instead, taking advantage of air cover and navigational data from global positioning satellites, U.S. General H. Norman Schwarzkopf redeployed the bulk of his forces westward, where they could strike deep into Iraq, pivot, and then quickly circle back to outflank Hussein's forces in Kuwait. The objectives of sweeping around enemy defenses were to envelop and then crush the Iraqi war machine.

Exhausted by weeks of aerial pounding and bewildered by Schwarzkopf's end run, the Iraqis began surrendering in droves. Those who fought were chewed up by the ground offensive. American troops were well-trained professionals; Iraqi front-line conscripts were riddled by poor morale. American equipment allowed soldiers to fire accurately while on the move and attack at night; Iraqi weaponry, though formidable, lacked the same level of technological sophistication and suffered from shortages of spare parts. Simply put, the mother of all battles was one of the most lopsided fights in the annals of military history. It quickly degenerated into the mother of all retreats.

The End Game

By the third day of the ground offensive, thousands of Iraqi troops began streaming northward out of Kuwait City. Forming a column almost thirty miles long and three or four abreast in places, the broken, defenseless units were ravaged by wave after wave of swarming coalition aircraft. Back in Washington, reports suggesting mass carnage created enormous pressure for a cease-fire.[46] Watching television coverage of what the media called the "highway of death," Bush worried that his triumph might be marred by charges of brutalization. Informed that the gate was closed on the encircled Iraqis and eradication of their heavy tanks and artillery imminent, the president now looked toward a cessation of hostilities. In the waning hours of the war, one last attempt was made to destroy a hardened command bunker where Saddam Hussein might be hiding. Late on the night of February 27, two five-thousand-pound penetration bombs were dropped on the al-Taji Air Base about fifteen miles outside Baghdad. The bunker was demolished, but it did not house the Iraqi leader. Shortly after the bombing raid, Bush suspended offensive action. "We were 150 miles from Baghdad and there was nobody between us and Baghdad," noted General Schwarzkopf. "If it had been our intention to take Iraq, if it had been our intention to destroy the country, if it had been our intention to overrun the country, we could have done it unopposed."[47]

The decision to halt the fighting was made on the basis of erroneous information, however. Contrary to Schwarzkopf's assertion that the gate had been closed, the retreating Iraqis were not completely surrounded. Another six to eight hours would have been needed to entrap them. With key choke points open, roughly half of Saddam Hussein's Republican Guard escaped with their weapons intact. Together with the twenty or so divisions not involved in the Kuwait theater of operations, these troops became the cornerstone for a reconstituted Iraqi army that would trouble the region for years to come.

The announcement of the war's end triggered celebrations throughout the United States. The war had been won with less than

"The time of reconstruction and recovery should not be the occasion for vengeful actions against a nation forced to war by a dictator's ambition."

— JAMES A. BAKER

150 American deaths. It was an impressive military victory. Unfortunately, the victory was tainted by lingering political problems. Little thought had gone into how the war's termination would affect the peace settlement. Could Saddam Hussein be removed from power without a U.S. march to Baghdad? If not, what would be the long-term consequences of his continued rule? How would the United States deal with those consequences? Anxious to secure a swift victory with minimal U.S. casualties, the Bush administration made a hasty decision to bring the war to a conclusion. Insufficient attention was devoted to how the United States would influence events in a postwar Iraq still ruled by Saddam Hussein, who was now, and remains, highly motivated to seek revenge for the destruction inflicted upon his country.

On March 3 General Schwarzkopf met with Iraqi representatives at the Safwan airfield in southern Iraq to finalize the terms of the truce. A lack of American planning for the peace settlement and the absence of a clear, coherent design for the future of Iraq soon became evident. The terms presented by the general called for Iraq to release all coalition prisoners of war and Kuwaiti detainees, provide information on the location of all sea and land mines, and comply with all relevant UN Security Council resolutions. When the Iraqis asked whether they would be allowed to fly helicopters over areas not populated by coalition forces, Schwarzkopf agreed. When they asked whether territory seized during the ground offensive would be returned to Iraq's control, he assured them his forces would soon depart. By granting Iraq the right to operate helicopters and promising to withdraw rapidly, Schwarzkopf inadvertently permitted Saddam Hussein to use a frightening weapon against his domestic opposition and relinquished the opportunity to use Iraqi land as leverage to ensure compliance with the terms of the truce. As one senior member of the Bush administration later admitted, "Norm went in uninstructed. He should have had instructions. But everything was moving so fast the process broke down."[48] "We never did have a plan to terminate the war," remarked another official.[49]

Given Iraq's military humiliation, President Bush assumed that a disgruntled army would rise against Saddam Hussein. On several occasions he called for a rebellion against the Baathist leader. A new government, Bush reasoned, would live in peace with its neighbors and act as a counterweight to Iranian ambitions. But rather than the army staging a coup, the Kurds in northern Iraq and the Shiite Muslims in the southern part of the country rebelled. Using the very Republican Guard forces that escaped American grasp and the helicopters he was now allowed to fly, Hussein viciously suppressed both uprisings, razing villages and sending hundreds of thousands of refugees fleeing in terror. Despite pleas for U.S. assistance from the minorities facing **genocide** as the penalty for their rebellion, the Bush administration initially stood on the sidelines. Defense Secretary Cheney explained that another American intervention would raise "the very real specter of getting us involved in a quagmire trying to figure out who the hell is going to govern Iraq."[50] According to another high-ranking official, Bush had "no, I mean absolutely no, intention of putting the United States in the middle of a civil war."[51] Ultimately, Bush responded to the threat against the *pesh marga* (literally, "those who face death") by creating a Kurdish safe haven above the thirty-sixth parallel and a Shiite haven below the thirty-second parallel, each patrolled by coalition forces. Although this provision of the truce settlement was designed to protect both groups while preventing the disintegration of Iraq, it enmeshed Washington in an ongoing commitment to uphold Gulf security. Aircraft, naval power, and prepositioned ground equipment would have to be maintained in the area for an extended period at considerable expense. On April 3, 1991, the UN Security Council approved Resolution 687, which specified the terms for a permanent cease-fire between Iraq and the American-led coalition. The formal truce went into effect eight days later. Saddam Hussein had been defeated on the battlefield, but he remained as truculent as ever. In the aftermath of the peace settlement, he tested allied determination to prevent him from rebuilding his military infrastructure and projecting his power beyond Baghdad. The following are a few examples of the carefully calculated probes Hussein initiated in the immediate wake of the Gulf War to undermine the victors' resolve in enforcing the punitive terms of the armistice:

- *Hiding and Developing Weapons of Mass Destruction*   UN Resolution 687 called for the disclosure and dismantling of Iraqi production facilities for chemical, biological, and nuclear weapons. The first UN inspection team visited the Al-Tuwaitha nuclear research facility on May 14, 1991, and discovered that much of the equipment had been moved to other locations. On the second inspection a few weeks later, UN personnel were denied entry to the Abu Ghurayb facility but noticed trucks removing uranium enrichment equipment. The next few visits revealed that Iraq had made considerable progress toward developing nuclear weapons, though controversy continued over whether Baghdad provided the United Nations with a complete inventory of its nuclear facilities. On September 13 Iraqi officials took documents away from inspectors and detained the UN team for a number of hours. Subsequent visits over the ensuing years were also marred by Iraqi efforts at evading and obstructing UN inspection, amid complaints that these monitoring activities were an unjust infringement of Iraq's sovereign right to arm for defense.
- *Rejecting Humanitarian Aid*   To prevent Saddam Hussein from rapidly rebuilding his arsenal, economic sanctions preventing the sale of Iraqi oil were maintained for a number of years following the war. A UN formula allowing limited sales to generate revenue for purchasing food and medical supplies was rejected by Baghdad as an unacceptable violation of its sovereignty. Hussein wanted to determine how revenue from the sale of Iraqi oil would be used. While the sanctions did not affect the living standard of Hussein and his entourage, they took a huge toll on ordinary Iraqis. In particular, cases of malnutrition-related diseases among children rose exponentially after the war. Only in the late spring of 1996

did Iraq begin serious negotiations on a deal to sell oil for emergency civilian needs. Until that point, Hussein used the plight of his people to gain sympathy from other Arab states.

- *Moving Troops into Forbidden Areas*   On several occasions after the Gulf War, Saddam Hussein massed troops along his borders in defiance of allied warnings. Sometimes they made limited incursions into forbidden areas. In early 1993, for instance, a small contingent of troops crossed into Kuwait to retrieve weapons.
- *Targeting Aircraft*   From time to time, Iraqi fighters entered the air exclusion zones, and in one instance on December 27, 1992, an Iraqi jet fired at an American plane. Surface-to-air missiles were moved in and around the exclusion zones over the years, and allied aircraft were tracked with radar from Iraqi antiaircraft batteries.

In a speech delivered on August 20, 1992, during his reelection campaign, George Bush told his supporters that he had "locked a tyrant in the prison of his own country."[52] Each of the probes by Saddam Hussein was a calculated exploration of the walls of that so-called prison. His tenacious poking and prodding served the twin ends of maneuvering for more latitude and demonstrating that he remained unbowed. The United States and its allies responded sporadically to Hussein, as illustrated by the limited retaliatory air strikes launched during January 1993 and the cruise missile attack of September 1996. But more often than not, warnings were issued and the matter was dropped—a strategy of "threat and forget." Whereas Saddam Hussein concentrated all of his energy at making a jailbreak, the guards experienced growing resource scarcities and fatigue. They found themselves frustrated and uncertain over what to do about the Iraqi leader. By not anticipating the political contours of postwar Iraq, the United States and its coalition partners won a hollow victory and lost the chance to show that **collective security** could work.

SADDAM THE UNVANQUISHED

The relationship between Saddam Hussein and the U.S.-led coalition that defeated him remained locked in an embittered confrontation for years after the Persian Gulf War ended. Triumph on the battlefield had been a cause for celebration in Washington. But the euphoria soon disappeared in a new round of military thrust and parry. Saddam Hussein desperately sought to overturn the sanctions that had strangled Iraq's economy and made his country an international pariah. With George Bush in retirement following his 1992 electoral defeat, the question of how to deal with a combative Iraq would now challenge U.S. President Bill Clinton.

In September 1996, as Clinton neared the end of his first term in office, Saddam Hussein once again tested American resolve. With the presidential election nearing its critical stage and public attention riveted on domestic issues, Hussein saw an opportunity in a civil war that had erupted among the Kurdish population in northern Iraq. Violating the provisions of the 1991 truce, he sent his tanks into the Kurdish city of Irbil with the intention of becoming the ultimate power broker between the two factions struggling for control of Kurdistan. By playing these factions

> "No promise of peace and no policy of patience can be without its limits."
>
> — BILL CLINTON

against one another, Hussein hoped to reverse the terms of the truce and resume his domination over that war-weary land.

This test of American resolve was met by an immediate response. To cripple Saddam Hussein's capacity to intervene into Kurdish politics, the United States fired twenty-two cruise missiles at Iraqi targets. President Clinton defended the retaliation as fully justified by Iraq's flagrant breach of the peace. Further underscoring his determination to contain Iraqi aggression, Clinton deployed additional forces in the Persian Gulf, where they would be poised to strike Iraq if Saddam Hussein persisted in his efforts to remove the shackles of the 1991 armistice agreement. As it turned out, the deployment proved insufficient. During the fall of 1997, Iraq once again barred UN weapons inspectors from examining key sites in Iraq, insisting on the right to influence the composition and activities undertaken by the inspection team. In addition, Iraq threatened to shoot down U-2 reconnaissance planes on surveillance missions over its territory. The Clinton administration replied by sending more U.S. forces into the region and threatening a military response. Just when a U.S. air strike on Iraq seemed imminent, Saddam Hussein backed down and the crisis appeared to be over.

In early 1998 Hussein resumed his obstreperous behavior, claiming that the American members of the UN team were spies who would not be allowed to inspect Iraqi facilities. The Clinton administration was now in a quandary. Having deployed additional troops, warships, and combat aircraft to the region, it found little international support for a punitive strike. Russia and France, backed by a chorus of African and Arab states, vigorously opposed military action against Iraq. Covert action against Saddam Hussein also appeared unpromising. The two major Iraqi opposition groups in exile—the Iraqi National Congress, based in London, and the Iraqi National Accord, based in Amman, Jordan—had been weakened by internal squabbles. Seven years after winning a crushing victory on the battlefield, the United States was still groping for a final political settlement to the Persian Gulf War.

The search for a viable solution to the problems in the Persian Gulf was complicated by distracting events in Washington. President Clinton, who had been embroiled in several previous controversies stemming from allegations about his sexual improprieties, was now under scrutiny for an affair with a White House intern. Coincidentally, a film titled *Wag the Dog* opened in theaters across the country. Portraying an embattled president who considers using a fabricated war to shift attention away from domestic issues, the film led the president's detractors to speculate about his foreign policy in terms of the **diversionary theory of war.** Thus, at the very time that the United States was poised to attack Iraq for violations of the 1991 cease-fire agreement, the Clinton administration had to deal with an unraveling international coalition and a host of domestic critics outraged over the White House sex scandal.

A military showdown was finally averted when UN Secretary-General Kofi Annan traveled to Baghdad in February and negotiated an arrangement that would allow weapons inspectors unrestricted access to sites suspected of housing weapons of mass destruction. The United States hoped to augment the agreement by obtaining UN Security Council authorization for an automatic military response in the event that Iraq violated its provisions. Russia, France, and China balked at the U.S. proposal, however, and only agreed to a more ambiguous resolution that threatened severe consequences would follow if there were any transgressions. With the threat of a U.S. strike now dissipated, Saddam Hussein returned to his long-standing effort to redefine the terms that ended the Persian Gulf War.

Losing a war against a hated adversary would, seemingly, leave the defeated leader humiliated and prostrate. Indeed, for Iraq, the outcome of the Persian Gulf War was truly devastating. But Saddam Hussein's stubborn response to his country's demise ironically strengthened his position at home by tightening his authoritarian grip on the population while hardening his resolve to settle scores with his foreign foes.

To hear the United States and its coalition partners tell it, the Gulf War was a complete victory. "The American people," wrote Colin Powell in his 1995 memoir, "fell in love again with their armed forces."[53] Yet defeat did not spell doom for Saddam Hussein, who launched a propaganda blitz over the next ten years to assure the Iraqi people that victory was theirs; they were better positioned than ever to rise to prominence on the international stage. There was no hint of guilt, no admission of wrongdoing for invading Kuwait, and no effort at reconciliation. To emphasize his lasting hatred of the United States, Saddam Hussein ordered that an unflattering portrait of George Bush in a major Baghdad hotel be "memorialized in a floor mosaic that visitors must walk upon as they enter."[54] He is also said to have commissioned a poem about himself written in the style of a *rajaz*, a traditional lyric composed to raise the spirits of warriors going into battle. One of its lines asserts: "He who is amongst the wolves, whose wounds turn into poison, frightens his enemies."[55]

Saddam Hussein's post–Gulf War strategy of revenge was scripted in harsh realpolitik. He completely suppressed internal opposition to his rule, and refused to back down in the face of UN economic sanctions, despite the harsh toll these sanctions exacted from his people: "Because of chronic malnutrition and a shortage of medicine, 500,000 more Iraqi children died under sanctions than would have been expected from prewar trends."[56] In 2000, a quarter of Iraq's children were malnourished, and the vast majority of Iraq's 23 million citizens were living in conditions of desperation.[57] In

response to the UN effort to impose **disarmament** and **arms controls,** he
made every effort to block the mandated site inspections of potential
weapons production facilities, and repeatedly tried to shoot down U.S and
British war planes that were enforcing the no-fly zones over northern and
southern Iraq in a somewhat successful endeavor to protect local rebels.
Equally indicative of his grand strategy was the mounting evidence that since
the Gulf War he has orchestrated a vigorous campaign of state-sponsored
terrorism against the United States.[58] Rather than knuckling under, Hussein
has hardened his resolve. As the *Wall Street Journal* summarized the situation in November 2000:

> American policy toward Iraq is falling apart. International economic sanctions
> remain in place but are being flouted on a regular basis as country after country
> sends airliners flying into Baghdad despite a flight ban. Arab countries that
> once supported sanctions now range between ambivalent and hostile toward
> them.
>
> Iraq is producing oil at full tilt, and, while most revenue still flows through
> the United Nations, the largesse from rising oil revenues is spreading in Iraq.
> American planes patrol northern and southern Iraq and bomb missile sites
> when threatened, but the exercise seems increasingly pointless. Iraqi airway
> passenger planes have begun violating those no-fly zones.[59]

Taking the interlude between the end of the Persian Gulf War and the start
of the twenty-first century into account, there is substantial reason to believe
that Saddam Hussein is unvanquished. "The American policy of containment against Iraq," concludes one assessment, "is leaking like a sieve. The
U.N. sanctions regime is crumbling. Iraq . . . earns more fuel oil sales that it
did prior to the embargo, and has been using those earnings to replenish its
military arsenal. . . . Meanwhile, Saddam Hussein is fast being rehabilitated
on the international scene. The emboldened Iraqi forces have violated the
no-fly zone with impunity, tested launched missiles, and massed troops on
their neighbors' borders. The Iraqi opposition, for its part, is weak and
divided."[60] Saddam Hussein, quipped one columnist, "seems to think he can
still win the Gulf War—and, with his oil reserves, he just might."[61]

Responsibility for dealing with Saddam has passed from Bill Clinton to
the son of former President George Bush, George W. Bush. Can he succeed
where the Clinton administration failed? Siege fatigue has set in among
many Western powers while the Iraqi dictator is enjoying the comforts of
wealth. According to one report, Saddam Hussein "has built a huge lakeside
resort as a playground for family and friends. . . . The compound boasts 625
homes for Saddam's current favorites, plus a safari park stocked with deer
and elephants. Spy satellites also have spotted stadiums, an amusement park,
hospitals, and advanced communication and irrigation systems. Meanwhile,
most Iraqis are battling unclean water supplies and fatal shortages of food
and medicine. . . ."[62]

Dealing with as complex and deceitful an enemy as Saddam Hussein
could well prove the acid test of statecraft for the new Bush administration.

CONTROVERSIES TO CONTEMPLATE

- Prior to the onset of the Persian Gulf War, the Iraqi economy appeared to be highly vulnerable to economic sanctions. Speaking before a joint session of Congress during the fall of 1990, President Bush indicated that sanctions needed time in order to succeed. However, approximately two months later, he abandoned sanctions in favor of an armed attack. Were sanctions given a chance to work? What would have been the likely consequences of continuing with a policy of economic sanctions in order to expel Iraq from Kuwait?

- What impact did perceived lessons from the Vietnam War have on the way the United States conducted the Persian Gulf War? Was the Vietnam experience applicable to Iraq? For the United States, what were the major similarities and differences between fighting in Southeast Asia versus fighting in the Middle East? Did the differences outweigh the similarities? If so, what were the consequences for the conduct of the war and the crafting of a postwar peace plan?

- Many military analysts assert that the armed forces of the U.S.-led coalition could have swept all the way to Baghdad without significant opposition. Why did President Bush decide to stop the war instead of continuing on to the Iraqi capital?

- Following the cease-fire, the Bush administration hoped that Saddam Hussein would be overthrown by an internal uprising. What was known about Saddam Hussein's opposition? What was unclear to policymakers about his opposition? What did they assume about the opposition? Were any of their assumptions unfounded? Were any of them treated as facts?

- Some political realists advised the Bush administration to design its postwar policies around the concept of a regional equilibrium. They cautioned the president against weakening Iraq to the point that it could not offset the power of such rivals as Iran and Syria. Others proposed that any balance of power policy would require that the United States play the role of the balancer, supporting whichever country was the weakest at a particular point in time. How useful is the balance of power concept as a mechanism for building a durable peace in the Gulf region?

In looking for a template for his Iraqi policy, the president is destined to be guided by his secretary of state, former chairman of the Joint Chiefs of Staff, General Colin Powell. The very personification of U.S. military power in the early 1990s, Powell favors a blend of caution and strength, as does National

Security Advisor Condoleezza Rice, who fashions a "velvet-glove forcefulness" in dealing with enemies.[63] It will be difficult for George W. Bush to avoid appearing "soft" on Saddam Hussein if military force is reserved only for overwhelming applications at the onset of a war. Moreover, any significant changes in U.S. policy toward Iraq might be interpreted as questioning the decisions his father made in office ten years ago.[64]

The question that must be faced is whether a strategy that failed in 1991 is useful today. Debate about the means to a just peace is likely to be intense in the foreseeable future, because there appears no all-purpose blueprint for bringing peace to places like Iraq where geopolitics is mixed with complex ethnic and religious conflicts. The following chapter explores these questions about effective peacemaking and peacekeeping in greater depth by investigating a civil war within a failed state — a type of conflict that appears to be increasingly prevalent and probable throughout the twenty-first century.[65] These new types of security challenges may necessitate different approaches to the making of peace than those which were pursued in the twentieth century, even if there remains a powerful temptation to apply old solutions to new problems.

To sum up, national leaders make crucial decisions when wars draw to a close. Victors from General Lysander of ancient Sparta to President George Bush of the United States typically think of **grand strategy** in the narrow terms of a military mission designed to coerce the enemy into submission and surrender. Rarely do they articulate the clear, long-term political goals that military missions ultimately serve. This inattention to political planning is troublesome because how an adversary is treated can exert a powerful influence on the prospects for lasting peace. As the Persian Gulf War illustrates, a seat-of-the-pants approach to making vital decisions in the waning days of battle can easily result in political defeat being snatched from the jaws of military victory. Peace is not something that happens spontaneously when the infernal engine of war is shut off; it must be cultivated and nourished by people of vision.

SUGGESTED READING

Byman, Daniel L., and Matthew C. Waxman. *Confronting Iraq: U.S. Policy and the Use of Force Since the Gulf War*. Santa Monica, Calif.: Rand, 2000.

Carmel, Hesi. *Intelligence for Peace*. Portland, Ore.: Frank Cass, 1999.

Cordesman, Anthony. *Iraq and the War of Sanctions*. Landam, Md.: Praeger, 1999.

Gordon, Michael R., and Bernard E. Trainor. *The General's War: The Inside Story of the Conflict in the Gulf*. Boston: Little, Brown, 1995.

Jentleson, Bruce W. *With Friends Like These: Reagan, Bush, and Saddam, 1982–1990*. New York: Norton, 1994.

Karsh, Efraim, and Inari Rautsi. *Saddam Hussein: A Political Biography*. New York: Free Press, 1991.

Miller, Judith, and Laurie Mylroie. *Saddam Hussein and the Crisis in The Gulf*. New York: Times Books/Random House, 1990.

Mylorie, Laurie. *Study of Revenge: Saddam Hussein's Unfinished War against America*. Washington, D.C.: American Enterprise Institute For Public Policy Research, 2000.

Sifry, Micah L., and Christopher Cerf. *The Gulf War Reader: History, Documents, Opinions.* New York: New York Times Books, 1991.
Simons, Geoff. *Scourging of Iraq.* New York: St. Martin's Press, 1998.

NOTES

1. Aspin, 1991, p. 10.
2. Buchanan, 1991; Kennedy as cited in *Time,* August 20, 1990, p. 82.
3. Schlesinger, 1991, p. 268.
4. *Washington Post,* March 2, 1991, p. A13.
5. Gordon and Trainor, 1995, p. 416.
6. *New York Times,* March 2, 1991, p. 5. It was U.S. Secretary of State Madeleine Albright who, on the eve of President George W. Bush's inauguration in January 2001, sarcastically noted that the Clinton administration had inherited the problem of Saddam Hussein's Iraq from President Bush, and now, ten years later, was passing the same foreign policy problem back to Bush's son, the new president-elect.
7. Waterman, 1996, p. 338.
8. Hersh, 2000, p. 81.
9. Trainor, 2000, p. A22.
10. Rosenthal, 2000, p. 8.
11. Dawisha, 1986, p. 30.
12. Post, 1993, p. 55; see also Henderson, 1991; Karsh, 1991; and Miller and Mylroie, 1990.
13. *New York Times,* August 3, 1990, pp. 8, 10.
14. Frankel, 1991, p. 17.
15. Stoessinger, 1993, p. 190.
16. Jentleson, 1994, p. 48.
17. Stoessinger, 1993, p. 190.
18. *U.S. News & World Report,* January 27, 1991, p. 31.
19. Bonafede, 1995, p. 99.
20. *New York Times,* March 3, 1991, p. 18.
21. Bush, 1990c, p. 674.
22. Bush, 1990a, p. 3.
23. Bush, 1990d, p. 739.
24. Bush, 1991, p. 261.
25. Bush, 1990b, p. 2.
26. Speech to the National Press Club on October 27, 1988, in Kegley and Raymond, 1994, p. 37.
27. Prepared statement delivered on September 4, 1990.
28. See Yergin, 1991.
29. Vaux, 1992, p. 18.
30. *Time,* August 20, 1990, p. 11.
31. Solarz, 1991, p. 270.
32. Jentleson, 1994, p. 170.
33. Ibid., p. 174.
34. Woodward, 1991, p. 237.
35. Gordon and Trainor, 1995, p. 37.
36. *Triumph without Victory,* 1992, p. 63.
37. See Aspin, 1990, pp. 2–3.
38. *Triumph without Victory,* 1992, p. 172.
39. Woodward, 1991, p. 311.
40. The letter was delivered to Iraqi Foreign Minister Tariq Aziz by Secretary of State Baker during their meeting in Geneva on January 9, 1991. Aziz refused to deliver it to Saddam Hussein because he felt the tone was inappropriate.

41. *Triumph without Victory,* 1992, p. 172.
42. Iraqi transcript of a meeting on July 25, 1990, with U.S. ambassador April Glaspie. Hussein voiced the same theme in a February 1990 speech before the Arab Cooperation Council when he reminded the audience that the United States withdrew from Lebanon after marines were killed in the bombing of Beirut airport.
43. Gordon and Trainor, 1995, p. 180.
44. Cohen, 1994, p. 110.
45. The technology used in the Gulf War was an outgrowth of a strategy devised in the 1970s to offset the numerical superiority of Warsaw Pact forces. According to a 1996 report issued by the General Accounting Office, the Pentagon exaggerated the effectiveness of this technology. See *International Herald Tribune,* July 10, 1996, pp. 1, 7.
46. Hersh, 2000.
47. Polmar, 1991, p. 212. Iraqi battle deaths have never been counted carefully. Estimates range from 6,500 to 200,000.
48. Gordon and Trainor, 1995, p. 444.
49. Ibid., p. 461.
50. *U.S. News & World Report,* April 15, 1991, p. 31.
51. Schneider, 1992, p. 66.
52. Bonafede, 1995, p. 119.
53. In Hersh, 2000, p. 70.
54. Finn, 2000, p. D5.
55. Anderson, 2000, p. 82.
56. Nordland, 2000, p. 32.
57. Whitelaw and Strobel, 2000, p. 53.
58. See Mylorie, 2000.
59. Seib, 2000, p. A28.
60. Kaplan, 2000, p. 28.
61. Anderson, 2000, p. 76.
62. Winik, 2000, p. 10.
63. Mufson, 2000a and 2000b, p. 8.
64. Fitts, 2001, p. A6.
65. See Wallensteen and Sollenberg, 2000.

· 8 ·

HUMANITARIAN INTERVENTION INTO KOSOVO: A QUIXOTIC CRUSADE?

Kosovo has cast in stark relief the dilemma of what has been called humanitarian intervention: on the one side, the question of the legitimacy of an action taken by a regional organization without a UN mandate; on the other, the universally recognized imperative of effectively halting violations of human rights with grave humanitarian consequences. The inability in the case of Kosovo to unify these two equally compelling interests of the international community . . . can only be viewed as a tragedy.

—KOFI ANNAN,
UN SECRETARY-GENERAL

PREVIEW

Ever since the Peace of Westphalia ended the Thirty Years' War in 1648, the twin principles of sovereignty and nonintervention have governed international politics. Sovereignty meant that no authority stood above the state, except that which the state voluntarily conferred on any organization it joined. Nonintervention meant that states could manage affairs inside their territorial boundaries without external interference. As the twentieth century drew to a close, several instances of foreign military involvement in the civil wars of other states raised questions about the Westphalian rules of international politics. Sovereignty no longer seemed sacrosanct. According to many political leaders, humanitarian intervention was not only legally justified but morally necessary in situations where brutal governments were violating the human rights of their citizens.

The case in this chapter describes the 1999 war in Kosovo, an armed conflict between the Federal Republic of Yugoslavia and the North Atlantic Treaty Organization (NATO) that highlights many of the issues surrounding the concept of humanitarian intervention. It is a tragic tale whose roots lie in the failure of what has been called the "Yugoslavia idea." The term refers to the conviction that despite being stitched together from several nations, a unique Yugoslav identity would eventually replace the affiliation citizens had with the constituent nations in the federation. Such an identity never took hold, and the country eventually collapsed in a series of vicious wars of succession.

Kosovo, a province within Yugoslavia, suffered through years of agonizing military conflict as its ethnic Albanian majority sought greater autonomy from the Serb republic of which it was a part. Shocked by the intensity of the conflict, U.S. Senator Daniel Patrick Moynihan once observed, "Yugoslavia's may be the war of the future: one waged between different tribes, harboring centuries-old grudges about language, religion, and territory, and provoking bitterness for generations to come." Although it may presage the shape wars may take in the early twenty-first century, a study of the origins and outcome of the war in Kosovo offers insights into many of the concepts that scholars and policymakers have long used to analyze international politics, including:

- sovereignty
- failed states
- nationalism
- ethno-nationalism
- international mediation
- state-sponsored terrorism
- humanitarian intervention
- coercive air power
- international peacekeeping

In addition to emphasizing these concepts, this case also provokes consideration of the adequacy of rational-actor conceptions of decision making. It encourages us to include the political psychology of grand passions in our understanding of how leaders make fateful decisions about war and peace. As you read through this chapter, consider how feelings of resentment, revenge, and rage may have affected the course of events on the Balkan peninsula.

Some Kosovar refugees left in a caravan of tractors, rickety Ladas, and worn-out Mercedes-Benzes. Thousands of others jammed into trains, cattle trucks, and horse-drawn carts. Many more hobbled along on foot, praying for the strength to endure the grueling trek. Stripped of valuables by unscrupulous border officials, the refugees poured out of Kosovo into neighboring Albania, Macedonia, and Montenegro. Not since World War II had Europe witnessed such an exodus.

On the eve this exodus, Kosovo was a province within Serbia, one of the republics that formed Yugoslavia. Roughly the size of Connecticut, 90 percent of Kosovo's 2 million inhabitants were ethnic Albanians. It had the highest birthrate in Europe and a population largely under the age of thirty, demographic trends which disturbed many Serbs, who saw Kosovo as their ancient homeland. Moreover, they were angered by what they believed were Albanian efforts to pressure the Serb minority into leaving. Slobodan Milosevic, who had risen to the presidency of Yugoslavia in 1997 under a banner of Serb jingoism, insisted that Kosovo would remain Serbian. "Every nation has a love which eternally warms its heart," he told a mass rally in Belgrade. "For Serbia it is Kosovo."[1]

Milosevic proposed to rid Kosovo of Albanians through a policy of state-supported terrorism, known euphemistically as "ethnic cleansing." His forces used rape, murder, and arson to forcibly expel the Albanians. On March 14, 1999, NATO launched air strikes against Yugoslavia to stave off what its members saw as a looming humanitarian catastrophe. U.S. policymakers assumed that a brief display of air power would compel Milosevic to stop the atrocities. "I don't see this as a long-term operation," declared Secretary of State Madeleine Albright on the first night of the bombing campaign.[2] However, much to the surprise of the Clinton administration, the Yugoslav leader did not immediately acquiesce; instead, he used scores of police and paramilitary forces to accelerate the ethnic cleansing of Kosovo. According to the United Nations High Commissioner for Refugees, 848,100 Kosovar Albanians eventually fled the province.[3] Rather than quickly bringing Milosevic to heel, the air campaign seemed to accelerate his pogrom against ethnic Albanians. As Pentagon spokesman Ken Bacon admitted, it was "difficult . . . to say that we have prevented [even] one act of brutality."[4]

Because only lightly armed paramilitary units were needed to purge entire villages of their inhabitants, NATO's attacks on Yugoslavia's industrial assets and mechanized units did not thwart Milosevic's plan. As a result, President Clinton faced a fateful decision: Should he escalate the air war, destroying an ever-widening array of targets until Milosevic capitulated? Or should he prepare for a protracted ground campaign against Yugoslavia? When weighing the use of air and ground forces, policymakers must consider what they seek to accomplish as well as what they seek to prevent.[5] Moreover, they must also calculate what public opinion at home and abroad will be. While the president was determined to stop the atrocities, could he do so without dismembering the Federal Republic of Yugoslavia and turning Kosovo into a permanent NATO protectorate? To better understand what brought Kosovo to this fateful point, it is necessary to first examine the history of Yugoslavia.

THE RISE AND FALL OF YUGOSLAVIA

Epic poetry from the Balkans tells of a confrontation in 1389 between the Ottoman Empire and a defiant Serbian nobleman. During the fourteenth century, Serbia was divided among various feudal lords. Prince Lazar, lord of a fiefdom in the Morava valley, incurred the wrath of invading Ottoman forces when he refused to become a vassal of Sultan Murad. In the words of a famous poem, the sultan proclaimed "we cannot both of us be ruler . . . [so] come to Kosovo meadow, and we shall do division with our swords."[6] The two armies clashed at the Field of Blackbirds (Kosovo Polje), near the modern city of Prestina. The Ottomans defeated the Serbs and ruled Kosovo for the next four centuries.

The defeat suffered by the Serbs at Kosovo Polje was a milestone in the evolution of Serbian national self-consciousness because it spawned a foundation myth. All societies, writes R. M. MacIver, are "held together by a myth-system."[7] Within such systems, foundation myths purport to explain the origins and destiny of a **nation**. Although they may be false in significant (though not very obvious) ways, foundation myths are accepted uncritically by many people. They tell dramatic stories about their nation's "sacred history" and thus serve as "the exemplary model for all significant human activities."[8]

At the heart of the Serbian foundation myth is a sense of continuity between ancient traumas and current events. "Concepts of the past and the present are so intermixed that a grievance of long ago is perceived as a present affliction," observes Paul Mojzes. "Likewise, it is believed that a present action may not only vindicate but actually eradicate and reverse a past defeat."[9] Kosovo is sacred ground for the Serbian nation. It contains the Patriarchate of Pec, the center of the Serbian Orthodox Church during the Ottoman period, as well as many important religious sites, including the Monastery of Michael the Archangel near Prizren as well as the fourteenth-century Gracanica and Decani monasteries. Owing to harsh Ottoman rule and difficult economic conditions, over the centuries many Serbs migrated to lands north of Kosovo. In the meantime, Albanians began moving from their rugged mountainous homeland on the Adriatic into the adjacent Kosovo basin, where they replaced the Serbs as Kosovo's largest ethnic group. From the Albanian perspective, they were merely seeking better economic opportunities. From the Serb perspective, the Albanians occupied Kosovo's sacred soil and converted to Islam to reinforce Turkish domination; hence they do not rightfully belong in Kosovo. For those under the sway of Serbia's foundation myth, these alleged injuries must be avenged, no matter how long ago they were committed. They believe steadfastness in the face of suffering will eventually turn defeat at Kosovo Polje into victory.[10]

Serbia and the Idea of Yugoslavism

The Serbian drive for independence began with a revolt against the Ottoman Empire in 1804 (see Table 8.1). It gathered momentum incrementally throughout the nineteenth century as one piece of territory after another was wrested from Turkish control. Patriotic fervor surged across the land as Serbs reveled in heroic tales about their collective history. Vuk Karajich

TABLE 8.1

A Chronology of Major Events in Serbian History

Date	Events
1389	Ottoman Turks defeat the Serbs in Kosovo at the Field of Blackbirds
1804	Serbian forces under Karageorge (George Petrovich) rise up against the Turks
1829	Serbia is granted autonomy within the Ottoman Empire
1876	With Russian support, Serbia and Montenegro declare war on Turkey; they block the Turks at Alexinatz but are defeated at Djunis
1877	Russia declares war on Turkey
1878	Serbia receives independence from Turkey under the Treaty of San Stefano, which is confirmed at the Congress of Berlin
1885	Serbian forces attack Bulgaria but are defeated at Slivnitza and Pirot
1908	Austria-Hungary annexes Bosnia-Herzegovina, creating discontent among Serbian nationalists
1912	Serbian, Bulgarian, and Greek forces attack Turkish forces in Macedonia and Thrace; Serbs win a decisive victory at the Battle of Monastir
1914	A Serbian nationalist assassinates Austrian Archduke Franz Ferdinand in Sarajevo; Austria attacks Serbia; World War I begins
1918	The Kingdom of Serbs, Croats, and Slovenes established (renamed Yugoslavia in 1929)
1941	Nazi Germany invades Yugoslavia; resistance forces begin guerrilla struggle
1946	Yugoslav communists acquire control of the Yugoslav government
1948	Conflict occurs between Yugoslav President Josip Tito and Joseph Stalin of the Soviet Union; Yugoslavia is expelled from the Cominform
1974	New constitution grants autonomy to Kosovo
1980	President Tito dies
1981	Student protest at Prestina University escalates to an anti-Serbian riot
1987	Slobodan Milosevic begins to consolidate his control over the Serbian Communist Party
1989	Milosevic elected president of Serbia; Kosovo's constitutional autonomy rescinded
1990	Free, multiparty parliamentary elections are held in all six of Yugoslavia's republics
1991	Slovenia declares independence and successfully defends its territory against the Yugoslav federal army; Croatia declares independence; war breaks out between Croatia and Serbia; Macedonia declares independence

Date	Events
1992	Bosnia-Herzegovina declares independence; civil war erupts among Bosnian Muslims, Serbs, and Croats; Serbia and Montenegro form a new, smaller Yugoslav federation
1995	The presidents of Serbia, Croatia, and Bosnia meet in Dayton, Ohio, and sign a peace agreement
1996	Conflict between Serbia and Kosovar Albanians escalates; Kosovo Liberation Army gains support from ethnic Albanians
1997	Molosevic is inaugurated as president of the Federal Republic of Yugoslavia
1999	The Rambouillet, France, peace talks between Serbs and Kosovar Albanians collapse; NATO air strikes against Serbia begin on March 24 and last for seventy-eight days; UN Mission in Kosovo is established on June 13; the NATO-led Kosovo Force (KFOR) is assigned peacekeeping duties
2000	Vojislav Kostunica defeats Slobodan Milosevic in the Yugoslav presidential election
2001	KFOR peacekeepers face a potential Albanian insurgency in southern Serbia led by the Liberation Army of Presevo, Bujanovac and Medvedja
	Slobodan Milosevic arrested on allegations of criminal conspiracy and diverting millions of dollars during his thirteen-year rule.

exemplified this rising tide of **nationalism** in 1814 when he published *Popular Songs and Epics of the Serbs*. As the Ottoman Empire continued to recede from Europe, many Serbs began dreaming of a state that would unite the other Southern Slavs (Croats, Macedonians, Montenegrins, and Slovenes) under their leadership. By 1829, the Ottoman Empire recognized Serbia as an autonomous principality. Roughly half a century later, following a war against the Turks that eventually brought Russia into the fray, Serbia achieved independence under a section of the Treaty of San Stefano (1878).

The first attempt to unify Southern Slavs occurred after World War I when the defeat of the Central Powers provided an opportunity to redraw the map of southeastern Europe. Rather than forming small, vulnerable countries, some of the ethnic groups on the Balkan Peninsula reluctantly decided to join with Serbia, which was already recognized by the European **great powers** as an independent state. On December 1, 1918, King Alexander of Serbia announced the establishment of the Kingdom of Serbs, Croats, and Slovenes. Renamed Yugoslavia in 1929 (*Yug* means "south" in many Slavic languages), the new country faced several grave problems. Externally, its boundaries were challenged by Italy in the west and Bulgaria in the east. Internally, it was divided by heritage, religion, and alphabet: Serbs had lived under Ottoman rule, they were Orthodox Christians, and they used the Cyrllic alphabet; Croats and Slovenes had lived under Austro-Hungarian rule, they were Catholics, and they used the Latin alphabet. Sharp disagreements over how Yugoslavia should be governed magnified these divisions. Whereas Serbs favored a centralized monarchy, Croats and Slovenes preferred a decentralized, federal republic. Plagued by constant bickering and brutal acts of political violence, the Yugoslavian government never enjoyed widespread legitimacy among the non-Serbian population. Already reeling from powerful forces within, it collapsed soon after the Germans invaded in April 1941.

The second effort at unifying the Southern Slavs came after World War II. Throughout the war, a resistance movement known as the Partisans conducted a relentless guerrilla campaign against German garrisons in Yugoslavia. Led by Josip Broz (who used the pseudonym "Tito"), the Partisans articulated a patriotic, federalist, and revolutionary vision of Yugoslavism. Projecting the image of anti-German liberators, transethnic conciliators, and harbingers of a new political order, they promised a future of "brotherhood and unity."[11] Tito was a dedicated communist who had risen to the rank of general secretary in the Yugoslav party by early 1939. As such, he believed that the ethnonationalist differences would eventually wither away in a socialist Yugoslavia. But, as historian Gale Stokes points out, the linkage between "socialist" and "Yugoslav" had a critical weakness: "As long as the communist movement remained strong, Yugoslavia was not in danger." If ethnonationalist outbursts flared up, they could be suppressed by the party. But if communism in Yugoslavia disintegrated, "then the Yugoslavia it championed would disintegrate too."[12]

Unlike in other Central and Eastern European states at the end of the Second World War, the communists in Yugoslavia possessed their own power base. Their country had not been liberated by Soviet troops and their leaders did not owe their positions to Joseph Stalin. To be sure, the war's toll was horrendous — over a tenth of Yugoslavia's population perished, and a fifth of the housing, half of the railways, and three-fifths of the roads were destroyed.[13] Yet out of this devastation arose a spirit of heroism that attracted people to Tito's cause. In the November 1945 elections for a two-chamber legislative assembly, the Communist People's Front won 91 percent of the vote in the Federal Chamber and 89 percent in the Chamber of Nationalities. As one student of the period observes, these lopsided results reflected "the deep reservoir of authentic popularity, prestige, and legitimacy that Tito, his Partisan movement, and his Communist party had amassed during the war."[14]

Cognizant of the ethnic discord that plagued the interwar years, Tito reconstituted Yugoslavia as a federation composed of six equal republics: Serbia, Croatia, Slovenia, Bosnia-Herzegovina, Macedonia, and Montenegro. Moreover, to assuage the feelings of Hungarian and Albanian minorities, two "autonomous regions" were created within the Serbian Republic: Vojvodina and Kosovo, respectively (see Map 8.1). The ethnic composition of the republics varied widely. Whereas 93 percent of Slovenia's population was Slovenian, only 43 percent of Bosnia-Herzegovina consisted of Bosnians (as the Slavic Muslims were called), while another 34 percent were Serbs, and roughly 17 percent were Croats.[15] In addition to variations in the ethnic composition of the republics, levels of economic development also differed. The northern third of the country (Slovenia, Croatia, and the autonomous

MAP 8.1 The Disintegration of Yugoslavia. The Yugoslav state forged by Tito after World War II began disintegrating a decade after his death. In 1991 Slovenia and Croatia declared their independence. They were followed later that year by Macedonia, and by Bosnia-Herzegovina the following year. During April 1992, the two remaining republics of Serbia and Montenegro formed a new Yugoslav federation that was little more than an expanded Serbia. The lightly shaded area of the map contains the republics that seceded from Yugoslavia after 1990.

region of Vojvodina within Serbia) had twice the per capita income of the rest of Yugoslavia, an inequality exacerbated by the desire of northerners to invest their earnings locally rather than have them used to subsidize the less industrialized southern republics.

During his years in power, Tito used a blend of personal diplomacy and brute force to muzzle ethnic discord. He also experimented with various mechanisms to defuse tensions among the republics. In 1952 the Yugoslav Communist Party was renamed the League of Communists of Yugoslavia to reflect a series of reforms aimed at decentralizing its structure. New constitutions were adopted in 1953, 1963, and 1974, gradually giving more equitable representation in the legislature and Federal Executive Council to the country's different ethnic groups. Finally, self-managed enterprises were promoted, which sought to take the interests of surrounding communities into consideration when making economic decisions. The son of a Croat father and Slovenian mother, Tito understood that Yugoslavia would be ripped apart if militant nationalism took hold in any of its republics.

Yugoslavia after Tito

After his death in 1980, Tito's socialist federated republic began to unravel. Rather than grooming a successor, Tito had established a collegial system where the presidency of the country was rotated annually within an executive committee containing one member from each republic and autonomous region. Historian Joseph Rothschild points out that as a result, "the leadership of Yugoslavia became kaleidoscopic and anonymous," which "badly eroded the prestige, authority, and residual unity of the state."[16] The lack of a president with Tito's stature could not have come at a worse time. Having borrowed heavily during the previous decade to finance salary increases for state employees and wasteful projects that duplicated in one republic what already existed in another, policymakers in Belgrade were caught between rising inflation and declining productivity. Deeply in debt and saddled with revolving leaders, Yugoslavia searched in vain throughout the 1980s for fiscal and monetary policies that would stabilize the economy.

A wave of regional grievances accompanied the economic downturn. In March 1981, a demonstration at Kosovo's Prestina University sparked by student frustration over living conditions quickly escalated to an anti-Serbian riot. Pointing out that the per capita income in Kosovo was less than one-third of the national average, many of the demonstrators insisted that the autonomous province be elevated to the legal status of a full republic. Others made more radical demands, including unification with Albania. Alarmed by the direction the protest was taking, the authorities declared a state of siege and sent in troops to quell the unrest. Estimates vary, but several hundred people may have died in the ensuing clashes between the military and the demonstrators.

Friction between Serbs and Kosovo's ethnic Albanians had existed since the end of the Second World War. Now it threatened to tear the country apart. An example of the widening rift could be seen in a controversial document prepared by the Serbian Academy of Sciences and leaked to the press in late 1986. Often referred to as the Memorandum, its authors alleged that poor economic conditions in the Serbian Republic were the result of discrimination by non-Serbian politicians, who gave the autonomous regions of Vojvodina and Kosovo so many special rights under the 1974 constitution that Serbia no longer controlled its own fate. In effect, the Memorandum alleged these provinces were self-governing entities within Serbia that could not be controlled by Serbs. In Kosovo, the Albanian majority was said to be taking advantage of the situation by harassing the Serbian minority to drive them from the very cradle of their nation. Serbs in that hallowed province, the document concluded, were suffering political and cultural genocide.[17]

"Only solidarity saves the Serbs" became the slogan of those who suspected that the federal government had orchestrated a policy of weakening Serbia to strengthen Yugoslavia. Kosovo bristled with tension as inflammatory rhetoric emanated from both Serbs and ethnic Albanians. Amidst the swirling accusations and denials, Slobodan Milosevic, the head of the Serbian branch of the League of Yugoslav Communists, traveled to Kosovo on April 24, 1987, to hear grievances from irate Serbs living in the province. Assembled at the Field of Blackbirds where the epic Battle of Kosovo had been fought against the Ottomans centuries earlier, the Serbs clashed with local Kosovo Albanian police. Milosovic, in a brief but electrifying speech, told the crowd:

> Comrades . . . you should stay here. This is your country, these are your houses, your fields and gardens, your memories. You are not going to abandon your lands because life is hard, because you are oppressed by injustice and humiliation. . . . You should stay here, both for your ancestors and your descendants. Otherwise you would shame your ancestors and disappoint your descendants. But I do not suggest you stay here suffering and enduring a situation with which you are not satisfied. On the contrary! It should be changed. . . . Yugoslavia does not exist without Kosovo! Yugoslavia would disintegrate without Kosovo! Yugoslavia and Serbia are not going to give up Kosovo.[18]

On television that night in the capital city of Belgrade, Serbia, a film clip of Milosevic declaring "No one will ever beat a Serb again" was replayed repeatedly. His popularity soared. A few months later, at the Eighth Session of the League of Communists of Serbia, Milosevic catapulted to the summit of political power in Serbia, though he would not formally assume the presidency until May 1989.

Yugoslavia under Milosevic

Slobodan Milosevic was born in 1941 on the outskirts of Belgrade. His mother was a communist activist and his father, who had trained as an Orthodox priest, taught language and religion. Both of his parents later committed suicide.

For most of his career, Milosevic was an undistinguished bureaucrat who rose from one position to the next on the coattails of his friend Ivan Stambolic, the nephew of an eminent Partisan leader. After studying law at Belgrade University, he worked for Technogas and then moved on to Beobanka. By the mid-1980s, he took a position with the League of Yugoslav Communists, where he initially showed little sympathy for ethnonationalist appeals. However, once he realized his political power could be enhanced by championing Serbian nationalism, he became a strident advocate of Serbian territorial ambitions.

In the aftermath of the Eighth Session of the League of Yugoslav Communists, Milosevic took a series of steps to consolidate his power. To install loyalists in key government offices, he initiated an "anti-bureaucratic revolution" —a removal of *foteljasi* (armchair sitters, a term implying nonproductive officials).[19] To eliminate opposition within the Serbian branch of the League of Yugoslav Communists, he undertook a process called "differentiation" that purged anyone who did not assure him of total loyalty.[20] Finally, to generate popular support, he organized hundreds of "meetings of truth" across Serbia that involved some 5 million people in anti-Albanian rallies.[21]

By late 1989, as communism was collapsing elsewhere in Eastern Europe, Slobodan Milosevic had become the most powerful figure in Yugoslavia. With his position solidified, he rescinded the **devolution** provisions of the 1974 Constitution that provided Kosovo's autonomy. Predictably, ethnic Albanians went on a rampage against Serbs living in the province, which further bolstered Milosevic's reputation. A clever opportunist, Milosevic could act charming one moment and brutal the next. Willing to incite Serbs living in Croatia, Bosnia, and Kosovo whenever their rebellions might advance his personal interests, he was equally prepared to sacrifice them if it was expedient. In short, as F. Stephen Larrabee puts it, Milosevic was "both the arsonist and the fire brigade."[22] He would start a crisis and then make himself essential for its resolution.

THE CIVIL WAR IN BOSNIA

Milosevic's demagoguery was watched with growing apprehension outside of Serbia. Citizens in the other republics were appalled by the repression he had unleashed in Kosovo, and they feared it would some day be used against them. In June 1991 the Slovene and Croatian parliaments declared independence from Yugoslavia. Belgrade responded by sending armored units into the breakaway republics. The Yugoslav National Army was forced into a humiliating retreat by the Slovenes, but hostilities in Croatia did not end as quickly. Assisted by paramilitary forces drawn from Serbs living in Croatia, the army seized land along the Sava River, overwhelmed the mining town of Vukovar, and soon controlled a fifth of Croatia.

The fighting spread to Bosnia-Herzegovina the following year. With large Serb and Croat minorities living among the Muslim population, Bosnian leaders feared their territory would be dismembered by the pull of rival **irredentist** claims. In a futile attempt to prevent partition along ethnic lines, they declared independence and sought security guarantees from the European Community. Bosnia's Serbs responded by proclaiming the formation of their own state, which they called the Serb Republic of Bosnia. Bosnian Serb paramilitary units proceeded to conduct a policy of ethnic cleansing, by which murder, torture, rape, and other horrific actions were used against non-Serbs to drive them out of the area. By early 1993, two-thirds of Bosnia was under Serb control, almost half of the population had been forced from their homes, and Sarajevo, the capital city and host of the 1984 Winter Olympics, suffered a brutal siege.[23] To make matters worse, Bosnian Croats began attacking Muslim positions around the medieval city of Mostar.

As the civil war in Bosnia raged on, discontent in Kosovo continued to fester. The voice of ethnic Albanians in Kosovo was Ibrahim Rugova, an urbane professor of Albanian literature known for his flamboyant silk scarf and a penchant for drinking huge quantities of coffee. Believing that Serbia possessed an insurmountable military advantage over the Albanians, Rugova counseled patience and passive resistance. He argued that because Kosovo already enjoyed self-government under the 1974 Constitution, by eschewing violence it would ultimately achieve republic status. Many Albanians disagreed, arguing that political conditions had not improved under Rugova's meek leadership. In May 1993 several of them gunned down a group of Serb police officers in Glogovac. Their attack was the opening salvo in a campaign waged against Kosovo's Serbs by an organization called the Kosovo Liberation Army (KLA). For the next two years, Albanian guerrillas launched sporadic attacks against Serbs, which provoked harsh reprisals against villages suspected of sheltering the guerrillas.

The KLA insurgency received an unexpected boost from the way the civil war in Bosnia ended. During the summer of 1995, Bosnian Serbs seized the Muslim town of Srebrenica, which had been declared a "safe area" by the UN Security Council. Referring to the bloody 1804 Serb rebellion against the Ottoman Empire, General Ratko Mladic, the Serb commander, announced that "the time has finally come to take revenge on the Turks in this region."[24] During the next week, the world witnessed a wave of brutality as his forces killed over seven thousand Bosnian Muslims in the most gruesome mass execution in Europe since World War II.

As the world recoiled in horror over the massacre at Srebrenica, several other developments began to turn the tide of battle against the Bosnian Serbs and their patrons in Belgrade. First, the combat effectiveness of the Bosnian and Croatian armies had improved: The former was now obtaining desperately needed weapons from Iran, while the latter was receiving military training from retired American officers. Second, the Croat minority in Bosnia agreed to join with Bosnia's Muslims in a new federation that would fight alongside the Republic of Croatia against the Serbs. Third, to supplement the economic sanctions already in place against Yugoslavia, increased diplomatic pressure was placed on Milosevic by the so-called Contact Group (the United States, Great Britain, France, Germany, and Russia) to restrain General Mladic and Radovan Karadzic, the political leader of the Bosnian Serbs. Finally, on August 30, over sixty NATO warplanes began a massive assault on Serb positions around Sarajevo.

As a result of these developments, the Bosnian Serbs faced a joint Croat-Bosnian Federation offensive in August and September. Serb forces were pushed out of the Krajina region of Croatia and began to fall back to Banja Luka, the largest Serb city in Bosnia. By October, the United States concluded that the time was ripe for a cease-fire. On the one hand, a rough **balance of**

power existed among the combatants. On the other hand, chronic disagreements between the Croats and Bosnian Muslims threatened to jeopardize their fragile coalition. By stopping the fighting before anyone had to capitulate, peace talks could commence without a heavy shroud of humiliation draped over one or more of the belligerents. None of them had achieved all they might have wished on the battlefield, but neither were they so dissatisfied with the military status quo that they would balk at negotiating a peace agreement.

In November 1995, at Wright-Patterson Air Force Base on the outskirts of Dayton, Ohio, President Alija Izetbegovic of Bosnia, Franjo Tudjman of Croatia, and Slobodan Milosevic of Serbia met to sign a peace accord. Under the terms of the agreement, a single Bosnian state would be established. It would possess a central government in Sarajevo and two regional entities: a Muslim-Croat Federation encompassing 51 percent of the country's territory, and a Serb Republic of Bosnia comprising 49 percent of the territory. An International Protection Force (IFOR) of sixty thousand NATO troops would oversee the disengagement of the rival armies and their withdrawal to predesignated locations. In addition, free elections would be held within nine months, displaced persons were allowed to recover lost property, and all citizens were guaranteed the right to move freely throughout the country.

Unfortunately, the Dayton Accords did not provide the foundation for a stable, multiethnic Bosnian state. Not only did the peace agreement leave two opposing armies in one country, but it placed an arbitrary time limit on the IFOR peacekeepers who stood between rival federation and Serb troops. Expecting IFOR soldiers to be withdrawn in the near future, both sides delayed implementing the Dayton Accord's provisions.[25] The fragile nature of the Croat-Muslim Federation created other problems. Military necessity encouraged Bosnian Croats to align with their Muslim neighbors during the war, but their sympathies remained with the Republic of Croatia. Hardly anyone felt allegiance to the Bosnian state cobbled together at Dayton. With ethnic animosities still seething and each group harboring fellow members responsible for hideous acts during the war, few people charged with war crimes were brought to justice, even though the International War Crimes Tribunal established in The Hague by the United Nations two years earlier had handed down over fifty indictments.

FROM THE DAYTON ACCORDS TO THE RAMBOUILLET PEACE CONFERENCE

Although Kosovo was not discussed at Dayton, the outcome of the peace talks over Bosnia marked a turning point in the ongoing conflict between Kosovar Albanians and Serbs. At issue was the Serb Republic of Bosnia. Kosovo's ethnic Albanians could not understand why those who had committed war crimes in Srebrenica and elsewhere were granted 49 percent of Bosnia under the Dayton Accords. In the words of one KLA member: "We all felt a deep, deep sense of betrayal. We mounted a peaceful, civilized protest [against Serbian policies in Kosovo and] . . . we were ignored." The Dayton peace negotiations "taught us a painful truth, [that] those that want freedom must fight for it."[26] Dayton, in other words, "was an extraordinary trauma for the Kosovo Albanians" because "it confirmed to them in the most dramatic and humiliating way that Rugova's policy of passive resistance had failed."[27] Recognition of the Serb Republic of Bosnia shattered all hopes for peaceful change in Kosovo.

As Kosovo's Albanians grew disenchanted with Rugova's nonviolent strategy, the KLA intensified its guerrilla campaign. Each attack prompted a more brutal Serb reprisal, which radicalized even more Albanians. Strengthened by the surge of new recruits and financial support from Albanian émigré communities in Italy, France, Switzerland, and Germany, the KLA began asserting control over an ever-widening area. Beginning in the late spring of 1998, the intermittent sniping and skirmishing of previous years escalated to fierce fighting. After weeks of KLA gains, a Serb counteroffensive began in mid-July and drove the overextended KLA guerrillas back into hiding. Some 200,000 ethnic Albanians were displaced by the fighting, with many seeking refuge in the hills along Kosovo's border with Albania.

Responding to images of burning homes and frightened villagers on the nightly news, the UN Security Council passed Resolution 1199 on September 23, which demanded that Yugoslavia "cease all action by the security forces affecting the civilian population" and alluded to the possibility of "further action" if it did not obey. NATO made similar demands the next day and, following reports of Serb massacres, U.S. Secretary of Defense William Cohen threatened Yugoslavia with air strikes. The crisis was temporarily diffused when U.S. Special Envoy Richard Holbrooke convinced Yugoslav President Slobodan Milosevic to allow unarmed Organization of Security and Cooperation in Europe (OSCE) troops to monitor **human rights** violations in Kosovo.

Violence broke out again in early 1999, when forty-five ethnic Albanians from Racak were killed in retaliation for the murder of three Serb police officers a week earlier. Sensing that the cease-fire agreement brokered by Holbrooke was unraveling, on January 29 the members of the Contact Group summoned the Serbs and Kosovar Albanians to attend peace talks in Ramouillet, a small town located about thirty miles from Paris. In effect, they had been given an ultimatum: The Serbs were threatened with NATO bombing if they declined, and the Albanians were warned that their refusal would result in being left to fend for themselves against the Serbs. Grudgingly, both sides agreed to send delegations. Whereas Milosevic dispatched a group that lacked decision-making authority but excelled at late-night carousing, the Albanians included virtually every Kosovar politican and guerrilla leader of stature, which led to frequent quarrels over who was in charge of their delegation.[28]

The peace proposal offered to the delegates at Rambouillet called for the disarmament of the KLA, the withdrawal of Yugoslav military units from Kosovo, deployment of a NATO-led **peacekeeping** force, restoration of

Kosovo's autonomy, and a referendum in three years on the region's political future. Much to the surprise of the United States, neither side accepted the proposal. As one member of the Clinton administration roared: "Here is the greatest nation on earth pleading with some nothing-balls to do something entirely in their own interest—which is to say yes to an interim agreement—and they defy us."[29]

With negotiations at an impasse, the peace talks were adjourned for nineteen days and then resumed in Paris on March 14. Tremendous pressure was placed on the Albanians during the recess to accept NATO's terms. Although they ultimately relented, the Serbs remained intransigent and rejected the peace proposal. The talks concluded on March 19, and OSCE monitors were withdrawn from Kosovo the following day. In a final effort to convince the Serbs to accept a cease-fire and the insertion of a NATO-led peacekeeping force in Kosovo, U.S. envoy Richard Holbrooke flew to Belgrade and met with Slobodan Milosevic on March 22. If anyone had a chance to salvage Rambouillet, it was Holbrooke. Labeled "the Muhammad Ali of diplomacy" by other foreign service officers for being able to wear down even the most difficult opponent,[30] he had enormous experience bargaining with Milosevic. Holbrooke told the Serbian leader that unless he accepted the proposed Rambouillet agreement, NATO would bomb Yugoslavia. Speaking in a firm, deliberate tone, Holbrooke promised: "It will be swift, it will be severe, it will be sustained."[31]

A WAR FOR HUMAN RIGHTS

In an televised address to the nation on March 24, the first night of NATO air strikes against the Federal Republic of Yugoslavia, President Clinton argued that "ending this tragedy is a moral imperative." The United States had learned a lesson in Bosnia: Firmness saves lives. "We must apply that lesson in Kosovo," he continued, "before what happened in Bosnia, happens there, too."[32] Clinton's appeal to moral necessity was echoed by other NATO leaders. NATO Secretary-General Javier Solana called the **intervention** "a moral duty."[33] British Prime Minister Tony Blair agreed: "The only peace that lasts is a peace based on justice . . . and we have a duty to see justice done."[34]

If NATO acted without a UN Security Council resolution specifically authorizing the use of force against Yugoslavia, it would violate the UN Charter. Article 2(4) prohibits "the threat or use of force against the territorial integrity or political independence of any state," except in self-defense (Article 51) or when authorized by the Security Council (Chapter VII). Although neither exception applied in Kosovo, NATO officials asserted that it was legally permissible and morally necessary to intervene with armed force to stop flagrant violations of human rights. Their argument rested on three propositions. The first proposition asserted that human rights are an international entitlement. Article 55 (c) of the UN Charter requires member states to promote "universal respect for, and observance of, human rights."

Over the past fifty years, the UN has developed a detailed list of inherent, inalienable rights of all human beings. The most important legal formulation of these rights is expressed in the so-called International Bill of Human Rights, the informal name given to the Universal Declaration of Human Rights (which was passed by a vote of the UN General Assembly in 1948), the International Covenant on Civil and Political Rights, and the International Covenant on Economic, Social, and Cultural Rights (which were both opened for signature in 1966 and entered into force a decade later). For NATO's advocates of **humanitarian intervention,** the legal rules governing these rights were regarded as *jus cogens*—peremptory norms from which no derogation was permitted.

The second proposition maintained that governments committing grave violations of human rights lose their legitimacy. Although Article 2 (7) of the UN Charter prevents member states from interfering in the domestic matters of another, the charter's legal protection does not extend to genocide, torture, or other horrific acts shocking to the conscience of the international community. As one legal theorist has expressed it, any government involved in egregious human rights abuses "betrays the very purpose for which it exists and so forfeits not only its domestic legitimacy, but its international legitimacy as well."[35] By forfeiting its political legitimacy, adds another scholar, it becomes an international outlaw—a rogue state that "forfeits the protection of international law."[36]

The third proposition declared that the international community had a legal responsibility to stop human rights violations. According to the International Court of Justice, there are some obligations that a state has "towards the international community as a whole," and all members of that community "have a legal interest in their protection."[37] According to NATO officials, the entitlement for protection against genocide gives rise to these legal obligations *erga omnes*. Any member of the international community has legal standing to call for a state to observe these obligations and to impose sanctions if wrongful acts continue.

To **realist** critics who dismissed Kosovo because it was too insignificant to engage NATO security interests, supporters of the intervention replied that anywhere people are being exterminated is a place that entreats us to demonstrate the moral code by which we live. Acknowledging that rules were needed to determine when and where humanitarian interventions should occur, British Prime Minister Tony Blair proposed the following criteria:

First, are we sure of our case? War is an imperfect instrument for righting humanitarian distress, but armed force is sometimes the only means of dealing with dictators. Second, have we exhausted all diplomatic options? We should always give peace every chance, as we have in the case of Kosovo. Third, on the basis of a practical assessment of the situation, are there military operations we can sensibly and prudently undertake? Fourth, are we prepared for the long term? In the past we talked too much of exit strategies. But having made a commitment we cannot simply walk away once the fight is over; better to stay with moderate numbers of troops than return for repeat performances with large numbers. And finally, do we have national interests involved? The mass expulsion of ethnic Albanians from Kosovo demanded the notice of the rest of the world. But it does make a difference that this is taking place in a combustible part of Europe.[38]

Confident that the Kosovo situation met these criteria, NATO braced for action. In so doing, the organization, which was founded in 1949 as a collective defense alliance to deter an attack on Western Europe by the Soviet Union, inaugurated its new Strategic Concept that expanded NATO security concerns to crisis management operations outside of its original scope.

> "What is wrong is not the impulse to give foreign policy a moral content, but the presumption that doing so is an uncomplicated business, one not requiring calculation and compromise but merely purity of intention."
>
> — OWEN HARRIES

Having made the case that NATO faced a moral imperative, President Clinton and his fellow NATO leaders confronted two alternatives for dealing with Milosevic's program of ethnic cleansing: (1) intervene exclusively with air power, or (2) intervene with air and ground forces. The first alternative seemed more attractive to the Clinton administration, which was still staggering from the president's sex scandal and the fight against impeachment. Many of the president's advisors believed that NATO air strikes against the Bosnian Serbs during the summer of 1995 forced them to negotiate at Dayton. Another dose of air power would presumably compel Milosevic to accept the Rambouillet accords, without the casualties that military planners feared would come from slugging it out with the Yugoslav army on the ground.

NATO INTERVENES

NATO's air attack began on March 24 at 8:00 P.M. local time. Its announced goals were to stop the use of terror against ethnic Albanians in Kosovo, deter what many NATO officials feared was an impending ethnic cleansing campaign, and reduce Serbia's capacity to wage war in the future. Because Clinton had indicated that he would not use ground troops to accomplish these goals, Milosevic believed that all he had to do was weather a short campaign of pinprick attacks.

Milosevic's strategy for outlasting the air offensive rested on two main pillars. The first pillar involved weakening NATO cohesion. The Serbs possessed a limited number of Soviet surface-to-air missiles, primarily obsolete SA-3 and SA-6 systems. To avoid suppressive fire early in the war, they camouflaged each missile battery, moved it whenever possible, and turned off the engagement radar to prevent detection. Although Milosevic's air-defense network did not produce the number of kills promised by his military leaders, it did force NATO pilots to fly above 15,000 feet. Conducting missions at this altitude minimized the chances of losing air crews, but it increased the risk of collateral damage around the intended targets. Milosevic predicted that some of NATO's European members would be squeamish about continuing the bombing runs in the face of mounting injuries to innocent civilians.[39] If the Serbs were able to acquire more advanced surface-to-air systems from the Russians, he assumed that rising casualties would cause them to demand the cessation of air operations over Yugoslavia.

The second pillar in the Serb strategy involved using Albanian refugees to create turmoil in the wider Balkan region. Code-named Operation Horseshoe, the plan called for Yugoslav troops to encircle the Kosovar Albanians in a U-shaped formation, and then drive them out of the province. The resulting flood of refugees would overwhelm neighboring states lacking the infrastructure to care for such a human tidal wave. It would also place enormous political pressure on Macedonia, which possessed a vocal Albanian minority that sought greater influence over the central government in Skopje. With hundreds of thousands of refugees spreading across the region, Milosevic expected NATO's beleaguered southern members to seek a negotiated end to the war.

Bombing for Peace

When Operation Allied Force began raining a hail of explosives on the Federal Republic of Yugoslavia, NATO's supreme allied commander in Europe, U.S. General Wesley Clark, promised to disrupt, degrade, and ultimately destroy the Serbian military. The theory behind the operation was called "parallel warfare," which envisioned using air power to sever an enemy's command and control systems while simultaneously whittling down its forces in the field. As described by Michael Ignatieff, an "enemy—without computers, telephones, or power—may still have forces capable of attack, but he no longer has the capability to order them into battle." Shattering the systems that enable an enemy to make military decisions is "just as effective as killing his people and wrecking his cities."[40]

Yet at the outset of the air campaign, this approach to combat did nothing to prevent over 800,000 ethnic Albanians from being evicted from Kosovo. Poor weather hampered the air offensive, often making targets difficult to locate. Meanwhile, crowded refugee camps began filling the borderlands of neighboring states, threatening to destabilize the entire region. To extinguish the flames of unrest that Milosevic hoped to foment, NATO undertook a massive program to feed, clothe, and shelter the refugees. Concurrently, reassurances were given to Albania, Bulgaria, and Macedonia to confirm NATO's willingness to protect them against Serbian aggression.

Phase two of the air campaign began on March 29, with NATO expanding its portfolio of targets to include oil refineries, radio and television broadcasting facilities, and, on May 24, the national power grid. General Clark quipped that until the power grid had been disabled, "this was the only air campaign in history in which lovers strolled down river banks in the gathering twilight and ate at outdoor cafés and watched the fireworks."[41] Once the grid went down, Milosevic's support in Yugoslavia began to erode as the civilian population became increasingly demoralized.

Public support for the air campaign began to waver in many NATO countries during late May following a series of accidental bombings of civilians, including attacks on a passenger train in Grdelica, a Serbian old-age home in Surdalica, the Chinese embassy in Belgrade, and even an Albanian refugee convoy near Djakovica. Critics complained that the erroneous anticipation of a quick Yugoslav surrender led to "a seemingly frantic selection of targets in the later phases of the intervention." Some targets, like the city of Novi Sad, "were bombed over and over again" despite being "firmly in [the] hands of the democratic opposition."[42]

By the end of the seventy-eight-day war, NATO aircraft had flown more than 37,000 sorties against Yugoslavia and did not suffer a single combat fatality. The United States flew 60 percent of the total, and was responsible for over 90 percent of the electronic warfare missions and over 95 percent of the cruise missiles that were fired. In contrast to the 1991 Persian Gulf War, where precision-guided munitions amounted to approximately 8 percent of the ordnance dropped on Iraq, smart weapons made up 35 percent of the ordnance used in Kosovo, with the overwhelming majority being deployed by the United States.[43] Surprisingly, the damage caused by this onslaught was modest. General Clark claimed to have destroyed 93 Yugoslav tanks, 53 armored fighting vehicles, and 389 artillery pieces, which comprised, respectively 8, 7, and 4 percent of these targets, thus leaving Milosevic's army virtually intact.[44]

The Final Settlement

For NATO to stop the bombing, Milosevic had to terminate all Yugoslav military action, withdraw his forces from Kosovo, allow the Albanian refugees to return, grant the province self-government, and accept a NATO peacekeeping force. On April 14, the German government proposed a modification of NATO's demands but added that the KLA should disarm, and the United Nations be given a role in administering postwar Kosovo. Three weeks later, in a meeting of foreign ministers from the G-8 industrialized states,[45] the German modification was incorporated within a set of "general principles" for settling the war. Following an endless stream of negotiations to mediate an agreement, President Martii Ahtisaari of Finland and Russian envoy Viktor Chernomyrdin presented a document based on the G-8 principles to Milosevic, who subsequently accepted. A Military Technical Agreement was then negotiated with Yugoslav authorities to specify the process for withdrawing their military forces. Civil administration in the province was turned over to the UN Mission in Kosovo (UNMIK) and peacekeeping was undertaken by the 45,000-strong Kosovo Force (KFOR), a NATO-led body that included contingents from twenty non-NATO countries, including Russia.[46]

The war in Kosovo did not end with the Federal Republic of Yugoslavia accepting the same proposal that it had previously rejected at Rambouillet. There were subtle but important differences between the two documents. First, Appendix B, paragraph 8 in the Rambouillet text, which allowed NATO troops "free and unrestricted passage and unimpeded access" throughout Yugoslavia, was not part of the final settlement. Second, the United Nations rather than NATO assumed political authority over Kosovo. Third, as stipulated in Article 19 of UN Security Resolution 1244, Rambouillet's three-year timetable for determining the final status of Kosovo was replaced by the establishment of "international civil and security presences . . . for an initial period of twelve months, to continue thereafter unless the Security Council decided otherwise." In short, the war ended in a manner that broadly suited the interests of each side: NATO could declare that most of its war aims had been achieved, and the Serbs could claim that they had won their argument about placing NATO forces under UN control.[47]

On June 10, NATO ended its bombing and British KFOR troops prepared to enter Kosovo. Shortly thereafter, a Russian military unit stationed in Bosnia drove to Prestina, Kosovo, and occupied Slatina airport before British troops arrived. Just hours earlier, Russian president Boris Yeltsin had assured NATO that his forces would not move until their role in Kosovo had been finalized. Not knowing whether the Russians were unilaterally establishing an occupation sector of their own, General Clark ordered General Michael Jackson, the British head of the peacekeeping force in Kosovo, to secure the airport. Jackson refused, replying that he was not going to start World War III. Unable to reinforce and supply their garrison, the Russians ultimately agreed to work within the guidelines of the final agreement that pertained to KFOR.[48]

Within days of the establishment of KFOR, hundreds of thousands of ethnic Albanians began returning to Kosovo. By late November, 808,913 refugees had returned and 247,391 people, primarily Serbs intimidated by KLA members bent on revenge, had departed.[49] The Serb departures were understandable—the murder rate immediately following the war averaged some fifty revenge killings a week.[50] Serb feelings have been described as *inat*, an old Turkish word meaning a mixture of anger, humiliation, defiance, and pride.[51] Chagrined by what happened to their nation, they insisted that they had been "caught between NATO's hammer and the Milosevic regime's anvil," condemned for things that Albanians, Bosnians, and Croats had also done at various times during Yugoslavia's wars of succession.

> "We won the war, but it will be a hollow victory if we lost the peace."
>
> — SAMUEL R. BERGER

As required by the settlement, the KLA turned in over ten thousand weapons and its leaders agreed to replace their organization with a smaller Kosovo Protection Force (KPC), allegedly designed to provide humanitarian assistance during emergencies. Confidentially, they admitted that the KPC had access to numerous secret arms caches and saw itself as the core of a future army for an independent Kosovo. The discovery of some seventy tons of hidden weapons during the summer of 2000 gave substance to suspicions that KLA members had never disarmed as promised.[52] Further complicating matters, a group calling itself the Liberation Army of Presevo, Medvedjc, and Bujanovac (named after three largely Albanian towns within Serbia) began an insurgency along Serbia's southern border with Kosovo, apparently to lure the Serbs into violating the cease-fire agreement.[53] Assumed to be linked to the former KLA, the group appeared determined to prevent a **rapprochement** between NATO and the Federal Republic of Yugoslavia.

Following the withdrawal of the Serb military, Kosovo continued to experience unrest as organized crime became rampant and different factions of ex-KLA guerrillas fought among themselves to carve out private fiefdoms. Evidence of popular disenchantment with the guerrillas surfaced during the October 2000 elections for local councils in Kosovo's thirty municipalities. Ibrahim Rugova's moderate Democratic League of Kosovo won nearly 60 percent of the vote, while the Democratic Party of Kosovo, the political organization of former KLA leader Hashim Thaci, garnered only 27 percent of the vote.[54]

While the electoral victory of the moderates was welcomed by many, the question of Kosovo's final status remains in limbo. How long will Kosovo be a UN/NATO protectorate within the Federal Republic of Yugoslavia? Given that ethnic Albanians insist that a return to Serb rule is unacceptable, will Kosovo eventually achieve independence? If so, will independence merely be a step toward Kosovo's amalgamation within a Greater Albania? Whatever direction political events take, the United Nations will play a major role in shaping Kosovo's future. Its presence in Kosovo is open-ended and can only be terminated by a UN Security Council vote, in which all of the permanent members have a veto over any schemes for autonomy, independence, or amalgamation.[55]

Even the most optimistic observers acknowledge the peacekeeping and nation-building missions underway in Kosovo will continue for years.[56] An independent task force studying the region has concluded that Kosovo's economy is in disarray: "Almost nothing is being produced, as most industrial facilities cannot operate due to war damage, lack of electrical power, the absence of key personnel, or years of inadequate plant and equipment maintenance."[57] The province is surviving on charity, foreign aid, and remittances from Albanians who had fled the country. Until the economy there rebounds, there is little hope for stability without significant foreign assistance.

THE COLLAPSE OF THE MILOSEVIC REGIME

Although Slobodan Milosevic remained in power when the war ended, NATO members continued their efforts to topple his regime. In addition to applying diplomatic pressure and **economic sanctions,** they offered assistance to strengthen student groups, rival political parties, and the anti-Milosevic media. Finally, after thirteen ruinous years in power, during which he dragged the country through four lost wars, Milosevic was defeated in the fall 2000 presidential elections by Vojislav Kostunica, a constitutional lawyer who received backing from eighteen disparate opposition parties. The new president of the Federal Republic of Yugoslavia is a moderate nationalist who was fired from Belgrade University for asserting that the 1974 constitution was unfair to Serbia. Kostunica supported the Serb Republic of Bosnia, though more recently he has indicated a willingness to recognize the independence and territorial integrity of Bosnia.[58]

The departure of Slobodan Milosevic, who the new Serbian justice minister announced in February 2001 would be arrested and tried for corruption and election fraud, has created a new context for building peace in Kosovo. As Richard Holbrooke points out, as long as Milosevic was in power "you couldn't deal with the problems there." Now that he is gone, "the real problems will emerge but at least you can deal with them."[59] The country's gross domestic product (GDP) has plummeted to half of what it was a decade ago, its external debt has climbed to $15 billion, and unemployment exceeds 35 percent. Aside from rebuilding a faltering economy whose infrastructure may cost $100 billion to reconstruct, Kostunica's primary problems include ending Yugoslavia's international isolation, keeping Montenegro in the federation, and dealing with Kosovo. He has admitted that KFOR peacekeepers "will have to stay for a while, and not a short while." Furthermore, he has called for "a real dialogue between Serbs and Albanians."[60] Yet the prospects for a durable peace in Kosovo remain clouded. As former Yugoslav prime minister Milan Panic notes, Milosevic may be gone but his die-hard supporters are still entrenched within the government, and they continue to threaten "to obstruct the rapid political and economic transformation that Serbia and the Balkans so badly need."[61] Although the Democratic Opposition of Serbia, the coalition backing Kostunica, holds 176 seats in the 250-seat Serbian parliament, ultranationalists from Milosevic's Socialist Party, the Radical Party, and the Party of Serbian Unity still control 74 seats.

Paradoxically, some Albanians fear that Milosevic's departure will hurt their cause. They argue that it will be more difficult to win NATO support for Kosovo's independence if Kostunica implements democratic reforms in Yugoslavia. When the European Union lifted economic sanctions on Yugoslavia two days after his victory, Albanians complained that the international community was merely interested in removing Milosevic, not punishing Serbs for what they had done in Kosovo.

Having peacefully ousted Solobodan Milosevic, the Serbs have an opportunity to begin building a lasting peace. Their challenge is to establish a level of civility in public life that has long been absent from the country. A

> "Let us beware of attempts to lay the blame for evil on whole peoples. That would be tantamount to adopting the ideology of ethical fanatics."
>
> — VACLAV HAVEL

CONTROVERSIES TO CONTEMPLATE

- If states that possess cruise missiles, stealth technology, and precision-guided munitions are able to wage war with impunity, will they avoid negotiating with obstinate opponents and resort instead to military force?
- As societies increasingly rely on interdependent power grids, telecommunication facilities, and computers to operate everything from air defense systems to sewage treatment facilities, will the traditional distinction between military and civilian targets disappear?
- Does NATO's lopsided victory over Yugoslavia demonstrate that national leaders can rely on coercive air power alone to achieve their political objectives? Can strategic bombing engender peace settlements without a collateral ground campaign?
- Does the NATO intervention in Kosovo mark the beginning of "post-heroic" warfare, a type of battle waged by computers and remote-controlled ordnance rather than by warriors?
- Can democratic power sharing in a multiethnic country work after an ethnic war? Or is partitioning the only viable approach to peace after such wars?
- Do national leaders have an obligation to alleviate human suffering no matter where it occurs? Must they protect foreign nationals even at the expense of their own citizens? If so, should it be done through a quick rescue operation? Or should it include an effort to eradicate the underlying cause of the suffering?
- Do the same criteria for waging a just war, as defined by just war theory, apply to internal wars within states?
- Is humanitarian intervention legal? If so, what criteria must be satisfied in order for humanitarian intervention to be permissible under international law?
- Should the permanent International Criminal Court be strengthened to prosecute and try individuals suspected of committing war crimes?
- Former U.S. envoy Richard Holbrooke was deeply involved in negotiations that ended the civil war in Bosnia as well as negotiations aimed at averting a war between NATO and Yugoslavia over Kosovo. Reflecting on his experiences, he observed: "The choice between 'realists' and 'idealists' was a false one: in the long run, our strategic interests and human rights supported and reinforced each other, and could be advanced at the same time." Can political leaders harmonize policy prescriptions from realist and liberal theories when crafting a peace settlement?

---

prerequisite for meeting this challenge is to manifest what historian Gale Stokes calls "the three Rs" of responsibility: reconciliation, remembrance, and regret.[62] Reconciliation not only means reaching a political accommodation with the Kosovar Albanians, it also entails entering voluntarily into larger European structures that internationalize and solidify the reconciliation. Remembrance involves openly confronting bitter, painful memories rather than leaving them hidden below the surface of public discourse, unattended and unhealed. Finally, regret means going beyond simply expressing sorrow for past actions and engaging in meaningful gestures of repentance. Ultranationalism is a device for avoiding responsibility. By identifying ethnic minorities as "the other," a threat to the people as one, ultranationalists like Milosevic shift the blame for every social ill to those who do not fit into their exclusionary categories. It may be some time before *all* of the peoples of the former Yugoslavia are able to accept responsibility for their collective past. "Without that acceptance," warns Stokes, "there will be no lasting peace."[63]

SUGGESTED READING

Allcock, John B. *Explaining Yugoslavia*. New York: Columbia University Press, 2000.

Buckley, William Joseph. *Kosovo: Contending Voices on Balkan Interventions*. Grand Rapids, Mich: Eerdmans, 2001.

Carmet, David, and Patrick James. *Peace in the Midst of Wars: Preventing and Managing International Ethnic Conflicts*. Columbia: University of South Carolina Press, 1998.

Carpenter, Ted Galen. *NATO's Empty Victory*. Washington, D.C.: Cato Institute, 2000.

Frye, Alton. *Humanitarian Intervention: Crafting a Workable Doctrine*. New York: Council on Foreign Relations, 2000.

Glenny, Misha. *The Balkans: Nationalism, War and the Great Powers, 1804–1999*. New York: Viking, 2001.

Holbrooke, Richard. *To End a War*. New York: Modern Library, 1999.

Howard, Michael. *The Invention of Peace: Reflections on War and International Order*. New Haven, Conn.: Yale University Press, 2001.

Judah, Tim. *Kosovo: War and Revenge*. New Haven, Conn.: Yale University Press, 2000.

Mazower, Mark. *The Balkans: A Short History*. New York: Modern Library, 2001.

NOTES

1. Judah, 2000, p. 55.
2. Layne, 2000, p. 11.
3. Judah, 2000, p. 250.
4. *Washington Post*, April 1, 1999, p. A3.
5. Byman and Waxman, 2000, p. 37.
6. Pennington and Levi, 1984, p. 13.
7. MacIver, 1963, p. 4.
8. Eliade, 1967, pp. 5–6; see also Tudor, 1972.
9. Mojzes, 1994, p. 40.
10. Ibid., p. 50. According to Mojzes, the characteristic of *prkos* reinforces the Serbian mythological conception of time. Variously translated as obstinacy or unyielding spite, it encourages avenging transgressions, even if they happened long ago.
11. Most of the other resistance groups had strong ethnic roots and thus fought for parochial interests rather than for a multinational Yugoslavia. The Chetniks, led by Draza Mihajlovic, were the largest of these organizations. Composed of Serbian remnants from Yugoslavia's defeated army, they were loyal to the royal government-in-exile in London and

supported a restoration of the Serbian monarchy after the war. Unlike those who resisted the Nazis, the Ustasha, a right-wing movement organized by Ante Pavelic, was supported by Germany and Italy in its effort to carve a Croatian state out of Yugoslavia. The Partisans and Chetniks spent the war fighting the Ustashes as well as the Axis powers. Following the war, Tito's Partisans executed Mihajlovic and thousands of Ustasha members for collaborating with the Germans.

12. Stokes, 1993, p. 223.
13. Rothschild, 1993, pp. 57–58.
14. Ibid., p. 105.
15. The Muslim inhabitants of Bosnia are the descendants of people who converted to Islam during the Ottoman period. Although they speak Serbo-Croatian, they consider themselves a distinct nation because of their unique culture. Stokes, 1993, p. 250.
16. Rothschild, 1993, p. 260. Leadership of the League of Yugoslav Communists also rotated within the party Presidium. Under this arrangement, each of the six Republican Central Committees was represented by a full Presidium member, and both provincial committees were represented by full ex officio members. Volgyes, 1986, p. 147.
17. See Banac, 1992.
18. Judah, 2000, p. 53.
19. Mojzes, 1994, p. 80.
20. Stokes, 1993, p. 234.
21. In Judah, 2000, p. 54.
22. F. Stephen Larrabee, as cited in *U.S. News & World Report,* April 5, 1999, p. 27.
23. Silber and Little, 1996, p. 252.
24. Holbrooke, 1998, p. 69.
25. Ibid., pp. 363–364. According to Carl Bildt, a former Swedish prime minister who served as the international community's High Representative in Bosnia from 1995 to 1997, for both sides "peace was just the continuation of war by other means. The peace process gave them a new battlefield in which they could continue their respective fights for their respective aims." *International Herald Tribune,* December 18, 2000, p. 12.
26. Quoted in Hedges, 1999, p. 29.
27. Judah, 2000, pp. 124–125.
28. Ibid., pp. 200–204.
29. Bandow, 2000, p. 31.
30. As one State Department official put it, Holbrooke has remarkable diagnostic skills for finding openings: "He hits a clean double, and then wants to stretch it into a triple." Traub, 2000, pp. 44, 66.
31. Judah, 2000, p. 227.
32. Text of the address at <http://www.nytimes.com/library/wor...pe/032599clinton-address -text.html>.
33. Text of the address at <http://www.nytimes.com/library/world/europe/032499solana-nato -text.html>.
34. Text of the address at <http://www.nytimes.com/library/world/europe/032499blair-nato -text.html>.
35. Tesón, 1988, p. 15.
36. Ellerman, 1993, p. 348.
37. *Case Concerning the Barcelona Traction, Light and Power Company, Ltd.* [Belgium v. Spain], I.C.J. Reports, 1970, para. 33.
38. Text of the address at <http://www.fco.gov.uk/news/speechestext.asp?2316>.
39. Posen, 2000, p. 51.
40. Ignatieff, 2000, pp. 169–170.
41. Ibid., p. 108.
42. Johnston, 2001, p. 6.
43. Ignatieff, 2000, pp. 198, 206.
44. Helprin, 2000, p. A26.

45. The Group of Eight (G-8) industrialized states meet in regular economic summit conferences. It consists of the United States, Canada, Japan, Britain, France, Germany, Italy, and Russia.
46. Reinhardt, 2000, p. 17.
47. Clark, 2000, p. 4.
48. It was unclear whether Yeltsin's assurances were false or simply ignored by a local commander. Regardless of the incident's cause, the conduct of the war greatly affected Russian leaders. According to Alexei Arbatov, deputy chairman of the Defense Committee of the Russian Parliament, they concluded that "the use of force is the most efficient problem solver, when applied decisively and massively . . . [and] limiting one's casualties is worth massive devastation and collateral fatalities among civilian populations." Arbatov, 2000, p. 22.
49. These statistics were reported by the UN High Commissioner for Refugees, as cited in Judah, 2000, pp. 286-287.
50. Reinhardt, 2000, p. 17.
51. *International Herald Tribune,* February 1, 2001, p. 8.
52. *New York Times,* July 17, 2000, p. A4; *The Economist,* August 19, 2000, p. 42.
53. *International Herald Tribune,* January 26, 2001, p. 4.
54. *The Economist,* November 4, 2000, p. 60.
55. Daalder and O'Hanlon, 1999, pp. 137–138.
56. Carpenter, 2000, p. 172.
57. *Promoting Sustainable Economies in the Balkans,* 2000, p. 13.
58. In *The Economist,* October 28, 2000, p. 45.
59. *New York Times,* October 8, 2000, p. 13.
60. In *Time,* October 16, 2000, p. 66.
61. Panic, 2000, p. 8.
62. Stokes, 1997, pp. 145–148.
63. Stokes, 1997, p. 153.

PART V

Paths to Peace in the Twenty-First Century: Moral Dilemmas and Policy Prescriptions

What is the best strategy to win a war and then win the peace? How should enemies fight and how should victors treat defeated foes? Are there sound lessons that can be learned from historical cases about the paths peacemakers should pursue as they make fateful decisions about peace settlements? What factors are likely to influence their capacity to make prudent and moral choices that can cement a lasting and just peace with a vanquished enemy? These are questions that were asked at the advent of the modern state system in the seventeenth century, and they will, in all likelihood, be asked throughout the twenty-first century.

The cases presented in *From War to Peace* provide a laboratory for deriving eternal principles that speak to the perpetual problems surrounding war and peace. A variety of past wars and peace settlements have been covered in the hope of capturing the complexities and controversies of this conundrum in the study of war and peace. In our concluding chapter, we draw on this rich and varied record to pull together the discrepant range of opinions, activities, and outcomes. Our focus centers on four major categories of evaluation.

First, we examine meaningful ways to look at war-waging and peacemaking practices. What are the major advantages and limitations of the realist and liberal schools of thought in interpreting why states go to war and how they make peace? What are the payoffs and pitfalls of relying on either perspective? Are either or both, to a degree, based on illusions? If neither theoretical tradition provides sound answers, should they be abandoned and a new or different theory be embraced? Or should future policymakers continue to see classical realism and liberalism — or some new fused version — as the only reasonable ways of organizing thought about these topics?

Second, we revisit the perils and politics of making decisions about war and peace and consider the many factors — international, domestic, and individual — that influence the capacity of victors to make rational and moral choices when they seek to promote peace.

Third, we advance twelve key policy prescriptions that the cases in this book and others throughout modern history suggest are worthy of consideration, and ask that an assessment be made about the boundaries of pragmatic and ethical peacemaking strategies.

Finally, we frame all the above controversies with a discussion of contrasting ethical arguments about the criteria for waging just wars, as well as how enemies can reconcile their differences and build a just peace after the war ends. Included is a summary of the major rules in international law and ethical discourse about when and how a just war might be waged. Our goal in this concluding chapter is to stimulate critical thinking about the rival approaches to making peace in contemporary international politics.

· 9 ·

WAGING PEACE:
CHOICES AND CONSEQUENCES

A phenomenon noticeable throughout history regardless
of place or period is the pursuit by governments
of policies contrary to their interests.
— BARBARA W. TUCHMAN

The victory won in 1991 by the U.S.-led coalition in the Persian Gulf War has been called a defining moment in military history — a victory as dramatic as those attained by Hannibal at Cannae or Wellington at Waterloo. Hyperbole aside, the coalition's battlefield success was predictable. Throughout modern history, when a significant imbalance of forces favored the side using a strategy of maneuver on flat, open terrain, circumstances which favored the United States in the Gulf War, it tended to win a decisive victory in a relatively short period of time.[1] What was new was that the United States relied so heavily on an air assault using precision-guided munitions to ravage Iraq's defenses before a ground attack commenced.

Whereas the Persian Gulf War introduced the world to hi-tech warfare, the 1999 war in Kosovo revealed how precision guidance had revolutionized military affairs. Through air strikes alone, with no NATO combat fatalities, the Federal Republic of Yugoslavia was defeated in just seventy-eight days. NATO ground forces never entered the battlefield.

With such stunning victories, almost everyone expected Iraq and Kosovo to disappear from America's national security agenda. Few people anticipated that the United States and its coalition partners would be unable to translate their military triumphs into durable peace settlements. Despite numerous attempts to make Saddam Hussein adhere to the UN resolutions that defined the terms of the Gulf War armistice, the truculent Iraqi leader continued for more than ten years after the war to flout the will of the international community. Slobodan Milosevic did not retain power as long as Saddam Hussein, but the future of Kosovo remains uncertain as it continues to suffer from an insurgency along its frontier with Serbia.

The German philosopher Johann Wolfgang Goethe once defined genius as knowing when to stop. According to Nissan Oren, political genius has been rare among victors: Some have gone too far, plundering the defeated in fits of avarice and rage; others have not gone far enough, humiliating them without weakening their capability to retaliate in the future. Prudent victories, he concludes, "are but small islands engulfed by an ocean of imprudence, like small specks of rationality afloat in a sea of insanity."[2]

THINKING THEORETICALLY ABOUT WAR TERMINATION

Mortal combat between **states** is rare, but its consequences are staggering. In the almost two centuries since the Congress of Vienna, 150 members of the interstate system never experienced warfare. Those that did suffered more than 30 million battle-connected fatalities and tens of millions of additional civilian deaths.[3] The human tragedy behind this horrific toll has led many scholars to undertake rigorous, systematic analyses of how wars begin. The question of how they end has received far less attention, despite the fact that the end of fighting does not necessarily mean the resolution of a conflict.[4] Indeed, if peace settlements are not handled properly, the end of one war can in fact become the beginning of the next. Because a cessation of hostilities can be engineered in ways that either dampen or inflame the underlying disagreement between combatants, some theorists maintain that the transition from war to peace is a more serious problem than the transition from peace to war.[5]

To build a theory that provides meaningful guidelines about how nations can successfully wage peace, one must begin with an inspection of past cases. The last seven chapters provide examples of efforts to build peace that illustrate the magnitude of the theoretical challenge.

In thinking theoretically about the origins and outcomes of different types of peace treaties, we will find that most interpretations have been informed by ideas derived from the **realist** and **liberal** intellectual traditions. As discussed in Chapter 1, realists "earn their label by emphasizing consequences over moral principles and necessity over choice. Liberals begin with opposite premises, emphasizing duty over consequences and moral imperatives over expediency."[6] These bodies of thought, ethicist Joel Rosenthal observes, provide the storehouse of concepts from which nearly all controversies in international politics can be examined, because "most of the literature of the past fifty years is an unwitting and curious combination of the two approaches."[7] The challenge now, Rosenthal cogently argues, "is to relate the insights of these traditions to the problems of our age."[8]

Waging peace remains our most important problem today, because failure can lead to mass destruction. For that reason, we advise readers to inspect and interpret the wars and peace settlements we have covered in previous chapters by applying the rich insights of both realism and liberalism to those cases.

Comparing the Cases

Although it is common for data-based analyses of interstate conflict to over-look temporal dynamics and treat violent incidents between the same pair of states as if they were independent of one another, these clashes generally do not happen out of the blue. Only 21 percent of the **militarized disputes** that erupted between 1816 and 1985 and 16 percent of the wars occurred in iso-lation.[9] Most violent clashes occurred within the context of a rivalry. Not only do states in protracted rivalries adopt more coercive bargaining strate-gies with each other in successive confrontations,[10] but the longer these alter-cations continue, the greater the likelihood of war.[11]

How belligerents conduct themselves on the battlefield, as well as how vic-tors treat the vanquished, have far-reaching implications for the durability of peace settlements between bitter rivals. Decisive military outcomes and imposed political settlements may temporarily reduce the prospects that the defeated will retaliate,[12] but people harboring an acute sense of injustice do not easily forget suffering at the hands of others. History is replete with examples of settlements that provoked a new round of hostilities by creating a sense of injus-tice among those on the losing side. Peace, in these situations, never endures; it is an interlude when one side or the other longs for revenge, and neither can overcome the rancor of their collective past to restore amicable relations.

The cases covered in this book comprise a special category of wars, namely, those where one side was a decisive winner on the battlefield and the other side a loser.[13] Table 9.1 lists the wars that we have examined in response to these questions. Whereas some were short, resulting in limited casualties (e.g., the Second Schleswig-Holstein, Austro-Prussian, Persian Gulf, and Kosovo wars), others stretched on for years causing enormous destruction (e.g., the Thirty Years' War, the Napoleonic, and the two World Wars). By selecting several cases from each type of war, we provided a basis for investigating whether the behavior of the winners in decisive military vic-tories followed a general pattern. Concentrating on a few cases allows us to examine the war-termination process in greater detail than if we had employed additional cases.[14] Of course, the drawback is that our ability to generalize is less than it would have been with a larger sample. There are costs and benefits to whichever choice a researcher makes, and these should be kept in mind when evaluating the results from our analysis.

Not only did the wars in our sample vary in terms of their duration, mag-nitude, and severity, but the termination agreements that ended them were also different. As shown in Table 9.2, victors' peacemaking strategies ranged from the highly punitive (e.g., the Franco-Prussian War and World War I) to the conciliatory (e.g., the Thirty Years' War, the Napoleonic, and Austro-Prussian Wars). Occupation, territorial losses, forced disarmament, financial reparations, and at times even assistance for economic recovery were used by the victors. Because winners employed so many approaches to deal with the defeated, we have ample opportunity to compare the results of punitive ver-sus conciliatory peace settlements.

TABLE 9.1
Selected Characteristics of the Wars under Investigation

War	Date	Number of Major Participants	Battle Deaths
Thirty Years'	1618–1648	15	750,000
Napoleonic	1803–1815	6	1,380,000
Second Schleswig-Holstein	1864	3	4,500
Austro-Prussian	1866	11	36,100
Franco-Prussian	1870–1871	5	187,500
World War I	1914–1918	15	9,000,000
World War II	1939–1945	29	15,000,000
Persian Gulf	1990–1991	21	100,000
Kosovo	1999	20*	1,000**

*Leaving aside nonstate actors such as the Kosovo Liberation Army (KLA), the formal partici-pants in the war included the Federal Republic of Yugoslavia and the nineteen-member North Atlantic Treaty Organization (NATO). Not all NATO members participated in combat, how-ever. In addition, several other states were involved with refugee support but were not involved in combat.
**Estimates vary due to uncertainties concerning the battle fatalities suffered by the KLA. NATO forces suffered no combat fatalities, Slobodan Milosevic cited 576 battle deaths among Serbs in his television address announcing the end of the war, and some KLA members have mentioned similar figures for their units.
Source: Clodfelter, 1992; Judah, 2000; Kegley and Raymond, 2002; Small and Singer, 1982. Persian Gulf statistics based on United Nations Information Office.

The relations among states are shaped by chance and the sequence of fateful choices made by the interacting parties. From antiquity down to the present, history has been used as a laboratory for discovering which choices in what contexts reduce the probability of committing those errors that precipitate avoidable policy disasters. "The future can never look exactly like the past," note social scientists Richard Neustadt and Ernest May, "but past conditions can offer clues to future possibilities."[15] Focused, structured comparisons of historical cases have the potential to stimulate our imagi-nation and help us frame sharper questions about how to build a durable peace.[16]

"What history teaches us is that men have never learned anything from it."

— GEORG WILHELM HEGEL

If the past can help us frame sharper ques-tions about peacemaking, can victors learn from this history? Learning from experience involves a change in beliefs or the degree of confidence in one's beliefs based on the interpretation of past events.[17] Unfortunately, there is mounting evidence that decisionmakers have difficulty learning from the experience of others. Rather than learning from the past, they often use it "to buttress pre-existing policy preferences."[18] To borrow a phrase from Edmund Burke, history for decisionmakers is "a magical mirror where everyone sees what he wants."[19]

One reason why decisionmakers have such problems with learning from the past can be found in their belief that history's "lessons and insights lie on

TABLE 9.2
A Comparison of Selected War-Termination Agreements

	Thirty Years' War	Napoleonic War	Second Schleswig-Holstein War	Austro-Prussian War	Franco-Prussian War	World War I	World War II — Germany	World War II — Japan	Persian Gulf War	Kosovo War
Treatment of loser										
Accused of responsibility for war	X	X				X	X	X	X	X
Condemnation of leaders		X			X	X	X	Yes, but Emperor not indicted	X	X
Occupied	X	X			X	X	X	X	X	X
Disarmed	X	X			X	X	X	X	X	X
Reparations	X	X			X	X	Light in U.S., British and French occupation zones/heavy in Soviet occupation zone	Light		
Territorial loss	X	X	X	Austria lost its rights in Schleswig-Holstein; Venetia ceded to Italy	X	X	X	X		X
Economic assistance	X						X	X	X	

Source: Adapted from Clemens, 1998, pp. 43, 53.

the surface for anyone to pick up, so that one can go at history like a looter at an archeological site."[20] Victors may remember a rousing success or a traumatic failure in postwar peace building, and assume that the situation they now confront is an exact parallel. Familiar episodes from the past are not always instructive, however. Drawing analogies between events that share only a superficial correspondence distorts reality, encourages premature cognitive closure, and may needlessly trigger negative feelings about the vanquished.[21] But when used carefully, history can provide a source of ideas, suggest alternatives that might otherwise have been overlooked, and encourage the search for additional information.[22]

What follows are twelve policy prescriptions suggested by the historical cases we have examined. Taken together, they sketch out an approach to peacemaking that abstains from heavy-handed oppression without embracing hope-for-the-best beneficence. As discussed in Chapter 1, harsh treatment and leniency are polar extremes on a continuum of possible peace settlements. Rather than conceiving of the victor's choice in dichotomous terms, these prescriptions embody a more nuanced approach to dealing with the defeated.

MORAL PRINCIPLES AND POLICY PRESCRIPTIONS FOR THE RESOLUTION OF ARMED CONFLICT

On November 7, 1941, with German tanks only eighty kilometers from Moscow, Soviet leader Josef Stalin spoke to local Communist Party workers at the Mayakovsky underground railway station. The invaders "would get their war of annihilation and be exterminated without mercy," he promised. "Our task is revenge," he thundered.[23]

The role of emotions in decision making has generally been neglected by contemporary students of international security. Yet, as suggested by recent neurological research, deep-seated emotions like Stalin's anger are central to decision making.[24] Emotions are like filters that narrow alternatives: They eliminate some options and draw those driven by passion to others.

Different emotions are brought into play by the manner in which a war begins and how it is conducted. For example, victors who have been targets of brutal, unprovoked aggression will have to grapple with feelings of treachery and betrayal, something unlikely to color the postwar policies of victors who initiated wars for opportunistic reasons. Regardless of how a war may have started and whether one was fighting to defend or overthrow the status quo, the longer the duration and the greater the costs, the more angry emotions will constrict the range of choices available to victor and vanquished alike. **Mirror imaging,** the propensity of each side in a conflict to see in its own actions only rectitude and in those of the adversary only malice, reduces the prospects for leniency by the winner and acquiescence by the loser. In such an atmosphere of mutual distrust, victors face difficult choices in sorting out short-term desires from long-term interests. What they want may not be what they need. Even from an advantaged position in which the enemy surrendered unconditionally, the victor still must decide what kind of peace agreement would enhance security. Should the peace be lenient or punitive? Can it combine elements of conciliation with retribution? How will the prostrate adversary respond? What countermoves are likely once the loser recovers from defeat? Military triumph solves certain problems but creates new ones. As we have seen in the preceding chapters, many wars have ended with a victor's peace rather than a victory for peace.

Given the far-reaching repercussions that result from how victors deal with the defeated, what steps can be taken to solidify a durable peace settlement? Based on the cases examined, we suggest the following policy prescriptions.

Prescription 1: Carefully define interests and priorities when making decisions about about war and peace.

It would seem prudent for states to specify their goals and carefully calculate the costs, risks, and benefits of alternative courses of action when formulating their foreign policies. Especially in the realm of national security, where the choices can spell the difference between life and death, states have enormous incentives to engage in long-range planning. This requires clarifying values, specifying objectives, and differentiating vital interests from those which are secondary.

Unfortunately, many states have not engaged in the kind of systematic, rigorous analyses necessary to meet these criteria. In a puzzling world where accurate, timely information is scarce, it is difficult to reach a clear consensus on national objectives; setting priorities presents a formidable challenge, especially when addressing some threats and needs can only be done at the risk of creating other threats or sacrificing other national needs. This trade-off is abundantly clear in the realm of peacemaking, when victors in war must reconcile their natural desire for retribution against the equally pressing need for reconciliation. As one diplomat has noted,

> A nation often does not recognize its own self-interest. One of the most vexing problems is to determine what is best for the nation. A related difficulty is to ascertain when a moth-eaten policy that once was viable is no longer valid. The international kaleidoscope is constantly changing; old formulas must be adjusted to new facts. . . .
>
> Improvisation is a risky procedure. Policies should be formed in advance of the emergency, not just after disaster strikes. A statesman should strive for a long-range major gain (sometimes with incidental losses) rather than a short-term minor gain. The United States was notoriously shortsighted during World War I and World War II; it fought for quick military victory without proper regard for long-range consequences. Too many Americans believe that once they have triumphed in the battlefield, all their troubles will be over. This attitude explains the psychology of "Whip the bullies and bring the boys home."[25]

The cases presented in *From War to Peace* suggest the wisdom of taking this recommendation into account when victors in war face the challenge of making peace. "No quarrel," warned British Prime Minister David Lloyd

George after World War I, "ought ever to be converted into a policy."[26] Yet all too frequently victors have pursued vendettas and the opportunity for building a durable peace was lost. Peacemaking is a complicated art whose success often hinges on being able to see long-term interests. Passion, however, obscures our time horizon. National leaders sometimes find it difficult to subordinate their private desire for revenge to the public good that would result from a sober assessment of how new, unanticipated problems may arise from the way immediate problems are solved.

Prescription 2: Military strategy in war-fighting should be coordinated with the political strategy for peacemaking.

Throughout this book we have argued that victory is not an end in itself. Military forces should be deployed for national purposes, not for promoting the interests of the military doing the fighting. However, this principle is sometimes overlooked and that exacerbates the problem of making peace.

At the root of the danger is the difficulty of separating military objectives from basic national goals. Although people tend to see a country's foreign policy as the product of a single calculating intelligence, in fact most governments are amalgams of large, semiautonomous bureaucratic organizations that have their own interests and hold different conceptions of national security. Because policy is often formulated by a small group of senior officials, each of whom may occupy a leadership position within one of these organizations, it can be difficult to orchestrate words and deeds in a coherent program that will be implemented faithfully by subordinates.[27] Fearing that **bureaucratic politics** contaminate military decisions, the armed forces sometimes are given substantial leeway in shaping the conduct of the war. Yet when crucial military and political decisions are compartmentalized, battlefield triumphs may not advance vital political aims.[28]

How wars are fought and won influences how peace agreements are designed and maintained. Without a mechanism to integrate the conduct of war with planning for peace, questions of **grand strategy** can devolve to questions of operational art.[29] In such circumstances, insufficient attention is devoted to the geopolitics of military victory. Where and when an adversary is forced to lay down its arms can have long-term political consequences. Consider the stab-in-the-back interpretation of Germany's defeat in World War I. At the end of the war, the German army was still in France. Given that a civilian government surrendered to the western allies, and no allied offensive ever reached Germany, disgruntled German officers later said that their army had not been defeated. Rather, it was betrayed by traitors who had negotiated a treaty of shame. This association between the allegedly perfidious Weimar Republic and the humiliating Treaty of Versailles haunted German political life for the next fourteen years.[30] Adolf Hitler made it a staple in his bombastic appeals to the German masses. To prevent a similar reinterpretation of history from souring the peace after World War II, the United States and Great Britain called for the "unconditional surrender" of Germany at the 1943 Casablanca conference, and together with France and the Soviet Union occupied German territory after the war. No German officers in 1945 could claim that their army had not been defeated.

Harmonizing military and political strategy does not mean politicians should consider themselves field commanders. Just as military leaders may be inattentive to how their actions affect the contours of the postwar settlement, political leaders ignorant of military matters may interfere with the conduct of crucial operations. According to Geoffrey Regan, Winston Churchill's "meddling in the military affairs of the Middle East Command in 1940–41 contributed to four separate yet connected disasters: the Greek expedition, the fall of Crete, Rommel's recapture of Cyrenaica, and the fall of Singapore."[31] Backseat driving by impatient political leaders may lead to assaults being launched too soon or in the wrong place. During the 1982 war between Argentina and Great Britain over the Falkland Islands, for example, British general Julian Thompson was ordered by his political superiors in London to seize an Argentinian position at Goose Green, despite its lack of military significance and serious logistical problems in mounting the attack.[32] The purpose of coordinating political and military strategy is to ensure that the process of war termination facilitates postwar peace building. Although political leaders decide war aims, they must avoid the temptation to micromanage the war effort, and never lose sight of their responsibility for seeing that military action should service the political goal of making peace.

Prescription 3: Planning for the postwar era must begin early.

The eve of victory is not the time to begin formulating plans for dealing with the many complicated problems that arise when wars end. Decisions must be made on the evacuation of wounded soldiers, the exchange of prisoners of war, the release of interned civilians, the repatriation of displaced persons, and the restitution of property. National leaders must also wrestle with questions pertaining to how many troops should be demobilized, how to absorb them into the labor force, and how to compensate those who have borne the costs of fighting. In some instances, they may have to confront additional challenges, including stationing occupation forces in conquered territory, retiring war-related debts, rebuilding damaged infrastructure, and converting armaments industries to the production of consumer goods. The nature of a war determines the complexity of these issues. Generally speaking, the longer the fighting continues and the greater the number of belligerents involved, the more difficult management of these issues becomes.[33]

Regardless of whether a war is terminated by a series of piecemeal agreements while the fighting drags on or through a comprehensive settlement after a truce, the bargaining position of victors erodes over time. As the United States discovered after the Persian Gulf War, and what was repeatedly reinforced for the next decade as an intractable Saddam Hussein hardened his resolve and plotted revenge, whatever is not exacted from the adversary during the shock of defeat becomes far more difficult to attain later.[34]

Unfortunately, as our cases reveal, postwar policies rarely emerge from deliberative plans; they unfold incrementally through a tyranny of small decisions, owing more to impulse than design. Lacking a grand strategy for the world of their making, victors usually improvise and muddle through the immediate aftermath of the war. "Few indeed are the occasions on which any statesman sees his objective clearly before him and marches toward it with undeviating stride," observed Harold Nicolson.[35]

To prevent policy drift, victors need to project what is likely to occur at the end of the war, anticipate the potential obstacles to a lasting peace settlement, and design a plan for surmounting them. Planning means forecasting the range of plausible futures, setting clear goals for attaining a specific desired future, and recommending actions for realizing that future. The sooner a formal attempt is undertaken to accomplish these tasks, the greater the chances that decisionmakers will be alerted to peacemaking opportunities they might otherwise miss.

Prescription 4: Know the character of your allies and your adversaries.

A common cause for the breakdown of peace and onset of war is that one or more of the participants failed to appreciate the character of their opponents, attributing to them interests and objectives at variance with their actual intentions. History is littered with numerous examples of such miscalculations. Consider the misjudgments made in the twentieth century that contributed to the outbreak of both world wars. For example, German leaders went to war in 1914 and again in 1939, in part, because they misread the isolationist impulses of the United States and Great Britain, and assumed that they would stay on the sidelines to preserve peace for themselves; moreover, the Germans underestimated the strength and resolve of the democracies and their willingness, once endangered, to fight for principle. After early setbacks, the democracies allied in World War I and World War II and finally triumphed.

Of course, democratic states also can misread the potentially belligerent motives of others. Adolf Hitler, for example, lulled many democracies into a false sense of security when he negotiated a series of nonaggression pacts with neighboring countries, as did Joseph Stalin of the Soviet Union. Ironically, Hitler signed such a pact with Stalin in 1939, who only discovered his miscalculations two years later, when to his shock Hitler attacked the Soviet Union, its "ally" in the nonaggression agreement. Neither the wily Stalin nor the naive Western European democracies read Hitler accurately. A practitioner of **realpolitik,** to Hitler diplomacy and treaties were merely a means to prepare for war.

When wars end, the same kinds of misperceptions about the character of a defeated adversary may doom the prospects for a durable peace. **Rapprochement**—a relaxation of tensions and restoration of friendly relations—may follow peace negotiations and calm fears of renewed aggression, but it is no guarantee of harmony. Victory is likely to produce a precarious peace if the vanquished state is ruled by someone whose philosophy allows them to redefine justice to serve their own self-interest. Often, warned military strategist Karl von Clausewitz, "the conquered nation sees [peace] as only a passing evil, to be repaired in after times . . ."[36] This is especially true of dictatorships, which, on the whole, have a demonstrably poor record of abiding by peace settlements. Despots can be vindictive — an attribute that can easily be ignored by a peace-loving country which, after defeating its enemy in battle, mistakenly projects its own values onto the vanquished. That appears to have been the case in the Persian Gulf War. At the start, Saddam Hussein totally misjudged U.S. intentions, initially thinking that the United States would not fight, and then assuming that U.S. forces would collapse because they could not take casualties.[37] Similarly, the United States misread Hussein's character and aims after the war when Americans mistakenly assumed that the leader of war-ravaged Iraq had learned his lesson and changed heart. Yet more than a decade after the war, the Iraqi dictator was still plotting revenge.

Modern history attests to the capacity of democratic states to keep peace with one another. This so-called **democratic peace** proposition asserts that "well-established democracies have never made war on one another [and] only republics have tended to form durable, peaceful leagues."[38] Because free governments tend to be pacific, encouraging the transition of nondemocratic states to democracies is a viable method of promoting global security. The Wilsonian ideal of "making the world safe for democracy" should be taken seriously as a path to peace since states that make their foreign policy decisions through democratic procedures can be expected to avoid fighting each other and adhere to peace accords negotiated with nondemocracies.[39]

Prescription 5: Prepare the public for the transition from war to peace.

Nationalistic fervor, so important for mobilizing the population for war, can become an obstacle to concluding a reasonable peace. Political leaders frequently stoke the fires of **xenophobia** on the home front to encourage sacrifice for the war effort. Denigrating the enemy's character is among the most common techniques to fuel these flames. Rhetorical appeals containing derogatory assertions about an enemy's character are a form of "ethotic" argument.[40] Typically, the thrust of these arguments during a war is to emphasize something diabolical about the character of the opponent in order to arouse a strong negative response. After highlighting these traits, an attempt is made to transfer the negative response to a conclusion about the intentions, actions, and motivations of the opponent.[41] Ethotic arguments appeal to the well-documented tendency of people to attribute their own behavior to situational factors while attributing the same behavior to an adversary's dispositional characteristics.[42] For example, if the leader of a particular country authorizes the strategic bombing of an enemy city, he might plead that he was driven to it by the exigencies of military necessity. However, when a rival engages in the same behavior, the leader probably would explain it by referring to his counterpart's inherent character flaws. Given that most people habitually overestimate the importance of dispositional causes when explaining the behavior of others, it is not surprising that ethotic arguments are common, politically acceptable, and persuasive during wartime.

Another reason for the effectiveness of ethotic arguments is the tendency of people to make facile connections between current problems and certain past events that they have personally or vicariously experienced. Research in cognitive psychology has found evidence that people are "classifiers" who attempt to understand the world by matching what is presently occurring with experiences that are stored in the form of memory schemata.[43] Simply put, **schematic reasoning** involves comparing the current situation with prototypes in one's memory. Among the types of schemata that influence decision making are stereotypical images that represent the character traits of vividly recalled or easily imagined individuals—the ruthless gangster, the sadistic bully, and so on. Despite the fact that an adversary may bear only a superficial resemblance to one of these stock characters, when little is known about someone our expectations will be shaped by presumed similarities to these stereotypes.

Finally, ethotic arguments are compelling because they allow people to evade responsibility. Combatants fall back on negative stereotypes and other discrediting devices to reduce guilt over their own repugnant acts by projecting blame on the enemy. Since the enemy allegedly is unscrupulous, one's own unethical behaviors are interpreted as preemptive measures.[44] According to the old saw, sometimes you have to fight fire with fire, and this way of thinking easily leads to the conviction that the end justifies the means, regardless of how evil are those means.

Heavy doses of ethotic argumentation have a dangerous side effect. When the war ends, the public may have little empathy for the losing side and expect to receive what it believes are justifiable spoils from the victory over a sinister enemy. For example, when it was learned that Russia refused to pay an indemnity or cede territory at the end of the Russo-Japanese War of 1904–1905, the *Asahi Shimbun,* a Japanese newspaper, printed the peace terms in a black frame, above a picture of a weeping soldier's skeleton. In response to this and similar editorials in other newspapers, tens of thousands of Japanese demonstrators clashed with police and set fire to government buildings on September 5 and 6, 1905, prompting the government to declare martial law and prohibit further criticism of the treaty.[45] Accentuating a diabolical image of the enemy may rally the populace when morale is low, but it will distort the peace settlement unless public expectations regarding the fruits of victory are attenuated before the fighting halts. Praise for an opponent's valor, differentiating between those who fought with honor and those who committed war crimes, and reminding one's own citizens of the plight of victims on both sides are critical in reversing the effects of wartime propaganda that denigrates the enemy's character.

Prescription 6: Victors should not ignore the passion for vengeance.

A passion for vengeance resides at the very core of our sense of justice. The moral vocabulary we use when discussing how to deal with perpetrators of grievous offenses is permeated with metaphors about debt ("repaying a wrong") and balance ("getting even") that underscore the central place of vengeance in our conception of punishment.[46] From the ghost of Clytemnestra who implores the Furies to avenge her murder by Orestes to the ghost of Hamlet's father who demands Hamlet avenge his murder by Claudius, playwrights through the ages have fascinated us with tales of vengeful anger. Although revenge themes are still common in film and literature today, we usually regard vengeance as the "sick vestige of a more primitive stage of human development," something that "falls within the province of detectives and other specialists in abnormal psychology."[47] Yet it is difficult to deny the satisfaction most humans feel when those guilty of some moral outrage receive their comeuppance, regardless of whether the penalty deters others from engaging in offensive conduct. Indeed, we often speak of "poetic justice" when miscreants who have evaded formal punishment experience a misfortune that nullifies ill-gotten gains.

The need for vengeance derives from powerful emotions that peacemakers ignore at great risk. It generally arises in the aftermath of premeditated campaigns of aggression that violate international humanitarian norms,[48] such as the those undertaken by the Axis powers in World War II. If the victims of these campaigns believe that wrongdoers failed to receive their just desserts, a sense of closure is never reached and private acts of retaliation are likely to follow.[49] Evil must be condemned and its perpetrators held responsible for their appalling deeds. The issue for victors is not whether angry emotions that demand punishment for wrongs are irrational and therefore inappropriate for consideration when crafting a peace settlement, but rather when and how it is reasonable to satisfy these demands.

Prescription 7: Avoid taking revenge, but seek retributive punishment for the culpably guilty.

To assert that a passion for vengeance is sometimes warranted is not to advocate wanton vindictiveness. Unrestrained vengeance has the potential to degenerate into an endless blood feud. In the culture of the vendetta, retaliation for an injury involves more than "an eye for an eye, a tooth for a tooth."[50] It is "an overpowering and consuming fire that burns away every other thought" and creates "the wildest, sweetest kind of drunkenness."[51] Under such a code of conduct, revenge is a duty. "He who cannot revenge himself is weak," proclaims an Italian proverb. "He who will not is contemptible."

The dangers of spiteful, measureless retaliation lead many theorists to differentiate between revenge and retribution. Revenge is an attempt "to impose suffering upon those who have made one suffer, because they have made one suffer."[52] It is a personal act — a self-righteous returning of wrong for wrong in which the avenger seeks pleasure from the suffering inflicted on the culprit.

Retribution lacks the resentful, vindictive spirit of revenge; it avenges a moral transgression dispassionately, without personal rancor. Retribution

has limits.[53] Since revenge has no objective limits, it is normally restricted by
social norms that specify what constitutes an affront, who is obliged to
respond, what means may be used, when it can occur, and what will be done
to those who fail to live up to their obligations. In some societies, these
norms transform revenge into ritualized acts of violence that extinguish
smoldering disagreements before they ignite into full-scale fighting.[54] More
typically, acts of revenge "overpay" rather than "even the score," thereby
adding new injuries that reinforce old hatreds.[55] **Retributive justice** attempts
to halt this escalatory momentum by taking jural-like activity out of private
hands, distinguishing between crimes and their punishment, and placing limits on the penalties wrongdoers pay.

Two basic schools of thought exist on the nature of retributive justice. The
maximalist school, represented by Immanuel Kant, holds that there is a duty to
punish anyone who is guilty and culpable for wrongdoing, and that the punishment should be equal to the seriousness of the offense.[56] Minimalism, the
second school of thought, also expresses moral indignation over the behavior
of the culpable. However, it asserts that punishment should be relative to the
seriousness of the offense and, unlike in a strict liability system, allows for mit-
igating circumstances that can partially or completely absolve the offender.

For victors seeking a durable peace, a minimalist conception of retributive
justice offers several important benefits. First, by holding specific individuals
accountable for any **war crimes** or crimes against humanity that they may
have committed, it defuses the possibility that charges of **collective guilt** will
be leveled against an entire defeated nation, as happened to Germany following World War I. Second, avoiding collective condemnation facilitates the
normalization of relations between victor and vanquished after the war.
Third, by showing that international humanitarian law cannot be violated
with impunity, it helps those who were victimized bring closure to the experience, thus avoiding the temptation toward revenge through violence in the
future. Finally, by eschewing revenge in favor of retributive justice through a
fair and impartial judicial process (ideally through an international tribunal),
reconciliation and the pursuit of **restorative justice** can begin.

Prescription 8: Victors should forgive the forgivable, but not forget.

Reconciliation is a process of developing a mutually conciliatory accommodation between former enemies.[57] It is a dynamic, sequential process that
requires actions by those who have suffered wrongs as well as by those who
have committed them. The former consists of forgiving; the latter, apologizing. Although it is common to hear references to forgiveness and apology in
our everyday conversations, rarely does anyone seriously reflect on their precise meaning. Because both are complex, multidimensional concepts, let us
briefly discuss each in turn.

Perhaps the most systematic contemporary work on the elusive concept of
forgiveness has been done by Donald Shriver.[58] Genuine forgiveness, he
explains, has four dimensions. First, forgiveness begins with a memory of

past evils suffused with a moral judgment of injustice. Second, forgiveness entails forbearance: Past wrongs are neither overlooked nor excused, but punishment is not reduced to revenge. Third, forgiveness includes empathy for the enemy; that is, a recognition of the other side's humanity. Fourth, genuine forgiveness is restorative; it seeks to repair fractured human relationships and promote social healing.

For social healing to occur, wrongdoers must shoulder the responsibility for apologizing. Like forgiveness, a sincere apology entails several things. First, it involves feelings of sorrow and regret for the injurious act.[59] Second, it expresses shame over what was done and repudiates that kind of behavior.[60] Third, it contains an avowal henceforth to conduct oneself in the proper way.[61] Finally, it includes a gesture of penance to atone for the transgression. In certain societies, apologies inaugurate a process of ceremonial purification. Rather than just stigmatizing the offender, the members of these societies follow their denunciations with a highly visible ritual of reacceptance.[62] In this way, the wrongdoer is reintegrated into the fold instead of remaining an outcast, forever condemned to the margins of public life. Public ceremonies of reconciliation, such as the ancient practice observed by some Native Americans of burying war axes, can help reverse relations among former adversaries.

Apology and forgiveness can jointly soothe raw postwar feelings, but not necessarily in every situation. No victor can force the vanquished to have feelings of sorrow and remorse for injurious acts. Even when someone has suffered directly from the misdeeds of a truly repentant person, deep introspection normally is required before the relationship can be repaired. Forgiving under ordinary circumstances is difficult. What happens when the injustice is far greater in scope and magnitude? Are certain offenses of such moral gravity and some perpetrators at such moral fault that apology is an empty gesture and forgiveness beyond human reach? Does anyone have the moral agency to forgive massive atrocities committed against others? How should we respond to existential evil? Consider the plight of Simon, a Jewish internee in a Nazi concentration camp.[63] One day he encountered a mortally wounded SS officer who asked forgiveness for the many heinous crimes he committed against other Jews. Did Simon have the power or the right to forgive him for his unspeakable acts? Perhaps there are some deeds so horrific that recompense for the victims and forgiveness for the perpetrators are outside of the victors' human capability.[64]

Prescription 9: A dictated peace is a precarious peace; victors should involve the vanquished in settlement negotiations.

History judges a state a winner in war if it can force the enemy to surrender. But winners can ultimately lose if they fail to include the defeated in the peace talks. There are many perils to the art of peacemaking. Perhaps none is as perilous as summoning the courage and skill to negotiate the terms of surrender with an enemy.

A classic example of the dangers of imposing a settlement is provided by the harsh treatment forced on France in 1871 at the conclusion of the Franco-Prussian War. The prostrate French were instructed about the terms of the peace treaty and were not given much of a chance to modify the settlement. Their thirst for revenge over this humiliation was one of the major factors that led to the outbreak of World War I in 1914. As Thomas Bailey notes, "The Germans forgot one of their own proverbs: 'Revenge does not long remain unrevenged.'"[65]

Victors should avoid treating grievances voiced by the defeated as if they were simply outrageous bargaining tactics. The losing side in a war may believe it has legitimate complaints and a right to express them. When victors deny that perceived right and proclaim that they alone can define the meaning of justice, they deprive the defeated a chance to express their ideas about what constitutes a fair peace settlement. Not only does this cause a loss of face, it also removes any stake the defeated might have in upholding the settlement. Even concessions by the victor on issues of low priority can assuage an adversary. As social scientists Roger Fisher and William Ury point out, giving the other side a small role in drafting the settlement creates a sense of ownership: "An outcome in which the other side gets absolutely nothing is worse for you than one which leaves them mollified."[66]

Showing disrespect to an adversary by precluding their participation in discussions about peace terms is also risky because it overlooks the possibility that yesterday's enemy may be needed as tomorrow's friend. Victors should be aware of the interests underlying their opponents' stated position and look for opportunities to work toward achieving superordinate goals that neither side could achieve alone.[67] Shared interests may not be immediately obvious, but there will almost always be elements in a peace settlement whereby victors can satisfy some interest of the vanquished without damaging significant interests of their own.[68]

In sum, victors in search of a durable peace settlement should apply the golden rule to diplomacy, treating the vanquished the way they would wish themselves to be treated were they in the same position. So long as one is not dealing with an utterly ruthless, depraved opponent, restraint and a readiness for conciliation can evoke gratitude and set in motion a positive spiral of tension-reducing reciprocation. Victors who couple firmness regarding their own interests with fairness toward the interests of others encourage defeated powers to work within the postwar system. Nowhere is this more important than in resolving outstanding territorial issues. A fair disposition of territorial claims, coupled with simple, unambiguous, and prominent lines of demarcation are critical to building a lasting peace.

Prescription 10: Beware of allies whose interest in the peace negotiations centers on gaining the spoils of victory.

Alliances are formal agreements between sovereign states "for the putative purpose of coordinating their behavior in the event of certain specified contingencies of a military nature."[69] Coordination may range from a detailed list of armed forces that will be furnished by each party to the broader requirement of consultation should a serious dispute occur. In addition to differing according to the level of coordination, **alliances** also vary in terms of the target and duration of their accords. The target of an alliance may be left implicit or may be identified as a single country, a group of states, or a geographic region. Alliance duration may be limited to a relatively short period of time or constructed to last indefinitely.

Rarely are alliances formed just to express friendship or some vague ideological affiliation. They are constructed for clear, calculated advantage. In the first place, alliances help states acquire benefits that might not have been attained by acting unilaterally. In the second place, they reduce the costs associated with foreign policy undertakings by spreading them among several partners. If the perceived benefits exceed the costs, and if the costs are politically sustainable, states worried about their security will join alliances despite the uneven burdens they necessitate and the unequal returns they provide.

It is always uncertain whether an alliance will serve the purposes for which it was originally created. Will it deter external attacks? If not, will the members uphold their treaty commitments when faced with the possibility of war? And if they do, will the alliance be able to defeat the aggressors? Fighting in concert with allies is a challenge. Enormous amounts of time and energy must be invested in resolving interallied disagreements on strategy. Even when a consensus exists, friction may still arise over the priorities assigned to specific theaters of the war. Further complicating matters, units from various countries — trained under different philosophies, armed with different weapons, and configured for different missions — must somehow work in tandem, occasionally in the midst of petty rivalries among allied commanders. As one observer of military partnerships has put it, alliances are "like a house built by jealous carpenters with no boss and with many different plans for the design of the building."[70]

Alliances, in other words, are rickety constructions whose structural integrity diminishes when the common external threat that brought them into being recedes. With victory in sight, aggressively self-interested members of large wartime coalitions will likely be tempted by the chance for plunder and begin jockeying for a peace settlement that furthers their own selfish aims. At this point it is crucial for those states with aspirations of building a durable peace settlement to use the waning days of the war to unite behind a collective peace plan. If major issues are left unresolved until a formal peace conference, the most determined ally will end up in possession of important assets which then can be removed only through a perilous confrontation.[71]

The success of a multilateral peace conference depends on the victors' capacity to transcend the desire for short-term relative gains and embrace the goal of avoiding mutual loss. Perhaps no statesman in the cases we have covered was better at framing the settlement process in these terms than Austria's Metternich. At the Congress of Vienna he was able to control events by defining their moral framework. Keenly aware of the importance of reducing the grandiose claims put forth by others—rather than simply promoting his own—Klemens von Metternich made concessions appear as sacrifices to a common cause. The legitimacy of a peace settlement, he always said, rests on acceptance, not imposition.[72]

Prescription 11: Victors should be prepared to use military force after the war ends.

Thomas Schelling has written, "it takes at least as much skill to end a war properly as to begin one to advantage."[73] Losers may still possess bargaining assets, even when they have no hope of winning a war. Not only can they struggle on and extract a price from the winner by making victory more costly, they may, like Saddam Hussein following the Persian Gulf War, be able to undermine postwar stability.[74] The durability of a peace settlement hinges on the victor's ability to anticipate how dissatisfied parties may challenge new security arrangements, and develop effective contingency plans for arresting these challenges. Ironically, "military victory is often a prelude to violence, not the end of it," notes Schelling.[75] The successful victor generally holds the threat of more pain to come in reserve as a way of inducing the vanquished to accommodate itself to defeat. Conciliation is unlikely to succeed without the backing of a credible deterrent.

By itself, restraint in victory may not be enough to diffuse the losers' desire for revenge. Occasionally restraint toward the vanquished must be combined with a convincing use of military force against someone else. Take, for instance, relations between Prussia and Austria after the Seven Weeks' War. As early as December 1866, Bismarck had sought a rapprochement with Austria, but was rebuffed. With Prussia's shocking victory over France at the Battle of Sedan, attitudes in Vienna began to change. Austrian Foreign Minister Friedrich Ferdinand Baron Beust, an ardent opponent of Bismarck, concluded that it was now in Austria's interest to distance itself from the French. In a memorandum written on May 18, 1871, Beust stated that Austria was detrimentally affected by the French loss at Sedan in two ways. First, Prussia could exert its immense military power against Austria directly. Second, it could interfere indirectly with Austria by manipulating German nationalist sentiments within Austria's multinational empire. Given the leverage Berlin would have over Austria, he recommended seeking an accommodation with Prussia.[76]

Prescription 12: The vanquished have responsibilities in making peace.

Winners in war have the power to exercise their will. As a result, they receive most of the praise when peace settlements succeed and most of the blame when they fail. Indeed, it is tempting to believe that the responsibilities for making peace rest exclusively with the choices of victors. That temptation should be overcome, however, because the actions of the defeated can influence the peace plans of the victors.

Losers, like winners, must also make hard choices. Should they resent their loss and strive to undermine the new postwar order? Or should they adjust to the painful turn of events and work within the new order? The choice is difficult even when the loser is guilty of wrongdoing; it becomes agonizing when the loser is innocent. How should the vanquished respond when it was responsible for the war? Conversely, what should it do when the winner provoked the showdown and then violated prevailing codes of military conduct? What should it do when blame is relatively equal? The answers depend in large measure on whether the war effort was regarded by the loser as being worth the costs. Wars perceived as not having been worth their costs engender a domestic political environment in which accommodationists rather than defiant hard-liners prevail. According to war and peace theorist John Vasquez, a repeat of war between the same two parties is less likely when accommodationists govern political life within the country that has lost the war.[77]

Defeated nations are always in a poor bargaining position. Yet they are not without power. In certain circumstances, a principled posture by accommodationists within the defeated country can influence how victors behave once the fighting ends. Assuming the loser is not annihilated (like Carthage after the Third Punic War), the victor must confront a series of questions about the role of its former enemy in the postwar world. Can the vanquished be trusted? Do they intend to stand by the peace agreement? Will they revert to battle at the first opportunity to avenge their losses? Uncertainty over the answers to these questions can plague a victor, leading it to expend scarce resources for contingencies it would prefer to avoid.

Consider the following scenario: What would a victor do if a defeated country accepted its part of the blame for the war's onset and its accommodationist government sought to work dutifully within the new international order? A pacific response by the subjugated can sometimes disarm the conqueror. Losing parties can win by practicing "moral jujitsu," in the terminology of Richard B. Gregg. Jujitsu is an Asian martial art that throws a powerful adversary off balance by countering its attack. In Gregg's conception, a repentant former enemy can encourage the victor to be merciful by throwing him off moral balance:

> He suddenly and unexpectedly loses the moral support which the usual violent resistance of most victims would render him. He plunges forward, as it were, into a new world of values. He feels insecure because of the novelty of the situation and his ignorance of how to handle it. He loses his poise and self-confidence. . . . [In this way, the vanquished party] uses the leverage of a superior wisdom to subdue the rough direct force of his opponent.[78]

Suffering may be a viable strategy for a state defeated in war. Principles can produce power. "Most advocates of principled nonviolence believe that unmerited suffering is the most forceful way to affect an opponent's conscience." Self-imposed suffering is often effective in changing the policies of one's opponents.[79] As the twentieth century's leading prophet of this philosophy, Mahatma Gandhi, explained, "suffering is infinitely more powerful than [war] for converting the opponent and opening his ears, which are otherwise shut, to the voice of reason."[80]

To heed this advice about encouraging compassion is to ask the loser in war to respond in an unusual way. Disarming the victor by appealing to morality is not easy. Tempers flare in the heat of battle, and enemies often dehumanize each other as accusations fly back and forth. Memories of war continue to smolder long after a truce is struck, threatening to ignite once again into an inferno of hatred. But if the defeated dutifully serves the victor after the war, and if it can identify itself with principles the victor accepts as just, it may be able to embarrass the victor into living up to its own beliefs about fair play. Of course, such a strategy assumes that the victor believes in fair play and is not committed to a policy of genocide or other unjust treatment.[81]

FROM JUST WAR TO JUST PEACE

The decision to wage war is perhaps the most fateful choice a state's leaders can make. Not only are the risks high, but the costs are certain to be extraordinary. Security, survival, and status are put at stake, alongside the lasting reputation by which history will remember the choices as being wise or foolish, moral or evil. Most leaders do not take such risks recklessly, for their place in history and their country's fate will ultimately be heavily determined by these choices.

Since the dawn of history, questions surrounding the decision to wage war have inspired people to think about when it is permissible, as well as how the war should be conducted. There is a rich and abundant literature in international law and in international ethics, known as **just war** theory, from which scholars and policymakers draw to make informed judgments about when and how to fight. Because just war theory has such an impact on contemporary foreign policy discourse, it is important to understand its origins and evolution.

Just War Doctrine

Many people are confused by international law because it both prohibits and justifies the use of force. Much of the confusion derives from the just war tradition in Christian realism, in which the rules of war are philosophically based on morals (principles of behavior) and ethics (explanations of why these principles are proper). In the fourth century, St. Augustine questioned the strict view that those who take another's life to defend the state necessarily violate the commandment "Thou shalt not kill." He counseled that it is the wrongdoing of the opposing party which compels the wise leader to wage war. The Christian was obligated, he felt, to fight against evil and wickedness. His logic was extended by Pope Nicholas I, who in 866 proclaimed that any defensive war was just. It was refined again in the seventeenth century by Hugo Grotius, who challenged the warring Catholic and Protestant powers in the Thirty Years' War to abide by humane standards of conduct. For war to be moral it must be fought by just means without harm to innocent noncombatants. From these and many other extensions of Augustine's theology a distinction emerged between two categories of argument, *jus ad bellum* (the justice of a war) and *jus in bello* (justice in a war). The former sets the criteria by which a political leader may determine whether a war should be waged. The latter specifies restraints on the range of permissible tactics to be used in fighting a just war.

These distinctions have been hotly debated since their inception. Drawing the line between murder and the just use of lethal force is a controversial task. At the core of the just war tradition is the conviction that the taking of human life may be a "lesser evil" when necessary to prevent further life-threatening aggression. For example, St. Thomas More contended that the assassination of an evil leader responsible for starting a war was justified if it would preclude the taking of innocent lives. From this premise, a number of other principles follow that provide a yardstick by which decisions to wage wars may be measured in terms of their legality and morality.

1. All other means to a morally just solution of conflict must be exhausted before a resort to arms can be justified.
2. War can be just only if employed to defend a stable political order or a morally preferable cause against a real threat or to restore justice after a real injury has been sustained.
3. A just war must have a reasonable chance of succeeding in these limited goals.
4. A just war must be proclaimed by a legitimate government authority.
5. War must be waged for the purpose of correcting a wrong rather than for malicious revenge.
6. Negotiations to end the war must be in continuous process as long as fighting continues.
7. Noncombatants must be immune from intentional attack.
8. Only legal and moral means may be employed in prosecuting the war.
9. The damage likely to be incurred from a war may not be disproportionate to the injury suffered.
10. The final goal of the war must be to reestablish peace and justice.

These criteria continue to color contemporary thinking about the rules of warfare and the circumstances under which the use of armed force is legally and morally permissible. They call upon political leaders not only to fight for a just cause, but to do so without violating the rights of their opponents.

Building a Just Peace

While scholars have argued for centuries about the conditions under which it is just to wage war, far less thought has gone into how to craft a just peace. "The real puzzle for social scientists is not war and violence," observe anthropologists Thomas Gregor and Clayton Robarchek, "but a more unusual phenomenon: peace."[82] While scholars rightly devote enormous effort to the scientific study of the causes of war, complementary research efforts on how states make peace lag far behind. The reasons why "just peace" theory does not benefit from an intellectual consensus and codified literature can be found in the lack of attention given to the subject, despite the existence of an energetic peace research community dedicated to understanding conflict resolution. War makes headlines; the long, hard process of peacemaking does not always attract commensurate interest. As philosopher Kenneth Burke notes, "The mere fact that something is to man's interest is no guarantee that he will be interested in it."[83]

Attaining peace is more difficult than desiring it. Sustaining peace once it has been attained is even more demanding. The victor in search of a lasting accord with the vanquished must somehow blend demands for security from domestic constituencies with policies the former enemy accepts as fitting. It must be able to quash challenges to the new international order while developing procedures that allow complaints to be aired and peaceful change to occur. The obstacles to these goals are numerous, and their existence explains why agreement about a blueprint for creating a lasting peace has proven so elusive. Postwar settlements that harmonize competing concerns are fragile and require constant care.

Trust and Mistrust

Achieving a just and lasting peace between former adversaries is difficult in international politics because mistrust is endemic among sovereign states in an anarchic environment. Without a higher authority possessing the legitimacy and coercive capability to preserve peace, states must fend for themselves while struggling with multiple fears: the fear of attack by enemies; the fear of exploitation by allies; and the fear of being victimized by an unfair treaty. These fears peak as war clouds gather, but scarcely dissipate when the fighting ends. As the belligerents face the task of rebuilding their relationship, insecurity persists.

The chronic suspicion infecting world politics does not augur well for building a lasting peace. Entrenched doubts about promises voiced by a former foe inhibit mutually beneficial collaboration and encourage defensive noncooperation. Yet, building peace requires building trust, even among states that have few reasons to have confidence in one another. At war's end, the victor must consider actions that seem counterintuitive, such as reconciling with an adversary previously perceived as without scruples. Obviously, many authorities recommend against this risky approach. They recognize that trusting involves believing the future actions of others are certain, even when these actions cannot be absolutely guaranteed. And should this trust be violated the trusting state would face negative consequences.[84] Trust can invite betrayal. Building trust by trusting unreliable former enemies is therefore highly controversial. As Bernhardt Lieberman has written, embedded within most foreign policy debates on these matters are two contending positions:

One group argues it is irrelevant, and possibly dangerous, to consider the notion of trust in the conduct of international relations. Nations, it is said, will act in their own self-interest and abrogate treaties, agreements, or their word informally given, whenever it is believed to be necessary to do so. It is said that a nation that does not act in its own self-interest is difficult to deal with; trustworthy behavior contrary to national interests is irresponsible and dangerous.

A second group believes that at the root of the difficulty in international affairs is the fact that nations cannot and do not trust each other. Aggressive behavior and conflicts arise not so much from genuinely irreconcilable conflicts, but more from mistrust, suspicion, and untrustworthy acts. They believe that one should impress upon one's opponent one's good intentions.[85]

These rival ideas about making peace are nested within the two major traditions of theoretical inquiry introduced in Chapter 1: liberalism and realism. As summarized in Table 9.3, liberals like Woodrow Wilson maintain that trust is possible and from it peace can be built. Realists from Cardinal Richelieu to Winston Churchill aver that it is better to put faith in your own power than to trust others. Let us briefly return to the ongoing conversation between these two traditions on how to craft a durable peace settlement.

Liberal Ideals and Illusions?

Observing the dismal regularity with which harsh peace settlements throughout history have disintegrated, liberal reformers have questioned the wisdom of punitive postwar policies. In fact, some liberal thinkers, like John Locke, believed that victors have ethical obligations to the vanquished.[86] Although there are several distinct theoretical traditions within liberalism, they share many elements of commonality. For today's liberals, foreign policy unfolds in a nascent global society populated by actors who recognize the costs of conflict and share significant interests. Believing in altruism, reason, and the capacity of people to change those practices that foster conflict, liberals emphasize how well-designed international institutions can bind victor and vanquished together in a web of overlapping and converging interests.

The European Coal and Steel Community (ECSC), formed by France, Germany, Italy, Belgium, Luxemburg, and the Netherlands in 1952, exemplified this integrative liberal approach to peace building through institutions. The ECSC contained a **supranational** body called the High Authority that made binding decisions by majority vote on the production and marketing of coal and steel. As part of the ECSC, Germany could revive its heavy industry after World War II without alarming its neighbors, who now possessed some degree of control over key German resources by virtue of their representation in the authority. Unfortunately, note some liberals, an earlier opportunity to build institutions

> "Wars occur because people prepare for conflict, rather than peace."
>
> — TRYGVE LIE

TABLE 9.3
Liberal and Realist Theories: Premises and Policy Prescriptions

	Liberalism	Realism
Premises		
Human nature	Cooperative, altruistic	Competitive, selfish
Primary global condition	Interdependence	Anarchy and self-help
Conception of politics	A struggle about principles	A struggle for power
Core concern	Global interests	National interests
Philosophical outlook	Optimistic	Pessimistic
Prescriptions		
Philosophy of action	Do what is morally right	Do what is strategically necessary
Boundary of state sovereignty	Moral duties supercede state sovereignty	State sovereignty is inviolable
View of negotiation	Negotiate rather than fight, but adjudicate when negotiations stall	Negotiate rather than fight, but fight rather than risk losing on an issue of importance
Range of national power	Limit national power through international law	Increase national power
Value of national autonomy	Promote international integration	Resist any reduction of national independence

in the metallurgical sector that could have brought the governments in Paris and Berlin closer together after World War I was missed, even though French iron ore complemented German coking coal. Nevertheless, from these humble origins emerged the fully integrated European Union that exists today—a **security community** dedicated to liberal democracy in which the prospect of war has virtually vanished.

Several steps are considered necessary in order to get former foes to participate in institutions like the ECSC: repentance, restitution, and reciprocity. To liberals, admitting injury and injustice are essential to the healing process. Peacemaking is not merely a matter of letting bygones be bygones. Reconciliation depends on a sincere effort to set the record straight through repentance and to build a new record through restitution.[87] Liberal theory also suggests that reconciliation depends on victors showing mercy to the defeated. Although mercy is a virtue that can conflict with the demands of justice, it nonetheless serves as a potential source of influence for the victor as well as a source of constraint for the vanquished. Recipients of magnanimity are placed in a position of social indebtedness. The greater their feeling of indebtedness, the greater their subsequent attempts to reduce it. Over time, this kind of relationship is thought to create obligations that generate **reciprocity.**[88]

Many liberals stress the importance of commerce in reinforcing the web of interdependence spun by international institutions. Free trade creates material incentives to resolve disputes peacefully. The cosmopolitan business elites who benefit most from trade are seen as comprising a powerful transnational interest group with a stake in promoting amicable solutions to festering disagreements. Furthermore, many liberal theorists argue that the flow of trade between former enemies increases communication, erodes parochialism, and encourages both sides to construct new institutions to coordinate their behavior in other issue areas.

Liberalism also advances a large number of other proposals for making peace between states: for example, human rights, international law, and democratic forms of governance. For our purposes, the important element in liberal theory is morality. Liberals see power in adherence to ethical principles, and see in conformity to rules the possibility of converting feuds into friendships. This applies directly to the question of the proper code of conduct for disputants after wars end. At the risk of oversimplifying the liberal argument, we can assert that most liberals would concur with the proposition that "Men will pay you back with the same measure you have used with them."[89] Good will be returned for good, bad for bad. Compassionate settlements, therefore, maximize the prospects for a lasting peace because they encourage the vanquished to return that good will.

The liberal approach to peacemaking is not without its problems, however. Ruthless opponents throughout history have taken advantage of mercy and forbearance, returning ill will for magnanimity. For this reason, various people have concluded that liberalism's peace proposals are illusory. The most severe of these critics are found in the realist camp.

The Realism of Realpolitik?

Any assessment of the virtues of repentance, restitution, and reciprocity must be balanced by a realist account of the dangers in this approach. Like liberalism, realism contains many strains of thought. As a political theory, realism traces its intellectual roots to the ancient Greek historian Thucydides, the Italian Renaissance theorist Niccoló Machiavelli, and the seventeenth-century English philosopher Thomas Hobbes. International politics, according to realists, is a ceaseless and repetitive struggle for power that occurs among ter-

> "Diplomacy without arms is like music without instruments."
>
> — FREDERICK THE GREAT

ritorially organized states of varying military and economic strength. Because the anarchic structure of the state system makes lasting peace impossible, realists envision the highest purpose of statecraft to be national survival. Wise leaders, they argue, will carefully weigh the perceived costs and benefits of alternative foreign policies with an eye toward marshaling the wherewithal needed to ensure security and advance national interests. From the realist perspective, security is a function of power, and power is primarily a function of military preparedness.

According to some versions of realist thought, concern over moral principles interferes with the pursuit of national power. Ethical preferences are neither good nor bad—what matters is whether the state's self-interest is served. As social scientist Albert O. Herschmann explains the realist philosophy:

> Modern political science owes a great deal to Machiavelli's shocking claim that ordinary notions of moral behavior for individuals may not be suitable as rules of conduct for states. More generally, it appeared, as a result of the wealth of insights discovered by Machiavelli, that the traditional concentration on the "ought," on the manner in which princes and statesmen ought to behave, interferes with the fuller understanding of the "is" that can be achieved when attention is closely and coldly riveted on the ways in which statecraft is in fact carried on.[90]

When it comes to designing a peace settlement, many realists argue that wise rulers on the winning side should be unrestrained in their sovereign right to choose whatever action they think is most likely to enhance their prospects for self-preservation. Any attempt to import moral principles into the settlement process would prove self-defeating. Looking at failed peace-making policies of the past, realist thought points to scenes of malevolence, deceit, and broken promises, concluding that postwar diplomatic conferences provide an opportunity to practice deception. Harsh punishment is the best way to keep a defeated enemy permanently down so it cannot rise again in retaliation. As a counter to the liberal claim that enemies should be forgiven, realists predict that crime unpunished will be repeated.

Like liberal theory, hard-boiled realism is not without its shortcomings. Contrary to what the nihilistic versions of this theory would predict, moderate treatment of France after the Napoleonic Wars ushered in a period of prolonged peace. Thus, while many realists scoff at the liberal suggestion that a defeated adversary will reciprocate with goodwill, some realists assert that pure power politics may not be as effective in dealing with the defeated as the exercise of power with a framework of accepted legitimacy.

Kautilya, the ancient Hindu practitioner of realism, embodies this tension between the roles of power and justice in a peace settlement. Kautilya urged caution when interacting with subjugated powers.[91] "An enemy who was defeated earlier and who has since become a friend should not be trusted," he warned. Because the remnants of such an enemy can spark an uprising, even "children of enemies who have surrendered" will "prove dangerous in due course." The "power born out of sorrow and resentment," he cautioned, "bestows bravery." Yet Kautilya recognized the importance of justice when dealing with the defeated. Wrong punishment angers while "good behavior wins even an enemy." He "who punishes severely is hated by the people, he who punishes mildly is despised, one who metes out deserving punishment is respected."

Proponents of liberalism and realism have long debated one another about the paths to peace and the perils of peacemaking, as this brief synopsis of their philosophies suggests. Whereas liberals believe in progress and place their faith in the improvement of individuals and institutions, realists discern no such capability in the human condition.[92] Notwithstanding these important distinctions, it would be wrong to conclude that there are no areas of agreement between the two traditions. Both agree on the importance of peace treaties in constructing a durable settlement, and both recognize the problems in designing such treaties. More importantly, all but the most vulgar exponents of realpolitik agree that prudence requires taking into account the moral values of those who the settlement will affect.[93] Peace agreements encapsulated by a web of collaborative, partner-specific norms of prudence are more resilient than those lacking normative support, because international norms add predictability to future relations by communicating the scope of each state's entitlements, the extent of its obligations, and the range of its jurisdiction. Liberals and realists agree that postwar diplomacy cannot be divorced from the normative climate in which it occurs. If victors do not reinforce international norms that buttress the war termination agreements they sign, the vanquished will attempt to establish alternative norms that can be used to undermine the peace settlement.

Embedding Peace within Justice

How can bitter adversaries overcome the rancor of their collective past and restore amicable relations? Peacemaking is a process without rigid rules. The only guidelines are those the winners choose. We have seen that victors tend to make up the rules as they go along. Sometimes their choices are made under time constraints. At other times, the peacemaking process is protracted, with no perceived incentives for a prompt settlement. Whether constructed quickly or patiently, either tack is likely to produce a series of problems in its wake if little thought has been given to questions of grand postwar strategy.

Like war itself, peacemaking can be likened to the game of chess. The players are able to make a vast number of interconnected moves and countermoves, each of which will alter the costs and benefits of the next round of decisions. Neither side can be sure of the opponent's sequence of moves over the course of the game, and each move alters the possibilities and payoffs of subsequent countermoves—thereby preventing anyone from knowing the long-term consequences of their choices. Just as there is no single formula to

> "War, the begetter of all things, the creature of all things, the river with a thousand sources, the sea without a shore: begetter of all things except peace, so ardently longed for, so rarely attained."
>
> — FERNAND BRAUDEL

win at chess, there is no simple formula for how nations should make peace. As Charles Doran has written, victors "must consider the unique aspects that characterize the [international] system" at the time of their victory and the impact the war's outcome will have on other major state actors.[94] In addition, they must recognize the moral dilemmas involved.

Recognition involves acknowledging the past. Wartime adversaries may have to face unpleasant truths about themselves and their enemies. They must both give up the self-righteous belief that virtue resides in their own behavior and that all blame can be ascribed to the enemy. Wars are seldom a struggle between total virtue and vice, between an honorable nation and a wicked nation. But when so conceived, they become crusades that remove the possibility of finding common ground after the battles are over.

Empathy is crucial for finding common ground. The architect of a peace settlement must understand the world of the defeated for the settlement to last. Victors must overcome what has been called "compassion fatigue" and the vanquished must move beyond recrimination.[95] Both parties need to see how their fates are intertwined. This requires that there be some general agreement as to the wrongs committed during the war, a consideration of the impact that those wrongs have had, and attempt to atone for them. The following steps are crucial for achieving these goals:

> First, the injured and the perpetrators openly acknowledge the reality of the terrible acts that were committed. Second, the injured are provided with prospects for security and well-being. Third, those who experienced injustices receive redress in some measure. Finally, the injured accept with compassion those who committed injurious conduct as well as acknowledge each other's suffering.[96]

In conclusion, when we think about making peace, we must think about justice. The end of a war requires calculations to be made about the allocation of benefits and burdens, rewards and punishment. These are ethical choices, not legal ones; they are decisions about values, not rights; they provide occasions when winners can determine what goods will be received and what goods will be lost.

The decision-making problem confronting winners is complicated by the pull of four central competing dimensions of justice: (1) distributive justice — the ethics of dividing the spoils of war at the loser's expense; (2) retributive justice — the ethics of administering punishment for wrongful deeds; (3) corrective justice — the ethics of compensating victims; and (4) restorative justice — the ethics of rebuilding broken relationships. All war-ending events raise difficult questions in each of these areas of moral inquiry. If this book inspires greater awareness of, and attention to, the broader ethical and policy issues of building a just world order, it will have accomplished its primary goal.

SUGGESTED READING

Barash, David P., ed. *Approaches to Peace*. New York: Oxford University Press, 2000.

Digeser, P. E. *Political Forgiveness*. Ithaca, N.Y.: Cornell University Press, 2001.

Halliday, Fred. *The World at 2000*. London: Macmillan, 2001.

Harbour, Francis V. *Thinking about International Ethics*. Boulder, Colo.: Westview, 1999.

Ikenberry, G. John. *After Victory: Institutions, Strategic Restraint, and the Building of World Order*. Princeton, N.J.: Princeton University Press, 2001.

Kegley, Charles W., Jr., ed. *Controversies in International Relations Theory: Realism and the Neoliberal Challenge*. New York: St. Martin's Press, 1995.

Kriesberg, Louis. *Constructive Conflicts: From Escalation to Resolution*. Lanham, Md.: Rowman & Littlefield, 1998.

Mitchell, Christopher. *Gestures of Conciliation: Factors Contributing to Successful Olive Branches*. New York: St. Martin's Press, 2000.

Pangle, Thomas L., and Peter J. Ahrensdorf. *Justice among Nations: On the Moral Basis of Power and Peace*. Lawrence: University Press of Kansas, 1999.

Wright, Robert. *Non Zero: The Logic of Human Destiny*. New York: Random House, 2000.

NOTES

1. Bennett and Stam, 1996, pp. 251–253.
2. Oren, 1982, p. 153.
3. Geller and Singer, 1998, p. 1. Of those states that have experienced war, forty-nine fought in one or two wars, sixteen participated in three or four, and only eight were involved in more than ten.
4. Massoud, 1996, p. 491.
5. Georg Simmel, in Beer and Mayer, 1986, p. 158.
6. Rosenthal, 1995, p. 317.
7. Ibid.
8. Ibid., p. 328.
9. Bennett, 1996, p. 158.
10. Leng, 1983.
11. See Brecher, 1984; Diehl et al., 1996; Goertz and Diehl, 1992a, 1992b.
12. Maoz, 1984, p. 239; Hensel, 1994. Although war winners tend to initiate new wars sooner than states that suffered a loss, the inhibiting effect of losing on future aggression is seldom long-lasting because losers have a high probability of initiating another war roughly a generation after they recover from a loss, largely due to treasured memories of previous victories. Nevin, 1996, p. 105.
13. As discussed earlier, for analytic reasons we have purposefully excluded those many armed conflicts that ended without a clear victor; hence, we will not focus on how to build peace following a military stalemate.
14. We have focused on those wars that have been most frequently cited by policymakers as evidence of why victors should act in a particular way when combat ends. Based on a comparison of those wars, we have advanced a prescriptive argument composed of didactic propositions about how states should act after wars to sustain durable peace settlements. In

the spirit of building policy-relevant theory that advances recommendations for making peace, we envision this tentative first step as a necessary preliminary to subsequent empirical testing.

15. Neustadt and May, 1986, pp. 91–92.
16. For suggestions on how policy-relevant theories can be built from the comparative study of cases, see George, 1979 and Raymond, 1987. See also Eckstein, 1975; Fry and Raymond, 1983, pp. 1–9; and McGowan, 1975.
17. Levy, 1994; Stern, 1997.
18. Levy, 1994, pp. 306–310.
19. Burke, 1989, p. 155.
20. Schroeder, 1994a, p. 148.
21. Khong, 1992, p. 225; Hybel, 1990.
22. Vertzberger, 1986, p. 243.
23. In *The European*, November, 8–10, 1991, p. 6.
24. Human behavior appears to be heavily influenced by "somatic markers," biases generated by emotions that give people a feeling about the outcome of doing one thing versus another. When a negative marker is associated with an anticipated future outcome, it functions like an alarm that warns against behaving in a certain way; but when a positive marker exists, it functions like a beacon of incentive. See Damasio, 1994, pp. 173–174; Devlin, 1997.
25. Bailey, 1968, pp. 84–85, 94–95.
26. Ibid., p. 96.
27. Thies, 1980, pp. 376–383.
28. Bailey, 1968, p. 247, observes, "Professional soldiers are seldom professional diplomats."
29. Operational art refers to managing tactical encounters during a sustained campaign to achieve strategic objectives. For a discussion of the linkages among strategy, operational art, and tactics, see Luttwak, 1987, p. 25.
30. On September 29, 1918, General Erich Ludendorff, who had assumed dictatorial powers over the war effort, informed the kaiser that Germany's military position on the western front was untenable and that he must seek immediate peace negotiations. Ludendorff called for the creation of a new democratic government, apparently so the military would not have to admit defeat and sue for peace. Our purpose in pointing out the way World War I ended gave reactionaries an opportunity to propagate a stab-in-the-back myth is not to suggest that the Allied powers should have refused the peace overtures and fought on until they could seize German territory. With some 10 million men killed and twice as many wounded, it was important to bring the fighting to a close as soon as possible. We use this case to illustrate the proposition that the geographic position of victorious troops has political consequences for the postwar period. Of course, we recognize that stab-in-the-back myths can surface even when the territory of the losing side is occupied. Following the Franco-Prussian War, for example, Captain Alfred Dreyfus, a Jewish officer in the French army, was falsely convicted of treason in a shameful effort to suggest that the war had been lost due to espionage rather than military failure.
31. Regan, 1987, p. 131.
32. Hastings and Jenkins, 1983, pp. 362.
33. Randle, 1973, pp. 36–52, 478–480.
34. See Anderson, 2000; Kissinger, 1994, p. 257; Mylorie, 2000. Colin Powell argued that Saddam Hussein should not have been ousted because a strong Iraq was needed to counterbalance Iran. In Rubin, 2001, p. A 9.
35. Nicolson, 1946, p. 19.
36. In Bailey, 1968, p. 261.
37. Rubin, 2001, p. A9.
38. Spencer Weart, in Kegley and Wittkopf, 2001, p. 641; see also Ray, 1995, and Russett, 1993.
39. See Hermann and Kegley, 2001, for a summary of evidence bearing on this proposition.
40. The term *ethotic* is derived from Aristotle's discussion of *ethos* (character) in deliberative rhetoric. For an analysis that applies Aristotle's example to foreign policy, see Raymond, 1991.

41. Brinton, 1986.
42. Nisbet and Ross, 1980.
43. Larson, 1985, pp. 50–57.
44. Blalock, 1989, p. 138. An illustration of this point can be found in Hume, 1948, p. 188: If "a civilized nation" was in a conflict with barbarians "who observed no rules even of war, the former must also suspend their observance of them . . . and must render every action or recounter as bloody as possible."
45. Shillony, 1982, p. 96.
46. Solomon, 1990, pp. 299–300.
47. Jacoby, 1983, p. 17. An example of the view that vengeance and justice are antithetical can be found in the criticisms Senator Robert A. Taft (R-OH) made of the Nuremberg and Tokyo war crimes trials at the end of World War II. In a speech delivered at Kenyon College, he asserted that a trial of the vanquished by the victors is animated by a "spirit of vengeance" and cannot be impartial. See Taft, 1946.
48. Some theorists differentiate between premeditated wars and two types of unwanted, unexpected wars: accidental and inadvertent wars. Whereas "a war that starts as a result of actions *not* properly authorized either by central decision makers or their legitimately pre-delegated command to those lower in the chain of command" is an accidental war, "a war that *is* authorized during the course of a crisis, even though at the outset of the crisis central decision makers did not want or expect a war" is an inadvertent war. Of course, both of these types of unwanted, unexpected wars may be conducted without restraint and involve actions that violate international humanitarian law. See George, 1991, p. 8.
49. Reflecting on the "accumulated passion" and "demand for retribution that rose like a plaintive chant from all the desolated lands" in the aftermath of the World War II, Herbert Wechsler defended the International Military Tribunal at Nuremberg on the grounds that a failure by the Allied Powers to proceed would have forsaken those who had suffered at the hands of the Nazi regime. "Who can doubt," he asked rhetorically, "that indiscriminate violence, a bloodbath beyond the power of control, would have followed an announcement by the responsible governments that they were unwilling to proceed?" Wechsler, 1972, p. 126.
50. *Exodus* 21:24–25; *Leviticus* 24:17–20; Cf. *Matthew* 5:38–42 and the comments on returning a wrong made by Socrates in Plato's *Crito*.
51. Djilas, 1958, pp. 105–107, 253.
52. Elster, 1990, p. 862.
53. Nozick, 1990, pp. 281–283. Some of these limits derive from an acceptance of the distinction between intentional and unintentional wrong.
54. Kiernan, 1989, p. 21.
55. Wolgast, 1987. For an analysis of social dynamics created by a code of revenge, see Marongiu and Newman, 1987.
56. Golding, 1975, p. 85.
57. Kriesberg, 1998a.
58. Shriver, 1995, pp. 6–9.
59. Tavuchis, 1991, p. 31.
60. Scheff, 1994, p. 135.
61. Goffman, 1971, p. 113.
62. Braithwaite, 1989.
63. Wiesenthal, 1976.
64. *Deuteronomy* 32:35.
65. Bailey, 1968, p. 267.
66. Fisher and Ury, 1981, p. 75.
67. Sherif and Sherif, 1953.
68. Fisher et al., 1994, p. 39.
69. Bueno de Mesquita and Singer, 1973, p. 241.
70. Gulick, 1955, p. 86.
71. Kissinger, 1994, p. 405.
72. Kissinger, 1973, pp. 21, 312.

73. Schelling, 1966, p. 128.
74. See Anderson, 2000.
75. Ibid., p. 12. For a discussion of the role of spoilers in peace processes aimed at ending civil wars, see Stedman, 1997.
76. Orme, 1996, p. 110.
77. Vasquez, 1993, pp. 202, 208–210. Accommodationists are defined as "individuals who have a personal predisposition (due to beliefs they hold) that finds the use of force, especially war, repugnant, and advocates a foreign policy that will avoid war through compromise, negotiation, and the creation of rules and norms for non-violent conflict resolution."
78. Gregg, 1966, p. 52.
79. Burgess and Burgess, 1994a, p. 14.
80. In Gregg, 1966, p. 150.
81. Obviously, pacific responses are not viable against everyone. The sack of Hamanu in the seventh century B.C.E. by the Assyrian leader Assurbanipal is one of many examples that testify to the inability of a vanquished people to prevent their utter destruction by a brutal conqueror. Even rulers who labored to integrate diverse populations into unified states occasionally responded to military adversaries with unmitigated fury. The sixteenth-century Mughal Emperor Akbar, for example, was so enraged by the resistance of the Rajput fortress of Chitor, that after overrunning the stronghold his forces massacred thousands of people.
82. Gregor and Robarchek, 1996, p. 160.
83. Kenneth Burke, in Sills and Merton, 1991, p. 32.
84. Liebermann, 1968, p. 361.
85. Ibid., p. 360.
86. Locke, 1952, pp. 104–105.
87. Graybill, 1998; Shriver, 1995, p. 224.
88. Dimuccio, 1998, p. 250.
89. *Matthew* 7:1–2.
90. In Sills and Merton, 1991, p. 90.
91. Kautilya, also known as Chanakya, lived during the period of approximately 350–275 B.C.E. He is credited with helping overthrow the last ruler of the Nanda Dynasty and making Chandragupta Maurya the Emperor of India. The citations that follow come from two of his most important works, the *Arthasastra* and the *Chanakyanitidarpana*, as reprinted and translated in Subramanian, 1990, pp. 42, 110–112, 161–162, 178.
92. Rosenthal, 1995, p. 322.
93. Wight, 1968, p. 128.
94. Doran, 1971, p. 194.
95. Ignatieff, 1998.
96. Kriesberg, 1998b, p. 5.

GLOSSARY

amnesty The decision by which a state's government grants a pardon to a former enemy state or its population for previous injuries.

adjudication A conflict-resolution procedure in which a third party makes a binding decision through an institutionalized tribunal.

alignments When a state threatened by foreign enemies forms a special relationship short of formal alliance with a stronger state able to protect it from attack.

alliance A formal agreement among states to coordinate their behavior in the event of certain specified military contingencies.

anarchy The absence of governmental authority to keep peace and enforce rules.

appeasement, appease A policy that attempts to satisfy a potential aggressor with significant concessions.

arbitration A conflict-resolution procedure in which a third party makes a binding decision through an ad hoc forum.

arms control Agreements designed to regulate arms levels.

arms race Intense competition between states in the acquisition of more or better weaponry.

balance of power The tendency of states to form counterpoised defensive alliances to prevent any single power or bloc from dominating the others.

balancer The role played by a great power that supports one side of a dispute to ensure that no one achieves preponderance, thus maintaining the international balance of power and deterring war.

bandwagoning The tendency for weak states to seek alliance with the strongest state, irrespective of that state's ideology or form of government, in order to increase national security.

bipolarity, bipolar An international system containing two dominant power centers.

bloc A rigid, highly cohesive alliance among a group of states that share a sense of solidarity about goals.

bounded rationality A concept which acknowledges that the decision-making capacity to choose the best option is often constrained by human and organizational factors.

bureaucratic politics model An interpretation of policy making which stresses the bargaining among contending governmental organizations that exert influence on the foreign policy choices of political leaders.

coercive diplomacy The use of threats or limited armed force to persuade another nation to take an action it would otherwise not take.

cognitive dissonance The tendency of people to ignore new information when it produces a distressing psychological reaction because it differs from their existing beliefs.

Cold War The forty-two-year rivalry between the United States and the Soviet Union, as well as their competing coalitions, which sought to contain each other's expansion through an arms race and military deterrence, and win worldwide predominance for capitalism (U.S.) or communism (U.S.S.R.).

collective guilt The belief that all members of a nation conducting a war are collectively responsible for the wrongs committed in pursuit of victory.

collective security A system of world order in which aggression by any state will be met by a collective response from other nations in the international community.

concert A cooperative agreement among great powers to jointly manage international relations.

conciliation The procedure in which a third party assists both sides in resolving their disputes.

containment A policy to prevent the expansion of an adversary's territory or influence beyond its present geostrategic reach.

corrective justice The ethical arguments in favor of inflicting either injury or providing rewards as a way to change another's behavior.

counterfactual analysis Investigations of and/or speculation about the relationship between cause and consequence in historical events, motivated by the quest to predict what outcome(s) would have occurred had different decisions been taken or conditions had prevailed different from what actually occurred in the past.

crisis decisions Made in high-threat situations, such as a probable war, these choices must be made under conditions of surprise and time pressure by the highest level of decisionmakers.

customs union A form of economic integration in which member states eliminate duties on commodities they trade among themselves while levying a common external tariff on commodities imported from nonmember states.

decision making theory, decision making An analytic approach to the determinants of states' foreign policy behavior that focuses on the settings and situations in which leaders find themselves when they make decisions.

democratic peace The propensity of democratically governed nations to settle conflicts among themselves through peaceful means rather than resorting to war, to form alliances among themselves for collective security, and to abide by the terms of the treaties they forge.

détente The relaxation of tension between adversaries.

deterrence A preventive strategy designed to dissuade an adversary from doing what it would otherwise do.

devolution States' granting of political power to minority ethnopolitical national groups and indigenous people in particular national regions with the expectation that greater autonomy will curtail their quest for independence as a new state.

disarmament Agreements designed to reduce or eliminate weapons.

distributive justice The ethical criteria used to evaluate how collective goods should be allocated to different parties.

diversionary theory of war The contention that leaders initiate conflict abroad as a way to increase their personal popularity and national cohesion at home.

domino effect A situation in which an expansionist state conquers another country and its aggression leads to the subsequent conquest of other neighboring countries.

domino theory A metaphor popular in the United States during the Cold War which predicted that the fall to communism in one country would in turn cause the fall of its neighbors.

economic sanctions Governmental actions designed to change an adversary's policies by inflicting deprivation on that state through the limitation or termination of economic exchanges.

embargo An order of a government prohibiting the export of commerce to a target state as a method of coercive diplomacy.

empire A political unit comprising extensive territory and many nations that is ruled by a single supreme authority.

enduring rivalries A condition pertaining to pairs of nations that, over a long period of time, relentlessly compete with one another and frequently take up arms to gain supremacy.

genocide The deliberate extermination of an ethnic, religious, or minority group.

grand strategy A nation's conception of its core security goals, military and nonmilitary methods for pursing them, and allocation of resources to support the means selected.

great powers The most powerful countries, militarily and economically, in the international system.

groupthink The propensity of members of cohesive, insulated groups to engage in excessive efforts to seek agreement at the expense of objectively analyzing policy problems and rigorously searching for solutions.

hegemon, hegemony A dominant military and economic state that uses its unrivaled power to create and enforce rules aimed at preserving the existing global or regional system and its own position in that order.

hegemonic stability theory A theory that focuses on the stabilizing impact of a preeminent state (a hegemon) in maintaining international cooperation.

high politics Geostrategic issues of national and international security that pertain to matters of war and peace.

humanitarian intervention A philosophy expressing concern and compassion for the welfare of humanity, as reflected in philanthropic policies and reforms to alleviate human suffering.

human rights The political rights and civil liberties recognized by the international community as inalienable and valid for individuals in all countries by virtue of their humanity.

imperialism, imperial The intentional imposition of one state's power over another, usually through territorial conquest and denial of the victim population's freedom to have a voice in the conquering regime's decisions.

inadvertent war A war that results from uncertainty, confusion, and circumstances beyond the control of those involved, rather than as the result of anyone's master plan.

international regime The set of rules, norms, and decision-making procedures that coordinates national behavior within a given area of activity, such as a security regime's rules to manage conflicts without recourse to war.

intervention An overt or covert use of force by one or more countries that crosses the borders of another country in order to affect the government and policies of the target country.

irredentism, irredentist The desire by one state to annex or reclaim territory held by another that was historically connected to the first state.

isolationism A national policy of withdrawing from active participation with other actors in world affairs by abstention from alliances and other political and economic relations.

just war theory The theory that identifies the conditions under which it is morally permissible for a state to go to war and the methods by which a war might be fought.

levels of analysis Alternative perspectives on world politics that may focus on the personal characteristics of decisionmakers, the attributes of states' societies and governing institutions, or the structure of the international system as factors influencing choices about war and peace.

liberalism The school of thought in international relations predicated on the assumption that applying reason to international relations can lead to institutional reforms conducive to the development of a more just and peaceful world.

limited war The restrained use of armed force for limited objectives.

long peace A prolonged period of peaceful great-power relations, such as that extending from the end of World War II until the present.

machtpolitik The German term for the practice of power politics.

mediation A conflict-resolution procedure in which a third party offers a nonbinding solution to the disputants.

militarized dispute Confrontations short of war, characterized by the reciprocated threat, deployment, mobilization, or use of limited armed force.

military intervention The overt or covert use of armed force by one or more countries, with troops crossing the border of another country to exercise influence over the decisions of the target country's government.

military necessity The legal doctrine that permits violations of the rules of warfare to be excused during periods of extreme emergency.

mirror images The tendency for each party in a conflict to see the other as the other sees it.

muddling through A model that stresses the tendency for foreign policy decisions to be made incrementally through trial and error rather than according to a comprehensive long-term strategy.

multiple advocacy The concept that high-quality decision making is most likely when leaders hear various policy recommendations from many different agencies within their government.

multipolarity, multipolar An international system containing three or more dominant power centers.

nation A collection of people who, on the basis of ethnic, linguistic, cultural affinity, or historic tradition, perceive themselves to be members of the same group.

national interest The goals that a state defines as foreign policy priorities in an effort to identify what objectives will parochially best serve the state's welfare.

nationalism The belief that one's nation is the ultimate object of political loyalty.

nation-state A polity (system of government) holding territory controlled by members of some nationality recognizing no higher authority.

negotiation The process of conferring with others when a conflict arises so disputing parties can reach a mutually satisfactory agreement that resolves the issue.

neutralization, neutralized The condition of permanent neutrality conferred on a state through treaties with guarantor states.

nonalignment, nonaligned A policy rejecting the decision to join either side when competitive alliances oppose each other.

noninterference principle The legal duty of states to refrain from uninvited involvement or intervention in another's internal affairs.

norms The generalized standards of behavior that prescribe certain actions but proscribe others.

opportunity costs The lost chance to undertake one rewarding activity because of involvement in another activity.

pacta sunt servanda The legal norm that treaties are binding and should not be violated even when defection would be expedient.

peace building Post-conflict actions, predominately diplomatic and economic, that strengthen and rebuild governmental infrastructure and institutions in order to avoid a relapse into conflict.

peace enforcement Military actions undertaken to impose a peace settlement, truce, or agreement to surrender by a warring party or to prevent the resumption of fighting by the participants in a past war.

peacekeeping The use of a military force as a buffer between disputants in order to prevent fighting.

peacemaking The process of diplomacy, mediation, negotiation, or other forms of peaceful settlements that seeks to end a war and resolve the issues that led to the original conflict.

peace research An epistemic community of scholars who seek to uncover the most useful paths to the preservation of peace through the systematic generation of evidence about the preconditions for world order.

polarization The clustering of smaller nations in alliances around the dominant power centers in the international system.

political integration The process or the product of efforts to build new political communities and supranational institutions that transcend nation-states.

popular sovereignty The belief embedded in liberal democratic theory that citizens should have a voice in governmental decisions and that government leaders should be accountable to the public.

power transition theory The contention that war is most likely when the differentials between the capabilities of rival states begin to narrow and that change provokes a pre-emptive attack to prevent the ascending rival from gaining supremacy.

preemption A quick first-strike attack that seeks to defeat an adversary before it can organize a retaliatory response.

preventive diplomacy Diplomatic actions taken in advance of a predictable crisis to prevent or limit violence.

raison d'etat Literally, "reason of state," a justification for the pursuit of national self-interest above all other foreign policy goals.

rapprochement In diplomacy, a policy to reestablish normal relations between enemies.

rational actor model, rational actor Decision-making procedures guided by a clear definition of the policy problem, the prioritization of goals, a careful weighing of all options, and the selection of the option most likely to achieve the highest priority goals.

rational choice The theory that decisionmakers choose on the basis of what they perceive to be the best interest of themselves and their states, based on their expectations about the relative usefulness of alternative options for realizing goals. Sometimes called "expected utility theory," it was derived from realist theories.

rationality, rational A conceptualization of decision making that assumes people have preferences and, when faced with two or more alternatives, will choose the one that yields the preferred outcome.

realism, realists A school of thought in international relations based on the premise that world politics is a struggle among self-interested nations for power and position within an anarchical global environment.

realpolitik The theoretical outlook prescribing that countries do whatever is expedient to advance their self-interests defined in terms of maximizing national power.

reciprocity A principle about international conduct holding that states should treat other states as they are treated.

regime A set of rules agreed to by states to regulate their interactions, for the purpose of managing common problems.

reparations Compensation paid by a defeated state for damages or expenditures sustained by the victor during hostilities.

restorative justice The ethical criteria addressing the means by which broken relationships can be restored and rebuilt.

retribution The punitive infliction of harm to an enemy in order to make it pay for acts perceived as unjust or illegal.

retributive justice The ethics of administering punishment for evil or illegal deeds.

revolution in military affairs Increase in military capabilities and effectiveness with new technology or tactics in warfare.

sanctions Punitive actions by one state against another to retaliate for previous objectionable behavior, often, but not always, through economic restrictions on trade with the target, such as by means of an embargo.

satisficing The tendency for decisionmakers to choose policy alternatives that are readily available and to select the first choice that meets minimally acceptable standards, even though it is barely satisfactory.

schematic reasoning Processing new information according to a memory structure that contains a network of generic scripts, metaphors, and stereotypical characters.

security community The achievement, among a group of states or within a region, of cooperation and attitudes of mutual trust, to such an extent that tension is minimal and fears that one member state of the community might attack another have virtually vanished.

security dilemma The propensity for one state's arming for ostensibly defensive purposes to be perceived by others as threatening, provoking them to arm in response, with the result that the security of all is reduced.

security regime Rules, norms, and decision-making procedures designed for the peaceful management of security problems or among countries.

self-determination The doctrine that asserts nationalities have the right to determine what political authority will represent and rule them.

self-help The dependence of the state on its own resources to promote its interests and protect itself against external attack.

sovereignty The legal principle that no authority is above the state to establish or enforce rules about foreign or domestic conduct.

sphere of influence A region or group of states within a particular territorial area dominated by a foreign great power.

standard operating procedures (SOPs) Established methods to be followed in performing designated tasks when bureaucratic units within governments make decisions about foreign policy choices and their implementation.

state A legal entity that possesses a permanent population, a well-defined territory, and a government capable of exercising sovereignty.

strategic surrender A tactic, when facing certain defeat in continued fighting, of accepting surrender in the hopes of evoking a lenient peace settlement from the victor.

structural realism A theory favored by some contemporary realists that sees the changing distribution of power within the global system as the primary determinant of nations' choices about international behavior and of whether peace will prevail.

summit conference Personal diplomatic negotiations between national leaders.

supranational International institutions authorized to make decisions binding on its national members without being subject to their individual approval, transcending national boundaries and authority in order to regulate shared problems.

total war Unrestrained battle against an enemy state's civilian population and economic resources to drive it into surrender.

unipolarity, unipolar An international system with a single dominant power center.

war crimes Acts performed during war that the international community defines as illegal crimes against humanity, such as atrocities committed on an enemy's prisoners of war and civilians or the state's own minority population.

war-weariness hypothesis The proposition that a state experiencing war will become exhausted after prolonged fighting and, whether victor or vanquished, will lose its enthusiasm for participating soon thereafter in another war.

war profiteer Opportunistic individuals who organize mercenary armies or manufacture armies for financial gain to states engaged in war.

xenophobia A fear of foreigners.

zero-sum The perception that gains for one side in a rivalry are losses for the other side.

REFERENCES

Adcock, F. E. "Fear of Carthage and Irrationality." In *Imperialism in the Roman Republic,* edited by Erich S. Gruen, 77–84. New York: Holt, Rhinehart & Winston, 1970.

Albrecht-Carrié, René. *A Diplomatic History of Europe Since the Congress of Vienna.* New York: Harper & Row, 1958.

———. *Europe 1500–1848.* Patterson, N.J.: Littlefield, Adams, 1964 and 1953.

Allen, Paul. *Philip III and the Pax Hispanica, 1598–1621.* New Haven, Conn.: Yale University Press, 2000.

Allison, Graham T. *Essence of Decision: Explaining the Cuban Missile Crisis.* Boston: Little, Brown, 1971.

———. "Conceptual Models and the Cuban Missile Crisis," *American Political Science Review* 63 (September 1969): 689–718.

Allison, Graham T., and Morton H. Halperin. "Bureaucratic Politics: A Paradigm and Some Policy Implications." In *American Foreign Policy: Theoretical Essays,* edited by G. John Ikenberry, 378–409. Glenview, Ill.: Scott, Foresman, 1989.

Anderson, Jon Lee. "The Unvanquished," *New Yorker,* December 8, 2000, 76–89.

Andocides. *Minor Attic Orators,* vol. I. Translated by K. J. Maidment. London: William Heinemann, 1941.

Angell, Norman. *The Great Illusion: A Study of the Relationship of Military Power in Nations to Their Economic and Social Advantage.* London: Heineman, 1910.

Arbatov, Alexei G. *The Kosovo Crisis: The End of the Post–Cold War Era.* Washington, D.C.: Atlantic Council, 2000.

Ardagh, John. *Germany and the Germans.* New York: Harper & Row, 1987.

Aristotle. *The Athenian Constitution.* Translated by H. Rackham. London: Heinemann, 1935.

———. *Nicomachean Ethics.* Translated by David Ross. London: Oxford University Press, 1925.

Armstrong, Donald. "Unilateral Disarmament: A Case History." In *Peace and War in the Modern Age: Premises, Myths, and Realities,* edited by Frank R. Barnett, William C. Mott, and John C. Neff, 5–13. Garden City, N.Y.: Doubleday, 1965.

Aron, Raymond. *Peace and War: A Theory of International Relations.* Translated by Richard Howard and Annette Baker Fox. New York: Praeger, 1968.

Arquilla, John. *Dubious Battles: Aggression, Defeat, and the International System.* Washington, D.C.: Crane, Russak, 1992.

Aspin, Les. "The Military Option: The Conduct and Consequences of War in the Persian Gulf," White Paper based on Hearings of the House Armed Services Committee, January 8, 1991. Washington, D.C.: U.S. Department of Defense.

———. "The Role of Sanctions in Securing U.S. Interests in the Persian Gulf," White Paper based on Hearings of the House Armed Services Committee, December 21, 1990. Washington, D.C.: U.S. Department of Defense.

Astin, Alan E. *Cato the Censor.* Oxford: Oxford University Press, 1978.

Bailey, Sydney D. *How Wars End: The United Nations and the Termination of Armed Conflict, 1946–1964,* 2 vols. Oxford: Clarendon Press, 1982.

Bailey, Thomas A. *The Art of Diplomacy.* New York: Appleton-Century-Crofts, 1968.

Balch-Lindsay, Dylan and Andrew J. Enterline. "Killing Time: The World Politics of Civil War Duration, 1820–1992," *International Studies Quarterly* 44 (December 2000): 615–642.

Baldwin, David A., ed. *Neorealism and Neoliberalism: The Contemporary Debate.* New York: Columbia University Press, 1993.

Banac, Ivo. *The National Question in Yugoslavia: Origins, History, Politics.* Ithaca, N.Y.: Cornell University Press, 1992.

Bandow, Doug. "NATO's Hypocritical Humanitarianism." In *NATO's Empty Victory,* edited by Ted Galen Carpenter, 31–47. Washington, D.C.: Cato Institute, 2000.

Barraclough, Geoffrey. *The Origins of Modern Germany.* Oxford: Basil Blackwell, 1946.

Bartlett, C. J. *The Global Conflict, 1880–1970.* London: Longman, 1984.

Beer, Francis A., and Thomas F. Mayer. "Why Wars End: Some Hypotheses," *Review of International Studies* 12 (April 1986): 95–106.

Bennett, D. Scott. "Democracy, Regime Change, and Rivalry Termination," *International Interactions* 22, no. 4 (1997): 369–397.

———. "Security, Bargaining, and the End of Interstate Rivalry," *International Studies Quarterly* 40 (June 1996): 157–184.

Bennett, D. Scott, and Allan C. Stam, III. "The Duration of Interstate Wars, 1816–1985," *American Political Science Review* 90 (June 1996): 239–257.

Bismarck, Otto von. *The Memoirs.* Translated by A. J. Butler. New York: Fertig, 1966.

———. "A Letter to Minister von Manteuffel." In *The Quest for a Principle of Authority in Europe 1715–Present,* edited by Thomas C. Mendenhall, Basil D. Henning, and Archibald S. Foord, 219–220. New York: Holt, Rhinehart & Winston, 1948.

Blainey, Geoffrey. *The Causes of War.* New York: Free Press, 1968.

Blalock, Hubert M., Jr. *Power and Conflict: Toward a General Theory.* Newbury Park, Calif.: Sage, 1989.

Blaney, David L., and Naeem Inayatullah. "The Westphalian Deferral," *International Studies Review* 2 (Summer 2000): 29–64.

Blum, Jerome, Rondo Cameron, and Thomas G. Barnes. *The Emergence of the European World,* 2nd ed. Boston: Little, Brown, 1970.

Bonafede, Dom. "George Bush and the Gulf War: A Tainted Triumph," *Miller Center Journal* 2 (Spring 1995): 95–123.

Bonfils, Henry. *Manuel de Droit International Public,* 4th ed. Paris: Fauchille, 1905.

Boulding, Kenneth E. *Stable Peace.* Austin: University of Texas Press, 1978.

Bradford, Ernle. *Hannibal.* New York: McGraw-Hill, 1951.

Braithwaite, John. *Crime, Shame, and Reintegration.* Cambridge: Cambridge University Press, 1989.

Brecher, Michael. "International Crises, Protracted Conflicts," *International Interactions* 11, nos. 3–4 (1984): 237–298.

Brinton, Alan. "Ethotic Argument," *History of Philosophy Quarterly* 3 (July 1986): 245–258.

Brodie, Bernard. *War and Politics.* New York: Macmillan, 1973.

Bronfenbrenner, Urie. "The Mirror Image in Soviet-American Relations," *Journal of Social Issues* 27, no. 1 (1971): 46–51.

Brown, Seyom. *The Causes and Prevention of War.* New York: St. Martin's Press, 1994.

Buchanan, Patrick. "Have the Neocons Thought This Through?" In *The Gulf Reader: History, Documents, Opinions,* edited by Micah L. Sifry and Christopher Cerf, 213–215. New York: Times Books/Random House, 1991.

Buckley, William Joseph. *Kosovo: Contending Voices on Balkan Interventions.* Grand Rapids, Mich.: Eerdmans, 2001.

Bueno de Mesquita, Bruce. "Popes, Kings, and Endogenous Institutions: The Concordat of Worms and the Origins of Sovereignty," *International Studies Review* 2 (Summer 2000): 93–118.

———. *The War Trap.* New Haven, Conn.: Yale University Press, 1981.

Bueno de Mesquita, Bruce, and David Lalman. *War and Reason.* New Haven, Conn.: Yale University Press, 1992.

Bull, Hedley. *The Anarchical Society: A Study of Order in World Politics.* New York: Columbia University Press, 1977.

Burgess, Guy, and Heidi Burgess. "Justice without Violence: Theoretical Foundations." In *Justice without Violence,* edited by Paul Wehr, Heidi Burgess, and Guy Burgess, 7–36. Boulder, Colo.: Lynne Rienner, 1994a.

Burgess, Heidi, and Burgess, Guy. "Justice without Violence: Theorectical Synthesis." In *Justice without Violence,* edited by Paul Wehr, Heidi Burgess, and Guy Burgess, 257–290. Boulder, Colo.: Lynne Rienner, 1994b.

Burke, Edmund. *Reflections on the Revolution in France.* New York: Anchor, 1989.

Buruma, Ian. *The Wages of Guilt: Memories of War in Germany and Japan.* New York: Farrar, Straus, Giroux, 1994.

Bush, George. "State of the Union." *Vital Speeches of the Day* 57, no. 9 (1991): 258–261.

———. "Aggression in the Gulf." *Vital Speeches of the Day,* no. 1 (1990a): 2–4.

———. "America's Stand against Aggression," no. 1294. Washington, D.C.: U.S. Department of State, Bureau of Public Affairs, 1990b.

———. "Iraq's Invasion of Kuwait." *Vital Speeches of the Day* 56, no. 22 (1990c): 674–675.

———. "The Persian Gulf." *Vital Speeches of the Day* 56, no. 24 (1990d): 738–741.

Butterfield, Herbert. "The Balance of Power." In *Diplomatic Investigations: Essays in the Theory of International Politics,* edited by Herbert Butterfield and Martin Wight, 132–175. Cambridge, Mass.: Harvard University Press, 1968.

Byman, Daniel L. and Waxman, Matthew C. "Kosovo and the Great Air Power Debate," *International Security* 24 (Spring 2000): 5–38.

Carpenter, Ted Galen. "Kosovo as an Omen: The Perils of the 'New NATO.'" In *NATO's Empty Victory,* edited by Ted Galen Carpenter, 171–183. Washington, D.C.: Cato Institute, 2000.

Carr, Edward Hallett. *The Twenty Years' Crisis, 1919–1939.* New York: Harper & Row, 1964.

———. *International Relations between the Two World Wars, 1919–1939.* New York: Harper & Row, 1947.

Carr, William. *The Origins of the Wars of German Unification.* London: Longman, 1991.

Caven, Brian. *The Punic Wars.* New York: St. Martin's Press, 1980.

Chandler, David G. *Atlas of Military Strategy: The Art, Theory and Practice of War, 1618–1878.* New York: Sterling, 1998.

Chazan, Naomi. *Irredentism and International Politics.* Boulder, Colo.: Lynne Rienner, 1991.

Church, William F. *Richelieu and Reason of State.* Princeton, N.J.: Princeton University Press, 1972.

Churchill, Winston. *Closing the Ring.* Boston: Houghton Mifflin, 1951.

Cicero, Marcus Tullius. *On Duties.* Edited by M. T. Griffin and E. M. Atkins. Cambridge: Cambridge University Press, 1991.

Cimbala, Stephen J., and Keith A. Dunn, eds. *Conflict Termination and Military Strategy: Coercion, Persuasion, and War.* Boulder, Colo.: Westview, 1987.

Clark, Bruce. "The Roots of Kosovo Calamity," *The Economist,* April 15, 2000, 3–4.

Clark, Ian. *Waging War: A Philosophical Introduction.* Oxford: Oxford University Press, 1990.

Claude, Inis L., Jr. *States and the Global System: Politics, Law, and Organization.* New York: St. Martin's Press, 1988.

Clausewitz, Karl von. *On War.* Edited and translated by Michael Howard and Peter Paret. Princeton, N.J.: Princeton University Press, 1984.

Clemens, Walter C., Jr. *Dynamics of International Relations: Conflict and Mutual Gain in an Era of Global Interdependence.* Lanham, Md.: Rowman & Littlefield, 1998.

Clodfelter, Michael. *Warfare and Armed Conflicts,* vol. 1. London: McFarland, 1992.

Cohen, Eliot A. "The Mystique of U.S. Air Power," *Foreign Affairs* 73 (January–February 1994): 109–124.

Cohen, Eliot A., and John Gooch. *Military Misfortunes: The Anatomy of Failure in War.* New York: Free Press, 1990.

Commager, Henry Steele. "Misconceptions Governing American Foreign Policy." In *Perspectives on American Foreign Policy,* edited by Charles W. Kegley, Jr., and Eugene R. Wittkopf, 510–517. New York: St. Martin's Press, 1983.

Cook, Don. *Forging the Alliance: NATO, 1945–1950.* New York: Arbor House/William Morrow, 1989.

Coplin, William D. *Introduction to International Politics: A Theoretical Overview.* Chicago: Markham, 1971.

Cordesman, Anthony. *Iraq and the War of Sanctions.* Landam, MD: Praeger, 1999.

Coser, Lewis. "The Termination of Conflict," *Journal of Conflict Resolution* 5 (December 1961): 351–357.

Craig, Gordon A. *The Germans.* New York: New American Library, 1982.

———. *The Battle of Koniggratz.* Philadelphia: J. B. Lippencott, 1964.

Craig, Gordon A., and Alexander L. George. *Force and Statecraft: Diplomatic Problems of Our Time.* 3rd ed. New York: Oxford University Press, 1995.

Crankshaw, Edward. *Bismarck.* New York: Viking, 1981.

Crocker, Chester A., and Fen Osler Hampson. "Making Peace Settlements Work," *Foreign Policy* 104 (Fall 1996): 54–71.

Cronin, Bruce. *Community under Anarchy: Transnational Identity and the Evolution of Cooperation.* New York: Columbia University Press, 1999.

Daalder, Ivo, and Michael O' Hanlon. "Unlearning the Lessons of Kosovo," *Foreign Policy* 116 (Fall 1999): 128–140.

Damasio, Antontio. *Descartes' Error: Emotion, Reason, and the Human Brain.* New York: Putnam's, 1994.

Davies, Norman. *Europe: A History.* Oxford: Oxford University Press, 1996.

———. "The Misunderstood War," *New York Review of Books,* June 9, 1994, 20–24.

Dawisha, Adeed. *The Arab Radicals.* New York: Council on Foreign Relations, 1986.

Dean, Jonathan. "No NATO Expansion Now," *Bulletin of the Atomic Scientists* 52 (May/June 1996): 18–19.

Dehio, Ludwig. *The Precarious Balance: Four Centuries of European Power Struggle.* Translated by Charles Fullman. New York: Alfred A. Knopf, 1962.

De Sousa, Ronald. *The Rationality of Emotion.* Cambridge, Mass.: MIT Press, 1987.

Destler, I. M., Leslie H. Gelb, and Anthony Lake. *Our Own Worst Enemy: The Unmaking of American Foreign Policy.* New York: Simon & Schuster, 1984.

Detwiler, Donald S. *Germany: A Short History.* Carbondale: Southern Illinois University Press, 1976.

Devlin, Keith. *Goodbye Descartes: The End of Logic and the Search for a New Cosmology of Mind.* New York: Wiley, 1997.

Diehl, Paul F. "What Are They Fighting For? The Importance of Issues in International Conflict Research," *Journal of Peace Research* 29 (August 1992): 333–344.

Diehl, Paul F., Jennifer Reifschneider, and Paul F. Hensel. "United Nations Intervention and Recurring Conflict," *International Organization* 50 (Autumn 1996): 683–700.

Dimuccio, Ralph B. "The Study of Appeasement in International Relations," *Journal of Peace Research* (March 1998): 245–259.

Diodorus of Sicily. *Fragments.* Translated by Francis R. Walton. London: Heinemann, 1967.

Dixon, William J. "Reciprocity in United States-Soviet Relations: Multiple Symmetry or Issue Linkage?" *American Journal of Political Science* 30, no. 2 (1986): 421–445.

Djilas, Miloven. *Land without Justice.* New York: Harcourt Brace, 1958.

Doran, Charles F. *The Politics of Assimilation: Hegemony and Its Aftermath.* Baltimore, Md.: Johns Hopkins Press, 1971.

Dorsey, T. H., and D. R. Dudley. *Rome against Carthage.* Garden City, N.Y.: Doubleday, 1972.

Dower, John W. *War without Mercy: Race and Power in the Pacific War.* New York: Pantheon, 1986.

Doyle, Michael W. *Ways of War and Peace.* New York: Norton, 1997.

Doyle, Michael W., and Nicholas Sambanis. "International Peacebuilding: A Theoretical and Quantitative Analysis," *American Political Science Review* 94 (December 2000): 779–801.

Duchhardt, Heinz. "Münster/Osnabrück as a Short-lived Peace System." In *Great Peace Congresses in History, 1649–1990,* edited by Albert P. van Goudoever, 13–19. Utrecht: Utrechtse Historische Cahiers, vol. 14, no. 2, 1993.

Dunnigan, James F., and William Martel. *How to Stop a War: The Lessons of Two Hundred Years of War and Peace.* New York: Doubleday, 1987.

Eckstein, Harry. "Case Study and Theory in Political Science." In *Strategies of Inquiry: Handbook of Political Science,* VII, edited by Fred I. Greenstein and Nelson W. Polsby, 104–113. Reading, Mass.: Addison-Wesley, 1975.

Eliade, Mircea. *Myths, Dreams, and Mysteries.* New York: Harper Torchbooks, 1967.

Ellerman, Christine. "Command of Sovereignty Gives Way to Concern for Humanity," *Vanderbilt Journal of Transnational Law* 26 (1993): 341–371.

Elrod, Richard. "The Concert of Europe: A Fresh Look at an International System," *World Politics* 28 (January 1976): 159–174.

Elster, Jon. "Norms of Revenge," *Ethics* 100 (July 1990): 862–885.

Esposito, David M. *The Legacy of Woodrow Wilson: American War Aims in World War I.* Westport, Conn.: Praeger, 1996.

Eyffinger, Arthur. *The Peace Palace.* The Hague: Carnegie Foundation, 1988.

Fair, Charles. *From the Jaws of Victory.* New York: Simon & Schuster, 1971.

Fallows, James. *Looking at the Sun: The Rise of the New East Asian Economic and Political System.* New York: Pantheon, 1994.

Fay, Sidney B. *The Origins of the World War.* 2nd ed., vol. I. New York: Free Press, 1966.

Ferguson, Niall, ed. *Virtual History.* New York: Basic Books, 1997.

Ferrill, Arthur. "The Grand Strategy of the Roman Empire." In *Grand Strategies in War and Peace,* edited by Paul Kennedy, 71–85. New Haven, Conn.: Yale University Press, 1991.

Festinger, Leon. *A Theory of Cognitive Dissonance.* Evanston, Ill.: Row, Peterson, 1957.

Finer, Samuel E. "State and Nation-Building in Europe: The Role of the Military." In *The Formation of Nation States in Western Europe,* edited by Charles Tilly, 84–163. Princeton, N.J.: Princeton University Press, 1975.

Finn, Peter. "New Team's Old Hands Reassure Other Nations," *The State* (Columbia, S.C.), December 17, 2000, D5.

Fisher, Roger, Elizabeth Kopelman, and Andrea Kupfer Schneider. *Beyond Machiavelli: Tools for Coping with Conflict.* Cambridge, Mass.: Harvard University Press, 1994.

Fisher, Roger, and William Ury. *Getting to Yes.* Boston: Houghton Mifflin, 1981.

Fitts, Mike. "New Team Has No Incentive to Fix Stagnant Iraq Mess," *The State* (Columbia, S.C.), January 13, 2001, A6.

Fowler, Wilton. *British-American Relations, 1917–1918.* Princeton, N.J.: Princeton University Press, 1969.

Fox, William T. R. "The Causes of Peace and Conditions of War," *The Annals* 392 (November 1970): 1–13.

Frankel, Glenn. "Lines in the Sand." In *The Gulf Reader: History, Documents, Opinions,* edited by Micah L. Sifry and Christopher Cerf, 16–20. New York: Times Books/Random House, 1991.

Freedman, Lawrence, ed. *War.* Oxford: Oxford University Press, 1994.

Frensley, Nathalie J. "Ratification Processes and Conflict Termination," *Journal of Peace Research* 35 (March 1998): 167–191.

Friedjung, Heinrich. *The Struggle for Supremacy in Germany, 1859–1866.* Translated by A. J. P. Taylor and W. McElwee. New York: Russell & Russell, 1966.

Fromkin, David. *The Independence of Nations.* New York: Praeger, 1981.

Fry, Earl H., and Gregory A. Raymond. *The Other Western Europe: A Political Analysis of the Smaller Democracies.* 2nd ed. Santa Barbara, Calif.: Clio Press, 1983.

Gallie, W. B. *Philosophers of Peace and War: Kant, Clausewitz, Engels, and Tolstoy.* Cambridge: Cambridge University Press, 1978.

Gardiner, S. Rawson. *Epochs of History: The Era of the Thirty Years' War, 1618–1648.* New York: Charles Scribner's Sons, 1895 and 1900.

Gardner, Lloyd C. *Architects of Illusion.* Chicago: Quadrangle, 1970.

Garfinkle, Adam. "Jumping to Confusions," *The National Interest* 62 (Winter 2001): 131–135.

Garrett, Stephen A. *Doing Good and Doing Well: An Examination of Humanitarian Intervention.* Westport, Conn.: Praeger, 1999.

Gay, Peter, and R. K. Webb. *Modern Europe to 1815.* New York: Harper & Row, 1973.

Geller, Daniel S., and J. David Singer. *Nations at War: A Scientific Study of International Conflict.* New York: Cambridge University Press, 1998.

George, Alexander L. "The Operational Code," *International Studies Quarterly* 13 (June 1969): 190–222.

———. "The Case for Multiple Advocacy in Making Foreign Policy," *American Political Science Review* 66 (September 1972): 751–785.

———. "Case Studies and Theory Development: The Method of Structured, Focused Comparison." In *Diplomacy: New Approaches in History, Theory, and Policy,* edited by Paul Gordon Lauren, 43–68. New York: Free Press, 1979.

———. "Plan of the Study." In *Avoiding War: Problems of Crisis Management,* edited by Alexander L. George, 7–12. Boulder, Colo.: Westview, 1991.

———. *Bridging the Gap: Theory and Practice in Foreign Policy.* Washington, D.C.: U.S. Institute of Peace Press, 1993.

Gibbard, Alan. *Wise Choices, Apt Feelings.* Cambridge, Mass.: Harvard University Press, 1990.

Gibbon, Edward. *The Decline and Fall of the Roman Empire.* New York: Viking, 1952.

Gibler, Douglas M. "Control the Issues, Control the Conflict: The Effects of Alliances That Settle Territorial Issues on Interstate Rivalries," *International Interactions* 22, no. 4 (1997): 341–368.

Giesberg, Robert I. *The Treaty of Frankfurt: A Study in Diplomatic History, September 1870–September 1873.* Philadelphia: University of Pennsylvania Press, 1966.

Gilbert, Martin. *The Roots of Appeasement.* New York: Plume Books, New American Library, 1966.

Gillis, John R. "Germany." In *Crises of Political Development in Europe and the United States,* edited by Raymond Grew, 313–345. Princeton, N.J.: Princeton University Press, 1978.

Gilpin, Robert. *War and Change in World Politics.* Cambridge: Cambridge University Press, 1981.

Glahn, Gerhard von. *Law among Nations,* 7th ed. Boston: Allyn & Bacon, 1996.

Goertz, Gary, and Paul F. Diehl. "The Initiation and Termination of Enduring Rivalries: The Impact of Political Shocks," *American Journal of Political Science* 39 (February 1995): 30–52.

———. "Enduring Rivalries: Theoretical Constructs and Empirical Patterns," *International Studies Quarterly* 37 (June 1993): 147–171.

———. "The Empirical Importance of Enduring Rivalries," *International Interactions* 18, no. 2 (1992a): 151–163.

———. *Territorial Changes and International Conflict.* London: Routledge, 1992b.

Goffman, E. *Relations in Public.* New York: Harper, 1971.

Golding, Martin P. *Philosophy of Law.* Englewood Cliffs, N.J.: Prentice-Hall, 1975.

Goldstein, Erik. *Wars and Peace Treaties 1816–1991.* London: Routledge, 1991.

Goldstein, Joshua S., and Jon C. Pevehouse. "Reciprocity, Bullying, and International Cooperation," *American Political Science Review* 91 (September 1997): 515–529.

Goodman, Allan E., and Sandra Clemens Bogart. *Making Peace: The United States and Conflict Resolution.* Boulder, Colo.: Westview, 1992.

Gordon, Michael R., and Bernard E. Trainor. *The Generals' War: The Inside Story of the Conflict in the Gulf.* Boston: Little, Brown, 1995.

Graybill, Lyn S. "South Africa's Truth and Reconciliation Commission: Ethical and Theological Perspectives," *Ethics and International Affairs* 12 (1998): 43–79.

Green, Jonathan. *The Book of Political Quotes.* New York: McGraw-Hill, 1982.

Gregg, Richard B. *The Power of Nonviolence,* rev. ed. New York: Schocken Books, 1966.

Gregor, Thomas, and Clayton A. Robarchek. "Two Paths to Peace: Semai and Mehinaku Nonviolence." In *A Natural History of Peace,* edited by Thomas Gregor, 159–188. Nashville, Tenn.: Vanderbilt University Press, 1996.

Grey, Edward. *Twenty-Five Years, 1892–1916.* New York: Stokes, 1925.

Gross, Leo. "The Peace of Westphalia, 1648–1948." In *International Law in the Twentieth Century,* edited by Leo Gross, 25–46. New York: Appleton Century-Crofts, 1969.

Gulick, Edward Vose. *Europe's Classical Balance of Power.* Ithaca, N.Y.: Cornell University Press, 1955.

Hackman, George G., Charles W. Kegley, and Viktjok Nikander. *Religion in Modern Life.* New York: Macmillan, 1957.

Hall, William Edward. *International Law.* 7th ed. Oxford: Clarendon Press, 1917.

Hamilton, Edith. *The Greek Way to Western Civilization.* New York: Norton, 1942.

Hammond, Grant T. *Plowshares into Swords: Arms Races in International Politics, 1840–1991.* Columbia: University of South Carolina Press, 1993.

Hampson, Fen Osler. *Nurturing Peace: Why Peace Settlements Succeed or Fail.* Washington, D.C.: U.S. Institute of Peace, 1996.

Handel, Michael I. "War Termination — A Critical Survey," *Jerusalem Papers on Peace Problems,* no. 24. Jerusalem: Leonard Davis Institute for International Relations, Hebrew University of Jerusalem, 1978.

Harris, Marvin. *Cultural Materialism.* New York: Random House, 1979.

Harris, W. V. *War and Imperialism in Republican Rome, 327–270 B.C.* Oxford: Oxford University Press, 1979.

Hartmann, Frederick H. *The Relations of Nations,* 6th ed. New York: Macmillan, 1983.

Hastings, Max, and Simon Jenkins. *The Battle for the Falklands.* New York: Norton, 1983.

Hedges, Chris. "Kosovo's Next Masters?" *Foreign Affairs* 78 (May/June 1999): 24–42.

Helprin, Mark. "Mr. Clinton's Army," *Wall Street Journal,* October 10, 2000, A26.

Hempel, Carl G. *Philosophy of Natural Science.* Englewood Cliffs, N.J.: Prentice Hall, 1966.

———. *Aspects of Scientific Explanation.* New York: Free Press, 1965.

Henderson, Simon. *Instant Empire: Saddam Hussein's Ambition for Iraq.* San Francisco: Mercury House, 1991.

Hensel, Paul R. "One Thing Leads to Another: Recurrent Militarized Disputes in Latin America, 1816–1986," *Journal of Peace Research* 31, no. 3 (1994): 281–297.

Hermann, Margaret G., and Joe D. Hagan. "International Decision Makers: Leadership Matters," *Foreign Policy* 110 (Spring 1998): 124–137.

Hermann, Margaret G., and Charles F. Hermann. "Who Makes Foreign Policy Decisions and How: An Empirical Inquiry," *International Studies Quarterly* 33 (December 1989): 361–387.

Hermann, Margaret G., and Charles W. Kegley, Jr. "Democracies and Intervention: Is There a Danger Zone in the Democratic Peace?" *Journal of Peace Research* 30 (March 2001): 237–245.

Herodotus. *The Histories,* 4 vols. Translated by A. D. Godley. London: Heinemann, 1920.

Hersh, Seymour M. "Overwhelming Force," *New Yorker,* May 22, 2000, 49–83.

Hershey, Amos S. *The Essentials of International Public Law and Organization,* rev. ed. New York: Macmillan, 1930.

Herz, John H. *Political Realism and Political Idealism.* Chicago: University of Chicago Press, 1951.

Hinsley, F. H. *Power and the Pursuit of Peace: Theory and Practice in the History of Relations between States.* Cambridge: Cambridge University Press, 1963.

Hoagland, Jim. "Candidates Gloss over Foreign Policy," *The State* (Columbia, S.C.), November, 2, 2000a, A11.

———. "Clinton's Most Daring Strategy on Iraq," *The State* (Columbia, S.C.), July 4, 2000b, A11.

Hoffmann, Stanley. *The Political Ethics of International Relations.* New York: Carnegie Council on Ethics and International Affairs, 1988.

———. "International Law and the Control of Force." In *The Relevance of International Law,* edited by Karl Deutsch and Stanley Hoffmann, 34–66. Garden City, N.Y.: Doubleday-Anchor, 1971.

Holborn, Hajo. *A History of Modern Germany, 1840–1945.* New York: Knopf, 1969.

———. "Moltke and Schieffen: The Prussian-German School." In *Makers of Modern Strategy: Military Thought from Machiavelli to Hitler,* edited by Edward Meade Earle, 172–205. Princeton, N.J.: Princeton University Press, 1943.

Holbraad, Carsten. *The Concert of Europe.* New York: Barnes & Noble, 1970.

Holbrooke, Richard. *To End a War.* New York: The Modern Library, 1999.

Holsti, Kalevi J. *The State, War, and the State of War.* Cambridge: Cambridge University Press, 1996.

———. *Peace and War: Armed Conflicts and International Order 1648–1989.* Cambridge: Cambridge University Press, 1991.

Holsti, Ole R. "Theories of International Relations, and Foreign Policy: Realism and Its Challengers." In *Controversies in International Relations Theory,* edited by Charles W. Kegley, Jr., 35–66. New York: St. Martin's Press, 1995.

Holt, Robert J., and John E. Turner, eds. *The Methodology of Comparative Research.* New York: Free Press, 1970.

Homer. *The Iliad.* Translated by W. H. D. Rouse. Edinburgh: Nelson & Sons, 1938.

Hopmann, P. Terrence. *The Negotiation Process and the Resolution of International Conflicts.* Columbia: University of South Carolina Press, 1996.

Horne, Alistair. *The Fall of Paris: The Siege and the Commune, 1870–71.* New York: St. Martin's Press, 1965.

Howard, Michael. *The Lessons of History.* New Haven, Conn.: Yale University Press, 1991.

———. *The Franco-Prussian War: The German Invasion of France, 1870–1871.* New York: Macmillan, 1962.

Hume, David. *A Treatise on Human Nature.* New York: Hafner Publishing, 1948.

Hunt, Michael H. *Crises in U.S. Foreign Policy.* New Haven, Conn.: Yale University Press, 1996.

Hybel, Alex Roberto. *How Leaders Reason.* Oxford: Basil Blackwell, 1990.

Ignatieff, Michael. *Virtual War: Kosovo and Beyond.* New York: Metropolitan Books, 2000.

———. *The Warrior's Honor: Ethnic War and the Modern Conscience.* New York: Metropolitan, 1998.

Iklé, Fred Charles. *Every War Must End,* 2nd ed. New York: Columbia University Press, 1991.

———. *How Nations Negotiate.* New York: Praeger, 1964.

Isard, Walter. *Understanding Conflict and the Science of Peace.* Cambridge, Mass.: Blackwell, 1992.

Jacobini, H. B. *International Law: A Text.* Homewood Ill.: Dorsey, 1962.

Jacoby, Susan. *Wild Justice: The Evolution of Revenge.* New York: Harper & Row, 1983.

Janis, Irving L. *Crucial Decisions: Leadership in Policymaking and Crisis Management.* New York: Free Press, 1989.

———. *Groupthink: Psychological Studies of Policy Decisions and Fiascoes,* 2nd ed. Boston: Houghton Mifflin, 1982.

———. *Victims of Groupthink.* Boston: Houghton Mifflin, 1972.

Jayatilleke, K. N. "The Principles of International Law in Buddhist Doctrine," *Recueil des Cours, 1967,* vol. I, no. 120, 445–567. Leyden: Sijthoff, 1968.

Jenkins, Simon. "Dresden: Time to Say We're Sorry," *Wall Street Journal,* February 14, 1995, A22.

Jentleson, Bruce W. *With Friends Like These: Reagan, Bush, and Saddam, 1982–1990.* New York: Norton, 1994.

Jervis, Robert. "Realism, Neoliberalism, and Cooperation: Understanding the Debate," *International Security* 24 (Summer, 1999): 42–63.

———. "The Future of World Politics: Will It Resemble the Past?" *International Security* 16 (Winter 1991–1992): 39–73.

———. Introduction: Approach and Assumptions." In *Psychology and Deterrence,* edited by Robert Jervis, Richard Ned Lebow, and Janice Gross Stein, 1–12. Baltimore, Md.: Johns Hopkins University Press, 1985.

———. "Cooperation under the Security Dilemma," *World Politics* 30 (January 1978): 167–214.

Joffe, Josef. "'Bismarck' or 'Britain'? Toward an American Grand Strategy after Bipolarity," *International Security* 19 (Spring 1995): 94–117.

Joll, James. *The Origins of the First World War.* London: Longman, 1984.

Johnson, James Turner. *Morality and Contemporary Warfare.* New Haven, Conn.: Yale University Press, 1999.

Johnston, Russell. "A Case of Depleted NATO Ethics in the Balkans," *International Herald Tribune,* January 16, 2001, 6.

Judah, Tim. *Kosovo War and Revenge*. New Haven, Conn.: Yale University Press, 2000.

Kagan, Donald. *On the Origins of War and the Preservation of Peace*. New York: Doubleday, 1995.

———. *The Fall of the Athenian Empire*. Ithaca, N.Y.: Cornell University Press, 1987.

Kaiser, David. *Politics and War: European Conflict from Philip II to Hitler*. Cambridge, Mass.: Harvard University Press, 1990.

Kaplan, Morton A. *System and Process in International Politics*. New York: Wiley, 1957.

Karsh, Efraim. *Saddam Hussein: A Political Biography*. New York: Free Press, 1991.

Kecskemeti, Paul. *Strategic Surrender: The Politics of Victory and Defeat*. Stanford, Calif.: Stanford University Press, 1958.

Kegley, Charles W., Jr. "International Peacemaking and Peacekeeping," *Ethics & International Affairs* 10 (1996): 25–46.

———. ed. *Controversies in International Relations Theory: Realism and the Neoliberal Challenge*. New York: St. Martin's Press, 1995.

———. "Decision Regimes and the Comparative Study of Foreign Policy." In *New Directions in the Study of Foreign Policy*, edited by Charles F. Hermann, Charles W. Kegley, and James N. Rosenau, 247–268. Boston: Allen & Unwin, 1987.

Kegley, Charles W., Jr., and Gregory A. Raymond. *Exorcising the Ghost of Westphalia: Building World Order in the New Millenium*. Upper Saddle River, N.J.: Prentice-Hall, 2002.

———. *A Multipolar Peace? Great-Power Politics in the Twenty-First Century*. New York: St. Martin's Press, 1994.

———. *When Trust Breaks Down: Alliance Norms and World Politics*. Columbia: University of South Carolina Press, 1990.

Kegley, Charles W., Jr., Gregory A. Raymond, and Margaret G. Hermann. "The Rise and Fall of the Nonintervention Norm: Some Correlates and Potential Consequences," *Fletcher Forum* 22 (Winter–Spring 1998): 81–101.

Kegley, Charles W., Jr., and Eugene R. Wittkopf. *World Politics: Trend and Transformation,* 8th ed. New York: Bedford/St. Martin, 2001.

———. *World Politics: Trend and Transformation,* 6th ed. New York: St. Martin's Press, 1997.

Kennan, George F. *The Fateful Alliance: France, Russia, and the Coming of the First World War*. New York: Pantheon, 1984.

———. "The United States and the Soviet Union, 1917–1976," *Foreign Affairs* 54 (July 1976): 670–690.

———. *American Diplomacy, 1900–1950*. New York: New American Library, 1951.

Kennedy, Paul. *The Rise and Fall of the Great Powers*. New York: Random House, 1987.

Kent, James. *International Law*. Cambridge: Deighton, Bell, 1866.

Keohane, Robert O. "International Liberalism Reconsidered." In *The Economic Limits to Modern Politics,* edited by John Dunn, 165–94. Cambridge: Cambridge University Press, 1992.

Keylor, William R. *The Twentieth-Century World: An International History,* 3rd ed. New York: Oxford University Press, 1996.

Khong, Yuen Foong. *Analogies at War*. Princeton, N.J.: Princeton University Press, 1992.

Kiernan, V. G. *The Duel in European History*. Oxford: Oxford University Press, 1989.

Kissinger, Henry A. *Diplomacy*. New York: Simon & Schuster, 1994.

———. *A World Restored*. Boston: Houghton Mifflin, 1973.

Klingberg, Frank L. "Predicting the Termination of War: Battle Casualties and Population Losses," *Journal of Conflict Resolution* 10 (June 1966): 129–171.

Knock, Thomas J. *To End All Wars: Woodrow Wilson and the Quest for a New World Order*. New York: Oxford University Press, 1992.

Koning, Hans. "Germanian Irredenta," *Atlantic Monthly,* July 1996, 30–33.

Korman, Sharon. *The Right of Conquest*. New York: Oxford University Press, 1996.

Kranzberg, Melvin. *The Siege of Paris, 1870–1871*. Ithaca, N.Y.: Cornell University Press, 1950.

Kriesberg, Louis. *Constructive Conflicts: From Escalation to Resolution*. Lanham, Md.: Rowman & Littlefield, 1998a.

———. "Reconciliation: Conceptual and Empirical Issues." Paper presented at the annual meeting of the International Studies Association, Minneapolis, Minn., March 17–21, 1998b.

Lane, Frederic C., Eric F. Goldman, and Erling M. Hunt. *The World's History,* 3rd ed. New York: Harcourt, Brace, 1959.

Langer, Herbert. *The Thirty Years' War.* New York: Hippocrene Books, 1980.

Langhorne, Richard. "Establishing International Organizations: The Concert and the League," *Diplomacy & Statecraft* 1 (March 1990): 1–18.

———. "Reflections on the Significance of the Congress of Vienna," *Review of International Studies* 12 (October 1986): 313–324.

Langsam, Walter Cunsuello. *The World since 1919.* New York: Macmillan, 1954.

Larson, Deborah Welch. *Origins of Containment.* Princeton, N.J.: Princeton University Press, 1985.

Lauterpacht, Hersch. "The Grotian Tradition in International Law." In *International Law,* edited by Richard Falk, Friedrich Krotochvil, and Saul H. Mendlovitz, 10–36. Boulder, Colo.: Westview, 1985.

Layne, Christopher. "Miscalculations and Blunders Lead to War." In *NATO's Empty Victory,* edited by Ted Galen Carpenter, 11–29. Washington, D.C.: Cato Institute, 2000.

Lazenby, J. F. *Hannibal's War: A Military History of the Second Punic War.* Warminster, England: Aris & Phillips, 1978.

Lederach, John Paul. *Building Peace: Sustainable Reconciliation in Divided Societies.* Washington, D.C.: U.S. Institute of Peace Press, 1997.

Lee, Stephen J. *Aspects of European History 1494–1789,* 2nd ed. London: Routledge, 1986.

Lefever, Ernest W. *The Irony of Virtue.* Boulder, Colo.: Westview, 1998.

Leng, Russell. *Interstate Crisis Behavior, 1816–1980: Realism versus Reciprocity.* Cambridge: Cambridge University Press, 1993.

———. "When Will They Ever Learn? Coercive Bargaining in Recurrent Crises," *Journal of Conflict Resolution* 27 (September 1983): 379–419.

Levy, Jack S. "Learning and Foreign Policy: Sweeping a Conceptual Minefield," *International Organization* 48 (Spring 1994): 279–312.

———. "An Introduction to Prospect Theory," *Political Psychology* 13 (June 1992): 171–186.

———. *War and the Modern Great Power System, 1495–1975.* Lexington: University of Kentucky Press, 1983.

Liberman, Peter. *Does Conquest Pay? The Exploitation of Occupied Industrial Societies.* Princeton, N.J.: Princeton University Press, 1996.

Liddell Hart, Basil Henry. *Strategy,* 2nd ed. New York: Praeger, 1967.

Lieberman, Bernhardt. "I-Trust: A Notion of Trust in Three-Person Games and International Affairs." In *Social Processes in International Relations,* edited by Louis Kriesberg, 359–371. New York: Wiley, 1968.

Limm, Peter. *The Thirty Years' War.* New York: Longman, 1984.

Lindblom, Charles E. "The Science of 'Muddling Through',," *Public Administration Review* 19 (Spring 1959): 79–88.

Link, Arthur S. *Wilson the Diplomatist.* Baltimore, Md.: Johns Hopkins University Press, 1957.

Liska, George. "Wars in Rounds: Termination and Erosion." In *Termination of Wars: Processes, Procedures, and Aftermaths,* edited by Nissan Oren, 114–146. Jerusalem: Magnes Press, Hebrew University, 1982.

Livy. *The War with Hannibal.* Translated by Aubrey De Sélincourt. Baltimore, Md.: Penguin, 1965.

———. *History of Rome,* vol. 1. Translated by B. O. Foster. London: Heinemann, 1919.

Lloyd, Alan. *Destroy Carthage! The Death Throes of an Ancient Culture.* London: Souvenir Press, 1977.

Locke, John. *The Second Treatise of Government.* Indianapolis, Ind.: Bobbs-Merrill, 1952.

Luard, Evan. *Types of International Society.* New York: Free Press, 1976.

Luttwack, Edward N. *Strategy: The Logic of War and Peace.* Cambridge, Mass.: Harvard University Press, 1987.

Lyons, William E. *Emotion.* Cambridge: Cambridge University Press, 1980.

Machiavelli, Niccolò. *The Prince*. Translated by Luigi Ricci. New York: Random House, 1950.

MacIver, R. M. *The Web of Government*. New York: Macmillan, 1963.

Mann, Golo. *The History of Germany since 1789*. Translated by Marian Jackson. New York: Praeger, 1968.

Manuel, Frank E. *The Age of Reason*. Ithaca, N.Y.: Cornell University, 1951.

Maoz, Zeev. "Peace by Empire? Conflict Outcomes and International Stability, 1816–1976," *Journal of Peace Research* 21, no. 3 (1984): 227–241.

Margolis, Howard. "Equilibrium Norms," *Ethics* 100 (July 1990): 821–837.

Marongiu, Pietro, and Graeme Newman. *Vengeance*. Toronga, N.J.: Rowman & Littlefield, 1987.

Massoud, Tansa George. "War Termination," *Journal of Peace Research* 33 (November 1996): 491–496.

May, Ernest R. *"Lessons" of the Past: The Use and Misuse of History in American Foreign Policy*. New York: Oxford University Press, 1973.

McGowan, Patrick J. "Meaningful Comparisons in the Study of Foreign Policy." In *International Events and the Comparative Analysis of Foreign Policy*, edited by Charles W. Kegley, Jr., Gregory A. Raymond, Robert M. Rood, and Richard Skinner, 52–87. Columbia: University of South Carolina Press, 1975.

McMahon, Matthew M. *Conquest and Modern International Law: The Legal Limitations on the Acquisition of Territory by Conquest*. Washington, D.C.: Catholic University of America Press, 1940.

McMurtry, Larry. *Lonesome Dove*. New York: Simon & Schuster, 1985.

McSweeney, Bill. *Security, Identity, and Interests: A Sociology of International Relations*. Cambridge: Cambridge University Press, 1999.

Merritt, Richard, and Dina Zinnes. "Democracies and War." In *On Measuring Democracy: Its Consequences and Commitments*, edited by Alex Inkeles, 207–234. New Brunswick, N.J.: Transaction Books, 1991.

Midlarsky, Manus I., ed. *Handbook of War Studies II*. Ann Arbor: University of Michigan Press, 2000.

Millar, T. B. "On Writing about Foreign Policy." In *International Politics and Foreign Policy*, 2nd ed., edited by James N. Rosenau, 57–64. New York: Free Press, 1969.

Miller, Judith, and Laurie Mylroie. *Saddam Hussein and the Crisis in the Gulf*. New York: Times Books/Random House, 1990.

Miller, Lynn H. *Global Order: Values and Power in International Politics*. Boulder, Colo.: Westview, 1985.

Modelski, George, and William R. Thompson. *Leading Sectors and World Powers*. Columbia: University of South Carolina Press, 1996.

Mojzes, Paul. *Yugoslavian Inferno: Ethnoreligious Warfare in the Balkans*. New York: Continuum, 1994.

Monod, Paul Kleber. *The Power of the Kings*. New Haven, Conn.: Yale University Press, 1999.

Monoson, S. Sara, and Michael Loriaux. "The Illusion of Power and the Disruption of Moral Norms: Thucydides' Critique of Periclean Policy," *American Political Science Review* 92 *(June 1998): 288–297.*

Montross, Lynn. *War through the Ages*. New York: Harper & Row, 1960.

Morgan, Patrick. "Examples of Strategic Surprise in the Far East." In *Strategic Military Surprise: Incentives and Opportunities,* edited by Klaus Knorr and Patrick Morgan, 43–76. New Brunswick, N.J.: Transaction Books, 1983.

Morgenthau, Hans J. *Politics among Nations: The Struggle for Power and Peace*, 6th ed. Revised by Kenneth W. Thompson. New York: Knopf, 1985.

———. "Defining the National Interest — Again." In *Perspectives on American Foreign Policy,* edited by Charles W. Kegley Jr. and Eugene R. Wittkopf, 32–39. New York: St. Martin's Press, 1983.

Mufson, Steven. "Condoleezza Rice Brings a 'Velvet-Glove' Forcefulness," *International Herald Tribune*, December 18, 2000a, 8.

———. "In Powell, Bush Finds a Seasoned Warrior," *International Herald Tribune,* December 18, 2000b, 8.

Mylorie, Laurie. *Study of Revenge: Saddam Hussein's Unfinished War against USA*. Washington, D.C.: American Enterprise Institute for Public Policy Research, 2000.

Nagel, Thomas. *Moral Questions*. Cambridge: Cambridge University Press, 1979.

Nardin, Terry. *Law, Morality, and the Relations of States*. Princeton, N.J.: Princeton University Press, 1983.

Nardin, Terry, and David R. Mapel, eds. *Traditions of International Ethics*. New York: Cambridge University Press, 1992.

Neustadt, Richard E., and Ernest R. May. *Thinking in Time: The Use of History for Decision Makers*. New York: Free Press, 1986.

Nevin, John A. "War Initiation and Selection by Consequences," *Journal of Peace Research* 33 (February 1996): 99–108.

Nicolson, Harold. *The Congress of Vienna*. New York: Viking, 1946.

Niebuhr, Reinhold. *Christianity and Power Politics*. New York: Scribner's, 1940.

———. *Moral Man and Immoral Society: A Study of International Politics*. New York: Scribner's, 1932.

Nino, Carlos Santiago. *Radical Evil on Trial*. New Haven, Conn.: Yale University Press, 1996.

Nisbet, Richard, and Lee Ross. *Human Inference*. Englewood Cliffs, N.J.: Prentice-Hall, 1980.

Norwine, Jim, and Jonathan M. Smith, eds. *Worldview Flux: Perplexed Values among Postmodern Peoples*. Lanham, Md.: Lexington Books, 2001.

Nozick, Robert. "Retribution and Revenge." In *What Is Justice?* edited by Robert C. Soloman and Mark C. Murphy, 281–284. Oxford: Oxford University Press, 1990.

Nye, Joseph S., and Roger K. Smith, eds. *After the Storm*. New York: Aspen Institute, 1992.

Ober, Josiah. "Classical Greek Times." In *The Laws of War: Constraints on Warfare in the Western World,* edited by Michael Howard, George J. Andreopoulos, and Mark R. Shulman, 12–26. New Haven, Conn.: Yale University Press, 1994.

O'Donovan, Oliver, and Joan Luckwood O'Donovan. *From Irenaeus to Grotius: A Sourcebook in Christian Political Thought*. Grand Rapids, Mich.: Eerdmans, 1999.

Ogg, David. *Europe in the Seventeenth Century*. New York: Collier Books, 1960.

O'Loughlin, John, Tom Mayer, and Edward S. Greenberg, eds. *War and Its Consequences: Lessons from the Persian Gulf Conflict*. New York: HarperCollins, 1994.

Oppenheim, Felix E. *The Place of Morality in Foreign Policy*. Lexington, Mass.: Lexington Books, 1991.

Oren, Nissan. "Prudence in Victory." In *Termination of Wars: Processes, Procedures, and Aftermaths,* edited by Nissan Oren, 147–163. Jerusalem: Magnes Press, Hebrew University, 1982.

Organski, A. F. K., and Jacek Kugler. *The War Ledger*. Chicago: University of Chicago Press, 1980.

Orme, John. "The Unexpected Origins of Peace: Three Case Studies," *Political Science Quarterly* 111 (Spring 1996): 105–125.

Owen, John M. *Liberal Peace, Liberal War: American Politics and International Security*. Ithaca, N.Y.: Cornell University Press, 1997.

Oz, Amos. "Israel's Wrath, Iran's Sweet Grapes," *New York Times,* April 25, 1996, A17.

Pages, Georges. *The Thirty Years' War*. London: Adam and Charles Black, 1970.

Palmer, R. R., and Joel Colton. *A History of the Modern World,* 7th ed. New York: Knopf, 1984.

Panic, Milan. "Don't Expect Renewal in Serbia with Milosevic Still Around," *International Herald Tribune,* October 10, 2000, 8.

Parker, Geoffrey. *The Thirty Years' War*. London: Routledge & Kegan Paul, 1984.

Parry, Clive. "The Function of Law in the International Community." In *Manual of Public International Law,* edited by Max Sørensen, 1–54. New York: St. Martin's, 1968.

Paskins, Barrie. "Obligations and the Understanding of International Relations." In *The Reason of States: The Study of International Political Theory,* edited by Michael Donelan, 153–170. London: Allen & Unwin, 1978.

Paterson, Thomas G. *On Every Front: The Making of the Cold War*. New York: Norton, 1978.

Pavithran, A. K. *Substance of Public International Law: Western and Eastern*. Bombay: Tripathi, 1965.

Pennington, Anne and Peter Levi. *Marko the Prince: Serbo-Croat Heroic Songs.* London: St. Martin's Press, 1984.

Pflanze, Otto. *Bismarck and the Development of Germany: The Period of Unification, 1815–1871.* Princeton, N.J.: Princeton University Press, 1963.

Phillimore, Robert Joseph. *Commentaries upon International Law.* 3rd ed. 4 vols. London: Butterworth, 1879–1889.

Phillimore, Walter Frank George. *Three Centuries of Treaties of Peace.* London: Murray, 1917.

Phillipson, Coleman. *Termination of War and Treaties of Peace.* London: Sweet & Maxwell, 1916.

Philpott, Daniel. "Sovereignty: An Introduction and Brief History," *Journal of International Affairs* 48 (Winter 1995): 353–368.

Picard, Gilbert Charles, and Colette Picard. *The Life and Death of Carthage.* London: Sidgewick & Jackson, 1968.

Pick, Daniel. *War Machine: The Rationalization of Slaughter in the Modern Age.* New Haven, Conn.: Yale University Press, 1993.

Pillar, Paul R. *Negotiating Peace: War Termination as a Bargaining Process.* Princeton, N.J.: Princeton University Press, 1983.

Pinson, Kappel. *Modern Germany.* New York: Macmillan, 1966.

Plato. *Laws.* Translated by R. G. Bury. London: Heinemann, 1926.

Plutarch. *Fall of the Roman Republic.* Translated by Rex Warner. Baltimore, Md.: Penguin, 1958.

Plutarch. *The Lives of the Noble Grecians and Romans.* Translated by John Dryden and revised by Arthur Hugh Clough. New York: Modern Library, 1864.

Polmar, Norman, ed. *CNN War in the Gulf.* Atlanta, Ga.: Turner Publications, 1991.

Polybius. *Polybius on Roman Imperialism.* Translated from the text of F. Hultsch by Evelyn S. Shuckburgh. Abridged, with an introduction by Alvin H. Bernstein. South Bend, Ind.: Regenery/Gateway, Inc., 1980.

Popper, Karl R. *The Logic of Scientific Discovery.* New York: Basic Books, 1959.

Porter, Bruce. *War and the Rise of the State.* New York: Free Press, 1994.

Posen, Barry P. "The War for Kosovo: Serbia's Political-Military Strategy," *International Security* 24 (Spring 2000): 39–84.

———. *The Sources of Military Doctrine: France, Britain, and Germany between the Wars.* Ithaca, N.Y.: Cornell University Press, 1984.

Post, Jerrold M. "The Defining Moment of Saddam's Life: A Political Psychology Perspective on the Leadership and Decision Making of Saddam Hussein during the Gulf Crisis." In *The Political Psychology of the Gulf War: Leaders, Publics, and Processes of Conflict,* edited by Stanley A. Renshon, 49–66. Pittsburgh, Pa.: University of Pittsburgh Press, 1993.

Promoting Sustainable Economies in the Balkans. New York: Council on Foreign Relations, 2000.

Pruitt, Dean G., and Jeffrey Z. Rubin. *Social Conflict: Escalation, Stalemate, and Settlement.* New York: Random House, 1986.

Public Papers and Addresses of Franklin D. Roosevelt, edited by Samuel I. Rosenman. New York: Harper Brothers, 1943.

Puchala, Donald J. "Fifty-Year Friendship with Germany: A Legacy of South Carolina's James F. Byrnes," *The State* (Columbia, S.C.), September 6, 1996, A9.

Quester, George H. *Offense and Defense in the International System.* New York: Wiley, 1977.

Raemdonck, Dirk C., and Paul F. Diehl. "After the Shooting Stops: Insights on Postwar Economic Growth," *Journal of Peace Research* 26 (August 1989): 249–264.

Raff, Diether. *A History of Germany from the Medieval Empire to the Present.* Translated by Bruce Little. New York: St. Martin's Press, 1988.

Rainor, Bernard E. "The Perfect War Led America's Military Astray," *Wall Street Journal,* August 2, 2000, A22.

Randle, Robert F. *The Origins of Peace.* New York: Free Press, 1973.

Ray, James Lee. *Democracy and International Conflict: An Evaluation of the Democratic Peace Proposition.* Columbia: University of South Carolina Press, 1995.

Raymond, Gregory A. "Necessity in Foreign Policy," *Political Science Quarterly* 113, no. 4 (1998–1999): 673–688.

———. "Democracies, Disputes, and Third-Party Intermediaries," *Journal of Conflict Resolution* 38 (March 1994): 24–42.

———. "The Use of Ethotic Argument in Foreign Policy." In *Proceedings of the Second International Conference of Argumentation,* edited by Frans H. Van Eemeren, et al., 1036–1040. Amsterdam: Stichting International Centrum voor de Studie van Argumentatie en Taalbeheersing, 1991.

———. "Demosthenes and Democracies: Regime Types and Arbitration Outcomes," *International Interactions* 22, no. 1 (1991): 1–20.

———. "Evaluation: A Neglected Task for the Comparative Study of Foreign Policy." In *New Directions in the Study of Foreign Policy,* edited by Charles F. Hermann, Charles W. Kegley, and James N. Rosenau, 96–110. Boston: Allen & Unwin, 1987.

———. "Comparative Analysis and Nomological Explanation." In *International Events and the Comparative Analysis of Foreign Policy,* edited by Charles W. Kegley, Jr., et al., 41–51. Columbia: University of South Carolina Press, 1975.

Reddaway, William F. *A History of Europe: From 1610 to 1715.* London: Methuen, 1948.

Regan, Geoffrey. *Great Military Disasters.* New York: Evans, 1987.

Regan, Patrick M. *Civil Wars and Foreign Powers: Outside Intervention in Intrastate Conflict.* Ann Arbor: University of Michigan Press, 2000.

Reinhardt, Klaus. "Commanding KFOR," *NATO Review* 48 (Summer/Autumn, 2000): 16–19.

Ritter, Gerhard. *The Sword and the Scepter: The Problem of Militarism in Germany,* vol. 1, *The Prussian Tradition, 1740–1890.* Translated by Heinz Norden. Coral Gables, Fla.: University of Miami Press, 1969.

Roberts, Michael. *Essays in Swedish History.* London: Weidenfeld & Nicolson, 1967.

Rock, Stephen R. *Why Peace Breaks Out: Great Power Rapprochement in Historical Perspective.* Chapel Hill: University of North Carolina Press, 1989.

Rodzinski, Witold. *A History of China.* Oxford: Pergamon Press, 1979.

Rorty, Amelie, ed. *Explaining Emotions.* Berkeley: University of California Press, 1980.

Rosecrance, Richard. *Action and Reaction in World Politics: International Systems in Perspective.* Boston: Little, Brown, 1963.

———. *The Rise of the Trading State: Commerce and Conquest in the Modern World.* New York: Basic Books, 1986.

Rosenau, James N. "Pre-Theories and Theories of Foreign Policy." In *Approaches to Comparative and International Politics,* edited by R. Barry Farrell, 27–92. Evanston, Ill.: Northwestern University Press, 1966.

———. "A Pre-theory Revisited: World Politics in an Era of Cascading Interdependence," *International Studies Quarterly* 28 (September 1984): 245–305.

Rosenthal, A. M. "Handing Triumph to the Enemy," *Washington Times,* September 18, 2000, 8.

Rosenthal, Joel H. "Rethinking the Moral Dimensions of Foreign Policy,." In *Controversies in International Relations Theory,* edited by Charles W. Kegley, Jr., 317–329. New York: St. Martin's Press, 1995.

———. *Righteous Realists.* Baton Rouge: Louisiana State University Press, 1991.

Rothschild, Joseph. *Return to Diversity: A Political History of East Central Europe since World War II,* 2nd ed. New York: Oxford University Press, 1993.

Royal, Robert. "Columbus and The Beginnings of the World," *First Things* 93 (May 1999): 32–38.

Rubin, Trudy. "Bush Will Face a Challenge in Handling Saddam Hussein," *The State* (Columbia, S.C.), January 16, 2001, A9.

Ruggie, John Gerard. *Constructing the World Polity: Essays on International Institutionalization.* New York: Routledge, 1998.

———. *Winning the Peace.* New York: Columbia University Press, 1996.

Russett, Bruce. *Grasping the Democratic Peace: Principles for a Post–Cold War World.* Princeton, N.J.: Princeton University Press, 1993.

Sagan, Carl. "Between Enemies," *Bulletin of the Atomic Scientists* 48 (May 1992): 24–26.

Sagey, I. "International Law Relating to Occupied Territory: Can Territory Be Acquired by Military Conquest under Modern International Law?" *Revue Egyptienne de Droit International* 28 (1972): 56–64.

Santayana, George. *The Life of Reason: Or the Phases of Human Progress.* New York: McGraw-Hill, 1953.

Santoro, Carlo M. "Bipolarity and War: What Makes the Difference?" In *Hegemonic Rivalry: From Thucydides to the Nuclear Age,* edited by Richard Ned Lebow and Barry S. Strauss, 71–88. Boulder, Colo.: Westview, 1991.

Scheff, Thomas J. *Bloody Revenge: Emotions, Nationalism, and War.* Boulder, Colo.: Westview, 1994.

Schelling, Thomas C. *Choice and Consequence.* Cambridge, Mass.: Harvard University Press, 1984.

———. *Arms and Influence.* New Haven, Conn.: Yale University Press, 1966.

———. *The Strategy of Conflict.* Oxford: Oxford University Press, 1960.

Schenk, H. G. *The Aftermath of the Napoleonic Wars: The Concert of Europe — An Experiment.* New York: Fertig, 1967.

Schiller, Friedrich von. *The History of the Thirty Years' War in Germany.* Translated by Captain Blaquiere. London, 1799.

Schlesinger, Arthur M., Jr. "White Slaves in the Persian Gulf." In *The Gulf Reader: History, Documents, Opinions,* edited by Micah L. Sifry and Christopher Cerf, 265–268. New York: Times Books/Random House, 1991.

Schneider, William. "The Old Politics and the New World Order." In *Eagle in a New World Order: American Grand Strategy in the Post–Cold War Era,* edited by Kenneth A. Oye, Robert J. Lieber, and Donald Rothchild, 35–68. New York: HarperCollins, 1992.

Schroeder, Paul W. "Historical Realty vs. Neo-realist Theory," *International Security* 19 (Summer 1994a): 108–148.

———. *The Transformation of European Politics, 1763–1848.* Oxford: Oxford University Press, 1994b.

———. "The Nineteenth Century System: Balance of Power or Political Equilibrium?" *Review of International Studies* 15 (April 1989): 135–153.

———. "The 19th-Century International System: Changes in the Structure," *World Politics* 39 (October 1986): 1–26.

Schuman, Frederick L. *International Politics,* 7th ed. New York: McGraw-Hill, 1958.

Schwebel, Stephen M. *Justice in International Law.* Cambridge: Cambridge University Press, 1994.

Seabury, Paul. *Power, Freedom, and Diplomacy.* New York: Random House, 1963.

Seib, Gerald F. "A New President, and Four Choices He Can't Dodge," *Wall Street Journal,* November 8, 2000, A28.

Seldes, George. *Great Thoughts.* New York: Ballantine, 1985.

Sengupta, Bama Prasanna. *Conquest of Territory and Subject Races in History and International Law.* Calcutta: Gouranga Press, 1925.

Shapiro, Michael J. *Violent Cartographies: Mapping Cultures of War.* Minneapolis: University of Minnesota Press, 1997.

Sherif, M., and C. W. Sherif. *Groups in Harmony and Tension.* New York: Harper & Row, 1953.

Sherman, Nancy. "Empathy, Respect, and Humanitarian Intervention," *Ethics & International Affairs* 12 (1998): 101–119.

Shillony, Ben-Ami. "The Japanese Experience." In *Termination of Wars: Processes, Procedures, and Aftermaths,* edited by Nissan Oren, 91–101. Jerusalem: Magnes Press, Hebrew University, 1982.

Shriver, Donald W., Jr. *An Ethic for Enemies: Forgiveness in Politics.* New York: Oxford University Press, 1995.

Sibert, M. "L'armistice dans le droit des gens," *Revue Générale de Droit International Public* 40 (1933): 657–714.

Sigal, Leon V. *Fighting to a Finish: The Politics of War Termination in the United States and Japan, 1945.* London: Cornell University Press, 1988.

Silber, Laura, and Allan Little. *Yugoslavia: Death of a Nation.* New York: Penguin, 1996.

Sills, David L., and Robert K. Merton, eds. *The Macmillan Book of Social Science Quotations.* New York: Macmillan, 1991.

Simon, Herbert A. *Models of Bounded Rationality.* Cambridge, Mass.: MIT Press, 1982.

———. *Administrative Behavior: A Study of Decision-Making Processes in Administration Organizations.* 2nd ed. New York: Macmillan, 1957.

Simons, Geoff. *Scourging of Iraq.* New York: St. Martin's Press, 1998.

Sinclair, T. A. *A History of Greek Political Thought.* Cleveland, Ohio: World Publishing, 1967.

Singer, J. David. "Peace in the Global System: Displacement, Interregnum, or Transformation?" In *The Long Post-War Peace: Contending Explanations and Projections,* edited by Charles W. Kegley, Jr., 56–84. New York: HarperCollins, 1991.

———. "The Level-of-Analysis Problem in International Relations." In *The International System: Theoretical Essays,* edited by Klaus Knorr and Sidney Verba, 79–92. Princeton, N.J.: Princeton University Press, 1961.

———. "Threat-Perception and the Armament-Tension Dilemma," *Journal of Conflict Resolution* 2 (1958): 90–105.

Singer, J. David, and Thomas Cusack. "Periodicity, Inexorability, and Steersmanship in International War." In *From National Development to Global Community,* edited by Richard L. Merritt and Bruce M. Russett, 404–422. London: Allen & Unwin, 1981.

Singer, J. David, and Melvin Small. *The Wages of War, 1816–1965: A Statistical Handbook.* New York: Wiley, 1972.

Small, Melvin, and J. David Singer. *Resort to Arms: International and Civil Wars, 1816–1980.* Beverly Hills, Calif.: Sage, 1982.

Smith, James D. *Stopping Wars: Defining the Obstacles to Cease-fire.* Boulder, Colo.: Westview, 1995.

Smith, Michael Joseph. *Realist Thought from Weber to Kissinger.* Baton Rouge: Louisiana State University Press, 1986.

Solarz, Stephen. "The Case for Intervention." In *The Gulf Reader: History, Documents, Opinions,* edited by Michael L. Sifry and Christopher Cerf, 269–283. New York: Times Books/Random House, 1991.

Solomon, Robert C. "Justice and a Passion for Vengeance." In *What Is Justice?* edited by Robert C. Solomon and Mark C. Murphy, 292–302. New York: Oxford University Press, 1990.

———. *The Passions.* Garden City, N.Y.: Doubleday, 1976.

Soren, David, Aicha Ben Abed Ben Khader, and Hedi Slim. *Carthage: Uncovering the Mysteries and Splendors of Ancient Tunisia.* New York: Simon & Schuster, 1990.

Sørensen, Max. *Manual of Public International Law.* New York: St. Martin's Press, 1968.

Stam, Allan. *Win, Lose, or Draw: Domestic Politics and the Crucible of War.* Ann Arbor: University of Michigan Press, 1996.

Starke, J. G. "Distinction Between a Suspension of Hostilities and a Cease-Fire," *Australian Law Journal* 65 (May 1991): 293–294.

Stedman, Stephen John. "Spoiler Problems in Peace Processes," *International Security* 22 (Fall 1997): 5–53.

Steefel, Lawrence D. *Bismarck, the Hohenzollern Candidacy, and the Origins of the Franco-German War of 1870.* Cambridge, Mass.: Harvard University Press, 1962.

Stein, Janice Gross. "War Termination and Conflict Reduction or How Wars Should End," *Jerusalem Journal of International Relations* 1 (Fall 1975): 1–27.

Stern, Eric. "Crisis and Learning: A Balance Sheet," *Journal of Contingencies and Crisis Management* 5 (June 1997): 69–86.

Stoessinger, John. *Why Nations Go to War,* 6th ed. New York: St. Martin's Press, 1993.

———. *Crusaders and Pragmatists: Movers of Modern American Foreign Policy.* New York: Norton, 1985.

Stokes, Gale. *Three Eras of Political Change in Eastern Europe.* New York: Oxford University Press, 1997.

———. *The Walls Came Tumbling Down: The Collapse of Communism in Eastern Europe.* New York: Oxford University Press, 1993.

Strauss, Barry S., and Josiah Ober. *The Anatomy of Error: Ancient Military Disasters and Their Lessons for Modern Strategists.* New York: St. Martin's Press, 1990.

Strong, C. F. *Dynamic Europe: A Background of Ferment and Change.* London: University of London Press, 1945.

Subramanian, V. K. *Maxims of Chanakya.* New Delhi: Abhinav Publications, 1990.

Suganami, Hidemi. *On the Causes of War.* New York: Oxford University Press, 1996.

Sylvan, David. "A World without Security and Foreign Policy: Thinking about the Future by Reflecting on Ancient Greece," *Mediterranean Quarterly* 6 (Spring 1995): 92–116.

Taft, Robert A. "Equal Justice Under Law: The Heritage of the English-Speaking Peoples and Their Responsibility," *Vital Speeches* 13 (November 1, 1946): 44–48.

Tavuchis, N. *Mea Culpa: A Sociology of Apology and Reconciliation.* Stanford, Calif.: Stanford University Press, 1991.

Taylor, A. J. P. *The Struggle for Mastery in Europe, 1847–1918.* Oxford: Oxford University Press, 1971.

———. *The Origins of the Second World War.* New York: Atheneum, 1962a.

———. *The Course of German History.* New York: Capricorn, 1962b.

Taylor, William J., Jr., and James Blockwell. "The Ground War in the Gulf," *Survival* 33 (May/June 1991): 230–245.

Tesón, Fernando R. *Humanitarian Intervention: Inquiry into Law and Morality.* New York: Transnational, 1988.

'tHart, Paul. *Groupthink in Government.* Amsterdam: Swets & Zeitlinger, 1990.

'tHart, Paul, Eric K. Stern, and Bengt Sundelius, eds. *Beyond Groupthink: Political Group Dynamics and Foreign Policy-making.* Ann Arbor: University of Michigan Press, 1997.

Thies, Wallace. *When Governments Collide: Coercion and Diplomacy in the Vietnam Conflict, 1964–1968.* Berkeley: University of California Press, 1980.

Thompson, William R. *On Global War: Historical-Structural Approaches to World Politics.* Columbia: University of South Carolina Press, 1988.

Thucydides. *The Peloponnesian War.* Translated by Richard Crawley. New York: Modern Library, 1951.

Timmerman, Kenneth R. "West Is Poised to Rearm Saddam," *Wall Street Journal,* September 27, 1994, A16.

Towle, Philip. *Enforced Disarmament.* New York: Oxford University Press, 1997.

Trainor, Bernard E. "The Perfect War Led America's Military Astray," *Wall Street Journal,* August 2, 2000, A22.

Traub, James. "Holbrooke's Campaign," *New York Times Magazine,* March 26, 2000, 41–45, 66, 69, 81.

Treitschke, Heinrich von. "What We Demand from France." In *The Quest for a Principle of Authority in Europe 1715–Present,* edited by Thomas C. Mendenhall, Basil D. Henning, and Archibald S. Foord, 226. New York: Holt, Rhinehart, & Winston, 1948.

Triumph without Victory: The Unreported History of the Persian Gulf War. New York: U.S. News & World Report, 1992.

Truman, Harry S. *Memoirs,* vol. I. Garden City, New York: Doubleday, 1955.

Tuchman, Barbara W. *The March of Folly: From Troy to Vietnam.* New York: Ballantine, 1984.

———. *The Guns of August.* New York: Macmillan, 1962.

Tucker, Robert W. "An Inner Circle of One: Woodrow Wilson and His Advisers," *National Interest* 51 (Spring 1998): 3–26.

Tudor, H. *Political Myth.* New York: Praeger, 1972.

Vasquez, John, ed. *What Do We Know about War?* Lanham, Md.: Rowman & Littlefield, 2000.

———. *The Power of Power Politics: From Classical Realism to Neotraditionalism.* Cambridge: Cambridge University Press, 1999.

———. "Distinguishing Rivals That Go to War from Those That Do Not," *International Studies Quarterly* 40 (December 1996): 531–558.

———. "Why Do Neighbors Fight — Territoriality, Proximity, or Interactions," *Journal of Peace Research* 32 (August 1995): 277–293.

———. *The War Puzzle*. Cambridge: Cambridge University Press, 1993.

Vaux, Kenneth L. *Ethics and the Gulf War: Religion, Rhetoric, and Righteousness*. Boulder, Colo.: Westview, 1992.

Verba, Sidney. "Assumptions of Rationality and Non-Rationality in Models of the International System." In *International Politics and Foreign Policy*, 2nd ed., edited by James N. Rosenau, 217–231. New York: Free Press, 1969.

Vertzberger, Yaacov Y. I. "Foreign Policy Decisionmakers and Practical-Intuitive Historians: Applied History and Its Shortcomings," *International Studies Quarterly* 30 (June 1986): 223–247.

Vitoria, Francisco de. *De Indis et de Jure Belli Relectiones*. Translated by John Pawley Bate. Washington, D.C.: Carnegie Institute, 1917.

Volgyes, Ivan. *Politics in Eastern Europe*. Chicago: Dorsey Press, 1986.

Von der Glotz, K. "The Growing Scale of Warfare." In *Basic Texts in International Relations: The Evaluation of Ideas about International Society*, edited by Evan Luard, 252–255. New York: St. Martin's Press, 1992.

Wallach, Jehuda L. *The Dogma of the Battle of Annihilation: The Theories of Clausewitz and Schlieffen and Their Impact on the German Conduct of Two World Wars*. Westport, Conn.: Greenwood Press, 1986.

Wallensteen, Peter, and Margareta Sollenberg. "Armed Conflict, 1989–99," *Journal of Peace Research* 37 (September 2000): 635–649.

Wallensteen, Peter. "Recurrent Détentes," *Journal of Peace Research* 26 (August 1989): 225–231.

Wallerstein, Immanuel. "The Rise and Future Demise of the World Capitalist System: Concepts for Comparative Analysis," *Comparative Studies in Society and History* 16 (September 1974): 387–415.

Walt, Stephen M. "The Case for Finite Containment: Analyzing U.S. Grand Strategy," *International Security* 14 (Summer 1989): 5–49.

Waltz, Kenneth N. "Structural Realism after the Cold War," *International Security* 25 (Summer 2000): 5–41.

———. *Theory of International Politics*. Reading, Mass.: Addison-Wesley, 1979.

———. *Man, the State, and War*. New York: Columbia University Press, 1954.

Walzer, Michael. *On Toleration*. New Haven, Conn.: Yale University Press, 1997.

———. *Just and Unjust Wars*. New York: Basic Books, 1977.

Ward, Robert Plummer. *An Enquiry into the Formation and History of the Law of Nations in Europe*, vol. 1. London: Butterworth, 1795.

Warmington, B. H. *Carthage*. London: Hale, 1960.

Warner, Rex. *The Greek Philosophers*. New York: New American Library, 1958.

Waterman, Richard W. "Storm Clouds on the Political Horizon: George Bush at the Dawn of the 1992 Presidential Election," *Presidential Studies Quarterly* 26 (Spring 1996): 337–349.

Watson, Adam. *The Evolution of International Society: A Comparative Historical Analysis*. London: Routledge, 1992.

Wayne, Stephen J. "President Bush Goes to War: A Psychological Interpretation from a Distance." In *The Political Psychology of the Gulf War: Leaders, Publics, and Processes of Conflict*, edited by Stanley A. Renshon, 29–48. Pittsburgh, Pa.: University of Pittsburgh Press, 1993.

Wechsler, Herbert. "The Issue of the Nuremberg Trial." In *From Nuremberg to My Lai*, edited by Jay W. Baird, 125–136. Lexington, Mass.: Heath, 1972.

Wedgwood, C. Veronica. *The Thirty Years' War*. London: Jonathan Cape, 1944.

Weinberg, Gerhard L. *A World at Arms: A Global History of World War II*. Cambridge: Cambridge University Press, 1994.

Weiner, Tim. "U.S. Holds Iraqis Who Aided CIA Plot to Oust Saddam," *International Herald Tribune*, May 12, 1997, 2.

Weir, William. *Fatal Victories*. New York: Avon, 1993.

Welch, David A. *Justice and the Genesis of War*. Cambridge: Cambridge University Press, 1993.

Westlake, John. *International Law*, 2nd ed., 2 vols. Cambridge: Cambridge University Press, 1910–1913.

White, Ralph K. "Why Aggressors Lose," *Political Psychology* 11 (June 1990): 227–242.

Whitelaw, Kevin, and Warren P. Strobel. "Inside Saddam's Iraq," *U.S. News & World Report*, September 11, 2000, 53–57.

Wiesenthal, Simon. *The Sunflower*. New York: Shocken, 1976.

Wight, Martin. "Western Values in International Relations." In *Diplomatic Investigations*, edited by Herbert Butterfield and Martin Wight, 89–131. Cambridge, Mass.: Harvard University Press, 1968.

———. *Power Politics*. London: Royal Institute of International Affairs, 1946.

Williamson, Samuel R., Jr. "World War I." In *The Oxford Companion to Politics of the World*, edited by Joel Krieger, 987–991. New York: Oxford University Press, 1993.

Winik, Lyric Wallwork. "Saddam's World," *Parade*, December 10, 2000, 10.

Wittman, Donald. "How a War Ends: A Rational Model Approach," *Journal of Conflict Resolution* 23 (1979): 743–763.

Wolfers, Arnold. *Discord and Collaboration*. Baltimore, Md.: Johns Hopkins University Press, 1962.

Wolgast, Elizabeth. *The Grammar of Justice*. Ithaca, N.Y.: Cornell University Press, 1987.

Woodruff, Paul, ed. *On Justice, Power, and Human Nature*. Indianapolis, Ind.: Hackett, 1993.

Woodward, Bob. *The Commanders*. New York: Simon & Schuster, 1991.

Wright, Morehead. "Reflections on Injustice and International Politics," *Review of International Studies* 12 (January 1986): 67–73.

Wright, Quincy. "How Hostilities Have Ended: Peace Treaties and Alternatives," *The Annals* 392 (November 1970): 51–61.

———. *A Study of War*. Chicago: University of Chicago Press, 1964.

Xenophon. *Hellenica*. Translated by Rex Warner. London: Penguin, 1979.

Yergin, Daniel. *The Prize: The Epic Quest for Oil, Money, and Power*. New York: Simon & Schuster, 1991.

———. *Shattered Peace*. Boston: Houghton Mifflin, 1977.

Yetiv, Steve A. *America and the Persian Gulf*. Westport, Conn.: Praeger, 1995.

Zartman, I. William. "Resolving the Toughness Dilemma." Paper presented at the 39th annual meeting of the International Studies Association, Minneapolis, Minn., March 17–22, 1998.

Zartman, I. William, and Jeffrey Z. Rubin. *Power and Negotiation*. Ann Arbor: University of Michigan Press, 1998.

Ziegler, David W. *War, Peace, and International Politics*, 6th ed. New York: HarperCollins, 1993.

INDEX